D1084622

ENGLAND UNDER THE YORKISTS
AND TUDORS
1471–1603

ENGLAND
UNDER THE
YORKISTS AND TUDORS
1471–1603

P. J. HELM, M.A.

LONDON
G. BELL & SON, LTD
1972

Copyright © 1968 by
G. BELL AND SONS, LTD
York House, Portugal Street
London, W.C.2

First published 1968
Reprinted 1972

GEN. EDN. ISBN 0 7135 0541 9
SCHL. EDN. ISBN 0 7135 0542 7

Printed in Great Britain by
The Camelot Press Ltd., London and Southampton

PREFACE

DURING the last thirty years a great deal of specialized work has been carried out on the period covered by this book. Old facts have been recovered and new assessments have been made. Together these have altered in some important respects the accepted picture of the age. I have tried to provide in outline an account which takes into consideration those changes that have become generally accepted. The sources on which I have drawn are indicated in the footnotes and in the suggestions for further reading, and here I should like to express my thanks for the help—and enjoyment—I have received from them.

I have drawn heavily on contemporary writers and speakers. Where necessary, spelling and punctuation have been modernized, but these changes have not, I think, affected the sense. The period is the earliest in which the ordinary reader can come to terms with the language used at the time: it is also one in which that language is particularly flexible, quotable, memorable.

Finally, I should like to thank all those who have helped with the production of this book, especially my publishers, my colleagues, and—not least—my pupils.

P. J. H.

SUGGESTIONS FOR GENERAL READING

AT the end of each chapter there is a short list of books and articles which refer to the topic dealt with in that chapter and which should also be used in connection with any later references to that topic. The following abbreviations are employed when referring to periodicals, etc.:

E.H.R. *English Historical Review*
Ec.H.R. *Economic History Review*
H.J. *Historical Journal*
H.A. Historical Association (Pamphlets, Aids for Teachers Series and Helps for Students of History)
P. and P. *Past and Present*
T.R.H.S. *The Transactions of the Royal Historical Society*

The following books are of general value and are not included in the lists at the end of the chapters:

1 THE EUROPEAN BACKGROUND

D. Hay, *Fourteenth and Fifteenth Century Europe*, Longmans, Green, 1966
The New Cambridge Modern History
    Vol. I *The Renaissance, 1493–1520*, ed. G. Potter, 1957
    Vol. II *The Reformation, 1520–1559*, ed. G. R. Elton, 1958
    Vol. III *The Counter-Reformation and Price Revolution, 1559–1610*, ed. R. B. Wernham, 1968
    Vol. XIV *Atlas*, 1970

2 THE ARTS

The Pelican History of Art
    M. Rickert, *Architecture in Britain in the Middle Ages*, 1954
    J. Summerson, *Architecture in Britain, 1530–1830*, 1955
    E. Waterhouse, *Painting in Britain, 1530–1790*, 1953
    M. Whinney, *Sculpture in Britain, 1530–1830*, 1964
The Oxford History of English Art
    E. Mercer, *English Art, 1553–1625*, 1962
The Oxford History of English Literature
    C. S. Lewis, *English Literature in the Sixteenth Century excluding Drama*, 1954
P. A. Scholes, ed., *The Oxford Companion to Music* (9th rev. edn.) 1955

3 GENERAL

The Oxford History of England
E. F. Jacob, *The Fifteenth Century*, 1961
J. D. Mackie, *The Earlier Tudors*, 1952
J. B. Black, *The Reign of Elizabeth*, 2nd ed., 1959
The Pelican History of England
A. R. Myers, *England in the Late Middle Ages*, 1952
S. T. Bindoff, *Tudor England*, 1950
S. B. Chrimes, *Lancastrians, Yorkists and Henry VII*, Macmillan, 1964
G. R. Elton, *England under the Tudors*, Methuen, 1955
C. Morris, *The Tudors*, Batsford, 1955
J. A. Williamson, *The Tudor Age*, Longmans; Green, 1957

4 FOREIGN POLICY

R. B. Wernham, *Before the Armada, the Growth of English Foreign Policy 1484–1588*, Cape, 1966

5 ECONOMIC HISTORY

P. J. Bowden, *The Wool Trade in Tudor and Stuart England*, Macmillan, 1962
E. M. Carus-Wilson, ed., *Essays in Economic History*, Arnold, *vol. I*, 1954, *vol. II*, 1962
F. J. Fisher, ed., *Essays in the Economic and Social History of Tudor and Stuart England*, C.U.P., 1961
P. Ramsey, *Tudor Economic Problems*, Gollancz, 1963
J. Thirsk, ed., *The Agrarian History of England and Wales, vol. IV, 1500–1640*, C.U.P., 1967

6 ORIGINAL MATERIAL

C. H. Williams, ed., *English Historical Documents, vol. V 1485–1558*, Eyre and Spottiswoode, 1967
G. R. Elton, *The Tudor Constitution*, C.U.P., 1960
J. R. Tanner, *Tudor Constitutional Documents*, C.U.P., 1922
R. H. Tawney and E. Power, ed., *Tudor Economic Documents*, 3 vols, Longmans, Green, 1924
J. D. Wilson, *Life in Shakespeare's England*, Penguin, 1944
The Oxford Book of Sixteenth Century Verse, 1932

CONTENTS

MAPS, GENEALOGICAL TABLES
AND GRAPHS

I · THE RESTORATION OF ROYAL POWER

Introduction

THIS book deals with the period during which England became a modern, rather than a medieval, state. Naturally there were some ways in which fifteenth-century England was already 'modern', and there were others in which the reign of Queen Elizabeth I was still 'medieval', but in general there is a change in quality observable between the England of 1450 and that of 1600, between the baronial wars of the fifteenth century, for example, and the sophisticated manœuvring for power at the Elizabethan court. Edward IV ascended the throne of a medievally governed kingdom, while Elizabeth handed to her successor a country administered on modern lines. It is easier to use the terms 'medieval' and 'modern' than to define them. The body of this book should, however, provide material for a definition. One might say, provisionally, that the changes are most obvious in the spheres of government and administration, and that the critical reign would seem to be that of Henry VIII.

'There are in history no beginnings and no endings. History books begin and end, but the events they describe do not.'[1] Nevertheless one must begin somewhere, and one of the problems of history is that of deciding just where to make a division in the seamless fabric. For many years historians were agreed that the year 1485 was a good point at which to make one of these cuts. Today they think differently. The years 1471 or 1529 seem more significant.

The advantages of the year 1485 as a limiting date are obvious. There is a nice finality about the battle of Bosworth. The death of Richard III removed the last of the great Yorkists. The accession of Henry VII introduced a new ruling family, the Tudors, whose descent from Edward III was relatively indirect. This new family ruled from 1485 to 1603 and during those years England became a powerful, unified state. Wise, modern Tudors replaced immoral, medieval Yorkists—this

---

[1] R. G. Collingwood, *The Idea of History*, O.U.P., 1946.

was the 'Tudor Myth' that grew up, partly as a result of Tudor propaganda, partly as an unconscious tribute paid by later writers to their success, partly in consequence of the coincidence in time of Tudor rule with a critical century in the history of England and of Europe.

Yet when historians consider not events but institutions the year 1485 loses much of its significance. What has been termed 'the Tudor revolution in government'—the extended use of parliament, the creation by statute of new instruments of administration, the break with Rome and the subsequent construction of a national church—began to take place after 1529, the year in which the Long Parliament of the Reformation was called. Before that date Henry VII (1485–1509) and Henry VIII (1509–47), or his 'prime man' Wolsey, were only concerned to refurbish the existing machinery of government so that it might function efficiently. They built on the foundations laid down by the Yorkists, Edward IV (1461–83) and Richard III (1483–5) There is continuity between Yorkist and early Tudor government. Indeed all the Tudor monarchs were to a large extent pragmatists. In the field of finance, for example, they continued throughout the century to refurbish the sources of revenue and the machinery of administration which they had inherited from earlier rulers.

Home Affairs and Foreign Policy

The struggle for power between the descendants of Edward III, which had first taken place in Richard II's reign, had broken out again in 1455 (the so-called 'Wars of the Roses'). Six years later the Lancastrian Henry VI had been deposed and the Yorkist Edward IV had, at the age of nineteen, been crowned king. He had been placed on the throne by the 'Kingmaker' Richard Neville, Earl of Warwick, and, though he might reign, the Earl ruled. It was ten years before Edward could free himself from the twin dangers of the defeated but not destroyed Lancastrians on the one hand, and the overmighty Warwick on the other. In 1470 Warwick changed sides and deposed Edward, who fled abroad. Within a year, helped by Burgundy, Brittany and the Hanseatic League, he was back. Warwick fell at the battle of Barnet, the Lancastrian heir, Prince Edward, was killed at the battle of Tewkesbury, and the captive Henry VI died in the Tower—officially 'of pure displeasure and melancholy'. By the end of 1471 Edward was king indeed.

Peace made possible the restoration of royal power. As in France and Spain, so too in England the elements of weakness in the king's position were the existence of powerful feudatories, fragmented jurisdiction and lack of money. A peaceful foreign policy would enable the king to concentrate on home affairs. Edward achieved his aims with the minimum necessary exertion. His attitude resembles that of Charles II. There is the same determination not to go on his travels again; the same love of wine, women and song; the same acute political judgement on the rare occasions when the king is prepared to shake off his lethargy and act.

Edward—a Renaissance prince, able, shrewd, magnificent and idle—seemed to live for pleasure, but observers recognized the political skill that lay concealed beneath the sloth. A contemporary chronicler marvelled that the king should have had

> a memory so retentive in all respects that the names and estates used to recur to him just as though he had been in the habit of seeing them daily of all persons dispersed throughout the counties of his kingdom and this, even if in the districts in which they lived they held the rank only of mere gentlemen.

A generation later More described him as

> of heart courageous, politic in counsel, in adversity nothing abashed, in peace just and merciful, in war sharp and fierce, in the field bold and hardy and nevertheless no farther than wisdom would adventure. Whose wars whoso will consider, he shall no less commend his wisdom where he avoided than his manhood where he vanquished. He was of visage lovely, of body mighty, strong and clean made.

More was anxious to point the contrast between the king and his brother Richard, but even so this remains an impressive testimonial.

The pattern of fifteenth-century Europe which faced Edward IV in 1471 was one that was becoming simpler as rulers consolidated their territories, extended their powers, destroyed foreign enclaves, and in general replaced the jigsaw pattern of

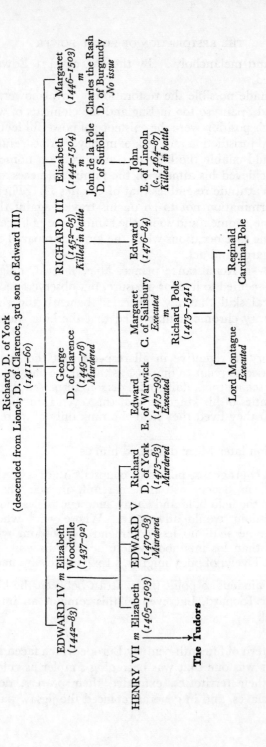

Richard, D. of York
(descended from Lionel, D. of Clarence, 3rd son of Edward III)
(1411–60)

EDWARD IV *m* Elizabeth
(1442–83)   Woodville
(1437–92)

George
D. of Clarence
(1449–78)
Murdered

RICHARD III
(1452–85)
Killed in battle

Elizabeth
(1444–1503)
m
John de la Pole
D. of Suffolk

Margaret
(1446–1503)
m
Charles the Rash
D. of Burgundy
No issue

HENRY VII *m* Elizabeth
(1465–1503)

The Tudors

EDWARD V
(1470–83)
Murdered

Richard
D. of York
(1473–83)
Murdered

Edward
E. of Warwick
(1475–99)
Executed

Margaret
C. of Salisbury
Executed
m
Richard Pole
(1473–1541)

Edward
(1476–84)

John
E. of Lincoln
(c. 1464–87)
Killed in battle

Lord Montague
Executed

Reginald
Cardinal Pole

THE YORKISTS

medieval 'liberties' by centralized administrations, a process in which England, France and Spain were among the leaders.

The Hundred Years' War with France had ended in 1453 with the defeat of the English at Castillon and the loss of Gascony. Henceforth of its former French dominions England held only Calais. Under Louis XI (1461–83) the French monarchy extended its control. The king acquired for the crown the semi-independent territories of Anjou and Maine, Provence, Picardy and Burgundy, while in 1491 Charles VIII (1483–98) added Brittany.

Portugal had no need to consolidate: already she had the same frontiers as today. Wealthy and united, she was leading the way round Africa to the riches of the East, but in power and enterprise she was soon to be overhauled by Spain and even temporarily (1580–1640) absorbed by that country. There the marriage in 1469 of Ferdinand of Aragon (1479–1516) and Isabella of Castile (1474–1504) led eventually to the union of their two states. Granada in the south was added in 1492, Spanish Navarre in 1512.

To the north France's old ally Scotland was still an independent kingdom. James IV (1488–1513), like other fifteenth-century monarchs, had begun to develop an efficient administration, though it did not survive his own death at the battle of Flodden. Scandinavia had been united under Danish rule since 1397. That area was an exception to the general process of unification, for in 1523 Sweden broke away from Denmark. Her new ruler, Gustavus I (1523–60), rapidly erected a strong centralized monarchy similar to those already built up in the rest of western Europe.

South of Scandinavia lay the Holy Roman Empire. The Emperors were unable to create the instruments of government necessary for unification and the Empire remained a medieval tangle of over three hundred Dukes and Counts, Margraves and Archbishops, Electors, Imperial Knights and Free Cities. The Emperor was chosen by seven Electors and from 1436 onwards it became customary to elect the Habsburg archduke of Austria. The family power of the Habsburgs was greatly strengthened by Maximilian I (1493–1519) through a series of dynastic marriages.

To the east of the Empire lay Poland and Russia. The process of Russian expansion and consolidation had begun in

B

1481, but for the time being eastern Europe was of no concern to England. To the south-east of the Empire lay the Balkan territories of the Ottoman Turks, a great and growing threat. In 1453 the Turks had taken Constantinople, soon they were to advance up the Danube to the gates of Vienna (1529), and across the sea to Rhodes (1522).

In Italy the seventy or eighty city states of earlier times had by 1471 reduced themselves to six, with a few attendant satellites: Naples, Florence, Genoa, Milan, Venice and the Papal States. Secular rulers picked up many hints on diplomacy, administration and financial efficiency from the last of these.

Two areas on the fringes of the Empire were important in 1471, but lost their significance within a generation. One, the Hanseatic League, was a federation of north German cities including at the height of its power about eighty towns lying along the waterways and coasts of north Germany. These had in the fourteenth century built up a network of commercial privileges which stretched from London to Novgorod and from Cologne to Bergen, and the League was designed to maintain this economic power by political action. By the end of the fifteenth century the Hanse was in decline—'most of its teeth were out and the rest loose', as an Englishman observed—but in 1471 it was still apparently a force to be reckoned with.

The other area was the disputed strip of territory between France and the Empire which included some of the richest, most densely populated, most urbanized districts north of the Alps. Here the Dukes of Burgundy, playing off their neighbours one against another, were slowly building their state. In 1471 Charles the Rash ruled lands that stretched from the Alps to the North Sea, that included in Flanders the richest area of northern Europe, and that contained perhaps twice the population of England.

Edward's foreign policy demonstrated a shrewd knowledge of where his country's real advantage lay. Peace would bring prosperity. The claim to the French crown might be a useful bargaining counter, but an attempt to reconquer the lost lands was clearly out of the question. England's economic interests demanded friendship with the Hanseatic League and with Burgundy. The League controlled the vital Baltic trade; moreover it had helped to equip Edward's expedition to recover the throne. Treaties were made in 1473 and 1474, and in the latter year the League was granted possession in perpetuity of the Steelyard, its London headquarters.

In 1474 Edward also concluded a treaty with Charles the Rash. Charles had married Edward's sister Margaret and he too had played a part in the king's recovery of the throne. Now Edward promised to support the duke against Louis XI. When they had won, France was to be divided between them, Edward taking the title of king.

In the summer of 1475 Edward himself led the expeditionary force to France. He landed at Calais and marched as far as St. Quentin, a hundred miles to the south, but Charles was short of men and money and sent no help. Edward halted, got in touch with Louis, and in August agreed to highly satisfactory terms at Picquigny. The two kings met on a bridge over the river Somme and embraced cautiously through a wooden grille which had been specially constructed halfway across, for fear of assassination. Commynes describes the preparations:

> . . . our next consultation was about a bridge which was ordered to be built, large and strong, for which purpose we furnished carpenters with materials. In the midst of the bridge there was contrived a strong wooden lattice, such as the lions' cages are made with, the hole between every bar being no wider than to thrust in a man's arm; the top was covered only with boards to keep off the rain, and the body of it was big enough to contain ten or twelve men of a side, with the bars running across to both sides of the bridge, to hinder any person from passing over it either to the one side or the other. . . .

Edward received a lump sum of 75,000 crowns and a pension of 50,000 crowns a year for life, and it was agreed that the English claim to the crown of France should be referred to four arbitrators. Within three months the English army was back home. Charles was justifiably annoyed, but he was far too busy fighting the Swiss to take any action. Two years later he was killed in battle and the greater part of his possessions, including Flanders, passed through marriage into the hands of the Emperor Maximilian.

In the north of England Edward's brother Richard was engaged in the usual border warfare with the Scots. In 1480 it was decided to launch a full-scale attack, and two years later Richard occupied Edinburgh. The Scots were forced to return Berwick (sold to them by the Lancastrians in 1461) which was incorporated in the East March of the Border.

Edward IV died suddenly in April 1483 at the early age of forty. For the next two years England was ruled by his brother Richard. It is comparatively easy to form an opinion of the characters of Edward IV and Henry VII, but around that of Richard there hangs darkness.

> I, that am curtail'd of this fair proportion,
> Cheated of feature by dissembling nature,
> Deform'd, unfinish'd, sent before my time
> Into this breathing world, scarce half made up, . . .
> I am determined to prove a villain, . . .

Shakespeare took his cue from the early Tudor propagandists, who had described Richard as 'ill featured of limbs, crookbacked, his left shoulder higher than his right, . . . malicious, wrathful, envious'—yet no one had remarked on these characteristics before Edward's death, and Richard had acquired a reputation for loyalty (unlike his brother Clarence), for ability as a general, and for quiet efficiency and expert administration in the North of England. There at York he had lived a respectable life, remote from the loose activities of Edward's court.

Edward IV left two sons, Edward V aged eleven, and his brother Richard Duke of York aged nine. Someone must rule until they came of age, either Richard of Gloucester, or the Woodvilles, the ambitious, numerous, jumped-up relations of the late king's widow. Edward had named Richard as protector and the title was confirmed by the council on 4 May. By that time the two princes were under Richard's control. On 13 June William Hastings, the late King's chamberlain, was accused by Richard of treason and executed on the same day. Perhaps Richard feared the opposition of a man who controlled a large force of indentured retainers. By 22 June Stillington, Bishop of Bath and Wells, had declared that Edward's heirs were technically illegitimate, since the King had been precontracted to Lady Eleanor Butler and had therefore not been free to marry the boys' mother, Elizabeth Woodville. The story was not impossible and if true made Richard the rightful heir. On 6 July he was crowned Richard III. For a time the little princes could be seen 'shooting and playing in the garden by the Tower', but they 'day by day began to be seen more rarely behind the bars and windows'. They were probably killed—'suddenly lapped up among the clothes . . . the feather bed and pillow hard unto their mouths . . . ' More wrote—some time between July 1483 and March 1484, the earlier months seeming the more likely. It is probable that they were killed on Richard's orders, but possible that the responsibility lies with the Duke of Buckingham who had inherited Hastings' retainers and who in October 1483 led a rebellion in support of Henry Tudor, then in Brittany. Buckingham was in London after Richard had left for the north and he then had the opportunity to eliminate these two inconvenient obstacles. The rebellion misfired, Henry failed in his attempt to seize Poole, and Buckingham was beheaded. Professor Chrimes, the leading authority on the period, has concluded: 'The weight of suspicion against Richard must remain heavy, but of proof there is none at present.'

Assuming his guilt, what had happened to the loyal, moral Richard? The temptation to act was considerable. Perhaps the princes *were* illegitimate. Certainly the boys' relatives, the Woodvilles, were his enemies, and it might be a question of their lives or his, 'For well he saw he could not live, unless he were King; that there was no safety but in sovereignty'.[1] The rules of succession were by no means invariable: in 1503, when Henry lay ill, officials discussed who might best succeed him, but none of them mentioned the Prince of Wales. Everything pointed to deposition, and from deposition to murder was only a short step, as Henry IV had once discovered. If Richard III had ruled peacefully for twenty years his success would have overlaid the dubious origins of his reign.

But Richard did not live long enough. In 1485 Henry Tudor set sail from Harfleur with a force of 1,800 mercenaries. He landed at Milford Haven on 7 August and marched north through central Wales to Shrewsbury. On 22 August Richard met him at Bosworth and was defeated and killed in battle. Some of the fire had gone out of the King's generalship, his wife and son had recently died and he can hardly have relished the prospect of fighting to keep the throne for Clarence's son, or for his nephew, de la Pole. Perhaps, too, he

[1] Sir William Cornwallis, *The Encomium of Richard III*, (*c.* 1603).

underestimated Henry—'an unknown Welshman, whose father I never knew. . . .'   Even so he might possibly have won had it not been for the inaction of Northumberland and the treachery of the Stanleys during the battle.

The news of Richard's defeat led the council at York to lament that the king '. . . was piteously slain and murdered to the great heaviness of this City, . . .' and the Prior of Crowland wrote 'Oh God! what security are our Kings to have henceforth, that in the day of battle they may not be deserted by their subjects?'   The greater part of the new King's reign was to be devoted to a search for that security.

Henry Tudor had been born at Pembroke in 1457. His father was the half-brother of the Lancastrian Henry VI, his

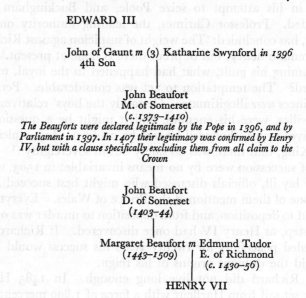

EDWARD III

John of Gaunt *m* (3) Katharine Swynford *in 1396*
4th Son

John Beaufort
M. of Somerset
(*c. 1373–1410*)
The Beauforts were declared legitimate by the Pope in 1396, and by Parliament in 1397. In 1407 their legitimacy was confirmed by Henry IV, but with a clause specifically excluding them from all claim to the Crown

John Beaufort
D. of Somerset
(*1403–44*)

Margaret Beaufort *m* Edmund Tudor
(*1443–1509*)   E. of Richmond
(*c. 1430–56*)

HENRY VII

THE DESCENT OF HENRY VII
FROM EDWARD III

mother the great-granddaughter of the Lancastrian John of Gaunt. In the sixties Henry had been brought up by Yorkists, but after the battle of Tewkesbury he had fled with his uncle Jasper to Brittany. In 1484 Richard had been negotiating for his extradition, but Henry had heard of the plot and had fled once more, this time to France. From there he had, against all likelihood, gained the throne. His task now was to keep it.

The Yorkists had based their claim on legitimacy, the Lancastrians had been forced to base theirs on the oath of allegiance. There were more than a dozen claimants with better titles than that of Henry. The Yorkist Earl of Warwick (Clarence's son) had the most direct claim, though some thought the attainder of his father had invalidated it. Fortunately for Henry he was in the Tower. Other Yorkist claimants were the four sons of the Duchess of Suffolk (Edward IV's sister), led by John de la Pole, Earl of Lincoln. The Lancastrian male line had been extinguished at Tewkesbury. The female line was represented by Henry's mother, Margaret Beaufort—but the Beauforts were illegitimate and, although they had been later legitimized, their right of succession had then been specifically excluded. In these circumstances it is not surprising that Henry spoke little of his royal blood and based his claim to rule on his *de facto* position as king. Though the cheers of his army after Bosworth might prove only a temporary endorsement, the victory that they celebrated was Henry's clearest title. He was king because he had conquered.

To his first Parliament (1485–6) Henry declared that he had inherited the crown, but he was careful not to develop this argument. Instead he pointed out that his victory at Bosworth indicated God's approval of his claim to rule. Parliament was invited to support the Almighty's judgement. They did not make Henry king: they recognized that he already was king (Edward IV and Richard III had had their titles confirmed in a similar way) and they declared that the succession should pass to Henry's children. Then—and only then—did Henry marry Elizabeth, the eldest daughter of Edward IV, thus ensuring that his descendants would combine the claims of York and Lancaster.

Henry ruled for twenty-five years and died in his bed, leaving a quiet and prosperous country to his son. Knowing this, one is apt to underestimate the insecurity of the early part of the reign. The first fifteen years were shadowed by plots and rebellions and it was not till 1497 that foreign observers

considered him secure. It was imposters rather than genuine
Yorkists who gave most of the trouble. Pollard has written
'. . . we misapprehend the nature of Henry's problem, if we
think of a party as being the greatest of his difficulties. The
problem was not a party, but a frame of mind . . . the issue was
one between order and disorder; . . . There was neither party
nor principle in the plots against Henry VII; they represented
merely personal discontents, abetted by foreign rivals, and fed
by endemic disorders.'[1]

It should be remembered that Henry's regular military
power was always small. Immediately on his accession he had
established a personal guard of yeoman 'hardy, strong, and of
agility' with a distinctive scarlet uniform, but they numbered
only about two hundred. Artillery was under the king's
control, but he does not appear to have used his gunners, except
against the Irish. In time of emergency Henry depended, as
earlier kings had done, on the shire-levies, the musters of able
men commissioned by the sheriffs from each shire. During the
reign six fighting ships were built, including the large, heavily-
armed *Regent* (she carried 225 guns) and the *Sovereign*, and in
1496 Henry ordered the construction of a dry dock at Portsmouth.

As soon as Henry moved north in the spring of 1486, a
rebellion broke out in southern England led by Richard's
chamberlain, Viscount Lovell, and by Humphrey and Thomas
Stafford. The plan collapsed, Lovell fled abroad, Humphrey
was executed and Thomas pardoned, but in the autumn of the
same year the Yorkists took up an Oxford boy, Lambert
Simnel, and announced that he was the Earl of Warwick.
The impersonation was supported by Edward IV's sister
Margaret, Dowager Duchess of Burgundy, by Lovell, and by
John de la Pole. Simnel was crowned king in Dublin early in
1487. In the summer the Yorkist forces, strengthened with
2,000 soldiers supplied by Margaret, landed in Lancashire.
Henry paraded the true Earl through the streets of London,
England remained hostile or apathetic, and the rebels were
defeated at Stoke. The leaders were executed, but Henry
sensibly put Simnel in the royal kitchens. He ultimately rose
to the rank of falconer. In 1489 the north murmured against

---

[1] A. F. Pollard ed., *The Reign of Henry VII from Contemporary Sources* (3 vols),
Longmans, Green, 1913–14, pp. xvii–xix.

taxation demands, 'the people of a sudden grew into a great mutiny', and the earl of Northumberland was murdered. The rising was put down by the Earl of Surrey.

In 1491 there began the most dangerous threat to Henry. Perkin Warbeck, servant to a Breton clothes merchant, made such an impression on the Irish that they decided he must be of royal blood. Taken up in his turn by the Irish Yorkists, it was decided that he was Richard, the younger of Richard III's two sons. Warbeck was passed from hand to hand: from Ireland to Charles VIII of France, until that King made peace with Henry; from France to the inevitable Margaret of Burgundy, and from her to the Emperor Maximilian; finally he was transferred from Vienna to the Austrian Netherlands. There a plan was prepared, but the conspirators were betrayed and those in England were executed, including the great Sir William Stanley whose treachery at Bosworth had ensured Henry's victory.

There followed a series of abortive attempts to invade Henry's lands; Warbeck's followers failed at Deal and at Waterford in 1495, failed to persuade the Scots to do more than launch a Border raid in 1496, failed again in Ireland and southwest England in 1497. (Earlier in that year the Cornishmen, protesting against paying taxes for 'a small commotion made of the Scots, which was assuaged and ended in a moment', had reached London, only to be defeated at Blackheath.) Warbeck fled from the west to Beaulieu Abbey, where he took sanctuary. He was persuaded to surrender himself and to make a public confession of his imposture. In 1498 he escaped from captivity, but was recaptured. Next year a new bogus Warwick appeared and was quickly seized, Warbeck and the real Earl were accused of plotting together to fire the Tower and were executed. The evidence suggests that they were encouraged by an *agent provocateur*. Henry must have felt that there would always be plots as long as Warwick lived, and it is certain that Ferdinand of Aragon was urging him to get rid of the Earl of Warwick.

It is certain, too, that the remainder of Henry's reign was one of domestic peace and quiet. In 1497 the Milanese ambassador Soncino had analysed the sources of the King's growing strength: 'Everything favours the king, especially an immense treasure, and because all the nobles of the realm know the royal wisdom and either fear him or bear him an extra-ordinary affection, . . .'. In 1498 the Spaniard Ayala wrote of Henry to Ferdinand, 'His government is strong in all respects' and in 1500 Soncino was able to write to Milan: 'England has never been so tranquil and obedient as at present.'

Security demanded friends abroad as well as peace at home. In so far as there existed any fixed principles in Henry's foreign policy they were that France was the potential enemy; that France and Scotland in alliance were more than doubly dangerous; that, as a market for England's cloth, Flanders was the area which concerned the country most closely (in 1496 De Puebla wrote to Ferdinand that Henry 'esteems Flanders more than any foreign power'); that the continent must be made unsafe for pretenders. Finally, Henry knew well that wars were becoming increasingly expensive and that peace was desirable for economic reasons. In the first year of the reign de Gigli, a Papal collector, wrote: 'The king shows himself very prudent and clement; all things appear disposed towards peace, if only the minds of men would remain constant'. Prestige, prosperity, safety—all depended on the pursuance of an astute foreign policy.

When Charles VIII of France threatened to annex the inde-pendent duchy of Brittany, Henry hastened to conclude the treaty of Medina del Campo (1489) with Ferdinand of Aragon. The two countries agreed to act together against France, and Henry's elder son Arthur was betrothed to Ferdinand's daughter Catherine. This Spanish alliance was, on the whole, maintained for the next seventy years.

Henry obtained from Parliament a grant of money to finance the war and in 1490 English forces were landed in Brittany and Calais. A sharp action was fought at Dixmude in Flanders and the port of Sluys was taken in 1492, but otherwise no move was made to seek out the enemy. Henry was wise—Ferdinand was accustomed to desert his allies without warning. Ferdi-nand seized the French south-eastern regions of Roussillon and the Cerdagne, while Charles VIII solved the Breton problem to his own satisfaction by marrying Anne, Duchess of Brittany, and the peninsula was incorporated in France. The time had come for Henry to make peace. By the Treaty of Etaples (1492) Charles agreed to pay 745,000 gold crowns (£159,000)

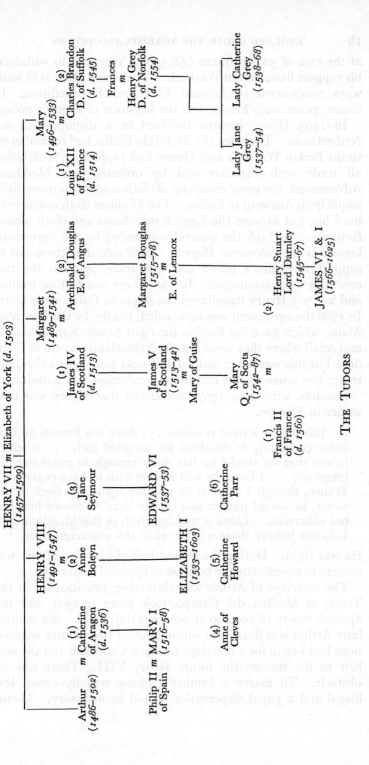

HENRY VII m Elizabeth of York (d. 1503)
(1457-1509)

Arthur (1486-1502) m Catherine of Aragon (d. 1536)

HENRY VIII (1491-1547)
m
(1) Catherine of Aragon (d. 1536)
(2) Anne Boleyn
(3) Jane Seymour
(4) Anne of Cleves
(5) Catherine Howard
(6) Catherine Parr

Philip II of Spain m MARY I (1516-58)
ELIZABETH I (1533-1603)
EDWARD VI (1537-53)

Margaret (1489-1541)
m
(1) James IV of Scotland (d. 1513)
(2) Archibald Douglas E. of Angus

James V of Scotland (1513-42) m Mary of Guise
Margaret Douglas (1515-78) m E. of Lennox

Mary Q. of Scots (1542-87)
m
(1) Francis II of France (d. 1560)
Henry Stuart Lord Darnley (1545-67)

JAMES VI & I (1566-1625)

Mary (1496-1533)
m
(1) Louis XII of France (d. 1514)
(2) Charles Brandon D. of Suffolk (d. 1545)

Frances m Henry Grey D. of Norfolk (d. 1554)

Lady Jane Grey (1537-54)
Lady Catherine Grey (1538-68)

THE TUDORS

at the rate of 50,000 francs (£2,500) a year and to withdraw his support from Perkin Warbeck. The whole affair is in some ways reminiscent of Edward IV's French expedition. In future, peace with France was the keystone of Henry's policy.

In 1493 Henry became involved in a dispute with the Netherlands. The ruler, the Archduke Philip, had refused to restrain Perkin Warbeck and Henry had replied by prohibiting all trade with Flanders and by ordering the Merchant Adventurers, the great company of cloth traders, to move their staple from Antwerp to Calais. The Flanders cloth towns were hard hit, but so were the English merchants and cloth manufacturers. In 1496 the quarrel was ended by the agreement known as the *Intercursus Magnus*. Each side undertook not to support the other's rebels and free trade between the two countries was encouraged. In 1504 there was further trouble and in 1505 Henry transferred the staple to Calais once more. In 1506 the agreement was superseded, briefly, by the *Intercursus Malus*, which gave the English the right to sell cloth wholesale and retail where they would in the Netherlands except in Flanders, but this was never ratified and next year, when the 1496 treaty was renewed, the additional concession was withdrawn.

Soncino, writing in 1497, considered that Henry was now secure in Europe:

> ... this prince is most prudent, ... there is a French ambassador constantly in Scotland for no good end, ... it seems to me that he thinks he has done enough in pacifying the kingdom; ... I fancy he will always wish to have peace with France, though I think if he saw her up to the neck in the water, he would put his foot on her head to drown her, but not otherwise. There is nothing fresh in this kingdom, and I do not believe there will be while this sovereign lives.

He was right. During the second half of his reign Henry was content to consolidate the position of England in Europe.

The marriage of Arthur and Catherine, provided for in the Treaty of Medina del Campo, took place in 1501 and the Spanish dowry of 100,000 crowns was duly paid. Six months later Arthur was dead, and within another two months negotiations had begun for a marriage between Catherine and the new heir to the throne, the future Henry VIII. There was an obstacle. To marry a brother's widow was by canon law illegal and a papal dispensation would be necessary. Meanwhile, for political reasons, the young Henry made a formal protest against the validity of the proposed marriage. It did not take place until 1509, after the death of Henry VII, and it had an unforseen consequence, the break with Rome.

Another marriage was to have equally far-reaching results of quite a different nature. In 1502 a peace treaty was made with Scotland (the first freely-agreed treaty since 1328). In addition to the usual pledge of 'perpetual peace' some attempt was made to end the interminable Border warfare, and the provisions were endorsed by the marriage of Henry's daughter Margaret and James IV of Scotland. It was from this marriage that the Stuarts derived their later claim to the English throne.

Henry took great pains over his foreign policy. At a time when permanent embassies did not exist, he was famous for the accuracy of his continental information, most of which was derived from unofficial, but trusted, sources. In 1497 the Milanese ambassador Soncino wrote to his master Ludovico Sforza:

> In many things I know this king to be admirably well informed, but above all because he is most thoroughly acquainted with the affairs of Italy, and receives especial information of every event.

Eighteen months later he wrote again on the subject:

> In his Highness's opinion he has need of no one, while everyone needs him, and although he clearly sees what may happen to the world, yet he considers it so unlikely as to be practically impossible. In the midst of all this, his Majesty can stand like one at the top of a tower looking on at what is passing in the plain. He also seems to believe that even if the King of France became master of Italy, which he would not like, he would be so distracted in ruling it that no harm would ensue either to his Majesty or to his heirs.

By the end of his reign the king had succeeded in strengthening or creating links with Spain, France, Flanders and Scotland, and in destroying foreign support for Yorkist claimants and imposters. His policy was not dramatic, but it was something better, it was effective.

Parliament

At some date before 1471 Sir John Fortescue, an able lawyer and a former Lancastrian, had written *The Governance of England*.

The earlier part of his book was a restatement of the medieval view of government as rule by consent (*dominium politicum et regale*), a view based on the political theories of writers such as the twelfth-century John of Salisbury. The latter part of the book stressed two dangers to a monarch, that of the overmighty subject 'of equal power to himself', and that of the king whose poverty leads inevitably to 'perversion of justice and perturbation of the peace'. Fortescue advised as cures the resumption of all alienated Crown lands, and the creation of a reformed council consisting of twelve spiritual and twelve temporal lords 'of the wisest and best disposed men that can be found'. Such a ruler would be powerful and popular, for

> If the King might have his livelihood for the sustenance of his estate in great lordships, manors, fee farms and such other demesnes, his people not charged, he should keep to him wholly their hearts, exceed in lordship all the lords of this realm and there should none of them grow to be like unto him, which thing is most to be feared of all the world.

This is very much the pattern of government followed by the Yorkists and by Henry VII, the rulers withdrawn a little from their supporters, preserving their power and their isolation by the revenue derived from carefully administered crown lands and by the employment of a small personally chosen council, using Parliament only occasionally and for exceptional purposes.

> The cause why I have called and summoned this my present Parliament is, that I purpose to live upon mine own, and not to charge my Subjects but in great and urgent causes, . . .

So Edward told the Commons in 1467, during his first period as King. As early as 1465 they had granted him tunnage and poundage, together with the proceeds from the customs, for life. Henceforth he would only need to call Parliament for extraordinary taxation. One of the two main functions of Parliament was to provide money for the king. The other was to give national support, as it were, to royal decisions. A declaration that one intended to live of one's own implied a restricted use of Parliament and Edward IV called only six Parliaments during the twenty-two years of his two periods as king. Richard III called one Parliament in two years; Henry VII called five in the first ten years of his reign, and only two between 1497 and 1509, moreover these five parliaments only sat for about twenty-five weeks in all—an average of hardly more than one week per year. It is quite clear that Parliament was not yet an essential part of the year-by-year machinery of government, but rather an aid to be used occasionally like a strong, and perhaps dangerous, drug.

In an emergency Parliament—and Parliament alone—might agree to the levying of direct taxation, the fifteenth and tenth, a tax on rural and urban property which had become fixed as early as 1334 and which represented about £30,000. When necessary several fifteenths and tenths might be voted.

Edward obtained grants from Parliament in preparation for his French adventure. Then the pension from Louis XI gave him increased financial independence, and only one Parliament was summoned between 1475 and 1483. That one was called for the sole purpose of passing a bill of attainder against the King's younger brother, George, Duke of Clarence. 'False, fleeting, perjured Clarence' had changed sides so often that his attainder came as no real surprise. Within a month he was dead, drowned in his bath or—some said—in a barrel of wine. In 1483 Edward called his last Parliament, to provide money to cover the costs of the successful Scottish expedition and those of a possible future war with France.

Richard III's only Parliament met in 1484. It confirmed his title to the throne adding that

> . . . the court of parliament is of such authority, and the people of this land of such nature and disposition, as experience teacheth, that manifestation and declaration of any truth or right made . . . by authority of the same, maketh, before all things, most faith and certainty, and quieting men's minds, removeth the occasion of all doubts and seditious language. . . .

In the same Parliament a number of measures were passed against local tyrannies and abuses such as the corruption of juries, and the imposition of benevolences (see p. 23) was declared illegal.

Like his Yorkist predecessors, Henry VII did what he could to 'live of his own', and in an emergency parliament was usually prepared to vote money. In 1497 he obtained £120,000 towards the cost of dealing with the threat of Perkin Warbeck and earlier in the reign parliament had voted £100,000 (of which rather less than £27,000 was finally collected) for the French war. Commynes commented sourly:

> . . . things of such importance [foreign expeditions] are managed very tediously there; for the king not being able to undertake such an affair without calling together his parliament, which is in the nature of our Three Estates, and, as it consists for the most part of sober and pious men, is very serviceable and strengthening to the king. At the meeting of this parliament the king declares his intention and desires aid of his subjects (for no money is raised in England but upon some expedition into France or Scotland, or some such extraordinary occasion); and then they supply him very liberally, especially against France; yet the Kings of England have this artifice when they want money, and have a desire to have any supplies granted, to raise men, and pretend quarrels with Scotland or France; and having encamped with their army for about three months, disband it, return home, and keep the remainder of the money for their own private use; . . .

Statute remained in theory declaratory, rather than innovatory. The author of the *Italian Relation* (see p. 48) thought that 'if the King should propose to change any old established rule, it would seem to every Englishman as if his life were taken from him; . . .', but in practice Henry's parliamentary measures frequently extended the scope of the royal power. They were of two main types, those designed to establish law and order, such as the statute of Liveries of 1504 which dealt with the great bands of retainers; and those designed to control trade and industry, such as the navigation act of 1485 which forbade merchants to use foreign shipping if native shipping were available.

The High Court of Parliament consists of Crown, Lords and Commons. At this time there was no doubt that the King was the dominant partner. Next in importance came the Lords, though in 1489 the Commons won a small but significant victory when the judges decided that an Act of Parliament was not valid unless they had given their assent to it. The Upper House consisted of two archbishops, nineteen bishops, twenty-eight abbots (though not all these attended), and between thirty and fifty lay lords. (Fifty-three lay lords had been summoned to the last Parliament before the civil wars, twenty-nine attended the first Parliament of Henry VII.)

In the Commons the counties were represented by seventy-four knights, and the boroughs by two hundred and twenty-four members. Technically the borough members should have been townsmen, but as early as 1422 a quarter had been non-residents, lesser gentry, lawyers, or officials, a tendency that was to become more pronounced, with important consequences, during the sixteenth century.

Finance, Administration and Justice

Throughout late fifteenth-century Europe financial independence was the key to a ruler's strength. To live of one's own was the goal which all sought but few achieved.

Yorkist and early Tudor revenue was drawn from four main sources: customs dues; crown lands; feudal prerogatives; and the profits of justice. To these must be added the occasional parliamentary grants already described, and such windfalls as a French pension or a Spanish dowry. Edward IV rebuilt the shattered royal finances. The contemporary Croyland Continuator described how

> ... he turned all his thoughts to the question, how he might in future collect an amount of treasure worthy of his royal station out of his own substance, and by the exercise of his own energies ... he resumed possession of nearly all the royal estates. ... Throughout all the ports of the kingdom he appointed inspectors of the customs, men of remarkable shrewdness, but too hard, according to general report, upon the merchants. The king himself, also, having procured merchant ships, put on board of them the finest wools, cloths, tin, and other productions of the kingdom, and, like a private individual living by trade, exchanged merchandise for merchandise, by means of his factors, among both Italians and Greeks. ... He also ... exacted heavy fines from those whom he found to have intruded and taken possession of estates without prosecuting their rights in form required by law. ... All these particulars, in the course of a very few years, rendered him an extremely wealthy prince. ...

The two anchors of revenue were the customs and the crown lands. While the ruler could do little about the former except ensure conditions favourable to trade, it was in his power to increase the yield from the latter source. The improved administration of crown lands, the resumption of alienated property, the confiscation of the forfeited estates of traitors—it

c

was these actions which enabled the Yorkists to rescue the monarchy from its dependence on the overmighty subject and thus to prepare the way for the independent rule of Henry VII and Henry VIII.

The customs dues had long been the chief item in the regular revenue. They were voted for life to all three kings and from them the Crown received an average income of perhaps £30,000 a year, rising to £40,000 at the close of Henry VII's reign.

By that time the customs had been overtaken and passed as the main source of revenue by receipts from the crown lands. Thanks to improved administration through the Chamber— and thanks also to the resumption of alienated lands (under Henry VII acts of resumption were passed in 1485, 1487 and 1488), to forfeitures (such as that of Clarence's lands in 1478, worth by 1485 £3,500 a year) and to deaths (Henry recovered in this way the lands he had granted to his mother and to his uncle Jasper)—the income from these lands rose to about £29,000 a year in 1485, and to an average of about £42,000 in the last five years of Henry's reign.

Of growing importance, though by their nature fluctuating wildly, were the profits of the king's feudal prerogatives. Feudalism as a military and administrative order was dying, but the Yorkists, and to an even greater extent the Tudors, saw to it that its financial aspect lived on. Technically, the feudal kings owned England, the landowners were their tenants. In consequence the king possessed certain rights: the right to financial 'aids' when his eldest son came of age, and when his eldest daughter married (Henry was the last ruler to collect these); purveyance and presumption, the right to obtain supplies and transport below cost price; the right to take over the estates of a tenant who left no heir; wardship, the right to arrange—at a profit to himself—the marriage of an heiress, and to administer the estates of a minor until he came of age. Pushed to their greatest extent these rights, especially that of wardship, formed a valuable source of royal income, and acted as a sort of primitive land tax. Richard III sent out commissioners to enquire into all alienations of land without licence and other infringements of the king's feudal rights. From the first year of his reign Henry also searched out concealed lands and in 1503 a master of the wards, Sir John

Hussey, was appointed as head of a regular organization designed to make the most of this valuable source of revenue.

The profits of justice were also uncertain but important. *Justitia magnum emolumentum est*—justice, said the lawyers, is a great source of profit. There were the fees which had to be paid before many sorts of legal action (for instance, the issue of writs) could take place. There were also the fines imposed on offenders. Here Henry was supreme: nobles, landowners, merchants, officials all paid if they broke the law. The west country handed over £15,000 for its ill-advised support of Perkin Warbeck.

Edward had introduced (1473) the custom of demanding 'voluntary' gifts from his richer subjects as a proof of their goodwill (*benevolentia*). These 'benevolences' were naturally not popular, and Richard III's parliament had declared them illegal, but Henry VII nevertheless levied one in 1491, as did his son Henry VIII in 1545. There were profits, too, for the king as a private merchant. As early as 1463 Edward was trading in wool and cloves with Italy. Later cargoes included woad, alum, wax, writing paper and white wine. It was good business, if shocking to conventional men who felt that a king should not dabble in trade. Henry VII followed the Yorkist example and in one year (1505–6) made £15,000 from the sale of alum.

In 1485 the royal income was about £70,000. After a temporary decline in the first years of Henry's reign it rose still further and by 1509 stood at £110–120,000.

Financial solvency implied administrative efficiency. The two main instruments of Yorkist and early Tudor rule were the Chamber and the Council.

In the sixties Edward IV had received sums of money directly into his own coffers in his chamber, by-passing the old department, the Exchequer of Receipt. Exchequer procedure was elaborate and formal, its officials cautious and conventional. Barricaded behind a heap of precedents and papers, they were well able to see that every traditional penny was accounted for, but they were quite unsuited to the adoption of new methods. They were, as Burke described them centuries later, 'impassive and immortal'.

In the seventies Edward made increasing use of his private

Chamber, with its household organization, and during the forty years between 1471 and 1509 'able kings in alliance with a confident professional class of lay administrators were busy creating a new royal administrative and financial web centred on the king's chamber'.[1]   The Chamber became the body that applied to the crown lands the new methods of large-scale, private estate management.   Much of what it did was drawn from the experience acquired in the running of the estates of the Duchy of Lancaster, which had for long handled its own revenues; something too was probably learnt from the practice of papal administrators in Italy.

The Chamber officials were professional civil servants— surveyors, receivers, and auditors, men trained in estate management, in accountancy and in the law.   Rents were raised and care was taken to see that the lands were properly farmed, and on at least one occasion instructions were given to '. . . stuff them with the king's cattle'.   One of the local receivers was John Hayes, who administered the lands formerly held by Clarence in Cornwall, Devon, Somerset, Dorset, Wiltshire and Hampshire, and who rode about the south-west 'Both to survey and guide the same manors and to levy the lord king's money both there and to conduct other business of the lord king there'.   (After fifteen years' service Hayes was dismissed in 1492 for having had contact with the agents of Perkin Warbeck.)

In consequence of this administrative revolution the Crown was solvent for the first time for generations.   Edward was probably more secure financially than any king had been since the twelfth century and by 1478 he was able to begin clearing the Crown's outstanding debts.

There was an instructive sequel.   When Henry VII came to the throne the ordered system of 'household' government, which depended on the king's personal supervision, started to break down as it always tended to do on the death of a king. The receivers once more paid their monies to the Exchequer and the lands they had administered began to slip out of their control, while the 'immortal' Exchequer recovered its complete powers of audit.   Revenue declined until Henry had restored the Yorkist system, which he quickly began to do.

[1] B. P. Wolffe, *The Management of English Royal Estates under the Yorkists Kings*, E.H.R., 278, 1956, p. 25.

In 1485–6 he set up a commission to discover his tenants-in-chief and where possible to add to their number. By 1488 many receivers and auditors had been appointed or reappointed and by 1493 the land revenues were once more securely back in the hands of the Chamber officials, supervised at first by Bray and Lovell, later by Empson and Dudley. The first ten years of the reign saw a great extension in the enforcement of the King's prerogative rights, and by the last years of the reign the Chamber was handling nine-tenths of the regular revenue, together with such occasional items as parliamentary grants and the Spanish dowries and French subsidies, leaving the Exchequer to account for only about £10,000 a year.

When Henry died the royal coffers were well-filled. Rumour said that his son inherited at least £1,300,000. Modern research is more cautious, suggesting that Henry left £300,000 in jewels and plate and that debts owed to him may have totalled another £300,000. The greater part of these represented loans to the Emperor Maximilian and it is doubtful if Henry regarded them as investments: more probably they were made as part of his policy of establishing his position in continental Europe. If the extent of the king's fortune was exaggerated the rumours nevertheless represent an accurate assessment of his financial stability, which was based on the use of the Chamber, the employment of modern methods, and on his own meticulous supervision. In 1498 the Spanish Ambassador Ayala informed Ferdinand that the King 'spends all the time he is not in public or in his Council in writing the accounts of his expenses with his own hand. . . .' The king's account-book for the years 1502–5 has survived. It begins with four sides in his writing, there follow pages checked by Henry with five or six signatures to a page, and after that the king's great angular initial H still continues to appear at least once on each page.

The Council was the other administrative instrument employed in the revival of royal personal government under the Yorkists and early Tudors. In membership it was not the meeting of great barons that it had once been, but rather a body of men who owed their importance not to their broad acres but to the king's favour. The Council consisted of whomsoever the king chose to summon. It could vary in size from that of the great councils of fifty or sixty members, meeting less than

once a year, to a mere handful.   For Edward IV's reign there
are records of 126 people called to at least one council during
the reign, for that Richard III 54, and for that of Henry VII
225, but the great bulk of the council's work was carried out by
a small group, slightly larger under Henry VII than under
Edward IV but in other ways much the same.   Indeed, at
least twenty of Henry's councillors had been councillors to
Edward IV, men like the Yorkists Northumberland and
Surrey, who had fought against Henry at Bosworth, and Oliver
King, Bishop of Bath and Wells, who served continuously from
1475–95.   To these Henry added Lancastrian supporters, such
as Oxford and Ormond, and Lord Daubeney, one of his own
creations.   The core of Henry's council was made up of a few
nobles and a number of clerics (such as Morton, Fox and
Warham), expert lawyers and country gentlemen—perhaps
fifteen or sixteen altogether.   The office of Secretary, which
dated at least from the reign of Richard II, now began to
assume importance.   The one qualification all councillors had
in common was that the king had chosen them as willing,
trusted servants.   Henry VII certainly did not employ, as a
matter of deliberate policy, only 'new men'.

The council's duty was to debate, usually in the king's
presence; to advise, though the king need not take the advice
offered—in 1507 De Puebla considered that 'The King of
England has no confidential advisers'; to judge cases brought
before it by petitioners; and to administer the government of
the country.   Often these roles overlapped and no distinction
was necessarily made between one activity and another.   The
same men carried them out, sitting in the same place, the two
rooms at Westminster known collectively as Star Chamber,
which had been council rooms since the days of Edward III.
Over fifteen hundred references to the Council have been
recovered for the years 1461–85.   The majority of these are
concerned with the judicial work of the Council, which would
naturally get recorded, but this was not necessarily the most
important of its activities.

Conciliar jurisdiction certainly grew in extent during
Edward's reign.   The councillors listened to petitions and
made it their business to see that the existing laws were obeyed.
Justice was swift, impartial and unbiased, and as time passed
the 'court of star chamber' (which was only the Council sitting

as a court) came to hear more and more civil pleas at West-minster. During Yorkist rule the Council's powers to expedite justice for the poor (powers which dated from the fourteenth century) were also more widely used.

Both Edward IV and Henry VII delegated specific work to small groups of councillors. A branch of the Council developed consisting of selected councillors specially chosen to deal with petitions for redress presented by those too poor to sue in the common law courts. This lapsed in 1485 but was revived in 1493, business being heard before the king's council-lors on progress, and by 1497 this Court of Requests was beginning to develop a life of its own, distinct from that of the main Council. In 1487 Henry VII caused an act to be passed setting up a specialized tribunal to deal with powerful offenders, to try those accused of seven specific offences against public order, and to deal with cases in which juries might be corrupted or intimidated. The new body was perhaps unnecessary, its job was already being done by the Council in Star Chamber, and its independent life was short.

Henry also established about 1500 a small standing committee of the Council, which came to be known as the 'Council Learned in the Law'. A group of a dozen councillors —under the control at first of Reginald Bray and later of Richard Empson and Edmund Dudley, harsh, competent rigorous administrators—was made responsible for collecting debts owed to the Crown. Before them came the great land-owners accused of keeping retainers, of failing to pay their feudal dues, or of occupying lands their title to which had not been registered, and those of Henry's subjects who were worthy of notice found themselves tied in a webby system of bonds and recognisances for loyalty, from which there was no escape. This Council made extensive use of informers, such as the mysterious Grimaldi, and eventually it was taking in some £40,000 a year, about a quarter in cash and the rest in bonds.

Local councils developed to administer special regions. In 1472 Richard became the real ruler, under Edward IV, of the north of England, with a council of his own based on York. In 1484 he reorganized the government of that area, appointing as his lieutenant his nephew the Earl of Lincoln, and drawing up instructions which established the manner in which the future Council of the North developed. This was essentially a judicial rather than an advisory council. The organization broke down in 1486, the existence of the council became intermittent and had ceased completely by 1509. The council was not established on a permanent basis until 1525.

The Council in the Marches of Wales had a rather similar history. It developed from a body which had looked after Edward's lands in that part of Britain, and Henry VII revived it as a council for his son Arthur, Prince of Wales. It too sank into the shadows, to be reconstituted by Wolsey in 1525.

Henry could neither afford to neglect Ireland nor to reconquer it. That country remained, as always, a problem. The early history of Britain can be interpreted in terms of a lowland zone (roughly defined as the area south and east of a line from Hull to Exeter) nowhere over six hundred feet in height, open to invasion and to civilisation from continental Europe, and a highland zone north and west of this area where communications are more difficult, the soil poorer, the climate wetter, the coastline more indented. Into this part of the British Isles the earlier forms of society were driven by successive waves of invaders from Europe, and there they lingered on. Ireland, though itself not particularly mountainous, forms part of this highland zone, isolated beyond the heights of the main island and the storms of the Irish sea.

A thousand years before the Tudors, in the sixth century, Ireland had been ahead of the mainland, a pocket of civilization saved from the barbarians, and had sent out missionaries to Scotland, scholars and works of art to Europe. Gradually it became a backwater. When in the twelfth century Henry II attempted to add it to his Angevin empire, Irish society was already an Iron Age anachronism in a feudal world. Henry's attempt failed. Like Mexico, Ireland absorbs its conquerors. The king's Anglo-Norman settlers, barons such as the Fitzgeralds and the Burkes, became more Irish than their subjects and Ireland remained unassimilated. At the end of the fifteenth century the king's deputy controlled only the Pale, a tiny area around Dublin (where there was a parliament of sorts) extending along the coast for about thirty miles and into the interior for less than twenty.

Henry VII would have been delighted, no doubt, to leave Ireland alone, but it was a Yorkist stronghold. The Lord Deputy was Fitzgerald, Earl of Kildare, who had been

appointed by Edward IV.   In 1487 and again in 1491, Kildare had accepted the claims first of Lambert Simnel and then
of Perkin Warbeck.   (The Irish Book of Howth says that after
Simnel's defeat Henry summoned those Irish lords on whom he
could lay hands and told them 'you will crown apes at length'.)

In 1492 Kildare was dismissed and two years later Henry
sent to Ireland one of his own household officials, Sir Edward
Poynings, with a small army and the title of Lord Deputy.
Poynings summoned the Irish Parliament and in 1494–5 it
passed the so-called 'Poynings' laws'.   By these, all laws passed
in England would automatically apply to Ireland, while no
legislation could be discussed by the Irish Parliament, nor
could a parliament even be summoned, without the king's
approval.   These provisions remained in force until the second
half of the eighteenth century.   Poynings failed to subdue
Ulster, but he secured the south-east and when Warbeck tried
to land at Waterford (1495) the pretender was driven off.

Henry was a realist.   Now that the danger was over, he
recalled Poynings and restored Kildare.   If Ireland could not
rule him, he should rule Ireland, or so the Irish declared that
'the king of the Saxons' had said, and for the remainder of
Henry's reign Kildare did rule Ireland—or at least Leinster—
from his palace at Maynooth.   Henry had adopted a moderate,
realist solution, adequate for his own needs, but one that might
pose problems in the future.

The structure of justice rested firmly on the three high courts
which sat, all together, in the great Westminster Hall—King's
Bench, Common Pleas, and Exchequer.   There the judges,
professional lawyers appointed by the king and removeable at
his pleasure, administered the common law.   They also advised
the king in council on points of law.   At Westminster too there
was the court of Chancery where the Lord Chancellor, the
'keeper of the King's conscience', remedied injustices that
might follow from a too strict interpretation of the common law
and heard cases which fell outside the latter's scope.   Justice
in Chancery was quick (therefore cheap) and efficient, and the
court sat out of term time.   For these reasons it tended to grow
in importance, particularly under an active chancellor.

The justice of the three central courts was applied throughout
the country by the high court justices when they held the assizes.

In the counties the king's representative was the sheriff, but during the fifteenth century his influence was declining, partly as a result of partisan activities during the civil war, and his tenure of office had been restricted to one year. The majority of his responsibilities were being transferred to the justices of the peace. These justices, chosen from the country gentry, were not a Yorkist or Tudor creation. They had their origins in the twelfth century and their statutory foundation in the fourteenth. In Edward IV's reign their powers were already extensive: as individuals it was their duty to arrest suspects, two or three sitting together in the petty sessions could deal with misdemeanours, and at the quarter sessions the whole body of justices could try any indictable offence save treason. Perhaps nine-tenths of the cases which came before King's Bench had first been heard by the J.P.s and referred by them to Westminster. Their powers were increased in Henry VII's reign by the acts of 1485 (extending their powers of arrest), 1487 (reorganizing the system of bail), 1495 (empowering them to investigate and punish the transgression of sheriffs) and 1504 (dealing with retainers). Already in 1485 there were in existence 133 statutes referring to their duties and during the sixteenth century the number grew to 309. Unpaid, influential and knowledgeable in local affairs, they proved an ideal instrument of government, and as their duties increased so did their numbers, from an average of under ten in a shire to over forty.

In great matters the Yorkists and Henry saw the needs of government and provided for them, in lesser matters likewise there was royal interference, probing and control. There is space to mention only a few examples: Edward IV set up a relay of mounted messengers between London and the Border, made a personal progress through those areas from which discontent had been reported following the demobilization of 1475, appointed royal surveyors in eleven of the principal ports (1481), and as early as 1474 caused commissions of enquiry into feudal tenures to be set up in ten counties. Henry VII's judges held that the privilege of sanctuary might not be claimed in cases of high treason (1487); laws passed in 1489 and 1497 enlarged the categories of those who were excluded from claiming 'benefit of clergy'.[1]

---

[1] By which those who could read, or pretend to read, a 'neck verse' claimed the right, as clerics, to be tried by the lenient church courts.

II · THE PATTERN OF TUDOR ENGLAND

The World Picture

THE sixteenth century was to be one of rapid changes that would destroy the medieval view of the world and of man's place in it. Earlier centuries had witnessed intellectual enquiry and the modification of accepted patterns of thought, but nevertheless the basic model, the fundamental view of the universe, the conventional world picture, had remained unaltered for a thousand years. The Church, universal and omnipotent, had given its authority to a philosophy which also on the whole satisfied the demands and ambitions of secular rulers.

The world had been created by God as the centre of an ordered universe finite in space and time. A harmonious chain of different orders of created matter existed. In the Great Chain of Being which hung from God's will there came first the different orders of angels, then man, then the animals, next the plants, and lastly the minerals. Freedom and happiness for members of each order consisted in accepting the duties of one's rank and enjoying the privileges that resulted from this correct behaviour, in carrying out the plan of God 'whose service', as the Elizabethan prayer-book later expressed it, 'is perfect freedom'. Man, part-angel and part-animal, occupied a special place.

Correspondences could be worked out between a member of one order of creation and its corresponding fellow in other orders. Thus there were similarities and appropriate parallels between gold, the king of metals; the lion, the king of beasts; earthly kings; and the sun, the king of the heavens. One could reach conclusions about the nature of each member by considering what such a group had in common.

The world, including of course man himself, was composed of four elements. When man ate, his liver turned the four elements into four liquids (*humours*) and these in turn affected his temperament:

Element	Humour	Quality	Temperament
Earth	Melancholy	Cold and dry	Melancholic
Water	Phlegm	Cold and moist	Phlegmatic

Element	Humour	Quality	Temperament
Air	Blood	Hot and moist	Sanguine
Fire	Choler	Hot and dry	Choleric

In the first chapter of *The Governor* (1531) Sir Thomas Elyot described the ordered pattern:

Take away order from all things, what should then remain? Certes nothing finally, except some man would imagine eftsoons chaos.   Also where there is any lack of order needs must be perpetual conflict.   And in things subject to nature nothing of himself only may be nourished but, when he hath destroyed that wherewith he doth participate by the order of his creation, he himself of necessity must then perish; whereof ensueth universal dissolution.

Hath not God set degrees and estates in all his glorious works?   First in his heavenly ministers, whom he hath constituted in divers degrees called hierarchies.   Behold the four elements, whereof the body of man is compact, how they be set in their places called spheres, higher or lower according to the sovereignty of their natures.   Behold also the order that God hath put generally in all his creatures, beginning at the most inferior or base and ascending upward.   He made not only herbs to garnish the earth but also trees of a more eminent stature than herbs.   Semblably in birds beasts and fishes some be good for the sustenance of man, some bear things profitable to sundry uses, other be apt to occupation and labour.   Every kind of trees herbs birds beasts and fishes have a peculiar disposition appropered unto them by God their creator so that in everything is order, and without order may be nothing stable or permanent.   And it may not be called order except it do contain in it degrees, high and base, according to the merit or estimation of the thing that is ordered.

The medieval world picture had a certain crossword puzzle quality and much of it remained a playground for intellectuals, but its basic assumptions were part of the mental climate of the times and these continued to influence sixteenth-century thought: the arts, especially poetry, discovered a stimulating source of metaphor in the correspondences between the different orders; scientific investigation found it difficult to escape from the model of the four elements and from the astrological implications of the pattern; political thought attempted to use the ideas of rank, order and obedience to justify the power of the ruler and to condemn the sin of rebellion.[1] At the same time the world picture was gradually destroyed by economic, religious and political developments.

The Monarchy

What had Henry become, and what had he and the Yorkists achieved?　In one year (1493) the Privy Purse expenses of Henry included the following items:

Jan. 1. To the choristers at Paul's and St. Stephen, 13s. 4d.
　　6. To Newark for making of a song, £1.
March 25. To one that brought the King a Mass of the Passion of our Lady, in reward, 6s. 8d.
May 13. To the waits of Northampton in reward, 13s. 4d.
　　16. To Padesey piper on the bagpipe, 6s. 8d.
Aug. 5. To the young damsel that danceth, £30
Sept. 24. To him that had his bull baited, in reward, 10s.
Nov. 12. To one Cornish for a prophecy, in reward, 13s. 4d.
　　30. Delivered to a merchant for a pair of organs, £30.
Dec. 6. To the King of France's fool in reward, £4.

Throughout the years the record of small luxuries continues: 'lost at the buttes to my lorde Marques, £1', 'for the kinges losse at chess 13 shillings and fourepence', 'for the kinges losse at cardes at Tauneton £8'; there are payments recorded to 'one that tumbled before the king', 'one that joculed before the king', and so on.　The king was a patron, too, of the new learning, with a King's Librarian (1492), a Latin Secretary (1495), and a Poet Laureate, the blind André of Toulouse.

The amusements, and the meticulous recording of them, throw light on two, perhaps contradictory, aspects of Henry's complex character.　The Venetian envoy Sanuto thought Henry 'a very great miser but a man of vast ability',[2] but the *Italian Relation* does not describe a money-grubber:

Though frugal to excess in his own person the king does not change any of the ancient usages of England at his court, keeping a sumptuous table, as I had an opportunity of witnessing twice that your Magnificence dined there, when I judged that there might be from six to seven hundred persons

[1] See, throughout, E. M. W. Tillyard, *The Elizabethan World Picture*, Chatto and Windus, 1943.
[2] Machiavelli would certainly have approved of Henry's care in money matters. In *The Prince* he wrote: 'We have not seen great things done in our time except by those who have been considered mean; the rest have failed.'

at dinner. And his people say that His Majesty spends upon his table £14,000 sterling annually . . . and it is possible that his own personal expenses, those of his Queen and of his children, and the military escort who compose his guard, and are from 150 to 200 in number, besides the many civilities that he pays to foreigners, may amount to £20,000 sterling as it is said they do.

The humanist whom Henry had himself invited to compile a history of England described his royal master as follows:

His body was slender but well built and strong; his height above the average. His appearance was remarkably attractive and his face was cheerful, especially when speaking; his eyes were small and blue, his teeth few, poor and blackish; his hair was thin and white; his complexion sallow. His spirit was distinguished, wise and prudent; his mind was brave and resolute and never, even at moments of greatest danger, deserted him. He had a most pertinacious memory. Withal he was not devoid of scholarship. In government he was shrewd and prudent, so that no one dared to get the better of him through deceit or guile. He was gracious and kind and was as attentive to visitors as he was easy of access. His hospitality was splendidly generous: he was fond of having foreigners at his court and he freely conferred favours on them. But those of his subjects who were indebted to him or who did not pay him due honour or who were generous only with promises, he treated with harsh severity[1]

In 1509 Henry died and was buried in his new chapel, still unfinished, at Westminster. The cautious exile had become one of the great kings of England, admired even by the super-sophisticated Italians, one of whom saw 'a man of vast ability, who had accumulated so much gold that he was supposed to have more than wellnigh all the other kings of Christendom'. The legendary metal was, to the observer, the outward and visible sign of that invisible security which the King, building on Yorkist models, had achieved.

Henry Tudor had put an end to civil warfare, the frame of mind that found security only in lordship or in the protection of a lord—'Get you lordship' one of the Pastons had written, '. . . on that hangs both the law and the prophets'—and had

---

[1] The *Anglica Historia of Polydore Vergil*, A.D. *1485–1537*, ed. and trans. by D. Hay (Camden Series, 1950), p. 142 et seq.

substituted for this the king's peace, concentrating in the Crown's hands all those fragments of royal power which had been alienated and divided among its subjects. Restoring solvency and power to the Crown, Henry brought as concomitants peace, justice and order to the land and in consequence firmly attached the loyalty of the propertied classes to his dynasty.

Pragmatic, empirical, a realist who never attempted more than he knew he could achieve, Henry VII stands as an equal with Henry II and with his own grand-daughter Elizabeth I. All three show a love for and grasp of statecraft, a firmness of purpose beneath a flexibility of means, and an almost unerring choice of servants to carry out their plans—servants who never became masters.

The Crown, clearly, was once again powerful—more powerful, perhaps, than at any earlier period. Was that power new, or was it the dying kick of medieval limited sovereignty? Today it is generally agreed that the strength of the Yorkists and of Henry VII rested largely on the past:

> . . . concentration of power in the hands of the sovereign effected no abrupt changes in either constitutional forms or procedures. The 'newness' of the Tudor rule lay, not in any novelty of the governmental system, but in the thoroughness with which it was administered. Old institutions were invigorated and adapted to new uses, while newer agencies followed the traditional pattern . . .[1]

> The period from the battle of Barnet (1471) to the death of Henry VII (1509) marks the recovery and renewed consolidation of medieval kingship . . . this period of reconstruction after the civil wars had considerably more affinity with the past than with the future.[2]

> The Tudor monarchy was the resurrection of a tradition.[3]

Three historians from different countries and with very different views on the sixteenth century speak with one voice on this point.

Edward IV, Richard III and Henry VII, so dissimilar in character, pursued the same limited ends with the same medieval means. Edward died when he was only forty years

[1] W. C. Richardson, *Tudor Chamber Administration, 1485–1547*, Baton Rouge, 1952, p. 1.
[2] G. R. Elton, *The Tudor Revolution in Government*, C.U.P., 1953, pp. 19–20.
[3] L. Cohen, *L'Evolution Politique de L'Angleterre*, Paris, 1960, p. 16.

old, and the work was less than half done.   He had governed
empirically, walking a knife-edge between order and disorder.
Richard's reign, though brief, gives indications that he intended
to pursue his brother's policy.   Henry, clearly, was concerned
simply to use efficiently the most effective institutions available:
'All he did was to endow existing institutions with more
precision; and above all with more force.'[1]

> The careful adjustment of his ambitions to his resources is the
> first of a statesman's duties; and it is Henry VII's singular
> merit that he accomplished the objects he set before him, and
> refrained from pursuing quests which could only lead to
> disaster.   A patient and grim diplomatist, he lacked the
> flamboyant spirit of Henry VIII and Elizabeth, and he
> never appealed to the mob, which never applauded; for
> wisdom is not a popular quality.   But no one knew his
> business better, or did his work more completely.   His
> prescription for England's disorders was a sedative toned
> with iron and administered with unflinching resolution.
> He confined to the bounds of law and order a liberty that
> had run riot over the land; and he gave the English State a
> framework of strength and unity that withstood the disrup-
> tive force of ecclesiastical revolution.[2]

Henry left to his son a strong, but not an absolute, monarchy.
The 'new' monarchies of the continent owned, or hoped to own,
standing armies and salaried officials.   Henry and the Yorkists
were content—were by force of circumstance compelled to be
content—to do things on the cheap, using existing machinery,
employing unpaid country gentry, while holding in reserve the
unlimited, undefined because undefinable, power of the royal
prerogative.   This method of government was to determine the
pattern of constitutional history for the next century and a
half.

The Social and Economic Scene

The country to which security and a measure of prosperity
had been restored was not a great power, but a small, under-
developed, thinly-peopled island on the misty fringe of civilized
Europe.

Large tracts of country were still waste, not only most of the

---

[1] J. D. Mackie, *The Earlier Tudors*, O.U.P., 1952, p. 208.
[2] A. F. Pollard, ed., *The Reign of Henry VII from Contemporary Sources* (3 vols),
Longmans, Green, 1913–14, p. lxx.

difficult highland zone—Quirini in 1506 wrote from Falmouth to his masters in Venice that he was in

> . . . a very wild place which no human being ever visits, in the midst of a most barbarous race, so different in language and custom from the Londoners and the rest of England that they are as unintelligible to these last as to the Venetians.

—but also parts of the potentially rich lowland areas, in the south and east. The vast majority of the people earned their living from subsistence agriculture or from sea fishing, while foreign trade depended on one product—sheep.

Nevertheless things were on the move. Population was growing. The old three-field system—never a static form nor a universal system, except in the history books[1]—changed rapidly in many areas as men began to consolidate and hedge their holdings, to take in the commons, to turn from arable to sheep-farming. The manor was losing its old stability and a brisk market in land was developing. As early as the fourteenth century the demesnes of many lords were cultivated almost entirely by wage labour. Great men made fortunes at court and became great landowners. A specialized food market supplied London's needs. The manufacturer of cloth tended to move from the established towns to villages. Cloth exports boomed. These developments had their origins in the fifteenth century or earlier, but their maximum impact was made in the sixteenth and seventeenth centuries.

Throughout western Europe the first half of the fifteenth century had been one of economic contraction. The second half witnessed, at least north of the Alps, the beginnings of a period of expansion. England, though perhaps lagging a little behind the continent, shared in these changes.

Between 1400 and 1475 the rent of agricultural lands fell generally (on lands belonging to the Duchy of Lancaster by as much as 20 per cent, on those of the Duchy manor of Leeds by 30 per cent to 50 per cent) while wages rose. In general, agricultural labourers' wages measured in terms of wheat rose from a base of 100 in 1300 to a figure of 220 for the period 1460–79, while artisans' wages rose to 196 in the years 1450–9.[2]

---

[1] The area where a three-field system was most common lay between Durham and Dorset, bounded on the west by Wales, and on the east by Cambridge.

[2] Postan, M., *Some Economic Evidence of Declining Population in the Later Middle Ages*, Ec.H.R., II, 1950.

The implication of these changes is that labour had become dearer because it had become scarcer; in other words, because the population was declining or had at least not recovered from the great Black Death of 1348–9 and the later attacks of 1360–1, 1369 and 1375. Before the plague the population had been in the region of 3·75 million, by 1400 it was down to about two million. Fewer people meant fewer mouths to feed and there was a consequent fall in the price of many, though not all, agricultural products.

Falling prices and rents, rising wages—it is not surprising that many landlords sought new ways of maintaining their income. They dabbled in commerce: they became more efficient, more business-like in their methods of estate management; they employed experts to help them; in particular, they turned arable land into pasture. Sheep-farming required fewer men than arable, and there was always a market for wool. The enclosure controversy—was it good for the country or bad for it—played a very large part in the economic discussions and discontents of the sixteenth century, but it is becoming clear that enclosures were well under way before the end of the fifteenth century. (The term *enclosures* came to cover many changes in land use, but essentially it referred to the hedging or fencing of land that had up to that time lain open as arable, meadow or common pasture, so that the common rights of grazing on that land were destroyed.)

Aubrey, writing in the seventeenth century, asserted that 'the destroying of petty manors began in Henry VII's time to be now common: . . . Inclosures are for the private, not for the public good. For a shepherd and his dogge, or a milk mayd, can manage that land, that upon arable employed the hands of severall scores of labourers.' There is independent evidence that Aubrey was not predating later developments. In 1548 the enclosure commissioner John Hales claimed that 'the greater part of the depopulation of towns was before the beginning of the reign of King Henry the Seventh' and John Rous, who died in 1491, listed fifty-eight places which had been depopulated in Warwickshire alone, most of which have been identified in the present century. He wrote:

> What shall be said of the modern destruction of villages which brings Dearth to the commonwealth? The root of this evil is greed. . . . How many outrageous things do men perform! . . .

They enclose the area of a village with mounds and surround it with ditches. In such places the king's highway is blocked and poor people cannot pass through. . . .

If such destruction as that in Warwickshire took place in other parts of the country it would be a national danger.[1]

It has been calculated that between 1485 and 1500 in the five counties of Warwickshire, Oxfordshire, Berkshire, Northamptonshire and Buckinghamshire almost 16,000 acres of land were enclosed, of which 13,000 acres were turned over to pasture. In another county, Leicestershire, one-third of the enclosures carried out between 1485 and 1607 had been effected before 1509. In general, depopulation by conversion to pasture seems to have reached its peak about the years 1485–1520.

Although the figures available concern only a small fraction of the total area of the counties involved, they represent a great upheaval in the lives of the people affected, and these 'depopulating' enclosures alarmed the government. In 1489 two acts were passed to reverse the process, one directed against 'the pulling down of towns' which declared 'where in some towns 200 persons were occupied and lived by their lawful labour, now be there occupied 2 or 3 herdsmen, and the residue fall in idleness. . . .' The second applied specifically to the Isle of Wight—'the which Isle is late decayed of people, by reason that many towns and villages be let down and the fields dyked and made pastures for beasts and cattle, ...'—if this depopulation continued, the French would seize the island! But sheep were profitable, already there may have been eight million (almost three to every man, woman and child) and government legislation proved quite ineffective.

In trade, as in agriculture, the century from 1350 to 1450 was one of arrested development, while the years after 1450 saw revival and expansion. The London merchants in particular showed their confidence in the stability of Edward IV's government, and a marked improvement in trade following the Treaty of Picquigny. At about this time, too, the population began to increase again and by 1500 had probably reached three million. Internal trade was far greater in volume than

---

[1] Extracts taken from M. Beresford; *The Lost Villages of England*, Lutterworth Press, 1954, p. 81. At the time of writing 1,353 deserted medieval villages have been located. Not all, of course, were depopulated in the fifteenth century.

external trade, but, by its nature, it is impossible to measure it. The exchange of local products at the local market was universal; the sale of more specialized products, such as Mendip lead, Cornish tin, or Tyneside coal, could be carried on wherever water transport was available. (In 1490 the Bishop of Durham was in communication with Sir John Paston of Norfolk, concerning the possibility of exchanging coal for corn, wax, wine and other products.) By 1500 the population of London was perhaps 50,000 and its demands were leading to the growth of a specialized food market, drawing on the home counties. In size London was unique: Norwich, York, Bristol, Newcastle, Coventry and Exeter had populations of not more than 10,000, and other 'towns' were only very large villages. It is possible that a limiting factor in the growth of many inland towns was the difficulty of feeding large numbers of town dwellers.

There is much more information about the nature and extent of overseas trade. Since at least the thirteenth century wool exports, controlled by the Company of the Staple with its headquarters in Calais, had been England's 'staple product', more than equal in value to all other exports together. In the fifteenth century these wool exports declined, their place being taken by exports of undyed cloth. The sheep remained supreme. As a fifteenth-century wool merchant's epitaph expressed it,

> God be praised and ever shall
> It is the sheep hath paid for all.

The cloth trade was a monopoly in the hands of a new company, the Merchant Adventurers, licensed to deal in any commodity except wool. Cloth exports passed through their hands into Flanders by way of the Company's headquarters, which they moved in Edward IV's reign from *Bruges le mort* to the rising centre of Antwerp.

By 1475 cloth exports had pulled ahead of wool, and they increased their lead during the reign of Henry VII. Steady progress over the years 1485–1503 was followed at the close of the reign by a boom which continued into the first years of Henry VIII's reign. Under Henry VII cloth exports increased by 61 per cent, while wool exports declined by about 30 per cent over the same period:

Years	Exports of wool (sacks)	Exports of broadcloth	Exports & imports of miscellaneous merchandise paying poundage (value in £)
1399–1402	15,023	27,760	
1462–5	7,044	25,855	57,449
1479–82	9,784	62,586	179,340
1503–9	3,839	81,835	116,003[1]

(for comparisons, reckon 4·3 cloths to the sack)

Who handled this growing volume of trade? As far as cloth was concerned the proportions exported by Englishmen and foreigners were as follows: Englishmen 53 per cent, Hansards 24 per cent, other aliens 23 per cent. Until about 1500 the outports shared in the general growth of England's trade. For instance, during the fifteenth century the population of Exeter trebled, an increase almost entirely due to its growing significance as a port. In the sixteenth century exports tended to be concentrated in the hands of London merchants who used either their home port or, for the last few years of Henry VII's reign, Southampton. Foreigners, too, concentrated their activities in London, the Hansards importing 96 per cent of their cloths through London in the period 1503–9.

The cloth boom was accompanied by the manufacture of new types of cloth in new areas, notably in East Anglia and the west country. The Stroud Valley began to acquire importance in Edward IV's reign, thanks to the existence of a plentiful supply of water for the fulling mills and dyeworks, and by the time of Henry VII 'Stroudwater reds' were famous for their quality. The cloth boom was the most important single industrial development, but one must not overestimate its importance in the daily life of the average Englishman—in 1450 there were probably not more than about 25,000 people employed in the cloth industry and although the numbers increased after that date they remained small in comparison with the total population.

There is evidence of growing royal interest in economic matters and the 1490's mark a peak (if only a small one) in the history of state planning by statute.

[1] Based on M. Postan and E. E. Rich, *The Cambridge Economic History of Europe*, Vol. II, C.U.P., 1952, p. 193, and P. Ramsey, *Overseas Trade in the Reign of Henry VII*, Ec.H.R., VI, 1953.

Commercial treaties were concluded with Spain and Portugal (1489), with the city of Riga (1498), with Ferdinand and Isabella (1499), with George, Duke of Saxony (1505). The rights of the Hanse and of Venice were a little restricted, while those of the English trader were enlarged, by the 'navigation acts' of 1485 (which enacted that no one was to buy or sell French wines '. . . but such wines as shall be adventured in an English, Irish, or Welsh man's ship. . . .') and 1489. In 1496 the Cabots were granted sole ownership of any heathen lands which they discovered, in return for a fifth of any profits made. In 1497 John Cabot sailed from Bristol under a royal commission, made his landfall in Newfoundland or Nova Scotia (probably at Cape Breton or Cape Race), and was rewarded by the king. Later entries in the King's account book include such items as:

> 1 April, 1498. To Thomas Bradley and Launcelot Thirkill going to the new Isle, £30.
> 'three men taken in the Newfound Island . . . clothed in beasts skins, and did eate raw flesh, and spake such speach that no man could understand them, and in their demeanour like to bruite beasts . . .'

Lorenzeo Pascuaglio wrote to his brothers on 23 August 1497:

> The Venetian, our countryman, who went with a ship from Bristol in quest of new islands, is returned, and says that 700 leagues hence he discovered land the territory of the Grand Cham. He coasted for three hundred leagues and landed; saw no human beings, but has brought hither to the King certain snares which had been set to catch game, and a needle for making nets; he also found some felled trees, wherefore he supposed there were inhabitants, and returned to his ship in alarm.
> . . . The King of England is much pleased with this intelligence . . . he is now at Bristol with his wife, who is also Venetian, and with his sons; his name is Zuan Cabot, and he is styled the great admiral. Vast honour is paid him; he dresses in silk, and these English run after him like mad people, so that he can enlist as many as he pleases, and a number of our own rogues besides.

In 1498 John sailed again and never returned. In 1506 the Bristol adventurers backed his son Sebastian and in 1508–9 he apparently reached Hudson Bay and then sailed as far south

as Delaware—early probings which were not followed up by
Henry VIII.

The policy of the Yorkists and of Henry, together with the
new economic trends, helped to make this period one of
mobility and change—movement and change that were to
some extent reflected in the social structure.

It would be unwise to overestimate the decline in the strength
of the nobility.   During the fifteenth-century civil wars twelve
of the descendants of Edward III in the male line were killed,
executed or murdered, and fifty-one lords and their heirs were
killed or executed, yet the old view that the blood-letting of
these wars permanently reduced their numbers can be shown to
be exaggerated.   The impact of attainders during the years
1453 to 1509 has been carefully analysed.   During the reign
of Edward IV 140 attainders were passed and 86 were reversed;
under Richard III the figures are respectively 100 and 99;
under Henry VII they are 138 and 52.   It was very much easier
for a noble to have his attainder reversed than for a lesser man;
34 nobles were attainted and of these attainders 29 were
eventually reversed.   The kings, especially Henry VII, were
glad 'to hold the sharpest of legal swords over recalcitrant
heads', but the sword was intended to intimidate, not to
destroy.[1]   The twenty-nine lords of Henry's first parliament
mark the lowest point.   During the next quarter of a century
attainders were reversed, suspended peerages revived, five new
creations were made.   By the end of the reign there were
as many lords as there had been before the civil wars.   Their
illegal activities had been cut back, but their legal rights
survived almost untouched.   They remained powers in the
land, though they were—to adapt Bacon—powers under the
king's throne.   They were not excluded from the Council.
Perhaps there were more new men than formerly, but these
had been summoned because of their *expertise* and not as part
of a deliberate policy of by-passing the nobility.

Nevertheless, new men were on the way up.   Except in
Spain and Portugal the tendency was general in western
Europe, as Rabelais genially observed a few years later:

---

[1] J. R. Lander, *Attainder and Forfeiture, 1453 to 1509*; H.J. IV/2, 1961.   The
detailed figures of attainders during the reign of Henry VII are as follows: 1485–6,
28; 1487, 28; 1489–90, 8; 1491–2, 1; 1495, 24; 1504, 51.

I think many are at this day Emperours, Kings, Dukes Princes, and Popes on earth, whose extraction is some porter, and pardon-pedlars . . .

The great names of the sixteenth century were often of 'middle-class' origin: the Herberts were sprung from Welsh gentry; the Russells were Dorset wine merchants; the ancestor of the Pagets was a London sergeant-at-arms, and that of the Cecils a yeoman of the wardrobe; Wolsey's father was an East Anglian grazier, Thomas Cromwell's a brewer, blacksmith and fuller.

There were two roads, not necessarily mutually exclusive, to power and a peerage; royal favour, usually at this period a consequence of faithful service, and money, with which one might buy lands, respectability, a place at court and royal favour. Indentured retainers and a hereditary title were no longer essential and might even prove perilous, as Mountjoy realized when, in 1485, he advised his sons 'to live right wisely and never take the state of baron upon them if they may leave it from them, nor to desire to be great about princes, for it is dangerous'. The personal bond gave place, slowly but inexorably, to the cash nexus. The legal distinction between bondsman and free gave place to one between the man who could pay his rent and the man who could not. A fifteenth-century poem had already recognized the power of money in its refrain:

> Above all thyng thow art a kyng
> And rulest the world over alle.

The esquires and the gentlemen—these were the groups from which the courtier and the J.P. alike were recruited. An examination of the position of the early Tudor gentry, based on five counties in the years 1524–7, concludes that esquires and gentlemen owned half the lay-owned land and that one in three —usually the wealthiest—executed Crown commissions and served as magistrates.[1] They formed about 2 per cent of the population. These ambitious, thrusting men hitched their fortunes to those of the great, pressed into parliament, climbed the staircase of State preferment, and sent their sons to the new schools and the old universities.

[1] J. Cornwall, *The Early Tudor Gentry:* Ec.H.R., XVII, 1965.

EXTRACTS

I. '*The Paston Letters*'—*over a thousand papers, dating from the years 1420–1503, and relating to the affairs of the Pastons, a Norfolk family. Mainly concerned with private matters, national crises loom distantly in the background but occasionally the family is caught up in them.*

1. The temporary restoration of Henry VI brings disaster to Edward IV's supporters:

1470, 12 October

... Tidings, the Earl of Worcester [John Tiptoft] is like to die this day or tomorrow at the farthest. John Pilkington, Master W. Attcliff, and Fowler are taken and in the castle of Pomfret, and are like to die hastily, without they be dead. Sir T. Montgomery and John Donne be taken; what shall fall of them I cannot say. ...

2. The Pastons fight on the losing side at Barnet:

1471, 18th April

... Mother, I recommend me to you, letting you wit [know] that, blessed be God, my brother John is alive and fareth well, and in no peril of death. Nevertheless he is hurt with an arrow on his right arm beneath the elbow, and I have sent him a surgeon, which hath dressed him, and he telleth me that he trusteth that he shall be all whole within right short time. It is so that John Milsent [the Milsents were in the Pastons' service] is dead, God have mercy on his soul, and William Milsent is alive, and his other servants all be escaped, by all likelihood ...

3. The Duke of Norfolk (who was killed at Bosworth) summons John Paston III to fight for Richard III:

1485, c. 12 August

... Well-beloved friend, I commend me to you, letting you to understand that the King's enemies be a land, and that the King would have set forth as upon Monday but only for Our Lady Day; but for certain he goeth forward as upon Tuesday, for a servant of mine brought to me the certainty. Wherefore I pray you that ye meet with me at Bury [St. Edmunds], for by the grace of God I purpose to lie at Bury as upon Tuesday night; and that ye bring with you such company of tall men as ye may goodly make at my cost and charge, beside that ye have promised the King. And I pray you ordain them jackets of my livery, and I shall content you at your meeting with me.

Your lover,
J. NORFOLK

4. William Paston prepares to join Henry VII's expedition to France:

1492, 18 February

. . . Sir, the King sendeth ordnance to the seaside, and his tents
and hales [pavilions] be a-making fast and many of them be
made. And there is also great provision made by gentlemen
that should go with his Grace for horse, harness, tents, hales,
gardevians [chests], carts, and other things that should serve
for this journey that the King intendeth to take on hand, so
that by likelihood His Grace will be going soon upon Easter.
And so I intended, after that I hear hereafter, to go to Calas to
purvey me of harness and such things as I shall need besides
horse, under that form that my costs shall be paid for. Sir, I
am as yet no better horsed than I was when I was with you, nor
I wot not where to have none, for horse-flesh is of such a price
here that my purse is scant able to buy one horse; wherefore
I beseech you to hearken for some in your country. . . . (*The
Paston Letters*, ed. N. Davis, 1963 (by permission of the Clarendon
Press, Oxford); pp. 195, 196, 256, 257–8.)

II. *Dominic Mancini, an Italian humanist who came to England in
1482, describes Edward IV:*

Edward was of a gentle and cheerful aspect: nevertheless should
he assume an angry countenance he could appear very terrible
to beholders. He was easy of access to his friends and to
others, even the least notable. Frequently he called to his side
complete strangers, when he thought that they had come with
the intention of addressing or beholding him more closely. He
was wont to show himself to those who wished to watch him,
and he seized any opportunity that the occasion offered of
showing his fine stature more protractedly and more evidently
to on-lookers. He was so genial in his greeting, that if he saw
a newcomer bewildered at his appearance and royal magnificence, he would give him courage to speak by laying a kindly
hand upon his shoulder. To plaintiffs and to those who complained of injustice he lent a willing ear; charges against himself
he contented with an excuse if he did not remove the cause.
He was more favourable than other princes to foreigners, who
visited his realm for trade or any other reason. He very
seldom showed munificence, and then only in moderation,
still he was very grateful to those from whom he had received
a favour. Though not rapacious of other men's goods, he was
yet so eager for money, that in pursuing it he acquired a reputation for avarice. (Mancini, *The Usurpation of Richard III*, ed.
C. A. J. Armstrong, 1936 (by permission of the Clarendon Press,
Oxford); pp. 79 et seq.)

III. *Francis Bacon describes Henry VII: Francis Bacon wrote in 1622, and based his 'Life' largely on Polydore Vergil, but he wrote with genius and is immensely quotable, if used with caution:*

... This King (to speak of him in terms equal to his deserving) was one of the best sort of wonders; a wonder for wise men ... He did much maintain and countenance his laws; which (nevertheless) was no impediment to him to work his will. For it was so handled that neither prerogative nor profit went to diminution. And yet as he would sometimes train up his laws to his prerogative, so would he also let down his prerogative to his Parliament. For mint and wars and martial discipline (things of absolute power) he would nevertheless bring to Parliament. Justice was well administered in his time, save where the King was party; save also that the counsel-table interfered too much with *meum* and *tuum*. For it was a very court of justice during his time, especially in the beginning. But in that part both of justice and policy which is the durable part, and cut as it were in brass or marble, which is the making of good laws, he did excel. ... But the less blood he drew the more he took of treasure: and as some construed it, he was the more sparing in the one that he might be the more pressing in the other; for both would have been intolerable. ... He was of an high mind and loved his own will and his own way; as one that revered himself and would reign indeed. Had he been a private man he would have been termed proud: but in a wise Prince, it was but keeping of distance; which indeed he did towards all; not admitting any near or full approach either to his power or to his secrets. For he was governed by none. ... Certain it is that though his reputation was great at home, yet it was greater abroad. ...

As for his secret spials which he did employ both at home and abroad, by them to discover what parties and conspiracies were against him, surely his case required it, he had such moles perpetually working and casting to undermine him. ...

To his counsel he did refer much, and sat oft in person; knowing it to be the way to assist his power and inform his judgement, in which respect also he was fairly patient of liberty both of advice and of vote, till himself were declared.

He kept a strait hand on his nobility, and chose rather to advance clergymen and lawyers, which were more obsequious to him, but had less interest in the people; which made for his absoluteness but not for his safety. ... For it is a strange thing, that though he were a dark prince and infinitely suspicious, and his times full of secret conspiracies and troubles, yet in twenty-four years reign he never put down or discomposed counsellor or near servant, save only Stanley the Lord Chamberlain.   As for the disposition of his subjects in general towards him, it stood thus with him, that of the three affections which naturally tie the hearts of the subjects to their sovereign,— love, fear, and reverence,—he had the last in height, the second in good measure, and so little of the first as he was beholding to the other two.

He was a Prince, sad, serious, and full of thoughts and secret observations, and full of notes and memorials of his own hand, especially touching persons; as whom to employ, whom to reward, whom to inquire of, whom to beware of, what were the dependencies, what were the factions, and the like; keeping (as it were) a journal of his thoughts. . . .

. . . Yet take him with all his defects, if a man should compare him with the kings his concurrents in France and Spain, he shall find him more politic than Lewis the Twelfth of France, and more entire and sincere than Ferdinando of Spain.   But if you shall change Lewis the Twelfth for Lewis the Eleventh, who lived a little before, then the consort is more perfect.   For that Lewis the Eleventh, Ferdinando, and Henry, may be esteemed for the *tres magi* of kings of those ages.   To conclude, if this King did no greater matters, it was long of himself, for what he minded he compassed.

He was a comely personage, a little above just stature, well and straight limbed, but slender.   His countenance was reverend and a little like a churchman: and as it was not strange or dark, so neither was it winning or pleasing, but as the face of one well disposed.   But it was to the disadvantage of the painter, for it was best when he spake.   (F. Bacon, *The Life of Henry VII.*)

IV. '*The Italian Relation*'.   *An Italian, probably a Venetian, describes England in Henry VII's reign.*

1. . . . The English are great lovers of themselves, and of everything belonging to them; they think that there are no other men than themselves, and no other world but England; and whenever they see a handsome foreigner, they say that 'he looks like an Englishman', and that 'it is a great pity that he should not be an Englishman'; and when they partake of any delicacy with a foreigner, they ask him, 'whether such a thing is made in *their* country?' . . . Few people keep wine in their own houses, but buy it, for the most part, at a tavern; and when they mean to drink a great deal, they go to the tavern, and this

is done not only by the men, but by ladies of distinction. . . . They are gifted with good understandings, and are very quick at every thing they apply their minds to; few, however, excepting the clergy, are addicted to the study of letters: . . . (*p. 20*)

2.   The riches of England are greater than those of any other country in Europe. . . .   This is owing in the first place, to the great fertility of the soil, which is such, that with the exception of wine, they import nothing from abroad for their subsistence. Next, the sale of their valuable tin brings in a large sum of money to the kingdom; but still more do they derive from their extraordinary abundance of wool, which bears such a high price and reputation throughout Europe.   (*p. 28*)

3.   The population of this island does not appear to me to bear any proportion to her fertility and riches.   I rode, as your Magnificence knows, from Dover to London, and from London to Oxford, a distance of more than 200 Italian miles, and it seemed to me to be very thinly inhabited; . . . .   (*p. 31*)

4.   They have a very high reputation in arms; and from the great fear the French entertain of them, one must believe it to be justly acquired.   But I have it on the best information, that when the war is raging most furiously, they will seek for good eating, and all their other comforts, without thinking of what harm might befall them.

They have an antipathy to foreigners, and imagine that they never come into their island, but to make themselves masters of it, and to usurp their goods; . . .

The want of affection in the English is strongly manifested towards their children; for after having kept them at home till they arrive at the age of seven or nine years at the utmost, they put them out, both males and females, to hard service in the houses of other people, binding them generally for another seven or nine years.   And these are called apprentices, . . . (*p. 33*)

5.   . . . all the beauty of this island is confined to London; which, although sixty miles distant from the sea, possesses all the advantages of a maritime town; . . . vessels of 100 tons burden can come up to the city, . . . Although this city has no buildings in the Italian style, but of timber or brick like the French, the Londoners live comfortably, and, it appears to me, that there are not fewer inhabitants than at Florence or Rome. It abounds with every article of luxury, as well as with the necessaries of life: but the most remarkable thing in London is the wonderful quantity of wrought silver. . . .   In one single street, named the Strand, leading to St. Paul's, there are

fifty-two goldsmith's shops, so rich and full of silver vessels, great and small, that in all the shops in Milan, Rome, Venice, and Florence put together, I do not think there would be found so many of the magnificence that are to be seen in London. (*p. 41*) (*A relation, or rather a true account, of the island of England . . . about the year 1500,* ed. C. A. Sneyd, Vol. 37, Camden Old Series.)

Further Reading

K. Pickthorn, *Early Tudor Government: Henry VII,* C.U.P., 1934

A. F. Pollard, ed., *The Reign of Henry VII from Contemporary Sources* (3 vols), Longmans, Green, 1913–14

F. W. Brooks, *The Council of the North,* H.A., Pamphlet G 25, 1953

G. A. J. Hodgett, *Agrarian England in the Later Middle Ages,* H.A., Aids for Teachers No. 13, 1966

K. B. McFarlane, *The Wars of the Roses,* Raleigh Lecture, O.U.P., 1964

B. P. Wolffe, *Yorkist and Early Tudor Government, 1461–1509,* H.A., Aids for Teachers No. 12, 1966

G. R. Elton, *Henry VII: Rapacity and Remorse,* H.J., I, 1958

J. R. Lander, *The Yorkist Council and Administration, 1461–85,* E.H.R., 286, 1958

— *Attainder and Forfeiture 1453–1509,* H.J., IV, 1961

P. Ramsey, *Overseas Trade in the Reign of Henry VII,* Ec.H.R., VI, 1953

B. P. Wolffe, *The Crown Lands 1461 to 1536,* Allen and Unwin, 1970

R. Lockyer, *Henry VII,* Longmans, 1968

III · HENRY VIII AND CARDINAL WOLSEY

Introduction

Two question marks hang over the character of Henry VIII.
Was he 'bluff King Hal', or was he a royal monster? Was he a
statesman-king content usually to rule through carefully chosen
ministers but able, when circumstances demanded it, to take
charge and frame policies himself, or was he an opportunist,
dependent on his ministers for a coherent course of action and
given to temperamental vacillation when left to himself?

The historian has no easy task with Henry VIII. He must
try to escape from the sheer physical presence of this handsome giant with his bright and penetrating eye, his frequent
joviality, his ready manipulation of men. On the other
hand, he must not surrender to a natural revulsion against
a man who constantly introduced personal emotion into
politics, pursued vendettas, displayed brutal indifference or
vindictive hatred where he had ceased to approve.[1]

At his accession Henry enjoyed three advantages. It was a
hundred years since an adult ruler had succeeded to the throne
of a peaceful and united England. It was even longer since a
king had inherited in addition a full treasury, a powerful and
efficient administrative machine, and a secure position in
Europe. Thirdly, the new king looked the part. Handsome,
strong, skilled in sport, an adequate linguist and musician,
above all young—Henry VIII appeared very different from
his old and careful father. Taken together, these facts help
to account for the impression he made on casual observers and
to explain the—to our ears—fulsome contemporary descriptions
of the young Henry.

Erasmus had already written that Prince Henry, at the age
of nine, exhibited 'a certain dignity combined with singular
courtesy'; soon after his accession an observer reported him to
be 'the handsomest potentate I have ever set eyes on; . . . sings
from the book at sight, draws the bow with greater strength than
any man in England, and jousts marvellously'. 'Love for the
king,' said another, 'is universal with all who see him, for his

[1] G. R. Elton, *Henry VIII*, H.A., Pamphlet G 51, 1962, pp. 26–27.

highness does not seem a person of this world, but one descended from heaven.' In 1509 Mountjoy had written to Erasmus, 'if you could see how the world here is rejoicing in the possession of so great a prince, how his life is all their desire, you could not contain your cheers for joy. Avarice is expelled the country; liberality scatters riches with bounteous hand. Our king does not desire gold or gems, but virtue, glory, immortality.' Ten years later the picture was unchanged when the Venetian ambassador, Giustiniani, described King Henry:

> His Majesty is twenty-nine years old and extremely hand-some. Nature could not have done more for him. He is much handsomer than any other sovereign in Christendom; a great deal handsomer than the King of France; very fair and his whole frame admirably proportioned. On hearing that Francis I wore a beard, he allowed his own to grow, and as it is reddish, he has now a beard that looks like gold. He is very accomplished, a good musician, composes well, is a most capital horseman, a fine jouster, speaks good French, Latin and Spanish, is very religious, hears three masses daily when he hunts, and sometimes five on other days. He hears the office every day in the Queen's chamber, that is to say, vesper and compline. He is very fond of hunting and never takes his diversion without tiring eight or ten horses, which he causes to be stationed beforehand along the line of the country he means to take, and when one is tired he mounts another, and before he gets home they are all exhausted. He is extremely fond of tennis, at which game it is the prettiest thing to see him play, his fair skin glowing through a shirt of the finest texture.

And, as late as 1531, another Venetian envoy was reporting that the King's face 'is angelic rather than handsome, his head imperial and bold . . .'

The court matched its ruler. Hall in his *Chronicle* described the Christmas festivities of 1511–12:

> The King this year kept the feast of Christmas at Greenwich, where was such abundance of viands served to all comers of any honest behaviour as hath been few times seen. And against New Year's night was made in the hall a castle, gates, towers and dungeon, garnished with artillery and weapon after the most warlike fashion: and on the front of the castle was written *Le Fortresse Dangerus*; and within the castle were six ladies, clothed in russet satin, laid all over with leaves of

gold, and every seam knit with laces of blue silk and gold, on their heads, coifs and caps all of gold.

After this castle had been carried about the hall, and the Queen had beheld it, in came the King with five others, apparelled in coats, the one half of russet satin, spangled with spangles of fine gold; the other half, rich cloth of gold, on their heads caps of russet satin, embroidered with work of fine gold bullion. These six assaulted the castle; the ladies seeing them so lusty and courageous were content to solace with them, and upon further communication to yield the castle; and so they came down and danced a long space, And, after, the ladies led the knights into the castle, and then the castle suddenly vanished out of their sights.

Within six weeks of his father's death Henry was married to Catherine of Aragon, a marriage that endured for over twenty years. Catherine was six years older than her husband and, at least initially, was able to use her influence in the interests of Spain. In her eyes England was a branch of the family business, as is clear from her letters to her father, Ferdinand of Aragon, in which she wrote: 'These kingdoms of your highness are in great tranquillity.'

The new king inherited his father's advisers and continued their employment; the lesser men such as Lovell, Poynings, and Harry Marney, Chancellor of the Duchy of Lancaster; the Treasurer, Thomas Howard, Earl of Surrey, who had served three previous kings; Warham, Archbishop of Canterbury and Lord Chancellor; above all, Richard Fox, Bishop of Winchester, a wary and resourceful man, whom the Venetian ambassador described as *alter rex*.

Two men were missing. Henry VII had in his last days promised a reformation of government, the punishment of unjust servants. Now Empson and Dudley, the officials who had done most to establish the real bases of the late king's power, were tried on a fictitious charge of treason and inevitably found guilty. It was a convenient method of establishing the popularity of the new régime, but it was also an omen of things to come. Before his death the fairy-book prince would have taken the lives of, among others, four descendants of Edward III, two wives and two of his chief ministers.

Parliament met in January 1510. Warham addressed the assembly, calling it the 'political stomach of the realm', and

E

defining its members' duties as being to 'repeal such laws as were bad, to temper such as were rigorous, and to issue such as were useful'. An act of attainder was passed against Empson and Dudley, the export of bullion was prohibited, all persons under the degree of knight of the garter were forbidden to wear foreign-made woollen cloth, supplies (including tunnage and poundage for life and the wool subsidy) were granted to the king, and then Henry VIII's first parliament was dissolved.

The reign falls fairly distinctly into five parts. The first (1509–14) is rather colourless, in many ways a continuation of Henry VII's rule, though there are some uncharacteristic foreign adventures; the second (1514–29) is dominated by the great panjandrum, Cardinal Wolsey; the third (1529–32) is concerned with a variety of desperate attempts to provide a satisfactory solution to the 'King's Matter'; there follows (1532–40) the final break with Rome and the administrative work of Thomas Cromwell. The last years, from 1540–7 are an unfortunate epilogue, a period of decline, debasement and disaster, best considered together with the reigns of Edward VI and Mary I as part of a mid-century period of crisis.

Foreign Affairs

England's basic needs remained unchanged; to keep a watchful eye on France and Scotland, to maintain the economically important link with the Netherlands, to avoid entanglement in European wars which did not concern her. These needs were not satisfied. England's intervention in Europe during the reign was intermittent, irrational and unprofitable. It is difficult to construct a coherent account of what was in many respects a disconnected series of escapades. Yet the pattern of European statecraft during the first half of the sixteenth century is basically very simple, though immensely complicated in detail. France fought Spain and the Empire for control of that debatable land which stretched south across Europe from the Netherlands up the left bank of the Rhine and through Italy to Rome itself, and both sides looked for allies of all sorts, from the Great Turk in the east to the King of England in the west. For much of the period three rulers dominated the scene; the Emperor Charles V (1519–56), Francis I of France (1515–47), and Henry VIII.

In December 1508 Pope Julius II had been prime mover in the formation of the League of Cambrai, directed against Venice. Six months later the French had defeated the Republic at Agnadello; 'In one day,' wrote Machiavelli, 'the Venetians lost all that they had acquired during eight hundred years of strenuous effort.' Yet none of the allies wanted to see France 'lord of Italy and monarch of the world' and Julius at once set to work to make a Holy League with Spain and Venice to drive the French from Italy. The Pope's flattery, his father-in-law's encouragement, a full war-chest and— perhaps most potent of all—his desire to play Henry V all combined to lure Henry VIII into joining the League (1511).

It was over fifty years since England had last fought with serious intent in Europe. The enemy, France, was traditional. So, unfortunately, were the English preparations. The shire musters provided the basis for the expeditionary force, feudal in origin and command. War was changing, and England lacked the heavy cavalry, the professional mercenaries, the mobile artillery and the practised commanders of her continental neighbour's and the king's new corps of Gentlemen Pensioners was much too small. The English fleet, though, was effective. It included five good ships built by Henry VII, among which were the 1,000 tonners, *Regent* and *Sovereign*.

Throughout his reign the King had a care for the navy. By 1514 Henry had built *Mary Rose* (600 tons), *Peter Pomegranate* (450 tons) and *Henry Grace à Dieu* (1,000 tons). Trinity House was organized, and in 1517 the King himself acted as Master at the launching of a new galley, the *Virgin Mary*, using a 'large whistle with which he whistled almost as loud as a trumpet'; in the same year a dry dock was built at Deptford and later that at Portsmouth was extended. Between 1509 and 1547 there were built 47 ships and another 35 were acquired by purchase or as prizes. Money, too, was available. In February 1512 the second parliament of the reign met and voted supplies for the war, two fifteenths and tenths.

Ferdinand persuaded Henry that he should reconquer the old English province of Guienne in the south-west of France. In fact he needed troops in that area to cover his flank while he seized Navarre. It was a trap into which he had often tried— and failed—to lure Henry VII. In June the English landed 10,000 men at Fuenterrabia on the border between Navarre and

Guienne. Lacking proper food, equipment and discipline they
were home again before Christmas, but meanwhile Ferdinand
had taken Spanish Navarre.

Next year Henry tried again. In May 1513 an expedition
of 14,000 men, prepared by Wolsey and commanded by the

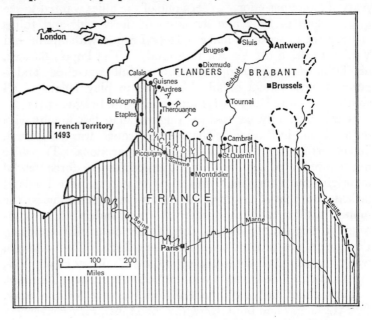

NORTH-EAST FRANCE AND THE LOW COUNTRIES, 1471–1559

earl of Shrewsbury, landed at Calais and invested Thérouanne,
thirty miles to the south-east. In June a further 11,000 men
followed under the command of Henry himself. In August
a French force sent to relieve the town was routed at Guinegate,
a mile or two to the south, in the 'Battle of the Spurs'—so called
from the speed of the French retreat. Thérouanne at once
capitulated, and in the following month Tournai followed suit,
'the wealthiest city in all Flanders, and the most populous of
any on this side of Paris'. By November Henry was back
in England, the fiasco of 1512 forgotten. 'Let all other
Christian princes take example by this unconquered king',
boasted a contemporary Englishman.

When England fought France it was almost routine that
Scotland, true to the 'auld alliance', should cross the Border to

threaten the English from the rear. In August 1513 James IV invaded England and won some early successes, but he could not move south while Berwick remained in the hands of the English.

Meanwhile the old earl of Surrey, who had been left in command of the home front, moved north with speed and efficiency, and in September he met James at Flodden, a dozen miles south-west of Berwick. The Scottish army at the outset held a strong position, but they abandoned it, partly as a result of Surrey's manœuvres, and were destroyed. Ten thousand were killed, including the king himself and many lords, and for a generation there was less danger from the Scots.

In 1514 Henry's former allies, Maximilian and Ferdinand, withdrew from the war and secretly promised France to make war on the King if he carried out the very treaty to which they had all three publicly agreed. The Spanish ambassador in London complained that when this secret promise became known he was treated 'like a bull at whom everyone throws darts', but it soon became clear that in matters of diplomacy Henry VIII now had little to learn. Within the year England had signed a perpetual peace with France, by which Louis XII agreed to increase the pension paid under the terms of the treaty of Etaples, Henry was to hold Tournai and his seventeen-year-old sister Mary was to marry the fifty-two year old Louis, whose wife Anne of Britanny had died a few months before.

England had emerged with some success from her activities of the last three years. 'I do not see any faith in the world save in me only, and therefore God Almighty, who knows this, prospers my affairs,' Henry piously concluded. It was an early hint of that belief in a working partnership between himself and the Almighty that was later to colour the king's actions to an alarming extent. In fact, the king's triumph was at least partly due to Thomas Wolsey, who had shown himself a competent royal servant, an efficient organizer and a shrewd diplomatist. 'I was the author of the peace,' he later claimed, and he received his reward. In January 1514 he was appointed bishop of Lincoln, Tournai soon followed, and within six months he became archbishop of York.

Thomas Wolsey was born about the year 1473, the son of an East Anglian grazier. At an early age he had gone up

to Magdalen College Oxford, and had subsequently been
advanced by a series of influential patrons who included the
marquess of Dorset, Henry Deane archbishop of Canterbury,
and the deputy lieutenant of Calais, Sir Richard Nanfan.   In
the last years of Henry VII he became one of the royal chaplains
and was employed on minor missions to Scotland and the
Netherlands.   At the beginning of the next reign his fortunes
appear to have been helped forward by Fox, who was concerned
to build up a group of his own men in opposition to the Earl of
Surrey.   Wolsey, with his eye already on the interests of Rome,
had encouraged Henry's adhesion to the Holy League and had
acted as a sort of quartermaster-general in the preparations for
the campaigns of 1513.   His advice and his activities had
proved successful.

For the next fifteen years England's foreign policy was
Wolsey's, a means to the acquisition of authority for himself.
To this end, the interests of the Papacy must be considered.
Before the close of 1514 the bishop of Durham observed
'. . . in the affairs of France, the policy of England will be that
of Rome.'   It was a more perceptive comment on the basic
principles of Wolsey's policy than that of many historians.

The old men were disappearing from the scene.   In 1515
Louis XII died, worn out it is said by Mary's ceaseless gaieties,
and was succeeded by his son Francis I.[1]   The new king was
two years younger than Henry.   The bishop of Winchester described him as follows: 'Francis is tall in stature, broad-
shouldered, oval and handsome in face, slender in the legs and
much inclined to corpulence.'   Francis at once invaded Italy,
and won a great victory at Marignano, a few miles south-east
of Milan.   This second phase of the Italian wars was to last
with brief intermissions till 1529.   Meanwhile in 1516 Ferdinand of Aragon died and was succeeded by his grandson
Charles, who was eight years younger than Henry.   Slow, ugly,
reserved, Charles was also honest and capable.   As the years
went by, experience made him a formidable monarch.

Both the new rulers looked to England for support and in
October 1518 Wolsey scored his only real diplomatic triumph.
By the treaty of London Charles, Francis, Henry and Maxi-
milian bound themselves to work together against the Turk.

[1] Mary took as her second husband Charles Brandon, Duke of Suffolk.   Lady
Jane Grey was their granddaughter.

Wolsey briefly occupied what he felt to be his proper position: 'As I was the author of the peace, so I will exert myself to confirm and preserve it', he proclaimed. The Venetian Giustiniani wrote 'Nothing pleases him more than to be called the arbiter of Christendom'—but within two years the fighting had started again.

Meanwhile the third of the old men, the unreliable Maximilian ('The Emperor is light and inconsistent, always begging for other men's money, which he wastes in hunting the chamois', Julius II had once commented) had died in 1519. Although Francis, and to a lesser extent Henry, poured money into the laps of the Imperial Electors, there was never any real doubt that a Habsburg would once again be elected and in due course Charles V succeeded his grandfather as ruler of the Empire. Now Francis felt himself encircled by Habsburg power, and looked for allies. In 1520 Henry met Francis at the Field of Cloth of Gold, between Guines and Ardres, a few miles to the south of Calais. There were great junketings, but Henry also had two meetings with Charles, one at Canterbury before that with Francis and another later at Gravelines and Calais. The result of all this diplomatic activity was that England entered the war on the side of Charles V and English armies moved across northern France, though to little effect, in 1522 (when Surrey passed through Morlaix and Artois) and again in 1523 (when Suffolk marched through Calais, Bray and Montdidier to reach the Oise within forty miles of Paris).

Wolsey's choice of sides is easy to understand; Spain was the traditional ally, France the traditional enemy; the Pope was anxious to get the French armies out of northern Italy; the Flemish trade was vital to England; and, finally, Charles V had promised to support Wolsey's candidature at the next election to the Papacy. The Emperor had a chance to redeem this promise rather earlier than he probably expected, for in 1521 and again in 1523 the papal throne fell vacant. The first time Charles' former tutor became Adrian VI, while on the second occasion one of the Medici was elected and took the title of Clement VII. One can sympathize with Wolsey's subsequent disenchantment, but the fact of the matter was that, whatever Charles might promise, Wolsey had no more chance of becoming Pope than Henry had of becoming Emperor—and the Cardinal ought to have recognized the fact.

Wolsey now began to turn towards France. The change of policy was no doubt also encouraged by lack of enthusiasm in England for the war. The fourth parliament of the reign had met in 1523 and voted only small supplies. At the very moment when Wolsey was deserting the Emperor's cause the troops of Charles V inflicted a crushing defeat on the French at Pavia (1525), about twenty miles to the south of Milan. Francis himself was captured and taken to Madrid where, in the following year, he swore to a treaty renouncing his claims in Italy, Burgundy and Flanders. Once back in France he disowned his oath and formed the League of Cognac (1526) by which he, the Pope, Florence, Milan and Venice agreed to resist the too-successful Charles. Henry VIII was named Protector of the new League.

During the war which followed, the Imperial army besieged Rome, got out of control, and sacked the city on 6 May 1527. From the King's point of view the Emperor's success could hardly have come at a more inopportune moment. On 17 May the legal battle to annul Henry's marriage to Catherine opened in England, at the very time when the Pope could no longer be expected to act as a free agent. In 1528 Henry declared war on Charles, but within a year the French had been defeated at Landriano and Charles and Francis had made peace at Cambrai (1529), on the borders of France and the Netherlands, without bothering to inform the King or his Cardinal. The Pope remained under the *de facto* control of Charles. He himself recognized this; 'I have quite made up my mind to become an Imperialist' he told the archbishop of Capua, and in 1530 the bishop of Auxerre declared 'If anyone was ever imprisoned in the power of his enemies, the Pope is now'.

Wolsey fell from power within two months of the signing of the peace of Cambrai. He fell because he could not obtain for his royal master the annulment that Henry desired. That he could not do so was in part a consequence of a foreign policy which since 1521 had been disastrous for England, for the Papacy, and for Wolsey himself. The alliance with France was impractical and unpopular, the French ambassador, Jean du Bellay, was himself amazed that the Cardinal should so blithely disregard the need to preserve the market for England's cloth: 'I believe he is the only English man who wishes war with Flanders.' The cloth trade suffered; there were riots in East

Anglia, Somerset and Wiltshire, and in Kent men said that, if they could get hold of Wolsey, they would send him to sea in a boat with holes bored in it.   When du Bellay heard the news of Cambrai he predicted correctly that it would be the cause of Wolsey's total ruin.

The Cardinal's pyrotechnics will not bear comparison with the patient statesmanship of Henry VII or Elizabeth I.   In 1524 Clement VII had expressed the general opinion of European observers when he declared: 'The aim of the King of England is as incomprehensible as the causes by which he is moved are futile.'   It was Wolsey who had supplied both the aim and the motion, and it was the peace of Cambrai which revealed the sterility of his manœuvres.

The Cardinal

In 1515 Wolsey reached the heights of power.   In that year he succeeded Archbishop Warham as Lord Chancellor and also received from Rome the cardinal's hat.   He was now, under the king, the head of both state and church, and from 1515 to 1529 it was apparently Cardinal Wolsey not Henry VIII who ruled England.   His activity—or, in certain directions, his lack of activity—effectively coloured every aspect of government.

In 1519 the Venetian ambassador, Giustiniani, wrote of him:

This Cardinal is the person who rules both the King and the entire Kingdom.   On the ambassador's first arrival in England he used to say to him, 'His Majesty will do so and so'; subsequently, by degrees, he began to forget himself, and started to say, 'We shall do so and so'; now he has reached such a height that he says, 'I shall do so and so'.

He is about forty-six years old, very handsome, learned, extremely eloquent, of great ability and untiring.   He himself transacts the same business as that which occupies all the magistracies, offices, and councils of Venice, both civil and criminal; and all state affairs are managed by him whatever their nature.

He is thoughtful, and has the reputation of being extremely just; he favours the people exceedingly, especially the poor, hearing their suits and seeking to despatch them at once; he also makes the lawyers plead *gratis* for all poor suitors.

He is in very great repute—seven times more so than if he were Pope.   He has a very fine palace, where one passes through eight rooms before reaching the audience chamber,

and they are all hung with tapestry, which is changed every
week. He always has a sideboard of plate worth 25,000
ducats, wherever he may be; and his silver is estimated at
150,000 ducats. In his own room there is always a cup-
board with vessels worth 30,000 ducats, this being customary
with the English nobility. He is supposed to be very rich
indeed, in money, plate, and household stuff.

Wolsey's work in foreign affairs has been described. Here
it is convenient to consider, separately, his work as Chancellor,
as the King's 'prime man', and as the effective head of the
Church in England.

It is arguable that Wolsey's most positive contribution lay in
the sphere of the law. As Chancellor the Cardinal was the head
of the judicial system in general and, in particular, the presiding
authority in Chancery. That court matched Wolsey's temperament in that it was not bound by the exact rules of
common law, but was 'the court of the king's conscience' in
which the Lord Chancellor was the only judge, a court therefore in which Wolsey could indulge to the full his penchant for
occupying the centre of the stage and distributing praise and
blame with an even-handed impartiality which should excite
the admiration of all observers. He achieved that aim: it was
his work in Chancery which most impressed contemporaries.
Wolsey's extensive use of Chancery helped to establish it as a
regular court of civil law, dealing with such matters as contracts,
property, trusts and testaments. Star Chamber, on the other
hand, was the place where the Chancellor could exercise
criminal jurisdiction. There seems no doubt that Wolsey
revived the Council's judicial activity, which had declined since
Henry VII's time. Writing forty years later, Sir Thomas
Smith believed that it 'took great augmentation and authority'
from Wolsey's use of it. To its jurisdiction over cases of riot
and too much force, he added those of forgery, libel and
perjury, matters formerly dealt with by the Church courts.
'His main achievement was to turn star chamber from a
tribunal of state into a court used freely by the king's subjects in
the settlement of their affairs; it was under Wolsey that it
became . . . a part of the regular system of law-administration
in England.'[1] Skelton, in his satirical attack on Wolsey, *Why*

---

[1] G. R. Elton, *England under the Tudors*, Methuen, pp. 82–83.

Come Ye Not to Court? (1522–3), seized on this as an outstanding characteristic of Wolsey's rule:

> He is set so high
> In his hierarchy
> Of frantic frenzy
> And foolish fantasy,
> That in the Chamber of Stars
> All matters there he mars.
> Clapping his rod on the board,
> No man dare speak a word,
> For he hath all the saying
> Without any renaying.
> He rolleth in his records,
> He saith 'How say ye, my lords?
> Is not my reason good?'
> 'Good even, good Robin Hood!'
> Some say 'Yes!' and some
> Sit still as they were dumb!
> Thus thwarting over them
> He ruleth all the roast
> With bragging and with boast.
> Borne up on every side
> With pomp and with pride.

The earl of Northumberland was sent to the Fleet prison, and Lord Hastings and Sir Richard Sacheverell were summoned before Star Chamber, all three for keeping liveried retainers.

There were other courts, outside the sphere of common law, in which Wolsey sat. The Court of Requests for poor men's causes was revived, and in 1518 four committees were set up to hear poor men's suits in civil cases. The Cardinal also revived the two moribund Conciliar Courts: by 1525 the Council of the North was restored under the titular presidency of Henry VIII's illegitimate son, the duke of Richmond, and in that year the Council in the Marches of Wales was reconstituted.

His work as a judge occupied a great part of the Chancellor's time. Star Chamber sat normally on Monday, Tuesday, Thursday and Saturday, while Chancery business was usually conducted on Wednesday and Friday, but Wolsey's biographer Cavendish described Wolsey carrying on the two types of work on the same day, writing that he would 'repair into Chancery and sit there until eleven of the clock, hearing suitors and determining diverse matters. And from thence he would divers times go into the Star Chamber, as occasion did serve, where he spared neither high nor low, but judged every estate according to their merits and deserts.' Wolsey's use of Star Chamber and Chancery did much to establish both institutions as regular machines for judicial administration, and his cheap, speedy and impartial judgements ensured good justice for all, including the feeble and the pauper, but it also earned him the jealousy of the common lawyers on whose territory his courts encroached—courts where, in Shakespeare's words, 'his own opinion was his law'.

Wolsey was an efficient administrator, and it is at first sight surprising that, controlling the whole machine of government he took such little interest in the apparatus. Yet there were good reasons for this neglect. The machine was functioning smoothly, Wolsey was much occupied with other matters, and obscure administration could not, for him, compare in attraction with the exhibitionist role of judge or diplomat. Consequently there was little change. The cardinal did prepare schemes of administrative reform in 1519 and in 1526 (the Eltham Ordinances), but they remained paper schemes. Henry VII's household methods were continued and officials were left undisturbed, the key post of treasurer of the chamber, for instance, being held successively by Sir John Heron (1492–1521), Sir Henry Wyatt (1524–8), and Sir Brian Tuke (1528–45). In this department, the only innovation was to appoint two General Surveyors of Crown Lands to administer that revenue and to audit the other accounts—an innovation made necessary by Henry VIII's disinclination to do this work himself, as his father had done. The first Act appointing General Surveyors was passed in 1515 and until 1535, when it was made permanent, the Act only operated from one Parliament to the next.

It is often said that Wolsey's greatest weakness lay in his handling of financial matters. Certainly he was not able greatly to increase the existing revenue, for the key to that lay in the manipulation of Parliament—an exercise he found uncongenial since that body gave him no opportunity to play the benevolent autocrat. Nevertheless, attempts were made to trap additional money. In 1512 Wolsey's predecessors had levied a poll tax, but it proved a failure for, estimated to bring in £160,000, it had in fact yielded only £50,000. In 1514 Wolsey made an important fiscal innovation when he introduced a new form of subsidy. This was a levy on wages, personal property and rents, which grew to be a regular part of the system of direct taxation, though it lost its flexibility and eventually became merely a conventional expression for a parliamentary grant of about £80,000 to £100,000.[1]

The manner in which war could inflate expenditure can be seen from this run of figures: 1509, £65,097; 1510, £26,735; 1511, £64,157; 1512, £269,564; (Guienne); 1513, £699,714 (Flanders); 1514, £155,757; 1515, £74,006; and Wolsey's foreign adventures proved even more expensive, the expeditions of 1522–3 costing almost £400,000.

In 1522 the cardinal imposed a forced loan on the rich, which brought in £200,000. In the next year Parliament was summoned and was asked for a tax of four shillings in the pound but the members were recalcitrant and eventually granted only two shillings. Consequently Wolsey tried in 1524 to supplement the Crown's revenue by another forced loan, which he euphemistically termed an Amicable Grant. (The gap between financial theory and practice is shown by the fact that there were in 1524 three sets of commissioners trying to collect money—for the loan of 1522, the subsidy of 1523, and the grant of 1524.) In East Anglia and Kent there was active resistance to the commissioners, and Henry eventually ordered the collection to stop and pardoned those who had resisted.

Wolsey's financial expedients created a group of potential enemies, that of the rich landowners, who were also made increasingly hostile by his attempt to deal with the problem of depopulating enclosures. In 1517 and 1518 the Cardinal appointed royal commissioners to enquire into the destruction of villages, the conversion of arable to pasture, and the imparking of land for hunting. The returns from twenty-two counties have been preserved. They show that the average rent of enclosed arable was 31 per cent more than that for open arable, while the rent for enclosed pasture exceeded that of enclosed arable by 27 per cent. Clearly, enclosed pasture was the most profitable form of land use. Some single enclosures were quite large; the abbot of Peterborough, it was

---

[1] Obtained from a fixed tax of 4s. in the £ on the annual value of land, and 2s. 8d. in the £ on the value of goods.

found, had taken in almost 1,000 acres; at Thornbury the duke
of Buckingham had imparked over 600 acres. Yet the commissioners' figures show that the total area affected was comparatively small. In Oxfordshire about 4 per cent and in
Berkshire less than 2 per cent had been enclosed, though these
were two of the counties most affected.

In 1518 a Chancery order was issued that enclosures made
since 1485 were to be demolished unless it could be shown that
they were for the good of the country. Further orders followed
in 1520, 1526 and 1528, but they remained largely dead letters.

It is easy to forget that Wolsey was a churchman, who
perhaps had it in his power to reform the Church from within.
It is important to understand the source of this power. The
Church in England consisted of the two provinces of York and
Canterbury, each with its own organization and its own
convocation, each subject individually to the Pope in Rome.
In addition, many monasteries and other religious communities
were outside the control of these provinces, being under their
own superiors and ultimately subject to the Pope. As Archbishop of York, Wolsey's ecclesiastical powers were confined to
the distant, backward, poverty-stricken, under-populated
province of York—a province that he never even visited until
after his fall from power. The much more important see of
Canterbury was in the hands of Archbishop Warham from
1503 to 1532, and therefore unobtainable by Wolsey. Given
this situation, if Wolsey were to rule the Church in England,
he must do so as the direct representative of the Pope, as papal
legate and Cardinal. It was these offices that gave him his
great administrative authority; they also earned for him the jealousy of English churchmen, and the hatred of English laymen.

Wolsey's cardinalate was the more dramatic of the two papal
appointments, but his legateship was by far the more useful to
him. To be a Cardinal was an honour, to be a legate was to
wield power. There were two types of legate, the *legatus natus*
and the *legatus a latere* (literally, a legate sent from the Pope's
side). Each archbishop was a *legatus natus*. A legate *a latere*
was a papal envoy and—theoretically at least—came direct
from Rome. Sometimes he was a sort of ambassador, sometimes a commissioner whose authority overrode that of all
ecclesiastical bodies in the area to which he was sent. In 1518

Wolsey persuaded the Pope to appoint him legate *a latere*—though the Cardinal was never nearer to Rome than Boulogne. Each year this overriding authority was renewed until at last in 1524 Wolsey was appointed legate *a latere* for life.

Wolsey declared his intention to reform the Church. Was he sincere in his declaration? It is hard to believe so. The legate was himself a laboratory specimen exhibiting conveniently in one body almost all the abuses against which Catholic and Protestant reformers were already protesting. He was a pluralist, always enjoying the revenue from at least one other bishopric in addition to that of York; he was a non-resident, a permanent absentee from his see; he was abbot of St. Albans' although as a secular priest he should have had no place amongst the Benedictine regulars;[1] he was a simoniac, coining money from the sale of offices and church patronage, and himself farming out three bishoprics for about £1,000 a year each; he was immoral and a nepotist, for he had a mistress and a natural son, Thomas Wynter, and obtained for the latter a number of preferments, together with the dispensations necessary on the grounds of his son's youth, non-residence and plurality, so that while still at school Wynter was dean of Wells, provost of Beverley, archdeacon of York and Richmond, Chancellor of Salisbury, Prebendary of York, Southwell, Lincoln, Wells and Salisbury, rector of Rudby in Yorkshire and of St. Matthew's, Ipswich. The annual revenues of these positions totalled about £2,700.

Wolsey, it is true, planned a number of reforms, but they were of a minor, piecemeal, administrative character. He intended to reduce the number of Irish archbishoprics from four to two, and the number of bishoprics from thirty to nine. In England he proposed to convert thirteen monasteries into new bishoprics, which were to be half regular and half secular, with the bishop as abbot *ex officio*. None of this work was carried out. Wolsey contented himself in practice with the dissolution of more than a score of small religious houses, partly at least so that he might endow new colleges of his own foundation at Oxford and at Ipswich. (Cardinal College at Oxford later became Christ Church; the foundation at Ipswich did not survive Wolsey's own disgrace.) These foundations do however reflect a genuine interest. Wolsey's support for the New

---

[1] *Regular*; following the *rule* of a religious or monastic order.

Learning was constant, and among his protégés were the humanists Richard Pace, secretary to the King in 1516, and Thomas Lupset, secretary to the Cardinal himself.

As legate Wolsey brought to the English church not reform but over-riding despotism. The two convocations never met, except when money was required from them. Heavy exactions were levied for the probate of wills, which was under the exclusive jurisdiction of the church courts. The Cardinal interfered continuously in the bishops' administration of their sees, making it clear that the exercise of episcopal jurisdiction was an act of grace on his part, and frequently withdrawing cases from the bishops' courts to his own legatine courts. He left sees vacant while he enjoyed their revenue himself and he encouraged the appointment of foreigners, since they might be paid a fixed income while he took the remainder, so that when he fell from power no less than five English bishoprics were held by non-resident foreigners. His hands also reached down to the lower clergy and when he was impeached the eighteenth article asserted that 'There is never a poor archdeacon in England, but that he paid yearly to him [Wolsey] a portion of his living'. Wolsey made use of his position as legate to visit through his agents dioceses in both provinces—and every visitation included a levy of 4 per cent on the value of each religious house and benefice concerned.

It is clear that Wolsey's legatine powers were not exercised in the interests of efficiency, regularity and orderly conduct, but were employed simply to the greater glory of Wolsey and for the augmentation of his own income. The last chance to reform the church from within was thus lost. Wolsey 'could not effect a reformation without obtaining the power to do so; but he was far more successful in securing the power than in effecting the reformation; and it was the concentration of the means rather than the achievement of their purpose that constitutes Wolsey's importance in English history'.[1]

For this concentration of all ecclesiastical power in the hands of one man had two far-reaching and unforeseen consequences. It created in the minds of bishop and layman alike a clear picture of the real extent of papal claims in England—claims which had not been asserted in this way for centuries. The laymen were by tradition anti-clerical, Wolsey now made the

1 A. F. Pollard, *Cardinal Wolsey*, Longmans, Green, rev. edn. 1953, p. 172.

bishops anti-papal. 'Whatever might be in store for them English bishops desired no more papal legates *a latere*. . . . There were ecclesiastical pastures into which no layman, not even Henry VIII, ventured to trespass; there were none from which Wolsey, as legate *a latere*, was debarred. . . . He always drove furiously; and as legate *a latere* of the pope he rode papal jurisdiction in England to its death.'[1] Secondly, Wolsey provided for the king and for his civil administrators a hint of the manner in which secular and religious control, vested in the hands of one man, might be used to destroy catholic and feudal liberties and, after victory, to create a national state-church. It was a hint which they were quick to take.

'*The King's Matter*'

A papal legate's administration had prepared the ground for the break with Rome, a king's political and psychological needs provided the occasion for that breach.

When in 1503 Henry VII had asked Pope Julius II for a dispensation to enable his second son Henry to marry his brother Arthur's widow, the Pope had replied that 'the dispensation was a great matter; nor did he well know, *prima facie*, if it were competent for the Pope to dispense in such a case'. No doubt the Pope's hesitation was in part a matter of diplomacy, but scripturally the matter was unclear, for while Leviticus xx, 21 forbade a man to marry his brother's widow, adding that such a marriage 'shall be childless' and canon law accepted this prohibition, Deuteronomy xxv, 5 appeared to command a brother to marry his brother's widow and raise up children.

The dispensation was issued by Julius in 1504, but the marriage did not take place immediately. Indeed in 1505, when his father wished to put pressure on Ferdinand of Aragon, the future Henry VIII, then fourteen, made a formal protest against the proposed union. The marriage was finally solemnized in June 1509. In the spring of 1510 there was a still-born daughter; in January 1511 a boy was born who died seven weeks later; in 1513 Catherine had a miscarriage; in December 1514 another son was born, but died after only a few hours. At last in February 1516 a daughter Mary lived. Henry was delighted, 'by the grace of God the sons will follow'.

---

[1] Pollard, pp. 215–16.

There was no son.   Ten years later one daughter still remained
the only product of Henry's marriage to a wife who was now
over forty.   It was natural that the king's mind should turn to
that text in Leviticus, accepted by canon law, *they shall be childless*.

Political expediency lent weight to theological argument.
There had been only one English queen regnant, Matilda, and
her reign had been one of disputed succession and unrelieved
civil war, many of the barons refusing to accept her right to
rule.   In the sixteenth century there were nobles with claims
to the throne by descent as good as those of Henry himself.   If
he died, one of their number might be preferred before a girl
and Tudor rule might end in renewed civil war.   The execution of the duke of Buckingham in 1521, nominally for treason,
was probably due at least in part to the duke's fondness for
reminding people of his descent from Edward III.

By 1527 desire had added its psychological pressure.   Henry
had fallen in love with Anne Boleyn.   The king had had
mistresses in the past.   His bastard son, the duke of Richmond,
born in 1519, was the child of Elizabeth Blount, and later there
had been a liaison with Anne's sister, Mary Boleyn.   Anne,
intending to be queen, refused to become the king's mistress.
Henry, requiring a legitimate heir to the throne, was prepared
to accept Anne's conditions.   Only Catherine remained as an
obstacle.

Doubts as to the validity of Henry's marriage were raised by
the bishop of Tarbes in 1527 when negotiations were afoot for a
marriage between Francis I and the princess Mary, and theological argument, political necessity and physical desire had
by that year already created a situation which made it almost
inevitable that Henry should attempt to rid himself of his ageing
wife.   Men will always sincerely believe what they wish to
believe and soon the king had convinced himself that he was
not married to Catherine.   It only remained to persuade
Clement VII to accept this point of view and to declare that the
dispensation granted by Julius II was null.   That should not
be difficult.   In 1527 Henry's sister Margaret obtained a
divorce on the thinnest of evidence and earlier in the century
the duke of Suffolk, now Henry's brother-in-law, had obtained
a declaration of nullity in very similar circumstances—a
declaration which was confirmed by Clement in 1528.   Moreover, Henry must have felt that he stood in a special relationship

to the Pope. Had he not composed, with perhaps some help from Sir Thomas More, a refutation of Luther's teaching under the title *An Assertion of the Seven Sacraments against Martin Luther*— and had he not been rewarded by Pope Leo X with the title *Fidei Defensor*? Finally, Wolsey's position as legate should enable the Cardinal to expedite matters.

In May 1527 Wolsey duly called Henry before the legatine court to explain why he was living with his brother's widow, but that same month the whole situation was changed. Charles V's troops took Rome. 'If the Pope be slain or taken, it will hinder the King's affairs not a little, which have hitherto been going so well,' Wolsey informed Henry. For Charles, Catherine's nephew, would not passively accept that weakening of Habsburg power and prestige which would automatically follow a papal declaration that Henry's marriage was null.

Meanwhile in England Catherine refused to recognize Wolsey's authority, which meant that the matter must be referred to the Pope. Clement temporized. At last, in October, 1528, he sent Cardinal Campeggio to England as legate to hear the case. Campeggio did not open his hearing until March 1529 and in July he adjourned it until the following October, on the grounds that in Italy courts did not sit in the hot Mediterranean summer! While the court was adjourned Clement revoked the case to Rome and in that same week the Peace of Cambrai marked the triumph of Charles V. In the circumstances, even were Henry to go to Rome, there could be no hope of a favourable verdict.

Wolsey had told Campeggio 'that if the King's desire were not complied with . . . there would follow the speedy and total ruin of the kingdom, of his Lordship and of the Church's influence in this kingdom'. The forecast was first fulfilled on the Cardinal himself. His enemies were delighted at his failure. Hearing that the case had been referred to Rome, Suffolk burst out: 'Now I see that the old-said saw is true, that never a cardinal or legate did good in England.' In September the Imperial ambassador Chapuys reported 'it is generally and almost publicly stated that the affairs of the Cardinal are getting worse every day'. A month later du Bellay wrote: 'At present the king takes the management of everything himself. . . . I see clearly that by this parliament Wolsey will completely lose his influence; I see no chance to the contrary.'

In two weeks the whole pattern of power which had endured for fifteen years was changed. Wolsey was indicted in King's Bench under the statute of *Praemunire*.[1] He surrendered the Great Seal and admitted his guilt. In November his enemies introduced a bill of attainder against him, but this ran counter to Henry's wishes, and was rejected. In the spring of 1530 he left London and proceeded slowly north towards his see of York. There he survived for a few months, but the lure of foreign intrigue exerted its fatal charm over him. Soon he was in touch with the Emperor and the King of France. In November 1530 he was arrested on a charge of high treason and conveyed towards London. He died at Leicester Abbey on 29 November 1530.

Wolsey's fall had been rapid and irrevocable. His power, his pride, his efficiency had all raised up enemies against him. The nobles, jealous of an upstart; the civil lawyers, seeing their courts and their fees eroded by conciliar jurisdiction; the anti-clerical gentry and townsmen; the bishops whose courts and whose incomes Wolsey had invaded—all echoed the words of the Duke of Suffolk, 'it was never merry in England whilst we had cardinals among us'. Yet it would be wrong to attribute Wolsey's destruction to these enemies. His fall from power depended, as his continuance in power had done, on one man— the King. Wolsey's position had rested, not on office nor on the support of a party, but on the favour of the Crown. When that was withdrawn, the whole superstructure collapsed. It was three years before the King again gave his backing to one man. When he did, it was to Wolsey's former man of business, Thomas Cromwell.

Modern historians see Wolsey as a disappointing figure, a man who exercised great authority for twenty years and yet made no positive use of that authority. Abroad his policy was over-ambitious and at the same time barren. At home he appeared content to demonstrate his own importance. His failure stemmed in part from his position as an essentially medieval man in a modern century. His methods and ideals were obsolescent and he remained largely unaware of the new world around him. Wolsey's historical significance lies in the

1 Designed to protect the king's rights against interference by foreign (i.e. papal) courts. See p. 94.

fact that he made papal and clerical claims increasingly obnoxious, and at the same time provided his royal master with the power to destroy those claims. Wolsey's reputation has varied greatly over the years. It is interesting to compare this assessment made by the nineteenth-century historian, Bishop Creighton, with that of twentieth-century writers:

'No statesman of such eminence ever died less lamented' is Dr. Brewer's remark on Wolsey's death. Indeed, the king had forgotten his old servant; his enemies rejoiced to be rid of a possible rival; the men whom he had trained in politics were busy in seeking their own advancement, which was not to be promoted by tears for a fallen minister; the people had never loved him, and were indifferent about one who was no longer powerful. In a time of universal uncertainty every one was speculating on the future, and saw that the future was not to be determined by Wolsey or by Wolsey's ideas. Not without reason has the story of Wolsey's fall passed into a parable of the heartlessness of the world.

For Wolsey lived for the world as few men have ever done; not for the larger world of intellectual thought or spiritual aspiration, but for the actual, immediate world of affairs. He limited himself to its problems, but within its limits he took a wider and juster view of the problems of his time than any English statesman has ever done. For politics in the largest sense, comprising all the relations of the nation at home and abroad, Wolsey had a capacity which amounted to genius, and it is doubtful if this can be said of any other Englishman. There have been many capable administrators, many excellent organizers, many who advocated particular reforms and achieved definite results. But Wolsey aimed at doing all these things together and more. Taking England as he found her, he aimed at developing all her latent possibilities, and leading Europe to follow in her train. In this project there was nothing chimerical or fantastic, for Wolsey's mind was eminently practical. Starting from the existing condition of affairs, he made England for a time the centre of European politics, and gave her an influence far higher than she could claim on material grounds. Moreover, his far-reaching schemes abroad did not interfere with strict attention to the details of England's interests. His foreign policy was to promote English trade, facilitate the union of Scotland, keep peace at small expense, prepare the way for internal re-organization, and secure the right of dealing judiciously with ecclesiastical reform. Wolsey's plans all hung together. However absorbed he might be in a particular point it was only part of a great design, and he used each advantage which he gained as a means of strengthening England's position for some future undertaking. He had a clear view of the future as a whole; he knew not only what he wished to make of England but of Europe as well. He never worked at a question from one motive only; what failed for one purpose was made useful for another; his resources were not bounded by the immediate result.

Politics to him was not a pursuit, it was a passion. He loved it as an artist loves his art, for he found in it a complete satisfaction for his nature. All that was best, and all that was worst, in Wolsey sprang from this exceptional attitude towards statecraft, which he practised with enthusiasm, not in the spirit of cold calculation.

EXTRACTS

I. *Sir Thomas More analyses some causes of unemployment, in* Utopia, *1516:*

. . . let us consider those things that chance daily before our eyes. First there is a great number of gentlemen, which cannot be content to live idle themselves, like daws, of that which others have laboured for, their tenants I mean, whom they poll and shave to the quick, by raising their rents . . . , those gentlemen, I say, do not only live in idleness themselves, but also carry about with them at their tails a great flock or train of idle and loitering serving-men, which never learned any craft whereby to get their livings. These men, as soon as their master is dead, or be sick themselves, be incontinent thrust out of doors . . . they that be thus destitute of service either starve for hunger or manfully play the thief. . . .

. . . your sheep that were wont to be so meek and tame and so small eaters now, as I hear say, be become so great devourers and so wild, that they eat up and swallow down the very men themselves. They consume, destroy, and devour whole fields, houses, and cities. For look in what parts of the realm do grow the finest, and therefore dearest wool, there noblemen, and gentlemen, yea and certain Abbots, holy men no doubt, not contenting themselves with the yearly revenues and profits, that were wont to grow to their forefathers and predecessors of their lands, nor being content that they live in rest and pleasure nothing profiting, yea much harming the public weal; leave no ground for tillage, they inclose all into pastures: they throw down houses; they pluck down towns, and leave nothing standing, but only the church to be made a sheep-house. . . .

Therefore that one covetous and unsatiable cormorant and very plague of his native country may compass about and enclose many thousand acres of ground together, within one pale or hedge, the husbandmen be thrust out of their own, . . . by one means or by other, either by hook or by crook, they must needs depart away, poor silly wretched souls, men, women, husbands, wives, fatherless children, widows, woeful mothers with their young babies, and their whole household, small in substance, and much in number, as husbandry requireth many hands. Away they trudge, I say, out of their known and accustomed houses, finding no place to rest in. . . . What can they else do but steal, and then justly, God wot, be hanged, or else go about a-begging? And yet then also they be cast into prison as vagabonds, because they go about and work not, whom no man will set a-work, though they never so willingly proffer themselves thereto. For one shepherd or herdsman is enough to eat up that ground with cattle, to the occupying whereof about husbandry many hands were requisite. And this is also the cause why victuals be now in many places dearer. (Sir Thomas More, *Utopia*, Dent, 1910.)

II. *Cromwell, in a speech to the parliament of 1523, opposes the sending of an army to France, and suggests a different pattern of foreign policy:*

. . . if it would please his [Henry VIII's] magnanimous courage to convert the first and chief his whole intent and purpose not only to the over-running and subduing of this Scotland but also to join the same realm unto his, . . . and of this act should follow the highest abasement to the said Francis [I] that ever happened to him or his progenitors afore him, not only for that he left the said Scots, his ancient allies and which have for his and their sakes provoked our nation so notably heretofore, at this time undefended by reason of our sovereign's navy which he dare not encounter with nor never dare send them succour so long as he shall know the narrow seas substantially to be kept, but also for so much as he shall know that we have changed our manner of war, . . . and though it be a common saying that in Scotland is nought to win but strokes, for that I allege another common saying, who that intendeth France to win with Scotland let him begin. Which interpret thus truly, it is but a simpleness for us to think to keep possessions in France, [which] is sundered from us by the ocean sea,

and suffer Scotland joined unto us by nature all in one island,
unto which we may have recourse at all times when we will, . . .
to live under another policy and to recognize another prince.
(R. B. Merriman, *Letters and Speeches of Thomas Cromwell*, 1902,
Vol. I, p. 43.)

III. *Edward Hall, sergeant-at-law, recounts the resistance in
East Anglia to Wolsey's taxation, 1525:*

The Duke of Suffolk sat in Suffolk this season in like commission
and by gentle handling he caused the rich clothiers to assent,
and grant the sixth part, and when they came home to their
houses they called to them their spinners, carders, fullers,
weavers, and other artificers, which were wont to be set a work
and have their livings by cloth-making, and said; Sirs, we be not
able to set you a work, our goods be taken from us, wherefore
trust to yourselves and not to us, for other wise it will not be.
Then began women to weep, and young folks to cry, and men
that had no work began to rage and assemble themselves in
companies. The Duke of Suffolk, hearing of this, commanded the Constables that every man's harness should be
taken from them, but when that was known, then the rumour
waxed more greater, and the people railed openly on the Duke
of Suffolk, and Sir Robert Dury, and threatened them with
death, and the Cardinal also, and so of Lanam [Lavenham],
Sudbury, Hadleigh and other towns about, there rebelled four
thousand men, and put themselves in harness, and rang the bells
Alarm, and began to come together still more! then the duke of
Suffolk perceiving this, began to raise men, but he could get but
a small number, and they that came to him said, that they
would defend him from all perils, if he hurt not their neighbours, but against their neighbours they would not fight! yet the
gentlemen that were with the duke did so much, that all the
bridges were broken, so that their assembly was somewhat
letted.

The Duke of Norfolk, High Treasurer and Admiral of England hearing of this, gathered a great power in Norfolk, and
came towards the Commons, and of his nobleness he sent to
the commons, to know their intent, which answered: that they
would live and die in the king's causes, and to the king to be
obedient: when the duke wist that, he came to them, and then
all spake at once, so that he wist not what they meant. Then
he asked who was their Captain, and bad that he should speak:
then a well aged man of fifty years and above, asked licence of

the Duke to speak, which [he] granted with good will. My lord, said this man, whose name was John Green, sith you ask who is our captain, forsooth his name is Poverty, for he and his cousin Necessity hath brought us to this doing, for all these persons and many more, which I would were not here, live not of ourselves, but all we live by the substantial occupiers of this country, and yet they give us so little wages for our workman-ship, that scarcely we be able to live, and thus in penury we pass the time, we, our wives and children, and if they by whom we live be brought in that case, that they of their little cannot help us to earn our living, then must we perish, and die miser-ably. I speak this my lord, the cloth makers have put all these people and a far greater number from work, the husband men have put away their servants, and given up household, they say the king asketh too much, that they be not able to do as they have done before this time, and then of necessity we must die wretchedly: wherefore my lord, now according to your wisdom consider our necessity. The Duke was sorry to hear their complaint, and well he knew it was true: then he said, neigh-bours, sever yourselves asunder, let every man depart to his home, and choose further four that shall answer for the remnant, and on my honour I will send to the king, and make humble intercession for your pardon, which I trust to obtain, so that you will depart. Then all they answered they would, and so they departed home. . . . Then the demand of money ceased in all the realm, for well it was perceived, that the commons would none pay. (E. Hall, *The Union of the Two Noble and Illustrious Families of Lancaster and York*, ed. Whibley 1904, Vol. II.)

IV. *George Cavendish, Wolsey's gentleman usher, describes, c. 1555, the last day of Catherine of Aragon's trial:*

. . . Thus went this strange case forward from court-day to court-day until it came to the judgment, so that every man expected the judgment to be given the next court-day. At which day the King came thither and sat within a gallery against the door of the same that looked unto the judges where they sat, whom he might both see and hear speak, to hear what judgment they would give in his suit: At which time all their proceedings were first openly read in Latin. And that done, the King's learned counsel at the bar called fast for judgment.

With that quoth Cardinal Campeggio, 'I will give no judgment herein until I have made relation unto the Pope of all our proceedings, whose counsel and commandment in this high case I will observe. The case is too high and notable [and] known throughout the world, for us to give any hasty judgment, considering the highness of the persons and the doubtful allegations; and also whose commissioners we be, under whose authority we sit here. It were, therefore, reason that we should make our Chief Head [the Pope] counsel in the same, before we proceed to judgment definitive.

'I come not so far to please any man for fear, meed, or favour, be he king or any other potentate. I have no such respect to the persons that I will offend my conscience. I will not for favour or displeasure of any high estate or mighty prince do that thing that should be against the law of God. I am an old man, both sick and impotent, looking daily for death. What should it then avail me to put my soul in the danger of God's displeasure, to my utter damnation, for the favour of any prince or high estate in this world? My coming and being here is only to see justice ministered according to my conscience, and I thought thereby, the matter either good or bad.

'And forasmuch as I do understand, and having perceivance by the allegations and negations in this matter laid for both parties, that the truth in this case is very doubtful to be known, and also that the party defendant will make no answer thereunto [but] doth rather appeal from us, supposing that we be not indifferent, considering the King's high dignity and authority within this his own realm which he hath over his own subjects; and we, being his subjects and having our livings and dignities in the same, she thinketh that we cannot minister true and indifferent justice for fear of his displeasure. Therefore to avoid all these ambiguities and obscure doubts, I intend not to damn my soul for no prince or potentate alive. I will therefore, God willing, wade no farther in this matter, unless I have the just opinion and judgment with the assent of the Pope and such other of his counsel as hath more experience and learning in such doubtful laws than I have.

'Wherefore I will adjourn this court for this time according to the order of the court in Rome from whence this court and jurisdiction is derived. And if we should go further than our commission doth warrant us, it were folly and vain and much to our slander and blame; and [we] might be accounted, for the same, breakers of the order of the higher court from whence we have, as I said, our original authorities.' With that the court was dissolved, and no more pleas holden.

With that stepped forth the Duke of Suffolk from the King, and by his commandment spake these words, with a stout and hault [haughty] countenance, 'It was never merry in England', quoth he, 'whilst we had cardinals among us.' Which words were set forth both with such a vehement countenance, that all men marvelled what he intended; to whom no man made answer. Then the Duke spake again in great despite.

To the which words my lord Cardinal, perceiving his vehemency, soberly made answers, and said, 'Sir, of all men within this realm, ye have least cause to dispraise or be offended with cardinals: for if I, simple Cardinal, had not been, you should have had at this present no head upon your shoulders, wherein you should not have a tongue to make any such report in despite of us who intend you no manner of displeasure; nor have we given you any occasion with such despite to be revenged with your *hault* words.'.... (*Cavendish's Life of Cardinal Wolsey*, Ed. Morley, London, 1885.)

Further Reading

J. J. Bagley, *Henry VIII*, Batsford, 1962
J. Bowles, *Henry VIII*, Allen and Unwin, 1964
A. F. Pollard, *Henry VIII*, Longmans, Green, 1905
— *Wolsey*, Longmans, Green, 1929
G. R. Elton, *Henry VIII*, H.A., Pamphlet G 51, 1962
W. Roper and N. Harpsfield, *Lives of Saint Thomas More*, Dent, 1963
R. W. Chambers, *Thomas More*, Cape, 1955
G. Mattingley, *Catherine of Aragon*, Cape, 1942
J. J. Scarisbrick, *Henry VIII*, Eyre and Spottiswoode, 1968

IV · THE BREAK WITH ROME

The Search for a Solution

In the years from 1529 to 1532 the government was, under Henry, in the hands of the new Chancellor, Thomas More, the Dukes of Norfolk and Suffolk, and the Earl of Wiltshire, Anne Boleyn's father. No clear line of policy was followed. One gets the impression of some great monster, threshing about in search of escape, as the king sought in vain for a solution that would be legally and theologically impeccable.

This was not how it appeared to foreign observers. As early as 1529 Chapuys had written that the English 'were thinking of nothing but how to do without Rome'. Yet if the King had any clearly formulated aims in 1529 they were no more than to make clear the dependence of the Church in England on himself, and to use the force of English lay anti-clericalism, on which Chapuys had commented, as an instrument with which to bend the Pope towards his wishes.

During the complex series of events that culminated in the breach with Rome and the establishment of an English Church, Parliament proved the King's most useful weapon. Called in November 1529, 'the Long Parliament of the Reformation' was not dissolved until April 1536. The continued existence and use of Parliament during these seven years marks an important stage in the development of that body. The first session took place during November and December 1529. Bills were introduced limiting church fees and mortuary fines, and forbidding pluralism and non-residence. These were reactions to church practice in general—as the saying went 'no penny, no paternoster'—and to Wolsey's oppressive actions and ostentatious display in particular. They were not directly connected with Henry's aims, but from the King's point of view they gave a valuable hint to the Pope of the fate which might overtake the Church in England. If the Pope did not understand the implications of the Commons' action, the Church in England certainly did. In the Lords Fisher warned his fellow bishops 'you see daily what bills come hither from the Commons House, and all to the destruction of the Church. . . .' The

Speaker, leading a deputation to the King of thirty members, retorted 'Are we infidels, are we Saracens, are we pagans and heathens, that the laws which we establish should be thought not worthy to be kept by Christian men?' The lines of conflict were already clear. Meanwhile, having curtailed these ecclesiastical privileges, Parliament was prorogued, and it did not sit again until January 1531, more than a year later. One must not antedate its main work. The Commons did not discuss the divorce itself until 1533, nor did they vote supplies until 1534.

During the year 1530 the King was following a different tack, one that had been suggested by a Cambridge don, Thomas Cranmer (1489–1556). Cranmer had become a Fellow of Jesus College, had married and resigned his Fellowship, and had recovered it after his wife's death. In his lectures he had, like Colet thirty years earlier, emphasized the superior authority of the Bible over that of the medieval schoolmen. In 1529 he had proposed to Henry's councillors that the theological question of the validity of Pope Julius II's dispensation might be submitted to the universities of Europe, there to be decided in a rational, impartial manner. The suggestion was taken up and during 1530 the King's envoys made the rounds, Cranmer himself visiting Italy. The outcome was disappointing, if predictable. Those universities in countries where anti-Habsburg feeling was strong—England, France, North Italy—gave their verdict for Henry, while Germany, Spain, and the remainder of Italy decided in favour of the Pope. The scheme and its failure illustrate the strength and the weakness of Cranmer's character. He remained to the end of his life an intellectual, scholarly, logical, responsive to theory and tradition, but completely unable to appreciate or to control the strong pressures that mould political decisions.

In the summer of 1530 a potent weapon was employed against the Church of England. Writs of *Praemunire* were issued against fifteen clergy, and then in December the whole body of the clergy were indicted, on the ground that they had unlawfully exercised their spiritual jurisdiction. The Church surrendered. Short of complete opposition, there was no intermediate position which it could adopt. In February 1531 the Convocation of York paid £18,840 and that of Canterbury £100,000 for a royal pardon. They did, however, refuse to

recognize Henry as their supreme head, substituting a compromise formula devised by Archbishop Warham, *singular
protector, only and supreme lord, and as far as the law of Christ allows
even supreme head*, a title which each man might interpret in his
own way.   The threat of future action remained: as Chancellor
Audley later reminded Gardiner, 'we will provide that the
Praemunire shall ever hang over your heads. . . .'   And no one
knew the limits of that threat for, as Chapuys observed, 'its
interpretation lies solely in the King's head, who amplifies it and
declares it at his pleasure, making it apply to any case he pleases'.
    Parliament had been recalled in January.   This second
session lasted till March, the main business being to register in
an act the royal pardon to the Convocations, and the remainder
of the year 1531 passed without any important new developments.   The King's attempt to put pressure on the Pope was
proving unsuccessful.   The Emperor urged Clement to declare
Catherine's marriage valid for 'it was a strange and abominable
proceeding that to suit the lust of two fools a law suit should be
held up. . . .'   Charles V was in a position to enforce his wishes,
while Henry VIII was not.   The King could only attack an
outlying part of that Church of which the Pope was head.
This he proceeded to do.

The Breach with Rome

    The second stage of the break with Rome opened when
Parliament reassembled in January 1532.   By that date
Thomas Cromwell was the King's chief adviser and events
marched in one sure and certain direction.   Cromwell introduced in Parliament the draft of a petition against the Church
courts which had been debated in 1529.   This was now revised
by the Commons.   The new version, the Supplication against
the Ordinaries (judges in spiritual courts), emphasized the
present independence of royal control enjoyed by these courts.
Henry despatched the Supplication to Convocation which, led
by Gardiner, reaffirmed the Church's prerogatives.   The king
then sent their reply to the Commons, with the significant
comment:

> We think their answer will smally please you, for it seemeth
> to us very slender.   You be a great sort of wise men, I doubt
> not but you will look circumspectly on the matter, and we
> will be indifferent between you.

To this clear hint Henry later added ingenuously that he had been surprised to discover the clergy to be 'but half our subjects, yea and scarce our subjects'.

Observers had for some time been prophesying the direction that events would take. As early as August 1529 du Bellay, the French ambassador, had written, 'It is intended to hold a Parliament here this winter and act by their own absolute power' and had prophesied:

> These Lords intend after he [Wolsey] is dead or ruined, to impeach the State of the Church, and take all its goods; which it is hardly needful for me to write in cipher, for they proclaim it openly. I expect they will do fine miracles. . . . I expect the priests will never have the great seal again; and that in this Parliament they will have terrible alarms.

The threat of parliamentary action had been hanging over the clergy for two years. In May 1532 they gave way and in the Submission of the Clergy yielded their right to legislate independently of the State. On the following day Sir Thomas More resigned his post as Chancellor. In the same month the first Act of Annates was passed. Annates were the payments made by bishops to the Pope when they succeeded to a new see, the first year's income. These were now to be paid to the Crown, though for the moment the act was not to come into effect but was to be held in reserve until such time as Henry should consider its use necessary.

It was in 1533-4 that the decisive steps were taken. The Church in England had given way, but in Rome the Pope remained immovable. In January 1533 Henry secretly married Anne. In the same month the Pope, anxious to conciliate when he could, ratified the appointment of Cranmer as Archbishop of Canterbury, Warham having died in the previous August. In March Parliament passed an Act in Restraint of Appeals to Rome, which made it possible for the new Archbishop to settle the 'King's Matter' in England, since it prohibited appeals to Rome from the decisions of the archbishops' courts. This was its immediate object, but the Act of Appeals had much wider and more far-reaching implications and is of the utmost importance, 'at once the most epoch-making, the most clear in its statement of principles, the most central to the Henrician Reformation . . . the banner in

Cromwell's hand when he led the nation across the Rubicon',[1] for the preamble to the Act laid down the theoretical basis of Henrician sovereignty over Church and State.

In May Cranmer's court at Dunstable declared Henry's marriage with Catherine null, nine days later Anne was crowned queen, and in the following September the future Queen Elizabeth was born at the palace of Greenwich. Meanwhile Clement had in July excommunicated Henry, Cranmer and the English bishops, while Henry in reply had confirmed the Act of Annates. Finally, in the following March (1534) Clement gave sentences in favour of Catherine. Flatterers wrote to Charles V congratulating him on the verdict; 'Other victories have been gained over men; this one is over enemies let loose from hell.' But the Church in England had been lost to Rome.

Four acts passed by Parliament in the spring of 1534 completed the administrative revolution. An Act in Restraint of Annates made absolute the former conditional restraint. More important, it laid down the rules for the future election of bishops and abbots. Chapters and monasteries would receive together with the royal permission to hold an election (congé d'élire) a letter nominating the person whom they were to choose—a proceeding still in force today. The Dispensations Act cut off the remaining payments to Rome, such as Peter's Pence (£200); it also transferred from Rome to Canterbury the administrative business of issuing dispensations, faculties and other licences, and added significantly in Article XIV that religious houses exempt from episcopal visitation would in the future be visited by royal commissioners. The Act for the Submission of the Clergy embodied the surrender of Convocation and also provided that appeals from church courts might be made to the king in Chancery. Fourthly, the first of a sequence of Succession Acts declared Mary illegitimate, vested the succession in the children of Henry and Anne, reminded the country of 'the great divisions which in times past had been in the realm by reason of several titles pretended to the imperial Crown of the same', and included a clause that every subject might be obliged to take an oath to observe the Act.

In the winter session of 1534 three more statutes were passed;

[1] Dickens, A. G., *Thomas Cromwell and the English Reformation*, E.U.P., 1959, p. 55. See also p. 113.

the Act of Supremacy; the Act for First Fruits and Tenths, annexing the first fruits of bishoprics, extending this tax to all benefices, and imposing an annual tax of one-tenth of the net income of each benefice; and a Treasons Act. The Act of Supremacy did not claim to make the King Supreme Head, on the contrary the preamble was careful to declare that 'the King's Majesty justly and rightfully is and ought to be the Supreme Head of the Church of England, and so is recognized by the clergy. . . .' The Treasons Act brought up to date the act of 1352. In the fifteenth century words had sometimes been held by the judges to constitute treason, the Act specifically declared that any who 'slanderously and maliciously publish and pronounce, by express writing or words, that the King our Sovereign Lord should be heretic, schismatic, tyrant, infidel, or usurper of the Crown . . .' should be adjudged a traitor. Of all the acts passed at this time, this was the only one which encountered significant resistance in parliament; 'There was never more sticking at the passing of any Act than at the passing of the same', wrote one observer. In 1536 a final Act Against the Authority of Rome summarized the existing position in England, but did not add to or change it in any way.

A profound revolution had been carried out and it is surprising—at first sight—that there was so little opposition and that there were so few martyrs.

In the beginning the open opponents of the royal policy were a mere handful. Among them were 'the Nun of Kent', Bishop Fisher, Sir Thomas More, and a number of Carthusians. Elizabeth Barton had first claimed to see visions as early as 1525. By 1530 she was already well known as 'the Holy Maid' or 'the Nun of Kent'. She was persuaded by a group of political clergy to prophecy disaster for Henry's second marriage; the King would die within six months. In 1533 she was arrested, and, together with those who were using her, was executed in April 1534.

In that same month commissioners began to administer the oath provided for in the Succession Act. Fisher and More refused to take the oath, since it included a condemnation of Henry's first marriage, which the Pope had pronounced valid only a month before. Since his resignation of the Chancellorship in 1532 More had shown himself quietly opposed to the

G

new dispensation.   Shortly before his imprisonment the Duke
of Norfolk had warned him:

> 'By the mass, Master More, it is perilous striving with princes.
> And therefore, I would wish you somewhat to incline to the
> King's pleasure; for by God's body, Master More, *Indignatio
> principis mors est.*'
>   'Is that all, my Lord?' quoth he [More].   'Then in good
> faith is there no more difference between your Grace and
> me, but that I shall die today and you tomorrow.'[1]

More and Fisher were imprisoned until the passing of the
Treasons Act, then they and the Carthusians were brought to
trial.   The Carthusians were executed between May and July.
Fisher had listened to the Nun of Kent and he had also spoken
very incautiously to foreign ambassadors.   More on the other
hand had maintained a scrupulously correct position.   At
More's trial, however, the new solicitor-general, Sir Richard
Rich, was prepared to swear that More had spoken treason to
him while in the Tower, saying that parliament could not make
the King Supreme Head of the Church.[2]

True or false, the reported statement served to condemn More.
For historians it neatly points the difference between those who
would, and those who would not, set limits to the powers of the
Tudor state.   More and Fisher were executed in the summer of
1535.

The Causes of the Reformation in England

When considering Henry's break with Rome one must always
bear in mind two questions, the answers to which are linked:
how did it come about; and why did it come about so easily?
The answer to the second of these questions is complex.

England, as part of Europe, shared in the general causes of
the Reformation, common to most parts of northern Europe.
It would be an over-simplification to say that the European
Reformation occurred because the Church in 1500 was worldly
and corrupt.   Certainly this was one important cause, but the
Church had been in a similar state in the past and yet had been
able to put its house in order.   The success of the Reformers
followed the failure of the Church to deal with their protests
either by assimilating the malcontents as saints, or suppressing

---

[1] W. Roper and N. Harpsfield, *Lives of St. Thomas More*, Dent, 1963, p. 145.
[2] See pp. 108–9.

them as heretics, the methods employed in the past. That it was unable to do so was due to a number of factors, among the most important of which were the critical eye of Renaissance philosophy; the financial needs of the Papacy; the growth of national feeling; and the invention of printing.

From the fourteenth century onwards the Church had been under fire from critics of the laxity in clerical behaviour and morals. In England, Chaucer (d. 1400) and Langland (d. *c.* 1400) had been satirical at the expense of monks, friars and the upper ranks of the clergy, though remaining full of admiration for the poor parish priest and accepting the dogma of the Church. Disapproval both in England and on the Continent was concentrated on the sins of the flesh, on indolence, and on ignorance. Priests have mistresses and children for whom they provide, they eat and drink to excess, they are proud and lazy. They preach poverty and charity, while they live idle and luxurious lives themselves. Sometimes the parish priests are no better than peasants, working in the fields six days a week and mumbling the services inaccurately on the seventh in only half-understood Latin. This is the burden of the criticism.

The richer clergy, and in particular the Roman Curia, exhibited their own specialized abuses—what may be termed sins of bureaucracy: simony, pluralism and nepotism, non-residence. Simony was the buying and selling of Church offices, taking its name from the sin of Simon Magus, described in Acts 8. Pluralism was the practice of holding several offices simultaneously. Nepotism, from the Latin word for a nephew, was the name given to the custom of giving Church preferment to relatives or illegitimate sons.

The Papacy itself was caught in the net of more insidious temptations arising from its position as a temporal monarchy, ruling a large part of central Italy. It developed what was at that time the most advanced system of foreign ambassadors and diplomatic techniques, which secular countries copied to their own advantage, and at the same time it became involved to an increasing extent in the struggles of the great powers for control of the Italian peninsula. The raising of armies by such men as Julius II was not only damaging to the Papal image, it was also expensive. From the early fifteenth century onwards the Papacy had restored its income, but often by undesirable methods and at a steep cost in lay resentment. Chancery taxes, imposed on those who required an official document from the Papal court, were increased; dispensations and the like were charged at a higher rate, and the sale of indulgences became financially important. The Papal income was further augmented by the profits of jurisdiction, cases being whenever possible referred to Rome. Many offices were put on the market, the purchase price being about ten times that of the salary involved. By 1520 there had grown up a kind of privileged stock exchange, entry to which was reserved for the officials of the Roman Curia—a fact which spelt failure to the many attempts made by the Popes to reform the administration, for the capital invested had grown to between two and a half and three million ducats, and the annual interest was correspondingly large.

It was in her judicial and financial activities in particular that the Church tended to come into conflict with the growing force of nationalism. The claim to control temporal princes, the claim to administer all clerical patronage, the claim of clerical immunity from lay jurisdiction, the claim that clerical property was exempt from lay taxation, the indirect taxation of the laity by the Church—even in the high Middle Ages these had provoked opposition from local rulers. Now, with the growth of new national monarchies intent on centralizing their administration, bringing all their subjects under one jurisdiction and increasing their revenue by all possible means, the Papal and clerical claims appeared intolerable. At the same time the Pope, since he was himself a temporal ruler, felt increasingly the need to augment his own income and strengthen his own position in Italy, at the very moment when such actions must arouse the greatest irritation.

Renaissance humanists, surveying this scene with their critical eyes, saw much that should be changed, much that was irrational, much that appeared to have no basis in the Biblical texts which they studied, and the new art of printing enabled them to broadcast their reactions, whether scholarly as in Erasmus' New Testament with notes (1516) or satirical as in the same writer's *Praise of Folly* (1509), to a wide secular audience, which included the new urban literate middle class. The work of destruction was carried a stage further by the continental reformers, Luther (1483–1546) and Zwingli (1484–1531).

In Germany the constructive part of Luther's work was carried out between 1517 and 1520. During these years he published three works which between them covered the main revolutionary aspects of his thought. The *Appeal to the Christian Nobility of the German Nation*, written in German, called on the German princes to resist the Papal tyranny, to reform the Church, to end papal taxation and to dissolve the regular orders. 'Our baptism consecrates us all without exception and makes us all priests.' The *Prelude concerning the Babylonish Captivity of the Church* was written in Latin and directed towards the clergy. In it Luther reduced the seven Catholic sacraments to three; confession, baptism and the Eucharist. With regard to the last, he denounced the withdrawal of the cup from the laity, and opposed to transubstantiation his own interpretation of the presence of Christ in the elements, consubstantiation: 'Fire and iron are two substances; yet they are so mingled in red-hot iron that any part is at once iron and fire.' Finally, in his *Liberty of a Christian Man*, Luther carved the keystone of his doctrine, the one tenet unparalleled in Wycliffism, Justification by Faith Alone, which he based on such texts from St. Paul as *Christ ends the law and brings righteousness for everyone who has faith* (Romans x, 4). To Luther this meant that Christ would save men only if they abandoned all reliance on personal merit and placed their trust solely in the merits of Christ. From this good works would follow, but in themselves they were valueless.

At about the time that Luther was influencing north and central Germany, Zwingli was carrying out an independent reformation of the church in Zurich, from which place it soon spread to the cantons of Bern and Basle (1518–31). There were profound differences between the two reformers. Luther was medieval, Zwingli was a humanist; Luther was in many ways traditional, Zwingli was much more radical—for him the service and the church must be at their most simple, and he saw in the Eucharist a commemorative feast, nothing more; Luther looked to the Princes, Zwingli drew his support from the town and his church was the congregation, united in faith and in direct communion with God.

This, in bare outline, was the European scene in which England shared—a mental climate hostile to the Church's practice and sometimes to its dogma; a Church that was particularly vulnerable to attack; and reformers who were already engaged in that attack.

The special situation in England must now be considered. There was a native tradition of lay mysticism going back to Richard Rolle (d. 1349), Walter Hilton (d. 1396) and the anonymous author of *The Cloud of Unknowing*, continued in the fifteenth century by such writers as Dame Julian of Norwich. With the introduction of printing it becomes possible to measure, if only crudely, the lay demand for religious works. In the years from 1470 to 1500 Caxton and his successor Wynkyn de Worde published 59 pious works out of a total list of 128 titles, and this high proportion continued until at least 1530. In passing, one notes that there was no English Bible, for in 1408 translation had been forbidden unless sanctioned by the bishops; in this England was out of step with the Continent where in France there was a translation in 1477, while in Germany there were twenty translations between 1466 and 1522.

If England lagged in Biblical translations, she had some claim to have produced the first Protestant. John Wycliffe (d. 1384), a North Country man educated at Oxford, had in the fourteenth century preached predestination, rejected transubstantiation, doubted Papal Supremacy, advocated clerical marriage, denounced monasticism, and seen in the lay ruler a godly prince. Justification by faith was the only major doctrine of the sixteenth-century Reformers that Wycliffe did not anticipate.[1] On the continent Wycliffe's work had its effect on the Bohemian, John Huss, and Huss in turn on Luther.

In England the followers of Wycliffe were known as Lollards. The name, first used in 1382, is from a Middle Dutch word meaning a *mutterer* of prayers. The Lollards drew up a manifesto in 1395 and in 1401 the statute *De Heretico Comburendo* was passed as one of the measures to crush the new heresy. The Lollards were driven underground. There they survived, an obscure proletarian movement, until in the late fifteenth century references to them begin to occur with increasing fre-

---

[1] For a different emphasis, see *John Wycliffe's Reputation* in P. and P. 30, where Margaret Aston argues that Wycliffe was a father figure for the Lollards, in no sense 'the morning star' of the English Reformation but simply 'a schoolman . . . whose concerns took him deeper into thought and study, rather than further into action and example'.

quency, notably in the Chiltern area of Buckinghamshire, in the city of London, and in the counties of Essex and Kent. In general they were poor—weavers, smiths, wheelrights, tailors and the like, much attached to that most revolutionary of the epistles, the *Epistle of St. James*, much given to provocative outbursts—they called the Cross 'Block-almighty', the church bell 'a cowbell' and referred to the font as 'a stinking tarn'. Sometimes the parish priest was himself a Lollard. Thus Robert Hemsted in 1518 described how he went to confession and the curate, Richard Fox, asked him:

How did he believe in the Sacrament of the altar: and then this respondent answered, and said as other men doth, that in the blessed Sacrament of the altar is the very body of Christ. To whom the said Sir Richard said, Nay thou must not do so. For that is not the best way; but believe thou in the Father, the Son, and the Holy Ghost, and not in the Sacrament of the altar.

It is clear that there were connections between Lollardy and Lutheranism. The Lollard cell would often accept the more sophisticated Lutheran heresy. By the end of Henry VIII's reign the former had been absorbed, having helped on the one hand to stiffen episcopal resistance to any concessions (for instance an English translation of the Bible) while on the other hand they had made easier the task of Lutheran missionaries. In 1523 Bishop Tunstall wrote that 'new arms are being added to the great crowd of Wycliffite heresies' and in 1528 he analysed the relationship: 'There have been found certain children of iniquity who are endeavouring to bring into our land the old and accursed Wycliffite heresy and along with it the Lutheran heresy, foster-daughter of Wycliffe's.'

The Church, split along what may be termed class lines, was unable to present a united front to its critics. Great chasms existed between priest and laity, secular and regular, upper and lower clergy, the cardinal-legate and the bishops.

The bishops and higher clergy were rigid in administration, wealthy in person, bureaucratic in outlook, pluralist in office. The parish clergy were ill-educated and underpaid—an analysis of the diocese of Coventry and Lichfield shows that 50 per cent of the rectories and 72 per cent of the vicarages were worth less than £10 a year, of which income Latimer said that it did not enable a man 'to buy him books, nor give his neighbour drink'.

A second division ran between the secular clergy and the regulars, the monks and nuns. The regulars were few in number (about 11,000) but enjoyed a total income of about £136,361—perhaps half the total wealth of the English church. Yet here, too, there were wide variations. There were altogether about 825 religious houses of all types and the average number of persons in the smaller houses was not more than seven or eight. Visitations suggest slackness rather than corruption. The traditional functions of monasticism had been prayer, hospitality, education and alms-giving. The monasteries do not appear to have spent more than between 3 and 5 per cent of their income on charity, and outside the universities they played an insignificant role in Tudor education. Too many heads of houses had become, not vicious, but—more insidious—indolent country gentlemen.

Directed against this divided body of the Church the criticism of the humanists (most of whom were themselves sincere Catholics) struck home and even their academic activities proved destructive. Symbolic was the return of Colet from Italy and the series of lectures on St. Paul's *Epistle to the Romans* which he delivered at Oxford (1496–7). Colet's theme was that Paul was a real man, the *Epistle* a real letter, and that consequently both must be considered critically in their historical context. Colet was thus at once a cause and a product of the changes that were taking place in English intellectual life. The international figure of Erasmus played a great part in encouraging men to turn their backs on the great heap of medieval traditions. Erasmus worked at Cambridge (1511–14) and the first established group of English Lutherans existed in that town in 1520, their meeting place the White Horse, known sarcastically as 'little Germany'. A list of Reformers who had spent some time at Cambridge would include the names of Tyndale, Coverdale, Cranmer, Latimer, Ridley and Parker.

From its earliest days the English Reformation was eclectic rather than sectarian, drawing on many sources, and though both Zwinglianism and Lutheranism affected the country, yet when they crossed the Channel they suffered a sea-change, so that one cannot say that at any specific moment England was

Lutheran or Zwinglian, though Luther's influence was, at first, the more potent.

A product of English Lutheranism was Tyndale's New Testament. William Tyndale (c. 1495–1536) was born in Gloucestershire and educated at Oxford and Cambridge. Later he went to London where, having failed to interest Tunstall, he came in contact with Humphrey Monmouth, a London cloth merchant who introduced Tyndale to the world of international Lutheranism. London had become second only to Cambridge as a centre of reforming activity. At the university the intellectual heretic predominated, in London and other large trading centres the stimulus came from laymen, merchants with money and cosmopolitan connections.

In 1524 Tyndale was at Wittenberg, but soon he moved to Cologne, and eventually he settled in the Merchant Adventurers' English House in Antwerp. There he was safe from both English and continental persecution, and in Flanders his translation of the New Testament was printed in 1525–6. In 1536 Tyndale was lured out of the English House and executed for heresy. Tyndale's version owed much to Erasmus's translation of 1516 and in its turn it greatly influenced later English translations, including the Authorized Version of the New Testament, nine-tenths of which is based on Tyndale.

Some years earlier Tyndale had made clear his aim that the common people might have the Bible 'plainly laid before their eyes in their mother tongue, that they might see the process, order and meaning of the text'. This democratic approach towards religion went, as in Luther's case, hand in hand with a strong belief in the divinely appointed nature of the office of the ruler.

The effect of Tyndale's Testament immediately began to be felt in England. As early as 1527 an English Lollard, John Tyball, described how he showed a Friar old translations of parts of the New Testament:

> Which books the said Friar did little regard, and made a twit of it, and said, A point for them, for they be not to be regarded toward the new printed Testament in English. For it is of more cleaner English. And then the said Friar Barnes delivered to them the said New Testament in English: for which they paid three shillings and two pence. . . .

The English Reformation developed without any support from Henry VIII, indeed in direct opposition to his wishes.

Doctrinally orthodox, the King and his ministers carried through in the thirties a double revolution: the English Church was cut off from the international Church of which it formed a part, and it was made subject to the King in Parliament. That these changes aroused so little opposition was due partly to the development of English reformed thought already described, but more to older English traditions of Erastianism (the doctrine of the supremacy of the State in ecclesiastical affairs) and anti-clericalism.

In the fourteenth century English national feeling had begun to run high. The Papacy was controlled by France (the Babylonish Captivity at Avignon 1305–77) or divided (the Great Schism 1379–1415) at a time when England was fighting France and was united. Men talked of the English Church, *Ecclesia Anglicana*. In this context one can understand the series of anti-papal laws (1351, 1353, 1365, 1389) which culminated in the great statute of *Praemunire* in 1393. This last was directed against anyone who should introduce papal bulls designed to put pressure in certain ways on the English bishops. Once its specialized aims had been achieved its powers were no longer invoked, but it remained on the statute book, a conveniently vague threat against ecclesiastical jurisdiction in general.

The great statute spoke of the independence of the English Crown 'which hath been so free at all times that it hath been in subjection to no earthly sovereign, but immediately to God and no other'. In Europe similar sentiments had been expressed, clearly and persuasively, by Marsiglio of Padua in 1324.[1]

Later Erastian legislation in England had been less spectacular. Henry VII had reduced the privileges of benefit of clergy and of sanctuary, and the right of sanctuary had been further restricted in 1512. The official lay view of the relations between Church and State at this time was expressed in Dudley's *Tree of Commonwealth*, though the manuscript itself was not printed until the nineteenth century. Dudley wrote of the ruler as a sort of umpire, standing apart from both clergy and laity and therefore able to judge impartially between them: 'no man can do it but the Prince'.

Anti-clerical feelings, symptomatic of the general shift in lay

[1] See pp. 128–9.

values, were exposed clearly in Hunne's case, a conflict between a prickly, conceited layman and hard, unscrupulous clerics. In 1511 Richard Hunne's child died. The rector demanded the bearing sheet as his due. Hunne refused the demand, and in 1512 a church court decided against him. In the following year Hunne retaliated, bringing a suit in King's Bench against the clergy, claiming that they were guilty of *Praemunire*. This case was never settled, for in 1514 Hunne was arrested by order of the bishop. His house was searched and heretical books were unearthed there. A little later Hunne was discovered hanging in his cell. A coroner's jury found, not suicide, but murder. Almost certainly they were correct. The Bishop's chancellor and two other men were indicted, but they were never brought to trial. Meanwhile the Church authorities declared Hunne a heretic and his body was burned. Laymen said that Hunne 'was made a heretic for suing a *Praemunire*', while on the other hand the bishop of London was sure that his chancellor would never get a fair trial, since a lay jury would convict any cleric 'though he were as innocent as Abel'.

National feeling resented papal taxes and papal claims. Englishmen believed that their country was being milked of money by Rome, though in actual fact the amount which left the country was not large, averaging less than £5,000 a year between 1485 and 1533. The significance of the part played by Wolsey in the growth of opposition to papal demands and of lay hostility to clerical claims has been described on pp. 66–9.

Literary attacks gave expression to this generalized anti-clericalism. The most picturesque of these was the satirical *Supplication of the Beggars* (*c.* 1529) by Simon Fish, which represented the professional beggars as complaining to the King that they were being ruined by the amateur beggars of the Church. Even in hospitals founded to look after the poor 'ever the fat of the whole foundation hangs on the priests' beards',

> And what do all these greedy sort of sturdy, idle, holy thieves with these yearly exactions that they take of the people? Truly nothing but exempt themselves from the obedience of your Grace. Nothing but translate all rule, power, lordship, authority, obedience, and dignity from your Grace unto them. Nothing but that all your subjects should fall into disobedience and rebellion against your Grace, and be under them.

A profound revolution had been carried out with so little open opposition largely because of this climate of opinion. Two other reasons also suggest themselves. One was the care taken to carry through the revolution in a strictly constitutional manner, with the support at every stage of political argument, parliamentary approval and at least the grudging acquiescence of the Church. In March 1534, for instance, the Convocation of Canterbury was persuaded to deny that 'the Roman pontiff has any greater jurisdiction conferred on him by God in Holy Scripture, within this realm of England, than any other foreign bishop', a valuable statement underpinning the new dispensation, not one that was legally essential in view of the statutes passed by parliament. Secondly, the revolution had so far been an administrative one, concerned with unemotive issues such as courts, appeals and clerical taxation, or questions of abstract political theory, neither of which touched the day-to-day practice of religion. The Pope was a remote foreigner and his disappearance from the liturgy did not much affect the ordinary worshipper's comfortable routine. In 1536, however, the government extended its activities and this extension led to widespread disturbances.

The Dissolution of the Monasteries

The dissolution of the monasteries is the most dramatic event in Henry's break with Rome and for contemporaries it must also have been the most prominent and the most spectacular, though the King was still moving within the ambit of national approval. In most parts of the country there was little support for monasticism: many of the attacks on the Church in late medieval England turn out on closer inspection to be aimed at monks and friars, rather than at the Church as a whole. Monasticism represented a spiritual level that was too high for many of its followers, and monastic failure to reach that level became a target for poet and satirist, humanist and reformer. It was, however, the monastic wealth which provided the final stimulus to action. The property of the Church represented between one-fifth and one-third of all the land in England, and Henry VIII needed money. A decline in wool exports had reduced the yield from the customs, Ireland was proving expensive, and in 1534 the French pension had been surrendered in an attempt to buy friendship in Europe. At a time when prices were rising, when land hunger was growing, and—above all—when the Crown was in financial difficulties, it is not surprising that the monastic lands should have been annexed. Something of the sort had been in the air for over a century. In the context of the Crown's needs, the landowners' greed, and the break with Rome, the dissolution of the monasteries became almost inevitable.

In 1535 Cromwell organized an assessment, needed for the levying of first fruits and tenths, of all church property in England. The work was completed in six months, and the information recorded in the *Valor Ecclesiasticus*. It revealed that the royal income from the taxes would be over £40,000 per annum. At the same time, having been appointed vicar-general and vicegerent of the Church, Cromwell despatched a second group of commissioners to visit the monasteries and gather evidence of slackness and immorality. The visitation duly produced plenty of ammunition for the attack, though not more than earlier ones had done. All this was followed in 1536 by a statute which ordered the dissolution of monasteries with incomes of £200 a year or less, 'forasmuch as manifest sin, vicious, casual and abominable living is daily used and committed. . . .' A second act established the Court of Augmentations to administer these new Crown lands. At once the royal officials began the work of dissolution and in October there occurred the first and last dangerous outburst against Henry's rule—a major crisis. Yet the Pilgrimage of Grace was not predominantly a rising in support of the monasteries. Fear of the consequences of dissolution, rather than the dissolution itself, was the precipitating cause. That fear released a host of other uncertainties and grievances, many of which had very little to do with religious protest.

What is known as the Pilgrimage of Grace was in fact four distinct movements: a brief rising in Lincolnshire (1–12 October 1536); the main rebellion centred in Yorkshire, Lancashire and the north-east (9 October–5 December 1536); a simultaneous but largely independent outburst in Cumberland and Westmorland; and a second rising in Yorkshire (January 1537) which in its turn sparked off further trouble in the Lake District.

The disconnected nature of these risings is explained in part by the variety of their causes. It is clear that the North had many complaints but no common aim. For historians the main interest of the Pilgrimage does not lie in its religious aspect nor even in its consequences, but rather in its open expression of the stresses—social, economic, political and personal—which had developed between the old feudal society, still almost unchanged in the Highland Zone, and the new, modern state that was being created so rapidly in the South.

The Lincolnshire rising was an explosion of the commons against the unpopular bishop of Lincoln and his servants, and against the royal officials who were collecting the subsidy of 1534. Within a fortnight it had collapsed, but not before it had led on to the main rising in the north. This was headed by Robert Aske, a lawyer and a religious idealist of strong personality. It was he who gave the movement whatever Roman Catholic character it possessed. In the Lake District the trouble was almost completely social and economic, directed against enclosures and against increased fines for the entry of new tenants into their lands (*gressums*). The rising in the North was supported by most of the leading families and their followers, men used to fighting the Scots, linked by clientage to the great, traditionally rebellious, feudal houses of Percy, Neville and Dacre. The force raised was formidable, and became even more so when Lord Darcy handed over Pontefract Castle, the key to the South.

The king sent the Duke of Norfolk and the Earl of Shrewsbury against the rebels. At Doncaster Norfolk, with vague promises, persuaded Aske to lay down his arms. The feudal army dispersed. In January a second minor wave of unrest, led by Sir Francis Bigod, gave Henry the excuse—if he had ever felt he needed it—to break his word. Norfolk suppressed the rising, and Aske, Lord Dacre, and a number of the other leaders were executed, together with between 220 and 250 of their followers, thus carrying out the king's orders to cause 'dreadful execution to be done upon a good number'.

The revolt had collapsed because it was haphazard and unplanned, and above all because it was not directed against the King, but against a diversity of targets. Aske, for all his religious enthusiasm, recognized the dominance of the economic motive, the fear that, when the monasteries were dissolved, the payment of rents, first-fruits and tenths would drain wealth from the north:

> By occasion whereof, within short space of years, there should be no money nor treasure in those parts, neither the tenant

to have to pay his rents to the lord, nor the lord to have money to do the King service withall, for so much as in those parts was neither the presence of his Grace, execution of his laws, nor yet but little recourse of merchandise, so that of necessity the said country should either patysh [make a treaty with] the Scots, or for very poverty be enforced to make commotion and rebellion.

Lord Darcy, on the other hand, saw the movement as one against the growing power of the centralizing authority:

Cromwell, it is thou that art the very original and chief causer of all this rebellion and mischief, and art likewise causer of the apprehension of us that be noblemen, and dost earnestly travail to bring us to one end to strike off our heads, and I trust that ere thou die, though thou wouldst procure all the nobleman's heads within the realm to be stricken off, yet shall there one head remain that shall strike off thy head.

Darcy spoke for many of the lords, to whom the Pilgrimage was a rejection of the whole direction of government action since 1471. Ironically, the most positive consequence of the Pilgrimage was to strengthen still further the machinery of government, for in 1537 Cromwell reorganized the Council of the North, giving it a permanent structure that endured for over a hundred years.

The Pilgrimage may have hastened the dissolution of the remaining monasteries. In 1536 two hundred and twenty of the smaller ones had been immediately dissolved, but the remainder had obtained exemptions. These now began to fall, usually by 'voluntary' surrender. In 1539 an act was passed confirming these surrenders. The dissolution of the remaining houses was soon completed. On 23 March 1540, the last of all the monasteries, the abbey of Waltham, surrendered.

The break with Rome brought a last flicker of opposition from the Yorkists. Reginald Pole (1500–58) was related through his mother Margaret, Countess of Salisbury, to both Edward IV and the Earl of Warwick. He was educated at Oxford and at Padua and in 1527 became Dean of Exeter. In 1532 he left England, returning eventually to Padua. In 1536 he published an attack on the royal Supremacy and early in the following year he was created Cardinal and Legate, the intention being that he should put himself at the head of the northern rising. By that time, though, the revolt had come to an end.   Henry Courtenay, Marquis of Exeter, a direct descendant of Edward IV, together with the brothers of Cardinal Pole, was encouraged by Chapuys to indulge in treasonable talk in the summer of 1538.   The new Treasons Act was used to convict them.   Courtenay and one of the Pole brothers were executed at once, while Pole's mother the Countess of Salisbury was imprisoned, and executed in 1541.   Behind much of the conspiring and half-conspiring of this period stood the Imperial ambassador Eustace Chapuys, the brilliant Swiss agent of Charles V.

What were the consequences of the Dissolution?   There were a number of administrative results.   In 1536 Cromwell instituted the Court of Augmentations, its methods based on those already successfully applied by the Duchy of Lancaster, to handle the huge royal revenues that would be derived from the monastic lands.   By 1544 these revenues totalled £253,292, but after that date the new Court, eyed jealously by older-established bodies, declined.   In 1547 it was united with the Court of General Surveyors of crown lands and in 1554 it was absorbed by the old Exchequer as part of the financial reforms introduced by the Marquis of Winchester, William Paulet.

Another result was the creation of new bishoprics based upon existing monastic foundations.   The King had originally intended to set up thirteen sees: in 1540 six were established, at Bristol, Chester, Gloucester, Oxford, Peterborough and Westminster.   (The last of these survived for only ten years, being reabsorbed into the see of London in 1550.)   A certain amount was done for learning.   All the new bishoprics except Oxford had cathedral schools attached to them; the old-established schools at Canterbury, Carlisle, Ely, Norwich, Rochester and Worcester were re-endowed; Trinity was founded at Cambridge and Christ Church completed at Oxford, and five Regius professorships were set up at each university in civil law, Greek, Hebrew, medicine and theology.

The last of the administrative decisions affected the future of the ex-religious.   The heads of religious houses received large pensions, and many of them continued as secular clergy, in some cases even becoming bishops.   The ordinary monk received a pension of about £5 per annum, which was equivalent to the income of a poor priest or an unskilled workman, but in 1552-3 an enquiry showed that often these pensions were not kept up to date. Out of 800 pensioners, 406 were in arrears and of these two-thirds had not been paid for one year. Nuns, unlike monks, received very small pensions and, like the monks, were forbidden to marry. Unable to continue a vocation in the Church, many must have suffered a psychological feeling of deprivation.

More general results of the Dissolution were a considerable destruction of works of art, an immense temporary increase in the wealth of the Crown, and the release on to the market of a great quantity of land, which had considerable social and economic effects.

The pulling-down of monastic buildings, the melting-down of medieval metal-work, the disappearance of manuscripts, represent a great artistic and antiquarian loss. The King did a little to lessen this. He allowed the antiquary John Leland to save some of the plums for him; the British Museum possesses 400 of King Henry's books and of these about 250 originated in medieval libraries, most of them monastic.

The most spectacular consequence was the transfer of vast amounts of land—the main source of wealth, of security and of status—to new owners. In the first instance it was of course the Crown which benefited. The *Valor Ecclesiasticus* had estimated a net monastic income of £136,361, an amount more than three times the income of the Crown lands at that time. Cromwell by the Dissolution provided the King with 'enormous rent-rolls, the true sinews of executive power. Yet within seven years these sinews had withered beyond all chance of recovery. The actual effects of the Dissolution upon our history seem as nothing compared with its potential importance at the moment when it was first consummated.'[1]

How did the King dispose of his new-found capital? Out of 1,593 grants only 41 were outright gifts, while another 28 were combinations of gifts and sale or exchange. Between 1543 and 1547 two-thirds of the lands were sold by the Crown to pay for the wars against France and Scotland. Most of these lands were bought at the standard purchase price of twenty years' rent. (Many buyers were buying to sell again, or were acting as proxies for other men, so that an analysis of the

---

[1] A. G. Dickens, *The English Reformation*, Batsford, 1964, p. 150.

H

original purchasers can only be used with caution.   Such an analysis gives the following percentages: miscellaneous, mainly gentry, 26; spiritual corporations, 22; peers, 18; royal officials, 15; courtiers, 8; industrials, 7; lawyers, 2.)   Regional surveys can add some important details regarding the history of the monastic lands during the next ten or twenty years.   In the West Riding 21 people held 60 per cent of the monastic lands in 1546 and, of these, 17 were connected with the peerage or with established families.   In Devon by 1558 almost a quarter of the old monastic lands was held by the Russells (to whom the King had given large grants in order that they might fill the power vacuum left there by the execution of the Courtenays) and by the canons of Windsor.   Less than 10 per cent was held by strangers.   'The ostensibly "new men" were in fact . . . of Devon gentry-stock, younger sons or heads of junior branches of well-known families, men who had earned money by active careers, often in the royal service . . . a most undramatic picture and exceedingly discouraging for the theory that the Dissolution introduced a new type of landlord to the countryside.'[1]   In Essex, though, near to the heart of affairs, it was new men like Rich and Petre who seem to have benefited.

Neither   rack-renting   nor   enclosures   originated,   nor apparently were they intensified, by the changes in ownership. The dispossessed had enclosed and raised rents like any other efficient landlord.   The new men continued to do so.   During the great period of land sales England was not a Protestant country and there is no evidence that future Protestants bought land more eagerly than those who later remained staunch Catholics.   Certainly in the fifties Simon Renard, the Spanish ambassador, thought that Catholics held more monastic land than did heretics, while in Cornwall it has been established that the leading figures in the Dissolution were all Catholics.

In general, it seems likely that the middling sort of man profited, that by the end of the century the gradual dis-appearance of the feudal aristocracy and the more dramatic removal of the ecclesiastical landlord had resulted in the enrichment of gentle families, ambiguously identified as the gentry and the yeomanry, a body which was already beginning to press into the House of Commons and to raise its voice in

---

[1] A. G. Dickens, pp. 158–9, summarizing J. Youings, *Devon and Cornwall Rec. Soc.*, new series, vol. i.

the nation's councils. They were great builders. Where the men they had displaced had raised castle and abbey they put their money into manor-houses, farm-houses, town-houses and, to a lesser but noticeable extent, into schools and almshouses.

National Catholicism

What was to be the theological position of the new Church? Two groups struggled for the King's favour. On the one hand there were those who were anxious to see some change in dogma, who were attracted by the established Lutheran church and who could see the political advantages of an alliance with the Protestant princes of the Empire. The chief spokes-men for this group were Thomas Cromwell and Thomas Cranmer.

Cromwell probably hoped to construct eventually some form of distinct national church. Such a creation would have been in keeping with his normal course of action and there are signs that he was preparing the ground. The Lutherans, notably Melanchthon, had developed the distinction between the essential matters of religion and *adiaphora*, the things indifferent, and in England in 1535 Thomas Starkey, one of Cromwell's publicists, had argued in *An Exhortation to the People*, that too many disputes on the continent had arisen over matters 'in no point necessary to man's salvation, but about ceremonies and traditions'. The right road lay between those who 'stiffly stick in the old ceremonies and rites of the Church' and those who 'under pretence of liberty, covertly purpose to destroy all Christian policy, and so in conclusion bring all to manifest ruin and utter confusion'.[1]

In 1536 and 1538 Cromwell imposed sets of Injunctions on the Church and these, too, give hints as to the way his mind was working. Those of 1536 included orders that the clergy were to teach their congregations the Pater Noster, the Articles of Faith (the 1538 Injunctions laid down that the parishioners were to be examined in these), and the Ten Commandments. They were to encourage parents to have their children edu-cated, or to apprentice them. Non-residents were to give a fifth of their income to repair the chancels of their churches and another fortieth to the poor, and the 1538 Injunctions added that they must appoint curates to do their work. Rich clergy

[1] See p. 129.

must support scholars at grammar schools and at the two universities.

Modesty, learning and a belief in the royal supremacy combined to make Thomas Cranmer a personal favourite of the King.' 'You were born in a happy time, for do or say what you will, the King will always take it at your hand', Cromwell observed. Cranmer was later accused of undue subservience to Henry, and his motives were said to be those of fear and of ambition. There is probably some truth in the accusation, but two points must be borne in mind when considering his character. The first is that his religious beliefs changed; what he sincerely believed in 1528 could no longer satisfy him in 1538 and, similarly, the tenets of 1538 had been superseded by very different ones, held with equal sincerity, in 1548. Secondly, he was a tactful man—in 1534 he advised Latimer not to preach for more than one and a half hours lest he bore the King—and tact often passes insensibly into compromise.

Cranmer and Cromwell, the man of letters and the man of affairs, were a strong team, but the King's natural impulse— and with Henry that was always the mainspring—was to make no change. Tudor caution counselled it and Henry's conscience approved. In consequence the conservative faction was powerful. It included most of the bishops and was headed by the Duke of Norfolk and Stephen Gardiner, Bishop of Winchester. They accepted the lay headship of the Church. Gardiner argued in De Vera Obedientia (1535) that God had appointed his representatives on earth, and the proclamation of Henry as Head of the Church had merely restored to the King a privilege and a position that had been temporarily usurped by the Bishop of Rome. He also accepted the dissolution of the monasteries, but nothing more.

On the surface the years from 1536 to 1547 are ones of triumph for this English Catholic party, which left Cranmer in an isolated position, though there are slight shifts of emphasis that indicate the struggle going on behind the scenes. In 1536 Convocation approved the Ten Articles, designed, it has been suggested, to achieve unity 'by ambiguity and silence'. These defined the three sacraments of baptism, penance and the Eucharist in a Catholic sense (presumably because the exact significance of these three was most in dispute); they approved auricular confession and prayers for the dead, and they declared that justification was 'by contrition and faith joined with charity'. The Ten Articles appear to be an attempt to define the English position in a traditional manner while yet leaving room for Lutherans to accept the country as an ally. In the following year a more conservative document was issued, the *Institution of a Christian Man*, soon known more simply as *The Bishops' Book*, which described the Church as being composed of free, equal, national churches, but which was in other respects strictly orthodox.

In 1539 Parliament passed the Act of Six Articles. The King had revised the earliest draft and later he himself addressed the Lords and, one said, 'confounded them all with God's learning'. This expression of the royal credo reasserted the Catholic position on transubstantiation, communion in one kind, the celibacy of priests, vows of chastity, masses for the dead, and auricular confession. The Act included penalties for heresy which were more ferocious than those of the church courts (for instance, a heretic who denied transubstantiation was in future to be burnt even though he abjured his heresy) and made it clear that the King was determined to enforce Catholic comformity on his kingdom. In the same summer this determination was emphasized by the execution of three Catholic traitors and the burning of three Protestant heretics on the same day and at the same place, Smithfield.

To the end of his life the King continued to balance old catholics against new protestants. Detesting the latter, he had nevertheless no intention of becoming the prisoner of the former. In 1539 the Great Bible, produced by Miles Coverdale (1488–1568) on Cromwell's instructions, enabled people openly to read the Bible in English. Yet printing ceased in 1541 and in 1543 Henry allowed an Act to be passed which limited, on a class basis, the circulation of the Bible. Noblemen and gentlemen might read it to their families, merchants and gentlewomen might read it to themselves, the 'base people' were forbidden to read it at all. (William Halden of Chelmsford later recalled how '. . . I and my father's prentice Thomas Jeffery laid our money together and bought the New Testament in English, and hid it in our bed straw. . . .') In 1543 doctrine was more narrowly defined in *The Necessary Doctrine and Erudition of a Christian Man*, known as *The King's Book*, which was specifically anti-Lutheran.

During these years Stephen Gardiner, an unimaginative choleric man, three times attempted to show that Cranmer himself was a heretic, but the King continued to protect his Archbishop. The latter's belief in royal supremacy had become as strong as his belief in the supremacy of the Bible. For Cranmer the King was still the one force that could preserve what had so far been won against false doctrine, reactionary nobles, rebellion at home and threats abroad. He spent his time translating portions of the liturgy into English, and in 1545 the King approved the use of his version of the Litany, in which the brief petitions of the Latin service are grouped in superb clusters: 'From all evil and mischief; from sin, from all crafts and assaults of the devil; from thy wrath, and from everlasting damnation, *Good Lord, deliver us.*'

Henry allowed his son to be educated by known reformers, and named in his will a council of regency which included a majority favourable to protestantism and omitted, conspicuously, the name of Gardiner. Yet at the same time he permitted the torture and burning of protestants, such as that of Anne Agnew in 1546. It is scarcely surprising that a contemporary protestant considered that 'there was no Reformation, but a deformation, in the time of that tyrant and lecherous monster'.

On Christmas Eve 1545 Henry addressed Parliament on the subject of religion:

> Charity and concord are not among you, but discord and dissension beareth rule in every place . . . Behold, then, what love and charity is among you, when one calleth another heretic and Anabaptist, and he calleth him again Papist, hypocrite and Pharisee! Be these tokens of charity among you? . . . Amend these crimes, I exhort you, and set forth God's word; or else, as God's vicar and High Minister, I will see these divisions extinct . . . Love, dread and serve God, to the which I, as your supreme Head and sovereign Lord, exhort and require you. . . .

The words *these divisions* provide a clue to Henry's religious policy at this time. The king, a perennial and unprincipled opportunist, demanded religious uniformity for the sake of political unity, and as a tribute to his own undivided authority as Supreme Head. He would die as he had lived, the secular pope of a catholic national church. After his death things would no doubt be different. This is the only interpretation that makes sense of the king's curious compromises. Luther, as usual, spoke rough sense when he said 'Junker Henry means to be God'. The cautious approach to any redefinition of dogma had infuriated him—'I dare say I have achieved bigger things and more work in the course of four weeks, and they have now been quarrelling over this one point for twelve years,' and on hearing of Henry's death Luther's natural reaction was '. . . good riddance, Head and Defender'.

Whatever his intentions, the ambiguity of Henry's actions led men towards a *via media*, a settlement neither Roman Catholic nor Lutheran but national, selective and detached from specific continental sects. The last years of the King's reign made much easier the acceptance of the changes that were soon to follow, for beneath the conservative surface the basis for those future changes was already beginning to develop.

EXTRACTS

I. *John Skelton satirizes new heresies and old jealousies in* Colin Clout (1519):

And some have a smack
Of Luther's sack,
And a burning spark
Of Luther's wark,
And are somewhat suspect
In Luther's sect;
And some of them bark,
Clatter and carp
Of that heresiarch
Called Wicliffista,
The devilish dogmatista;
And some be Hussians,
And some be Arians,
And some be Pelagians,
And make much variance
Between the clergy
And the temporalty,
How the Church hath too mickle,
And they have too little, . . .

II. *Edward Hall describes the reception in England of Tyndale's translation of the New Testament:*

In the beginning of this two and twentieth year [1530–1], the king like a politic and prudent prince, perceived that his

subjects and other persons had divers times within four years
last past, brought into his realm great number of printed books
of the New Testament, translated into the English tongue by
Tyndal, Joy, and others, which books the common people
used and daily read privily, which the clergy would not admit,
for they punished such persons as had read, studied or taught
the same with great extremity, but because the multitude was
so great, it was not in their power to redress their grief: wherefore they made complaint to the Chancellor (which leaned
much to the spiritual men's part in all causes) whereupon he
imprisoned and punished a great number, so that for this cause
a great rumour and controversy rose daily amongst the people:
wherefore the king, considering what good might come of
reading the New Testament with reverence and following the
same, and what evil might come of the reading of the same if it
were evil translated, and not followed: came into the star
chamber the five and twentieth day of May, and there com-
muned with his council and the prelates concerning this cause,
and after long debating it was alleged that the translations of
Tyndal and Joy were not truly translated, and also that in
them were prologues and prefaces which sounded to heresy,
the bishops uncharitably, wherefore all such books were
prohibited and commandment given by the king to the bishops,
that they calling to them the best learned men of the universities should cause a new translation to be made, so that the
people should not be ignorant in the law of God: and notwithstanding this commandment the bishops did nothing at all
to set forth a new translation, which caused the people to
study Tyndal's translation, by reason whereof many things
came to light, as you shall hear after.   (E. Hall, *The Union of
the Two Noble and Illustrious Families of Lancaster and York*, ed.
Whibley, 1904, Vol. II.

III.   *William Roper recounts the evidence given against his father-
in-law, Thomas More:*
Shortly hereupon, Master Rich, afterwards Lord Rich, then
newly made the King's Solicitor, Sir Richard Southwell, and
one Master Palmer, servant to the Secretary, were sent to Sir
Thomas More into the Tower to fetch away his books from
him.   And while Sir Richard Southwell and Master Palmer
were busy in the trussing up of his books, Master Rich, pretending friendly talk with him, among other things, of a set course,
as it seemed, said thus unto him:
'Forasmuch as it is well known, Master More, that you are a

man both wise and well learned as well in the laws of the Realm as otherwise, I pray you therefore, sir, let me be so bold as of good will to put unto you this case. Admit there were, sir,' quoth he, 'an Act of Parliament that all the Realm should take me for King. Would not you, Master More, take me for King?'

'Yes, sir,' quoth Sir Thomas More, 'that would I.'

'I put case further', quoth Master Rich, 'that there were an Act of Parliament that all the Realm should take me for Pope. Would not you then, Master More, take me for Pope?'

'For answer, sir,' quoth Sir Thomas More, 'to your first case, the Parliament may well, Master Rich, meddle with the state of temporal Princes. But to make answer to your other cause, I will put this case—suppose the Parliament would make a law that God should not be God. Would you then, Master Rich, say that God were not God?'

'No, sir,' quoth he, 'that would I not since no Parliament may make any such law.'

'No more,' said Sir Thomas More, as Master Rich reported him, 'could the Parliament make the King Supreme Head of the Church.'

Upon whose only report was Sir Thomas More indicted for treason upon the statute whereby it was made treason to deny the King to be Supreme Head of the Church. . . . (William Roper, *The Life of Sir Thomas More, c.* 1556.)

IV. *Edward Hall writes on some of the causes of the Pilgrimage of Grace:*

The inhabitants of the North parts being at that time very ignorant and rude, knowing not what true religion meant, but altogether noseled in superstition and popery, and also by the means of certain Abbots and ignorant priests not a little stirred and provoked for the suppression of certain monasteries, and for the extirpation and abolishing of the bishop of Rome, now taking an occasion at this book [the Act of Ten Articles], saying, 'See friends now is taken from us four of the seven sacraments and shortly ye shall lose the other three also, and thus the faith of holy church shall be utterly suppressed and abolished. . . .' Among these were many priests which deceived also the people with many false fables and venomous lies and imaginations (which could never enter nor take place in the heart of any good man, nor faithful subject) saying that all manner of prayer and fasting and all God's service should utterly be destroyed and taken away, that no man should marry a wife or be partaker of the sacraments, or at length should eat a piece of roast meat, but he should for the same first pay unto the king a certain sum of money, and that they should be in more bondage and in a more wicked manner of life than the Saracens be under the great Turk.   (E. Hall, Vol. II, pp. 269–71.)

V.   *Cromwell writes to the Duke of Norfolk, May 22, 1537, concerning the property of Bridlington Priory and Jervaulx Abbey:*

As for the shrine, the King's highness, to the intent that his people should not be seduced in the offering of their money, would have taken down, which and all other plate and jewels appertaining to his Highness, except such as you desire to have for your money, which his Highness is content with, his pleasure is shall be sent up hither with all speed, being also contented that you according to your desire shall have such vestments and ornaments of the church, not being meet for his Highness' use, the same being appraised for your reasonable money as shall appertain.   And also that the corn and cattle, specially such as be meet to be sold, be uttered, his Highness thinks to be best now, remitting the discretion and order thereof unto you, and also the lands likewise, at this time of the year being both sown, and of other nature his Highness doubteth not but that ye will substantially order the same as shall be most for his Highness' profit.   And the pleasure of his Highness is that the due debts of the said houses, well proved without covin, shall be contented of the goods of the same.

And as to the lead, and all other things, wherein ye be willing to know the King's pleasure, your lordship shall understand that upon the view and survey thereof now at this time by your grace and his commissioners to be eftsoons unto his Highness, in all things he will upon the sight of the same determine his pleasure.   (R. B. Merriman, *Letter and Speeches of Thomas Cromwell*, Vol. II, pp. 57–58.)

VI.   *Cromwell's Injunctions to the Clergy, Sept. 5, 1538; they are to keep a register of christenings, weddings and burials:*

Item, that you and every parson, vicar or curate within this diocese shall for every church keep one book or register wherein ye shall write the day and year of every wedding, christening and burying made within your parish for your time, and so every man succeeding you likewise.   And shall there insert every person's name that shall be so wedded, christened or buried, And for the safe keeping of the same book the parish shall be bound to provide of their common charges one sure coffer with two locks and keys, whereof the one to remain with you, and the other with the said wardens, wherein the said book shall be laid up.   Which book ye shall every Sunday take forth and, in the presence of the said wardens or one of them, write and record in the same all the weddings, christenings and buryings made the whole week before, And that done to lay up the book in the said coffer as afore.   And for every time that the same shall be omitted the party that shall be in the fault thereof shall forfeit to the said church iij s iiij d to be employed on the reparation of the said church.   (R. B. Merriman, Vol. II, pp. 154–5.)

FURTHER READING

The New Cambridge Modern History, Vol. II, The Reformation (1520–59) ed. G. R. Elton, Chapter II, 'The Reformation in England', C.U.P., 1958
T. M. Parker, *The English Reformation to 1558*, O.U.P., 1950
A. G. Dickens, *The English Reformation*, Batsford, 1964
Map of Monastic Britain, two sheets, Ordnance Survey, 1950
D. Knowles, *The Religious Orders in England, Vol. III: The Tudor Age*, C.U.P., 1959
G. Baskerville, *English Monks and the Suppression of the Monasteries*, Cape, 1937
A. G. Dickens, *Thomas Cromwell and the English Reformation*, E.U.P., 1959
J. Ridley, *Thomas Cranmer*, O.U.P., 1962
G. W. O. Woodward, *The Dissolution of the Monasteries*, Blandford, 1966

V · THOMAS CROMWELL

Introduction

THOMAS CROMWELL was born about 1485. His father was a fuller and blacksmith in Putney. Little is known of his son's early life, except that he travelled about Europe, picking up new ideas and techniques. He served as a mercenary in the Italian wars and later traded in Antwerp, and somewhere on his journeys he studied law and the new Italian methods of book-keeping. By about the year 1512 he was back in England, making a living out of the variety of skills he had acquired, and eight years later he was in Wolsey's service, where he remained until his master's disgrace. His work included the dissolution of those monasteries the funds of which were used to endow Wolsey's two colleges. Already there were signs of a restless activity, prepared to question the established pattern. In 1523 he attacked in the Commons the traditional foreign policy, in 1527 he was in touch with the protestant exile, Miles Coverdale, and in 1530 he tried to persuade another exile, William Tyndale, to return to England.

Wolsey's fall did not involve Cromwell. 'I am like to lose all that I have laboured for' he lamented, but in fact he sat in 1529 for Taunton in that Parliament of which he was to make such revolutionary use. In 1530 he was sworn a member of the Council and towards the close of 1531 he became a member of the inner circle of the King's advisers. Power came first, office followed. Cromwell was made Master of the King's Jewels and Clerk of the Hanaper, a department of Chancery dealing with the enrolment of charters (1532), Chancellor of the Exchequer (1533), principal Secretary and Master of the Rolls (1534), Vicegerent (1535), and Lord Privy Seal. These posts were rewards and sometimes administrative conveniences, but they did not in themselves matter—though Cromwell made the Secretaryship a key office, and the Vicegerency was a unique creation—for, as with Wolsey and indeed as with all Tudor ministers, the basis of Cromwell's authority rested not on office but on the King's confidence, which he enjoyed from 1532 to 1540. In the latter year Henry withdrew that confidence and within a few weeks Cromwell had been imprisoned, found guilty of treason, and executed.

The years from 1530 to 1540 contain a revolution in administration for which Thomas Cromwell was directly responsible. During these years work inspired or initiated by him affected every form of government activity. This work had five main aspects, though naturally these interlock and overlap: the Church; the Crown; Parliament; the destruction of 'liberties'; administrative changes. The assessment of Cromwell's achievement and the interpretation of it is primarily the work of Dr. Elton, and it seems unlikely that this will be essentially altered in the future, though some of its details have been criticized.[1]

The Crown

'The essential ingredient of the Tudor revolution was the concept of national sovereignty.'[2] This is the basis on which Cromwell's work rests. This national sovereignty expresses itself in parliamentary statute and operates through new or reformed institutions, staffed not by household servants but by government officials.

In 1533 the political philosophy behind these changes was stated in the preamble to the Act of Appeals:

Where by divers sundry old authentic histories and chronicles it is manifestly declared and expressed that this realm of England is an empire, and so hath been accepted in the world, governed by one supreme head and king having the dignity and royal estate of the imperial crown of the same, unto whom a body politic, compact of all sorts and degrees of people divided in terms and by names of spirituality and temporalty, be bounden and owe to bear next to God a natural and humble obedience; . . .

Here England is defined as a self-governing state (*empire*), under the Crown, which is itself under God. No external ties, political or spiritual are recognized—this is the novel statement.

---

[1] For a full statement of Dr. Elton's views see his book *The Tudor Revolution in Government*, C.U.P., 1953. For the most detailed criticism of these views see the article by P. Williams and G. L. Harriss *A Revolution in Tudor History?* in P. and P., No. 25, July 1963. The argument is continued in Nos. 29 and 31. A brief statement of the Elton interpretation, by one not directly involved, can be read in A. G. Dickens, *Thomas Cromwell and the English Reformation*, E.U.P., pp. 55–57.

[2] G. R. Elton, *England under the Tudors*, Methuen, 1955, p. 160.

To Henry in his capacity as king is due the allegiance of his subjects in temporal matters, while in spiritual affairs they owe him their obedience as supreme head of the church. In the sixteenth century men did not declare—and often did not think—that they were revolutionaries. They based their arguments on tradition (*old authentic histories*). Cromwell was concerned to show that Henry's authority as supreme head of the church rested on the past. Consequently the King's minister uses traditional terminology, but he fills the old bottles with new wine. Thus the word *empire* was an impeccably medieval term implying *imperial authority*: now Cromwell extended its meaning to that of *self-governing in matters temporal and spiritual*, and by using the old term he gave respectability to the enlarged meaning.

The clear statement of national sovereignty and the equally clear rejection of any outside authority released great power, power which found its most obvious expression in the administrative and legislative steps by which the Catholic Church in England became the Catholic Church of England, a profound revolution which was nevertheless a revolution of administrative control rather than of theological belief—though there are signs that Cromwell's tidy mind was looking towards the creation in the future of a national church, distinct in liturgy as in administration, which might also serve as the ground for a European alliance.

Parliament

Cromwell used parliament in a way that was new in extent though not in character. Increased use meant increased importance, increased importance would lead to increased authority for the members. As early as 1523 Thomas More, as Speaker, had requested for those members free speech 'without doubt of your dreadful displeasure, every man to discharge his conscience and boldly in every thing incident among us to declare his advice; and whatsoever happen any man to say, that it may like your noble Majesty, of your inestimable goodness, to take all in good part . . .' and there are examples of opposition by individual M.P.'s to royal desires in the Reformation parliament. In 1529 John Petite opposed a bill to cancel the King's debts, saying that in this matter he could not commit other men's estates. In 1533 Sir George Throckmorton spoke against the Act of Appeals, and the Act was in fact only passed by the Commons after they had amended it. There was general opposition from 1529–36 to the proposed Statute of Uses.[1]

A Commons then with a mind of its own, but nevertheless a Commons by means of which there was carried through a great packet of new legislation. Fear of the King's wrath influenced members, as did the flattering knowledge that they were playing a great part in affairs of state—between 1509 and 1531 about 150 public Acts had been passed, but in Cromwell's brief eight years 200 bills became law. Outsiders noted the emphasis on Parliament. Charles V's ambassador wrote of Henry: 'He has always fortified himself by the consent of Parliament', while in 1540 those who did not approve scoffed at 'this newfound article of our creed, that Parliament cannot err'.

More effective than either fear or self-importance was the care that Cromwell took to see that the Government's point of view was well represented. He did what he could to organize local influences so that men might be returned who would serve the interests of the Crown. It was not a question of packing parliament, which was not possible, but rather of attempting to manage it in a manner that looks forward to the methods of Shaftesbury in the seventeenth century and beyond him to the party managers of the eighteenth century. Cromwell understood how important it was that a good number of the King's Councillors should sit in the Commons, and one of the complaints of the Pilgrims of Grace was that the 'old custom was that none of the King's servants should be of the commons house, yet most of the house were the King's servants'.

The preambles to the new acts represent statements of Cromwellian policy; from these statements the body of the acts draw conclusions and decree punishments for infringement. The acts still claim, as in earlier times, to be declaratory rather than creative, to discover the law and then to make deductions from it rather than to innovate, but whatever they may say, they are in fact creative government by statute, the legal enforcement of a new royal policy. For the time being Parliament and Crown acted together, and to this extent there is truth in the old cliché that Tudor government was despotism

[1] See below, pp. 116–117.

by consent. Revolution by statute meant revolution through
the common law and the effect of the mass of acts passed in the
thirties was to strengthen that law. 'Indeed, it was Cromwell's
administration that saved the medieval common law, as it saved
the medieval parliament, and used both in the service of the
modern state.'[1] In the future state-made law might destroy
the idea of moral law (as Sir Thomas More so early realized),
but for the moment the value of the instrument outweighed its
dangers. Parliament, too, might grow in strength until it
challenged royal despotism but, for the time being at least, the
interests of its members coincided with those of the government
and a working partnership was possible.

Three Acts designed to increase the royal power illustrate
the varying relations in that partnership. The Treasons Act
of 1534, which made spoken words treasonable, undoubtedly
strengthened Henry's hand, yet at the same time it symbolized
the growing importance of parliamentary recognition, since it
gave statutory approval to a treason which had already been
accepted in the law courts. Somewhat similar was the
Proclamations Act of 1539. This gave statutory force to
proclamations issued by the king with the advice of his council.
This time the Commons amended the bill, inserting a clause
excluding proclamations which interfered with the life or
property of a subject. The growth in the use of proclamations
can be seen from the fact that of the proclamations surviving
from the period 1485–1553 (388 in all) two-thirds date from
the years 1529–53. At first sight the act appears to acknowledge the king's right to legislate but in fact by defining proclamations it limits their scope. Here parliament is used to
delineate one of the boundaries of royal activity.[2]

When the king and the Commons were working to the same
ends, there was no difficulty, but when their interests were
diametrically opposed, matters were not so simple. It took
Henry seven years to get his Statute of Uses through the
Reformation parliament. In order to avoid feudal dues
tenants adopted the device of conveying their estates to a third
person who would hold (*use*) them in trust for the heir. In

---

[1] G. R. Elton, *England Under the Tudors*, p. 169.

[2] See J. D. Mackie, *The Earlier Tudors*, O.U.P., 1959, pp. 438–9, and G. R.
Elton, *England under the Tudors*, pp. 169–70 for the legal position regarding proclamations.

1529 Henry offered to recognize uses on part of an estate.   The
Commons would not accept this.   In 1532 the King tried
again, and again the Commons refused the compromise.
Henry then addressed a delegation from the Lower House and
told them 'you should not contend with me that I am your
sovereign lord and king, considering that I seek peace and
quietness of you; . . . I have offered you reason, as I think, yea,
and so thinketh all the Lords, for they have set their hands to
the book; therefore I assure you, if you will not take some
reasonable end now when it is offered, I will search out the
extremity of the law and then will I not offer you so much
again.'   In 1535 a Statute of Uses was finally passed.   It laid
down that the user of the land was to be under the same
obligations as if he were the heir—and this for the whole of the
estate.

Local administration; the destruction of 'liberties'

Cromwell was concerned to destroy the 'liberties' (rights of
exemption from royal control) that existed within the 'empire'
as he had destroyed the external liberties of the Church.

In 1534 he received a report on the northern franchises, 'the
king's rights are attacked by all manner of liberties . . . and his
laws are not dreaded'.   Two years later Cromwell made a
note to speak to the king 'for the dissolution of all franchises
and liberties throughout the realm, . . .'

The independence of the county palatine of Durham and of
other judicial enclaves was taken away, so that for the first
time the whole country was directly subject to government
from Westminster through the king's judges and the local
justices appointed by the Crown.

In 1534 Cromwell revived the moribund Council of the
Marches of Wales, under the presidency of Rowland Lee,
Bishop of Coventry.   The bishop had a low opinion of the
Welsh—'Thieves I found them, and thieves I shall leave them'
—and, perhaps for this very reason, he worked indefatigably
to establish English law and order.   In 1536 the marcher lordships were abolished and all Wales was shired.   Six counties
(Flint, Anglesey, Caernarvon, Merioneth, Cardigan and
Carmarthen) already existed, to these were now added the
royal lands of Pembroke and Glamorgan and four new counties
along the border between England and Wales (Denbigh,

I

Montgomery, Radnor and Brecknock). Each shire was to send one knight to parliament and—except for Merioneth—one burgess to represent the county town. Monmouthshire was incorporated in the English system, being represented by two knights and two burgesses.

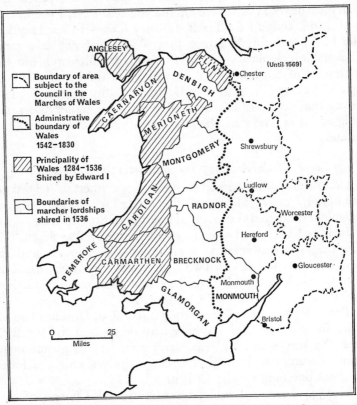

THE UNION OF ENGLAND AND WALES 1536–43

In 1543 the administrative changes that followed the act of 1536 were summarized in a comprehensive statute. Sheriffs, constables, coroners, English law, the English pattern of assize circuits, justices of the peace—Wales received all these and was completely assimilated to the English administrative system. The Council of the Marches was now given statutory recognition for the first time. It was directly responsible to the Crown and from its centre at Ludlow it controlled the twelve counties of Wales, Monmouthshire, Hereford, Worcester, Shropshire, Gloucester and, until 1569, Cheshire. Dissolved in 1641, the Council was revived in 1660 and then finally abolished in 1689. Calais, too, was drawn into the governmental structure, being represented by two members of parliament from 1536 until its loss in 1558.

In Wales the government was successful in its aims; in Ireland, as usual, there was failure. At the close of Henry VII's reign the Lord Deputy had been Gerald, the Earl of Kildare, and on his death in 1513 he was succeeded by his son. The Fitzgerald Earls of Kildare were the traditional Lords Deputy, but their otherwise continuous tenure was punctuated by regular bouts of treason. In 1519 the new Earl became involved in intrigue. Henry VIII sent Thomas Howard, Earl of Surrey, to Ireland with the title of Lord Lieutenant to put down disorder, unify the Church, collect the taxes. It was easier said than done. Kildare was arrested and sent to London, but soon Surrey was writing that his force in Ireland 'have not amongst us £20 in money' and that he would require £10,000 a year. He was recalled in 1521 and in the following year Kildare's rival Piers Butler, Earl of Ormond, was appointed Lord Deputy. For a time Henry tried, not very successfully, to play off Kildare against Butler.

When Cromwell came to power Kildare was enjoying the Deputyship, but in 1533 he was accused of plotting with Charles V and the Pope, was summoned to England and was imprisoned in the Tower. In Ireland his son, 'silken Thomas', acted as his deputy. In 1534 a rumour of his father's death, together with news of the growing breach with Rome, led Thomas to rebel. The archbishop of Dublin was murdered, and the city besieged. The rebellion was put down (1535-6) by an English force under Lord Leonard Grey and Sir William 'Gunner' Skeffington. Silken Thomas and five of his uncles were dispatched to London and executed in 1537.

Beyond this Cromwell's rule made no impact on Ireland. Shortly after his fall from power the King adopted the title of King of Ireland (1541). The Irish chiefs were induced to surrender their lands to the Crown and they then received them back again as tenants-in-chief. In this way it was hoped that Irish administration—since administration depended in the last analysis on land tenure—would be assimilated to that of England. The hope rested on a misunderstanding of the Irish structure of civilization. Ireland was a Celtic society in which the clan held the land, the chief merely having a life-tenure and hence it was not in his power to hand over the lands to the King. In 1543 an Act of Succession declared Henry Head of the Church in Ireland. Within six months the first Jesuit missionaries had landed. The pattern of Elizabethan conflict was already being drawn. It would take more than changes of title to control that island.

THE NORTHERN MARCHES

In 1537 the Pilgrimage of Grace provided an excuse and an incentive for the creation of a permanent Council of the

North replacing the series of temporary, personal councils which had been intermittently in existence since the days of Edward IV. The Council governed the five northern counties, usually from York (after 1582 always from that city), and derived its authority directly from the Crown, though the Privy Council kept a supervisory eye on affairs. Its jurisdiction covered both criminal and civil matters. The Council was abolished by the Long Parliament in 1641.

The conspiracies of the Courtenay family led in 1537 to the establishment of a third Council, that of the West, to administer from Exeter the counties of Dorset, Somerset, Devon and Cornwall. Clearly this was soon found to be unnecessary, for the Council disappeared at some date before 1547.

Central Administration

Cromwell's reforms of the day-to-day machinery of government took place almost as by-products of his major concerns, yet they were perhaps those which lay nearest to his heart. He was by nature bureaucratic; he loved the institution and the record. When he received authority he found a system in existence in which daily routine was largely vested in the king's household servants. It was a very personal form of government, depending for its power and its efficiency on either an active king like Henry VII or an active minister like Wolsey. In the absence of such men the system tended to fall apart, or at the very least to slow down. The effect of the changes which took place in the thirties was to depersonalize the structure, though the personal element was not removed entirely and executive *control* remained personal for a very long time to come.

At the beginning of Henry's reign the Council was still an amorphous body with a tendency to split into an inner ring of councillors attendant on the King and an outer body of occasional advisers. The King seems to have played a smaller part than his father had done, and there are signs that the most important councillors were beginning to meet regularly and formally. Wolsey's period in power checked this change, for the Cardinal was, so to speak, his own inner ring. In 1526, he produced a scheme, the Eltham Ordinances, by which it was proposed to reduce the Council to twenty office-holders and to exlude law officers from this body altogether.

Like so many of Wolsey's plans, the Eltham Ordinances remained a paper plan, but they provided a basis for Cromwell's changes. At some date between 1534 and 1536 a council of nineteen members came into existence, and in August 1540 this body appointed its own clerk and started its own minute book, from which date at the latest it clearly had a life of its own. It is convenient to call this new institution the Privy Council. In the mid-thirties its members consisted of nobles, such as Thomas Howard Duke of Norfolk; of clerics such as Cranmer; and of officials such as Cromwell himself and the Chancellor of the Court of Augmentations, Sir Richard Rich. The Council could work without the King's presence and in the middle years of the century it became the administrative heart of government, while the outer ring of councillors ceased to exist.

Cromwell made the office of Secretary the key position in the state—or perhaps one should say that the office of Secretary gave Cromwell the scope to act as the key man in the state. There is some truth in both these aspects of the situation. The Secretary had long been the king's private servant. Cromwell, replacing Gardiner, received the position in 1534 and made of the appointment what was virtually a new office. To an active, enquiring, pushing man the unspecified nature of its powers proved a great advantage and during Cromwell's tenure—he was the first layman to hold the post—the Secretary acquired control over almost everything. By 1539 he ranked as one of the great ones in the state and had taken over the functions formerly exercised by the holders of the privy seal and the royal signet. In 1540, after Cromwell's death, the Secretaryship was divided between two holders and for the next eighteen years the office declined in importance. Then, under the great William Cecil, it became once again the chief executive office in the state.

By the time of Cromwell's execution the financial administration centred on the Chamber had been greatly restricted in its activities, and had to a large extent been superseded by six departments, each with its own officials, seals and offices. The Exchequer continued to handle the ancient revenues, notably those derived from customs and from parliamentary taxation (£40,000); the Duchy of Lancaster looked after its own lands

(£13,000); the General Surveyors administered the old crown lands (£25,000). To these three departments Cromwell added the Court of First Fruits and Tenths to handle clerical monies (£40,000); the Court of Wards and Liveries to administer the feudal income of the Crown (£7,000); and the Court of Augmentations to deal with the former monastic lands (£100,000). The church lands and the better administration of earlier sources of income combined to increase the King's income from about £100,000 to about £220,000.

Foreign Policy

In the sphere of foreign policy Cromwell was both something of a pragmatist and something of a theorist: 'So often may we observe this antithesis between opportunities and doctrinairism in the chequered story of Tudor diplomacy. Always the opportunists like Henry VII and Elizabeth emerge unscathed, while the doctrinaires, the would-be builders of systems like Wolsey and Mary Tudor, end in confusion. Henry VIII and Cromwell both stood between the extremes. . . .'[1]

From 1529 to 1536 England's foreign policy was cautious and negative. This is hardly to be wondered at. During these years Henry was flouting the power of the Pope and offending Charles V, thus antagonizing the most powerful spiritual and temporal powers in Christendom. More to the point, perhaps, these were the very years during which the Habsburg-Valois struggle was in abeyance. There was a danger that Francis and Charles might with the Pope's blessing unite, if only temporarily and for purely selfish reasons, in a crusade against the heretic king of England. In 1533, following the first excommunication of Henry, the Imperial ambassador Chapuys wrote to his master, urging that he should prepare an invasion: 'You cannot imagine the great desire of all this people that your Majesty should send men. Every day I have been applied to about it by Englishmen of rank, wit and learning, who give me to understand that the last King was never so much hated by his people as this King' and Bishop Fisher had told Chapuys, so the latter claimed, that an invasion of England would be 'a work as agreeable to God as going against the Turk'.

Yet the crusade did not take place, for with good reason neither Charles nor Francis trusted the other. Thus Charles

[1] A. G. Dickens, p. 159.

rejected a suggestion that Francis might be encouraged to take Calais. That city, he thought, 'is better as it is, for the security of Flanders'. Then, too, Charles had other pressing problems. From 1530 to 1532 he was in Germany vainly attempting to settle the Lutheran crisis there, and also preparing to move against the Turks in the Danube valley. In 1534 the Lutheran Philip of Hesse was conspiring with Francis I against him. In 1535 he was busy campaigning in North Africa, capturing Tunis. It was not only in Germany but also in England that 'Protestantism was saved by the Frenchman and the Turk'. The English cloth trade also helped to protect the country. The richest region in the Emperor's dominions was the Netherlands, and in 1533 Henry closed the staple at Calais, ostensibly as part of a dispute between himself and the merchants. The Regent protested and Henry replied that this was an internal matter and no concern of any foreign power. Three months later the Staple was reopened. The King had demonstrated the value of the English imports to that area.

During these years English diplomatic activity was limited to some tentative attempts to find allies among the Lutheran princes as an insurance policy against the possibility of the Catholic crusade. In 1531 Henry suggested to Francis a joint mission to the Duke of Saxony; in 1532 Sir William Paget was instructed to sound out the princes on their attitude to the divorce; in 1534 envoys were sent to explain the king's cause, and in the same year a treaty was signed between England and the Hanseatic city of Lübeck; two years later this last was superseded by a treaty with the new king of Denmark, the Lutheran Christian III, who now controlled Lübeck.

By the end of 1536, the year of the Danish treaty, the situation had improved. Catherine was no longer a living reproach to the Emperor, having died early in the year. (Henry's reaction was characteristic: 'God be praised; we are free from all suspicion of war'.) Francis had overrun Savoy and Piedmont, and Charles had retaliated by occupying Provence. It was as well for England that the Habsburg-Valois quarrel had broken out again, for in the Pilgrimage of Grace Henry faced the most serious threat of his reign and had there been peace in Europe foreign support might have been available for the rebels. Fear of invasion led to the construction of coastal defences and a line of batteries and squat castles, the last in

English history, was built between the Thames estuary and the Isles of Scilly.

The death of Catherine was followed within four months by the execution of Anne Boleyn on charges of adultery. Two days earlier Cranmer's court at Lambeth had declared the King's marriage to Anne null and void, and less than a fortnight later Henry married the daughter of a Wiltshire knight, Jane Seymour. In October 1537 Jane gave birth to a son, the future Edward VI, but herself died a few days later.

Henry now began to consider the possibility of a diplomatic marriage, perhaps with Charles V's niece, the Duchess of Milan, or perhaps with one of the French princesses. Might several of the latter be sent over for his inspection? The French replied that their ladies were not to be trotted out like ponies, Henry had better send someone to the French court to report on them. 'By God', said the king, 'I trust no one but myself. The thing touches me too near. I wish to see them and know them some time before deciding.' Then in 1538 Francis and Charles concluded the Truce of Nice and for the moment the marriage plans lost their point. 'I am resolved,' Henry then told Chatillon, 'not to marry unless the Emperor or the King my brother prefer my friendship to that which they have together.'

In December 1538 the final bull of excommunication was issued and next month Francis and Charles bound themselves to make no alliance with Henry except by mutual agreement. Once more England was dangerously isolated. In February 1539 the government played its strongest card. For seven years Flemish goods, except for wool, were to pay no higher customs or subsidy than that paid by the king's own subjects. This met the threat of economic sanctions against England, for Flanders could not resist the bribe. At the same time Thomas Cromwell put forward another plan for a diplomatic marriage. Duke William of Cleves had inherited Gelderland and his territories now lay in a crescent round the Netherlands and threatened the communications between that area, the Rhineland and Germany, and though the Duke was not a Lutheran he had established a compromise religion rather similar to that which now obtained in England. It was suggested that Henry should marry William's sister Anne. The marriage would form a link between England, Cleves, and the German Lutheran princes' League of Schmalkalde.

Cromwell hurried the scheme along and Henry, forgetting his own principle of personal inspection, accepted the favourable reports of others. In October 1539 the marriage treaty was signed. Anne was thirty-four, plain and homely, fond of needlework and a German card game known as *Skat*, and Henry was appalled when he saw her; 'Say what they will, she is nothing so fair as has been reported. . . . Is there no remedy but I must needs, against my will, put my neck in the yoke?' They were married in January 1540.

There were weaknesses in Cromwell's policy: Henry had no intention of becoming closely attached to the Lutherans, regarding himself as an orthodox Catholic; the strength of the princes was suspect, for they were still divided among themselves; England's prime aim should have been to play on the differences between Francis and Charles and break their alliance. The methods employed in diplomacy can rarely be so direct as those used at home, and Cromwell's flaw as a foreign minister was his inclination to move too directly towards his goal.

The Pilgrimage of Grace had combined loyalty to the Catholic faith with resentment at the centralizing policy of the government and conservative fear of Cromwell's activities— what Lord Darcy had described as 'the apprehension of us that be noblemen'—an apprehension that appeared well-founded when they were told, as the Duke of Norfolk was by Cromwell, 'If it shall please his Majesty to appoint the meanest man . . . to rule and govern in that place [the Welsh Marches], is not his Grace's authority sufficient to cause all men to serve his Grace under him without respect of the very estate of the personage?' This remained the pattern of an aristocratic and Catholic opposition to Cromwell's ideas and achievements which grew in strength as the years went by.

The King's disgust at the Cleves marriage gave these opponents their chance. In April matters were still uncertain. Cromwell resigned the Secretaryship and the French ambassador Marillac believed him to be tottering, yet added cautiously: 'If he remains in his former credit and authority, it will only be because he is very assiduous in affairs . . . and does nothing without consulting the king.' In the same month, when parliament met, Cromwell sat in the Lords as the newly-created Earl of Essex. In May 'the King did cast a fantasy on

Catherine Howard the first time that ever his Grace saw her'. Catherine was the niece of Cromwell's enemy the Duke of Norfolk. At this time another adversary, Bishop Gardiner, was involved in a long and complicated attack on Protestant preachers. Cromwell, without advising the King, ordered the arrest of the Bishop of Chichester, a supporter of Gardiner. The old Catholic leaders denounced Cromwell to the King and he was arrested early in June. An Act of Attainder was quickly passed which emphasized Cromwell's low birth and alleged that he had boasted that 'if the lords would handle him so, that he would give them such a breakfast as never was made in England, and that the proudest should know'. From the Tower he helped the King to dissolve the Cleves marriage. Then he was executed. Four weeks later the King's marriage was declared null and void, on the grounds that Anne had been precontracted to the son of the Duke of Lorraine. When Charles V's secretary heard the news he declared that God was bringing good out of evil.

There are obvious parallels with Wolsey's fall. Of the Cardinal, Skelton had jibed:

> It is a busy thing,
> For one man to rule a king
> Alone and make reckoning,

and from his prison Cromwell wrote to Henry: 'I have meddled in so many matters under your Highness that I am not able to answer them all.' Royal frustration, aristocratic resentment, and 'snuffling prelates' destroyed a man whose great power had nevertheless always only rested on the narrow point of the King's favour. In the course of his efforts Cromwell had pushed his master faster and farther than the latter had intended to go—and he had made him look a fool into the bargain. It is hard to resist the conclusion that these two facts were the real causes of Cromwell's destruction.

Cromwellian Ideas

It would be incorrect to think of Thomas Cromwell as an iron-fisted dictator, the 'hammer of the monks', a conscious disciple of Machiavelli, a would-be Renaissance minister, concerned to place the King above the law. He was rather a manager of men, a civil servant with executive power, a political agent supported by devoted, almost anonymous, constituency workers. There is no evidence that he had read Machiavelli's *Prince* before, at the earliest, 1537. He did possess in 1530 a copy of the much more conventional Castiligione's *Book of the Courtier*. 'The office of a good courtier is to know the prince's character and inclinations, and thus to enter tactfully into his favour according to need and opportunity', Castiligione had written, and when Cromwell forgot that lesson he fell from power. It would be equally mistaken to see Cromwell as a kind of Benthamite, enforcing a Utilitarian policy by Act of Parliament, one of the Whigs of 1832. Yet there is a very modern flavour about the events of these years and many of the Cromwellian innovations lasted with little change until the nineteenth century. One can get nearest to Cromwell's political philosophy by considering the ideas he expressed, or paid others to express for him. As already mentioned, the preambles to the acts of the period contain much of this, in particular the preamble to the Act of Appeals (see p. 113).

Cromwell's receptivity to new techniques shows itself in a variety of ways, but in none more clearly than in his appreciation of the value of printed propaganda, for which purpose he employed a brains trust of humanist clerics and bourgeois intellectuals, the 'Commonwealth men' who believed that the state was supreme in all matters, that it had a duty to improve the lot of all men, and that this improvement could best be carried out through the machinery of government. There still exist nearly fifty books published during these years written with the specific aim of defending the new religious settlement, and of this number twenty-eight came from the King's printer, Berthelet. Cromwell's reaction to public opinion was always rapid; within a few weeks of the outbreak of the Pilgrimage of Grace, four books had been published denouncing the sin of rebellion!

In 1535 one of Cromwell's men, William Marshall, published the first English translation of the *Defensor Pacis*. Cromwell lent Marshall £20, almost two-thirds of the cost of publication. Marsiglio of Padua had completed the *Defensor Pacis* in 1324. In it he had described the nation-state, deriving its authority from the legislative power of the people, omnipotent and omnicompetent in the affairs of this world. The Church would look after men's souls, but it must operate within the framework of the State, deriving the authority of its officials, the powers of its courts, its property, from the State. The clergy were spiritual doctors, and no more deserved secular powers and privileges than did lay physicians (Marsiglio was himself a doctor). The book had proved a valuable weapon in the fourteenth-century struggles between Pope and Emperor, and both Marsiglio and the Emperor Lewis IV had been excommunicated by Pope John XXII. Now, two centuries later, Marsiglio's doctrine could prove of value in the struggle between Henry VIII and Pope Paul III. In the same year that Marshall produced his translation another of Cromwell's protégés, Thomas Starkey, who had earlier prepared for his patron an essay on Aristotle's *Politics*, wrote what may be termed a plain man's guide to Marsiglio, *An Exhortation to the People, instructing them to Unity and Obedience*.

Another of Cromwell's men was John Bale, a former Carmelite now converted to Protestantism. Among his works is a play, *King John*, probably first produced at Christmas 1538 in Cranmer's household, designed to show that John was a staunch defender of English national liberty against Papal pretensions and attempted tyrannies.

The Cromwellian writers' general political philosophy was Marsiglian. In theological matters their most fertile concept was that of *adiaphora*, 'matters indifferent' such as pilgrimages, fasting, prayers to the saints, and even—most valuable from Cromwell's point of view—the authority of the Pope. Starkey, among others, stressed the point that such matters were not worth fighting over. They were not essential to the main fabric of religion, being only applied ornament, and when a referee was required the business of laying down the law in these affairs should be left to the secular government of the State.

Cromwell, clearly, was concerned to provide a framework of theory, and of propaganda, for the great extension of national authority over spiritual territory. To what extent was he consciously—and successfully—also carrying through a revolution in government? That something changed is agreed, it is the extent and the originality of the changes that is debated. It is safe, perhaps, to make three points and from these to draw one general conclusion. During this period the somewhat haphazard, personal, household administration was, over large areas, replaced by institutions, by state officials; these changes were a transformation of, rather than a break with, the past; and consequently there is in the new bottles at least some medieval wine.   In all that he did Cromwell was both revolutionary and conservative, '. . . he did not create from nothing, but though he invariably and necessarily built up on what there was before him, he altered the very concepts and basic nature of things'.[1]   When all is said and done, the thirties still mark a decisive administrative change.   In Dr. Elton's words, 'government by the king gave way to government under the king'.[2]

FURTHER READING

G. R. Elton, *The Tudor Revolution in Government*, C.U.P., 1953
— *King or Minister?*, History 39, 1954
— *The Political Creed of Thomas Cromwell*, T.R.H.S., 1956
W. Penry and G. L. Harriss, *A Revolution in Tudory History?*, P. and P., 25, 1963
G. R. Elton, *The Tudor Revolution: A Reply*, P. and P., 29, 1964
H. R. Trevor-Roper, *Historical Essays*, Chapter X, 'England's Moderniser: Thomas Cromwell', Macmillan, 1957

[1] G. R. Elton, *England Under the Tudors*, p. 184.
[2] G. R. Elton, *The Tudor Revolution in Government*, p. 369.

VI · THE MIDDLE YEARS

Introduction

THE poet Surrey had expressed the fears of those who felt themselves threatened by Cromwell's apparently unending reforms when he said: 'These newly erected men would by their wills leave no nobleman on life.' Yet it was Henry who had Surrey's head and for those at court the closing years of the reign were the most perilous. Meanwhile the King lamented, apparently sincerely, the loss of 'the best servant I ever had'.

Henry's reign declined in its last scenes, not glorious ones: three wives; pointless foreign wars wasting the rich endowment of crown lands by which Cromwell had made Henry temporarily the richest king in Christendom; noble heads rolling in answer to the purposeless shifts of palace pressures; the Church uneasily balanced between Pope and Protestant.

After the fumbling uncertainties of Henry's final years the crown passed first to a minor, Jane Seymour's son, Edward VI (1547–53), and then to a half-Spanish queen, Catherine of Aragon's daughter, Mary I (1553–8). During these years the social structure was shaken by the greatest price rise England had yet known.[1] In spite of some attempts in Mary's reign to set the house in order, the years from the summer of 1540 to the winter of 1558 are in many ways an interlude in the development of the Tudor state—a period of almost twenty years in brackets as it were.

Henry's Last Years

In the same month that Henry's marriage with Anne was declared void[2] the King wedded Catherine Howard, the favourite of the Catholic party. Next year a Catholic plot in the north was discovered and a wave of executions followed which included that of the old Countess of Salisbury, Margaret Pole, while in 1541 the Queen was accused of immorality, found guilty, and executed in 1542. For a little over a year Henry

[1] See pp. 282–86.

[2] Anne accepted her dismissal placidly, and the French Ambassador was soon able to report: 'As to her who is now called Madame de Cleves, far from pretending to be married, she is as joyous as ever, and wears new dresses every day.'

remained unmarried, then he chose Catherine Parr, thirty-one years old and already twice a widow. A north country woman of Protestant leanings but no political principles, she safely outlived her husband.

As at the beginning of his reign, so too at the end Henry frittered away a fortune in fruitless foreign escapades. By 1542 Francis and Charles were at war, and danger from that quarter was at an end. In October the King declared war on Scotland. Intervention there continued, on and off, from 1542 to 1550, while from 1544 to 1546 Henry involved the country in war with France.

These unnecessary and unprofitable adventures are important for their effect on the royal finances. In order to wage useless wars the King sold his lands, and debased his coinage, thereby destroying the Crown's financial independence and aggravating the great mid-century price rise. Expenditure on the war with France ran at between £600,000 and £700,000 per annum and the total cost of the two wars during Henry's remaining years was about two million pounds. That cost was largely covered, but only by recourse to disastrous expedients. In 1545 Wriothesley, the Lord Chancellor, informed the Council that '. . . this year and last year the King has spent about £1,300,000. His subsidy and benevolence ministering scant £300,000, and the lands being consumed and the plate of the realm molten and coined, I lament the danger of the time to come. . . .' Taxation brought in about £650,000 (1540–7), and to this was added £250,000 raised by a return to the bad old expedient of forced loans and benevolences, while between 1544 and 1547 money was raised by loans at high rates of up to 14 per cent on the Antwerp money market. But over half the cost was met by the sale of crown lands, realizing £770,000 between 1542 and 1547 and, over the same period, by the debasement of the coinage.

Cromwell's Court of Augmentations became merely an instrument for raising ready money. By the end of the reign two-thirds of the monastic lands had been sold—capital assets lost to the crown for ever. The debasement of the coinage had consequences at least as serious. It was not a new expedient. The weight of coins had been reduced several times in the fourteenth and fifteenth centuries and more recently in 1526 by Cardinal Wolsey. Henry made further reductions in the weight and also increased the proportion of alloy to such an extent that the coins minted in 1544 contained only half their weight in fine silver, while those of 1545 contained no more than a third. By increasing the amount of alloy the crown could mint a greater number of coins from the same amount of precious metal, the difference between the true value and the stated value representing sheer profit. Between 1544 and 1547 this yielded £363,000. It was a confidence trick worked at the expense of the nation. In the long run, though, debasement led to inflation when men realized that more coins were required to give the same real value. Coming at a time when prices were already rising, the debasement made matters much worse.

Henry died early in 1547, holding Cranmer's hand. A few hours earlier he had told his courtiers that 'the mercy of Christ could pardon all his sins, though they were greater than they be'. For some time the great, gross man had been very ill, 'he had a body and a half, very abdominous and unwieldy with fat. And it was death to him to be dieted, so great his appetite, and death to him not to be dieted, so great his corpulency.'[1]

Like all the Tudors—and this is a great part of their fascination—Henry VIII remains an ambiguous enigma. 'The problem facing all Henry's biographers', Professor Barraclough has written, 'is to avoid surrendering either to revulsion against the king's sheer nastiness or to admiration for his real but shallow political instincts.'[2] The Royal monster, the Tudor terrorist, stands larger than life, dominating the scene as he straddles the fireplace in Holbein's painting, dominating the imagination in Ralegh's words: 'For King Henry the Eighth, if all the Patterns and Pictures of a merciless Prince were lost in the world, they might all be painted to the Life, out of the Story of this King. . . .'

Yet when one looks at the achievements of the reign, what is there behind the big, bluff façade? Thirty-seven years of—on the whole—internal peace, the break with Rome, the administrative reforms of Cromwell. These are important events, but they raise a second query concerning the royal character, one more important than that of its 'niceness' or 'nastiness'. To what extent were Henry's achievements the result of deliberate policy? Was the king the able architect of his

[1] Fuller, *The Church History of Britain*, Vol. v, p. 254.   [2] In the *Observer*.

K

success, or was he an essentially backward-looking medieval man hauled, kicking and screaming, into modern history by the combined efforts of his advisers and of circumstance? One historian has struck the balance as follows:

> In the hands of Henry VIII personal monarchy did not mean personal attention to the business of government, though it had done so in the hands of Henry VII. Nor did it mean the constant weighing up of conflicting counsel and the pursuit of a personal policy based upon a personal assessment as it did for Elizabeth. It meant the putting of the king's personal force behind policies not of his devising. His greatness lay in the rapid and accurate interpretation of the immediate situation, in a dauntless will, and in his choice of advisers; but not in originality and it is doubtful if he was the architect of anything, least of all of the English Reformation.[1]

Edward VI

Edward VI was nine years old when he came to the throne. The late king had nominated sixteen councillors as regents, and his choice showed a heavy bias towards the new men. There was no lord whose title was more than twelve years old; Howard, the leader of the Catholics, was in the Tower and only saved from execution by Henry's death; Gardiner was not named; 'I could myself use him', Henry had said, 'and rule him to all manner of purposes, . . . but so will you never do.' Wriothesley and Tunstall were conservative, but Hertford, Dudley, Paget, Russell, Herbert and Sir Anthony Denny were all men known to support new ideas in church and state.

Edward died young and he had not the time or opportunity to make enemies or show faults. Greek, Latin, theology and politics were all packed neatly into his little head. He had received an intensive humanist education from such men as John Cheke of Cambridge; Roger Ascham, who taught him 'penmanship'; and Anthony Cooke. The last wrote of Edward when the king was not yet eight that he had 'conquered a great number of the captains of ignorance', that he could conjugate any Latin verb that was not irregular, that he had 'made already forty or fifty pretty Latin verses', and that he was then studying the book of Proverbs, where he learnt 'to beware of strange and wanton women'—a side glance at Henry VIII, or merely at the Catholic church?

[1] G. R. Elton, *Henry VIII*, H.A., Pamphlet G51, 1962, p. 27.

The new king was small for his age, with fair hair and grey short-sighted eyes. He understood the lute, enjoyed music, and played some games; in 1550 he wrote in his journal, 'I lost the challenge shooting at rounds and won at rovers', and again, when tilting at the ring, 'My hand touched often, which counted as nothing, and took never, which seemed very strange, and so the prize was of my side lost.'

On other pages the journal indicates a reserved nature and a narrow protestantism. Both were perhaps necessary defences against the environment in which he lived, but they suggest that he might have developed into a hard, bigoted man, perhaps the ablest and most cold-blooded of the Tudors. He composed a memorandum recommending that the Order of the Garter should be detached from all connection with St. George, for fear of superstition; later, when Cheke was thought to be dying, he explained, 'He will not die at this time, for this morning I begged his life from God in my prayers, and obtained it.'

The King's eldest uncle, Edward Seymour, Earl of Hertford, seized power together with the King's person, helped by Sir William Paget. The Council, accustomed to one man's rule, raised no objection and were easily persuaded to accept promotion for Hertford and for themselves. Hertford became Lord Protector and Duke of Somerset while John Dudley (son of Henry VII's minister) was created Earl of Warwick.

Somerset was in many ways an attractive figure; mature, able, affable, moderate, an idealist out of key with the tone of the sixteenth century. He re-established the Court of Requests, repealed the treason laws of Henry VIII, and got rid of the heresy laws. Under his rule no one lost his life for religious nonconformity, but this very moderation angered the realists on the Council, as did his pride, ostentation and avarice— during his brief tenure of power he doubled his income—while at the same time his half-hearted reforms caused widespread unrest which gave his enemies their chance to displace him. In the autumn of 1549 Somerset was overthrown by Warwick and imprisoned in the Tower. Early in 1550 he was released but was re-imprisoned eighteen months later and executed early in 1552, the King recording in his journal the bald statement: 'The Duke of Somerset had his head cut off between eight and nine o'clock in the morning.' Meanwhile Edward had fallen completely under the influence of Warwick ('He is like a father to His Majesty—and governs all'), whom he created Duke of Northumberland. In 1553 the new Duke persuaded the King to alter the succession and bequeath the Crown to Lady Jane Grey, Northumberland's daughter-in-law, whose claim to the throne rested on her descent from Henry VII through his daughter Mary.

These rapid shifts in power demonstrate both the strength and the weakness of Tudor government. That it survived and continued to function fairly smoothly is a tribute to the solidity of the day-to-day administration. That it could fall so easily into the hands of ambitious men emphasizes how much depended on the strength of the ruler himself. (In 1549 the outspoken Latimer chose as one of his texts, 'Woe to the land where a boy is king'.)

The government faced grave problems: the war with Scotland; the economic strains produced by enclosures, the price rise and the debasement; the question of the future religion of the country.

In September 1547 Somerset himself marched north at the head of about twenty thousand men and defeated the Scots at Pinkie, half a dozen miles from Edinburgh. Somerset suggested a marriage between Mary, Queen of Scots, and Edward. The two countries should unite under 'The old indifferent name of Britons . . . having the sea for a wall, mutual love for garrison, and God for defence, . . .' Then affairs in England called him south again. The war dragged on until 1550, by which time the Scots had sent the young Queen Mary to France, where she eventually married the Dauphin. Henri II, king of France, boasted: 'France and Scotland are now one country.' Somerset's schemes had been exactly reversed. Unofficial French aggression in 1548 gave place to official war the next year when the French invaded the Boulonnais. By the ignominious treaty of Boulogne in 1550 England surrendered that town in return for 400,000 crowns, while at the same time English forces withdrew from Scotland, leaving the French firmly established there. In 1551 a further treaty was signed at Angers, by which Edward gave up his claim to the hand of Mary and was betrothed instead to Elizabeth de Valois.

At home plotting and rebellion, never far below the surface during the sixteenth century, threatened the government. Somerset's brother Thomas, a boisterous, ambitious man who had married Catherine Parr—and had hoped, after her death, to marry the Princess Elizabeth—was involved in a number of shady transactions. In 1549 he was attainted by parliament and executed. Somerset made no effort to defend him, a fact which may help to explain the ease with which he was himself deposed later in the year.

In 1549 the government faced open rebellion in the east and in the west. The introduction of the new prayer book (see p. 147) led to a rising in Devon and Cornwall, where the rebels complained that the service in English was 'like a Christmas game . . . and so we Cornish men (whereof certain of us understand no English) utterly refuse this new English'. The authorities explained that there was no real change, that the new liturgy was 'none other but the old; the selfsame words in English which were in Latin saving a few things taken out', but this disingenuous reply cut no ice. As so often in this century, men were protesting, at least in part, not against specific details so much as against the arbitrary actions of a distant government which seemed to them to be intent on changing the old order in every way. For six weeks the rebels besieged Exeter and then Russell and Herbert, both of them new men anxious for the safety of their monastic estates, crushed the rising, using Italian mercenaries for the purpose. Lesser disturbances in Oxfordshire and in Yorkshire were suppressed very easily.

In Norfolk men were also in arms, not against the religious innovations (of which they specifically approved), but against economic and social changes.

The Norfolk rebels had been encouraged by Somerset's actions. He and others were concerned at the economic situation. The 'Commonwealth Men' (the name occurs first in this connection in 1549), the civil servants who had survived the fall of their master Cromwell, saw in 'the great dearth of all things' the most pressing problem of the time. The preachers Latimer and Lever, the pamphleteers Crowley and Starkey, the men of affairs John Hales and Thomas Smith, the radical Bishops Hooper and Latimer—all had their preferred solutions to the problem.

Thomas Starkey (1499–1538) was educated at Oxford, singled out by Wolsey, and studied law at Avignon and Padua, where he served as Reginald Pole's secretary from 1524 to 1534. He then came back to England and became one of Cromwell's publicists (see p. 129). Amongst other works he produced, probably in 1535, *A Dialogue between Reginald Pole and Thomas Lupset*. Starkey was a humanist and his work lies in the Utopian tradition of Thomas More. Pole and Lupset are not real people, they are voices arguing as to what is best rather than discussing what can be done. Thus the *Dialogue* is in favour of a revision of common and canon law (in another work Starkey described the latter as 'founded by mere policy', which must have pleased Cromwell), the reception of Roman law, the transformation of monasteries into schools for nobles, the setting-up of an elective and limited monarchy, and a tax on bachelors.

Starkey's economic analysis is more down to earth. He defines a Commonwealth as '... the most perfect and prosperous state (and for this is every man bound to live) having before his eyes the commonwealth, without regard to his own vain pleasures and singular profit'. It is clear that England is not at present in this state, and Starkey proceeds to discuss the diseases—decayed towns, untilled fields, poverty. Lupset would attribute these ills to the fact that the people are idle and 'ill-occupied'; Pole thinks rather that there is a lack of people in the towns and a lack of due proportion between different occupations. Discord arises from the absence of justice and equity. It is agreed that 'The parts of this body be not knit together'; the nobility take no thought for the good of the commons, the justices are swayed by personal considerations—'matters are ended as they are friended', the commons are idle, and in general 'some have too much, some too little, and some never a whit'.

Remedies suggested include the encouragement of larger families and of married clergy, and every child is to be educated or apprenticed. The manufacture of luxuries is to be rooted out at home and their import from abroad forbidden, while England's exports are to be limited to commodities of which there is abundance, such as lead, wool and tin. These are not to be exported in their raw state, but to be worked up at home. Men tend to gravitate towards the easiest work. To counteract this committees should be set up to decide what each youth is best suited for. Each man should 'mind his own craft' and not meddle with another's, the Enclosure Acts should be strictly enforced, and rents should be reduced. Crowley laid great store by this last suggestion. He argued that if rents were reduced, the price of food (and hence of manufactures) would fall and consequently 'dearth' and the sturdy vagabond would disappear. Only the impotent poor would be left, and they could be looked after in hospitals, as was already the practice on the continent at Ypres.

Starkey represents English humanism; Robert Crowley (1518–88) may be termed a conservative Puritan. The protestant emphasis on such matters as stewardship and vocation are dovetailed neatly into the old framework of the Great Chain of Being, where every man has his part to play in that state of life to which it has pleased God to call him. In both *An Information and Petition against the oppressors of the poor Commons* (*1548*) and in the *Way to Wealth* (*1550*) Crowley urged this philosophy as a solution to the social crisis, writing in the *Petition*, 'Content yourself with that state wherein your fathers left you', and in the *Way to Wealth*:

> A hell without order I may it well call,
> Where each man is for himself and no man for all.

He perceptively observed the appearance of a new type of men, the *entrepreneurs*, 'men that have no names because they are doers in all things'.

More outspoken, and yet in some ways more traditional than Crowley, was the radical Hugh Latimer (*c.* 1485–1555). Born in Leicestershire the son of a yeoman, educated at Cambridge, created bishop of Worcester in 1535, but later forced to resign for criticizing the Act of Six Articles, influential in Edward's reign though he refused a bishopric, Latimer was burnt at Oxford in 1555. There is a Cobbett-like simplicity in his sermon preached at St. Paul's before Edward VI on Plough Sunday, 18 January 1548:

> You landlords, you rent-raisers, I may say you steplords, you unnatural lords, you have for your possessions yearly too much. For that heretofore went for xx or xl pound by year (which is an honest portion to be had *gratis* in one lordship, of another man's sweat and labour) now is it let for fifty or a hundred pound by year.

My father was a yeoman, and had no lands of his own, only he had a farm of three or four pound by year at the uttermost, and thereupon he tilled so much as kept half a dozen men. He had walk for a hundred sheep, and my mother milked thirty kine. He was able and did find the King a harness, with himself and his horse, while he came to the place he should receive the King's wages. I can remember that I buckled his harness, when he went unto Blackheath field. He kept me to school, or else I had not been able to have preached before the King's Majesty now. He married my sisters with five pound or twenty nobles apiece, so that he brought them up in godliness and fear of God.

He kept hospitality for his poor neighbours. And some alms he gave to the poor, and all this he did of the said farm, where he that now hath it payeth sixteen pound by year or more, and is not able to do anything for his prince, for himself nor for his children, or give a cup of drink to the poor. Thus all the enhancing and rearing goeth to your private commodity and wealth; so that where ye had a single too much, you have that; and since the same, ye have enhanced the rent, and so have increased another too much; so now ye have double too much, which is two too much. But let the preacher preach till his tongue be worn to the stumps, nothing is amended. We have good statutes made for the common wealth as touching commoners, enclosers; many meetings and sessions, but in the end of the matter there cometh nothing forth. Well, well, this is one thing I will say unto you, from whence it cometh I know, even from the devil.

In the first parliament of the new reign bills were introduced to maintain tillage, to prevent regrating (cornering the market), to confirm the rights of copyholders and leaseholders, to educate poor children. But none of these was passed in a parliament where the landed gentleman and the well-to-do townsman held the controlling interest. Instead, the most savage poor law of the century was enacted, by which the able-bodied poor might be branded and, if recalcitrant, reduced to slavery.

In June 1548 Somerset had issued a proclamation condemning enclosures and had at the same time sent out commissions of enquiry to discover to what extent earlier acts were being disobeyed. Representatives of the counties were asked seventeen questions concerning enclosures, the decay of houses, and the numbers of sheep in their areas. (John Hales was a member of the commission operating in the counties of Oxfordshire, Berkshire, Warwickshire, Leicestershire, Bedfordshire, Buckinghamshire and Northamptonshire.) These enquiries led men to take matters into their own hands and agricultural disorders followed. At the same time Somerset's policy met with opposition from within the Council led by Warwick, himself an enclosing landlord. Nevertheless, Somerset issued in the following year a second proclamation against enclosures, together with a free pardon for those who had broken down fences.

That same month fences were thrown down in Norfolk. The leader was Robert Ket, a well-to-do tanner and landowner, who not only pulled down his own enclosures, but also those of his neighbours. Eventually his supporters numbered about twelve thousand, drawn from twenty-four of the thirty-two hundreds of Norfolk and from some parts of Suffolk. The insurgents moved on Norwich, the second city of the kingdom, and though they failed at first to enter the city they remained outside for six weeks at their Great Camp on Mousehold Heath to the north. There good order was kept. East Anglia was traditionally protestant in sympathy and the rebels used the new prayer-book for regular services, asking Norwich to supply preachers (one of whom was Matthew Parker, Elizabeth's future Archbishop).

The men refused a royal pardon on the grounds that they were not rebels. A small force under Northampton was sent to quell the rising, but was beaten off. The Council then despatched an army of twelve thousand men under the command of Warwick. He occupied Norwich, and when the rebels began to abandon their camp he sent in his own cavalry, together with twelve hundred German mercenaries. Three thousand of Ket's followers were slaughtered in the rout which followed and a further three hundred were executed more formally later. What had begun as a local riot over agricultural matters had grown into a rising against the government, and had ended in complete defeat for the rebels.

What had they wanted? Not, primarily, the destruction of enclosures, since these were not an issue that greatly affected East Anglia, and there is only one reference to them among the twenty-seven articles of complaint. Thirteen of those articles were directed against the overstocking of commons or against other forms of interference by large sheep-owners in the affairs of the small arable worker. Significantly, the rebels demanded that no man worth £40 or more a year should keep cattle or sheep, save for his own use. When the revolt began suspicion had naturally fallen on Mary, who was living at Eccles close by. She had replied 'that all the rising about the parts where she was, was touching no part of religion', and mention has already been made of the rebels' protestant sympathies. At the same time many of their complaints did have a general anti-clerical flavour, and there is a hint of Anabaptist radical protest which carried echoes, terrifying to the ears of those in authority, of the German Peasants' War. There the peasant had declared 'Lord Christ has freed us all' (*Dan Christus hat uns alle befriet*); Ket's followers petitioned 'that all bondmen may be made free, for God made all free with his precious blood-letting'. These echoes do much to explain the violent terms in which the rebels were described; 'not men but brute beasts', 'the refuse of the people', fellows who had 'conceived a wonderful hate against gentlemen and taketh them all as their enemies. . . .'

The successful destruction by Warwick of these potentially dangerous social revolutionaries accelerated the fall of Somerset. As early as July Paget had warned the Duke:

> Look well whether you have either law or religion at home and I fear you shall find neither. . . .   Would to God that at the first stir you had followed the matter hotly and caused justice to be administered in solemn fashion to the terror of others and then to have granted a pardon. . . .   I know in this matter of the Commons every man in the Council hath misliked your proceeding and wished it otherwise.

A few months later the King was persuaded to create Warwick Duke of Northumberland and to allow Somerset to be imprisoned.

The new Duke of Northumberland was in most ways very different from the man he had supplanted. Both were fond of power and both made money from their position, but there the similarities end. Somerset was a moderate idealist, Northumberland an extreme realist; the former was doctrinaire, the latter opportunist; Somerset's religious settlement was cautious, Northumberland's was radical. Somerset's permissive rule had produced disorder, Northumberland planned a personal autocracy and the establishment of a Dudley dynasty. His friends were allowed to raise bands of men-at-arms and all the authority of government was concentrated in the hands of those friends and of himself.

Under both Somerset and Northumberland the Council remained the instrument of government if not the prime mover. On Henry's death it had numbered twenty-six, the great majority of its members holding an office of state. Under Somerset the membership changed little, but by the end of 1551 Northumberland had added twelve of his own supporters, bringing the numbers up to forty. Early in the reign the Council's efficiency had been improved by the allocation of particular days to particular business. From their head-quarters at Westminster members supervised the whole work of government, determined policy, issued proclamations regulating such diverse matters as war and peace, religion, enclosures and the currency, and acted as a judicial court exercising its powers usually—though not invariably—in the star chamber. (In 1540 the Court of Star Chamber had at last acquired its own clerk and minutes and had achieved an autonomous existence.)

During Edward's reign two parliaments were called. The first held four sessions: November–December 1547; November 1548–March 1549; November 1549–February 1550; January–April 1552; the second sat only during March 1553. The development of government business had led to an increase in the number of office-holders in the Commons. In the first parliament 'Of the one hundred and eighty-nine members, ... whose names occur in the returns, at least a third either held some office about the court, or were closely related to ministers. ...'[1] Thirty-four members[2] were added during the reign, in consequence of pressure from the boroughs and from the local gentry. There is little evidence for the packing of the first parliament and though Northumberland tried hard to affect the composition of the 1553 assembly, he does not appear

[1] A. F. Pollard, *England under the Protector Somerset*, Kegan Paul Trench and Trübner, 1900, p. 74.

[2] The boroughs they represented were Boston, Bossiney, Brackley, Camelford, Grampound, Heydon, Lichfield, Liverpool, Michael (Cornwall), Penryn, Peterborough, Petersfield, Saltash, Thirsk, West Looe, Westminster and Wigan.

to have been very successful. The Commons consolidated the position they had achieved in Henry's reign and there are signs of the growth of a feeling of corporate identity—it is significant that the Commons' *Journals* begin in 1547 and that two years later the members acquired a permanent home, moving from the Chapter House of Westminster Abbey to the disused chapel of St. Stephen's, where they were to remain for almost three hundred years. In their first session important legislation included the Poor Law already referred to, an act dissolving the chantries, and a new Treasons Act, which swept away all save one of the treasons created by Henry VIII, repealed the Proclamations Act of 1539 and the heresy laws, but reaffirmed that to deny the royal Supremacy was treason.

The financial situation inherited from Henry VIII was bad and soon grew worse. The revenue from the Customs fell from £40,000 to £25,900, and while the total direct taxation during the reign amounted to only £300,000, military expenditure exceeded £1,500,000. Somerset persuaded parliament to introduce a new tax, levied in part on sheep and wool, but this was abandoned by Northumberland. The latter made some attempt to clear the foreign debts and to improve the audit of accounts, but the effect of these reforms was more than counter-balanced by embezzlement and by the continued debasement of the coinage between 1547 and 1551. In 1542 the English pound had been valued at 27 Flemish shillings; by 1551 it was worth only 15 shillings. Then Northumberland stopped the practice: no attempt was made to call in the debased coins, on which the copper showed clearly, as a contemporary jingle observed:

These testons [shillings] look red, how like you the same?
'Tis a token of grace; they blush for shame.

Crown lands were sold to the value of £435,000 and further lands to the value of £550,000 were given away.

In 1550 the savage Poor Law of 1547 was repealed and the Act of 1531 was revived. In 1552 an Act 'for the provision and relief of the poor', which emphasized the distinction between the vagabond and the impotent, was passed 'to the intent that valiant beggars, idle and loitering persons, may be avoided, and the impotent, feeble, and lame provided for, which are poor in very deed'. Amended on minor points in 1555, this Act remained in force until 1563. In each parish two Collectors of Alms were to be chosen to 'gently ask' for contributions. The Bishop was to 'induce and persuade' the recalcitrant. The Act is important rather for the distinction made between those who could not, and those who would not, work than for the bishops' inducements. In London the palace of Bridewell, St. Thomas's and Grey Friars were also used for the relief of the poor.

Undoubtedly the government actions which were of the greatest importance were those affecting religion. The country could hardly remain indefinitely in the ambiguous position in which Henry VIII had left it. Somerset, weighing the contradictory advice of Gardiner and Cranmer, chose that of the latter, a policy of moderate reform:

> There be some so ticklish and so fearful one way and so tender stomached that they can abide no abuses to be reformed, but think every reformation to be a capital enterprise against all religion and good order. As there be on the contrary side some, too rash, who having no consideration what is to be done, headlong will set upon everything. The magistrate's duty is betwixt these so in a mean to set and provide that old doting should not take further or deeper rust in the Commonwealth, neither ancient error overcome the seen and tried truth; nor long abuse, for the age and space of time only, still be suffered; and yet all these with quietness and gentleness and without all contention, if it were possible to be reformed. (*Somerset to Gardiner, c. 1547.*)

Somerset and Cranmer, the chief forces in the liturgical revolution, were both convinced reformers. Cranmer's protestantism was by this time eclectic, drawing something from each of the main continental sources, which now included not only Lutheranism and Zwinglianism, but also the newer, tougher, more missionary Calvinism. Though Zwingli's was probably still the main weight throughout the reign of Edward, Calvinism, entering England from Strassburg, Zurich and Geneva, was to become eventually the strongest of foreign influences on the English reformers.

John Calvin (1509–64), the son of a Picard lawyer, educated at Paris, suddenly converted—probably in 1533, had published his *Institutes of the Christian Religion* in 1536, and had finally settled at Geneva in 1541. 'By an unsurpassed feat of committee-government, pyschological tyranny and social engineering Calvin and his successors turned this confused and demoralized town into one of the proud centres of European culture.'[1] Geneva became 'the Protestant Rome'; to the Venetian Suriano it was 'the mine whence came the ore of heresy', while to John Knox it seemed '. . . the most perfect school of Christ that ever was in earth since the days of the Apostles'.

Theologically, Calvinism was distinguished by its emphasis on the doctrine of predestination, what Calvin himself called 'this hair-raising decree' (*decretum quidem horribile*) by which God had from the beginning chosen some, the Elect, for eternal salvation and others for eternal damnation. For Calvin the Eucharist was a commemorative feast; Christ was in Heaven and, as the *Geneva Catechism* (1541) expressed it, 'we are not to seek Him in these corruptible elements'. Church and State must work together, but the Church must be free to manage its own affairs and the State must be prepared to use its power to protect the Church and enforce the latter's decisions. The strength of Calvinism lay in its organization. Men worshipped and fought in small groups, capable of leading an autonomous existence yet linked in a pyramid of cellular structure. Most important of all, Calvinism, with its lay elders supervising the congregations, had found a means of uniting the ecclesiastical revolution and the social revolution, of harnessing in the interests of both Church and State the energy and aspirations of the pious, educated, individual layman.

What, in the simplest possible terms, were the common aims of English reformers in Edward's reign? They shared the doctrine of justification by faith alone. This in turn led them to reject much in the Catholic liturgy, and to emphasize the importance of the individual. From this it follows that their aims can be defined as twofold; to remove false doctrine, and secondly, to make plain the true doctrine by means of sermons, translations and simplifications.

In 1547 Injunctions were issued introducing a certain amount of English into the services and compelling each church to provide two books, Erasmus' *Paraphrase of the New Testament* and

---

[1] A. G. Dickens, *Thomas Cromwell and the English Reformation*, E.U.P., 1959, p. 198.

a *Book of Homilies* which amongst other matters included a moderately-phrased version of the doctrine of justification by faith.   Acts were passed permitting communion in both kinds and assigning to the Crown all chantries,[1] colleges and hospitals. Their lands were now confiscated by the Crown and almost immediately sold.   The contemporary Camden estimated that 2,374 chantries and chapels, 90 colleges and 110 hospitals were involved.   The disappearance of these institutions probably affected the day-to-day life of the people more than the dissolution of the monasteries had done, but it is a misconception to think that teaching was one of the normal duties of chantry priests and that education suffered from their disappearance.   In Shropshire and Yorkshire, for instance, only about 10 per cent of these priests conducted schools, and a careful census in the latter county has shown that there were about 46 grammar-schools there in the first half of the century and that very few of these vanished as a result of the Chantries Act, while 58 new lay schools appeared between 1545 and 1603.

In February 1549 the clergy received permission to marry. Such figures as are available suggest that in the south about one in four did so, while in the north the figure was much lower, perhaps one in ten.   In the same year Cranmer's First Prayer Book was passed by Parliament and came into operation in June.   The book combined in one volume, written in English, all the rites required by clergy and congregations.   It drew largely on the Sarum use, the order of service in use at Salisbury since the eleventh century.   An Act of Uniformity laid down penalties for clergy refusing to use the new prayer book, but no punishment was provided for laymen who did not attend church.   An ingenious masterpiece of compromise and ambiguity, it did not attack Catholic doctrine, but '. . . at every point upon which there was a vital doctrinal difference between the Old Learning and the New, one finds a careful use of words which would enable a Protestant to use the service with a good conscience'.[2]   Thus in the Mass the Sarum Use had prayed that the bread and wine might 'become unto us' the Body and Blood of Christ, but the new book used instead the phrase 'that

---

[1] A chantry was an endowment, usually in property, to provide masses for the souls of those named in the grant and the chapel thus endowed.

[2] T. M. Parker, *The English Reformation to 1558*, O.U.P., 1952, p. 130.

they may be unto us', so avoiding the suggestion of any change in the elements.   The form of Communion service was nevertheless sufficiently traditional for Bishop Gardiner, then in the Tower, to declare that he was quite prepared to use it.

The fall of Somerset and the triumph of Northumberland coincided with the opening of the second stage of the Protestant revolution.   Of Northumberland Pollard has written that he 'covered his hypocrisy by the vehemence of his protestations' and certainly his religious policy seems to have sprung from expediency rather than from principle.   Certainly, too, there could have been no further stage without his approval.   Yet there were other factors making for change.   The Emperor Charles V's victory at Mühlberg in 1547 had led to an influx of German religious refugees, and other continental protestants were arriving to observe—and if possible influence—the changes taking place in England.   Before the end of the reign there were perhaps five thousand foreign protestants in London.   These included distinguished theologians; John à Lasco from Poland, Martin Bucer from Strassburg, John Knox from France.   Partly due to the arguments of these, especially Bucer, partly through conversation with Ridley and partly under the impact of his own meditations, Cranmer's views on the Eucharist moved towards a more protestant interpretation, never exactly defined by him, but lying somewhere between those of Luther and Zwingli.   In England itself a host of varying criticisms and opinions had been let loose, ranging from the licensed attacks of preachers who called the Host 'Round Robin', or 'Jack-in-the-box', or more temperately argued against 'a carnal change, a carnal presence, a carnal sacrifice; a piece of paste, as we say, flesh and blood as ye say, to be carnally worshipped with fond gestures, a creature to be made a creator, a vile cake to be made God and man', to the generally feared heresies of the Anabaptists.   All these factors combined to convince the government that it was desirable to authorize a more definite and at the same time a more protestant form of service.

The Second Prayer Book, together with an Act of Uniformity, was passed in 1552.   Matins and evensong were little changed, but the communion service was rewritten in an attempt to restore its Apostolic simplicity.   The 1549 book had referred to *The Supper of the Lord and Holy Communion, commonly called the*

Mass; the 1552 book referred instead to *The Order for the Administration of the Lord's Supper, or Holy Communion.* In the earlier book the rubric and words of administration had been: '*And when he delivereth the Sacrament of the body of Christ, he shall say to everyone these words.* The body of our Lord Jesus Christ which was given for thee, preserve thy body and soul unto everlasting life.' In the new book the rubric and words of administration were amended to: '*And when he delivereth the bread, he shall say.* Take and eat this, in remembrance that Christ died for thee, and feed on him in thy heart by faith, with thanksgiving.' The changes were significant. The altar was to be placed table-wise in the church, the wearing of vestments was forbidden, only the surplice being required. At the last moment, due to Knox's influence, the Council inserted a 'Black Rubric' to make clear that kneeling did not imply adoration of the bread and wine in the communion service. The new book was an original composition, but closer to Zwinglianism than to any other continental model. There was no intention of allowing liberty to more extreme opinions, in 1550 an Englishwoman was burned for denying the humanity of Christ and in 1551 a Dutchman went to the stake for denying His divinity.

In 1553 the Forty-two Articles were published, defining the beliefs of the new Church. These, too, were largely the work of Cranmer. They were Calvinist in tone and seem to have been designed to make clear the new Church's abhorrence of Anabaptist doctrines. They were never in force, since within a month of their publication Edward was dead and Mary on the throne: their importance lies in the fact that they were the basis of the Elizabethan Thirty-nine Articles.

Mary I

Henry VIII had three times altered the line of succession (1534, 1536, 1543). Northumberland worked on Edward to do likewise. If Mary were to be set aside, the next heir should be Elizabeth, but Northumberland had decided that Lady Jane Grey would be a more malleable choice. She was descended from Henry VII's daughter Mary through the latter's second marriage to Charles Brandon, Duke of Suffolk.

In May 1553 Lady Jane Grey was wedded to Northumberland's son Lord Guilford Dudley. In June Edward was persuaded to compose a 'device' by which the claims of Mary,

Elizabeth and Lady Jane's own mother, Frances, were all set aside in favour of Lady Jane Grey and her male descendants. Six weeks later the king was dead and Lady Jane was proclaimed Queen. Mary raised her standard at Framlingham in East Anglia and wrote to the Council, ordering them to declare her Queen. This they refused to do, but Mary's determined resistance saved the day for her. Men everywhere could see through the hurried composition of the 'device', and Lady Jane was only accepted as Queen in the City of London for nine days. Exactly four weeks after the death of Edward, Mary was in London and Northumberland was in the Tower, soon to be executed. For the time being Lady Jane, her husband and a handful of others, including Cranmer, were kept in confinement.

The new Queen was thirty-seven years old, half-Spanish and wholly Catholic. She was virtuous, stubborn, unimaginative. The Spanish ambassador Simon Renard summed her up accurately: 'I know the Queen to be good, easily influenced, inexpert in worldly matters, and a novice all round.' Two immediate problems that faced Mary, as they were later to face her half-sister Elizabeth, were those of religion and of marriage. To some extent they were inter-linked. Mary's solutions to both arose from the fact that she was essentially a Catholic Spaniard. In 1554 she married Philip of Spain and in the same year England was reconciled to the Catholic Church. Both decisions proved dangerously unpopular.

The proposed Spanish match was the direct cause of Wyatt's rebellion (see below). It was then said that England would become 'a little cock-boat in the wake of the Spanish galleon', and the fear proved justified. In 1557, the country was drawn into the Spanish Habsburg war against France and six months later, early in 1558, Calais fell to the French. For England this was a blessing in disguise. Calais was expensive to maintain, strategically untenable, a will-o'-the-wisp always beckoning England to try to recover her lost French territories. This is historian's hindsight however, and at the time the loss of the city seemed one more proof of the disastrous nature of the Queen's Catholic Habsburg policy. Mary died later in 1558 having lost almost all the support which had only five years earlier helped her to hold the throne. 'When I am dead and opened,' she lamented, 'you shall find Calais lying in my heart.'

On hearing that Mary had become Queen, the Emperor Charles V gave his cousin three pieces of advice: punish the rebels; beware of France; above all, be *une bonne Anglaise*. This last was what Mary could never be. The Venetian ambassador specifically noted that she scorned her English descent and boasted of her Spanish blood. It was easy therefore for Simon Renard to persuade her of the desirability of the Spanish match, a suggestion that was itself in line with the traditional Habsburg policy of gaining territory by marriage rather than by warfare. To English eyes the matter looked very different. Mary was the first Queen of England to rule in her own right since the days of Matilda in the twelfth century, and that Queen's reign had been one of almost continuous civil war. Naturally she must marry, but whom? For a king the matter was easy, a foreign marriage brought continental alliances, the possibility of acquiring foreign territories. For a Queen the matter was exactly reversed. To ensure the country's independence, she must marry at home. There was, unfortunately, no obvious candidate. Men spoke of Courtenay, a great-grandson of Edward IV, but he was self-willed and weak, had spent the last fifteen years in the Tower, and had no strong following. Meanwhile to Mary's mind there were strong arguments in favour of the marriage to her cousin Philip II. Philip was Spanish, Catholic, powerful; friendship with Spain was the traditional English policy, designed to counter the Franco-Spanish alliance; the King of Spain had inherited the Netherlands, the essential key to England's foreign trade.

Mary's reasons were cogent, yet there was from the start considerable opposition, led by Gardiner with the support of about one-third of the Council. Nevertheless by October Mary had agreed to marry Philip. While the London street-urchins attacked the unpopular Imperial envoys with snowballs, the terms were hammered out. Philip was to have the title of king and was to share in the government of the country, but Mary alone was to appoint officials, all of whom must be English. She was not to be taken out of the country without her own consent and England was not to be expected to go to war with France. If there were no children, Philip was to lose all claim to the throne on his wife's death, but if there were children they were to inherit not only England but also Franche Comté and the Netherlands.

On paper the terms were good, but men distrusted the outcome and already rebellion was being planned in Hereford, Devon, Leicester and Kent, its aim being to replace Mary by Elizabeth, who would then marry Courtenay. In Hereford nothing happened, in Leicester and Devon the movements were abortive, but in Kent Sir Thomas Wyatt raised a force.

Wyatt's rebellion (1554) was dangerously close to the capital; however it was very much an individual affair. There had been agricultural riots in Kent in 1543 and again in 1548–9, yet there do not appear to have been any strong economic motives in 1554. Wyatt himself was a gentleman who had held the office of sheriff and whose father had been one of the largest landowners in the county. The distribution of known rebels strongly suggests that where local gentlemen were involved ordinary men joined the rising, otherwise they remained unmoved—a personal pattern reminiscent of the civil wars of the fifteenth century and of the Civil War of the seventeenth.

The rebellion began in January in that part of the county around Maidstone. Trainbands dispatched against Wyatt went over to him and soon he was marching on Southwark at the head of between two and three thousand men. Thence he moved west, crossed the Thames at Kingston, and approached London, but he received little support when he reached the City itself and the rising, outnumbered and outgunned, suddenly collapsed. Wyatt himself was executed, as were Suffolk, Lady Jane Grey, and Dudley. Elizabeth was lucky to escape with her life; the Spaniard, Mendoza, had reported, 'it is considered that she will have to be executed . . .'. About 480 of Wyatt's followers were convicted, of whom 350 were from Kent, 76 from London, and 37 from Southwark. In the end only seventy-five of these were executed.

In June 1554 Philip II arrived in England and next month the marriage took place. Wyatt's rebellion had failed in its objective, but it was only the sharpest expression of a crisis of confidence that continued throughout the resign. Opposition took both constitutional and illegal forms. The fourth parliament[1] of the reign proved particularly independent, fore-

---

1 Mary's parliaments sat from October to December 1553; April to May 1554; November 1554 to January 1555; October to December 1555; January to March, and November 1558. Twenty-five additional members took their seats, represent-

shadowing developments under Elizabeth. The royal decision to relinquish the Crown's claim to first-fruits and tenths only passed the Commons by 193 votes to 126 after the doors of the House had been locked. The same parliament used force to prevent members from leaving the House until they had rejected a government bill to confiscate the property of those Protestants who had fled abroad. Of this body, Michieli, the Venetian ambassador, wrote:

> The present House of Commons whether by accident or design, a thing not seen for many years in any Parliament, is quite full of gentry and nobility (for the most part suspected in matters of religion) and therefore more daring and licentious than former houses which consisted of burgesses and plebeians, by nature timid and respectful, who easily inclined towards the will of the sovereign.

There was also constant scheming against Mary's rule, originating mainly among English exiles. The Marian exiles were of two types, the religious enthusiasts who went to Germany, and the political malcontents who went to France. It was the latter group, encouraged by Henri II, who plotted steadily, if to little effect. The most serious threat came from a conspiracy of Sir Henry Dudley's in 1556, intended to set Elizabeth on the throne.

In that year, too, the duc de Guise attacked Spanish possessions in north Italy, encouraged by Spain's inveterate enemy Pope Paul IV, and in the following year Philip paid a diplomatic visit to England (he had left the country in 1555) with the object of enlisting English help. Mary declared war on France in June 1557 and cited among her reasons the French support given to the English political exiles. In August Philip won a clear-cut victory over the French at St. Quentin (east of Amiens on the Somme), one of the few in the long series of Habsburg–Valois wars, but Guise hurried north and redressed the military balance by capturing Calais and Guisnes in 1558. For the first time since 1066 there was no territorial connection between France and England.

Mary's marriage had brought not only unpopularity, but also failure. Her religious policy had similar consequences.

ing Abingdon, Aldborough (Yorks.), Aylesbury, Banbury, Boroughbridge, Castle Rising, Droitwich, Higham Ferrers, Knaresborough, Morpeth, Ripon, St. Albans, St. Ives and Woodstock.

It is perhaps surprising that the restoration of Catholicism was not more popular, for about the year 1550 Cecil had considered that a demand for the restoration of the Pope's former position in England would be supported by

> The great body of the peers, some of the Council, all the Bishops except three or four, almost all the judges, almost all the justices of the peace, the priests, and vicars will be on the same side; . . .

Yet in the same memorandum he laid his finger perceptively on one reason for England's fear of continental Catholicism—its political implications:

> The Emperor is aiming at the sovereignty of Europe, which he cannot obtain without the suppression of the Reformed religion, and unless he crushes the English nation he cannot crush the Reformation. . . .

It seems clear that from the start of Mary's reign there was little enthusiasm for the change.   Charles V had advised Mary to temporize at first, and Edward's funeral took place at Westminster, where Cranmer used the protestant service, while Mary attended a requiem Mass sung by Gardiner at the Tower. A proclamation declared that the Queen 'meaneth not to constrain or compel other men's consciences'.   Nevertheless about eight hundred protestants, mainly the more well-to-do, soon left the country.[1]

The restoration of the old religion took about eighteen months to accomplish.   The first steps were administrative. Control over preachers was given to Gardiner, a number of Protestant bishops were removed on various grounds (Hooper for instance was imprisoned for an alleged debt to the Crown), and former Catholic bishops, including Tunstall, Bonner and Gardiner himself, were restored to their old sees.

In October 1553 Mary's first parliament removed from the statute book Edward VI's ecclesiastical legislation.   This Act of Repeal was opposed by about one-third of the Commons. In it nothing was said of the position of the Papacy, nor of the problem of the future of the monastic lands,[2] a particularly tricky question since, as Simon Renard noted, the Catholics held more church property than did the heretics.   The royal

[1] See pp. 165–6.
[2] Mary later restored six monasteries still in her possession, including Greenwich, Sheen, Sion and Westminster.

supremacy was maintained, and for the time being worship was to be conducted as at the end of Henry VIII's reign. In the following spring Royal Injunctions were issued by which those priests who would not accept the doctrine of transubstantiation were deprived of their livings, as were those married priests who would not put away their wives. As a result of these Injunctions about 1,500 priests were removed, one-fifth of all the clergy.

These measures completed the first stage. Had Mary been content to rest for a while at that point, the Henrician compromise might have proved acceptable and union with Rome could perhaps have come later. The English do not mind revolutions provided their attention is not drawn to the changes that are taking place. Mary could not adopt such a policy. She was an enthusiast in a hurry. Every day that complete union was postponed, souls went to perdition—indeed, by not moving as quickly as possible towards reunion, the Queen would herself be sinning.

The second stage opened in the winter of 1554 with the return of Cardinal Pole. On 30 November the country was formally received back into the Catholic Church. The heresy laws, which parliament had earlier refused to revive, were now restored, and in the following February the first victims went to the stake. The total number during the reign was certainly more than two hundred and eighty, but probably less than three hundred. Condemnation of those accused was a matter for the Church courts, technically their burning depended on the secular arm and many of Mary's councillors advised moderation, if only for the time being. Convinced that she was right, convinced that she was acting for the good of her people, Mary must carry the responsibility for the extent of the persecution.

Hooper, Latimer and Ridley were burnt in 1555, Cranmer early in 1556. Cranmer was particularly repugnant to the authorities as the prime agent of Henry's desires: 'What may we conjecture hereby', they accused, 'but that there was a compact between you, being then Queen Anne's chaplain, and the King: Give me the archbishopric of Canterbury, and I will give you licence to live in adultery.' Cranmer himself was tossed between his belief in royal supremacy and his belief in the supremacy of Scripture. He recanted his protestant views, but then at the end withdrew his recantation and died bravely, putting his right hand, which had written the recantation, into the flame and holding it there steadfast and immovable.   The example of the bishops was important, as Latimer emphasized in his words to Ridley: 'We shall this day light such a candle, by God's grace, in England as shall never be put out.'   Yet the majority of the victims were common people and this certainly increased resentment.   The great ought not to escape, for them execution was an occupational hazard; 'mercy will soon pardon the meanest: but mighty men shall be mightily tormented'.

The status is known of a little over half of those who were burnt.   They included seventy-five labourers, twenty-six weavers and cloth-workers, four tradesmen, nine gentry, sixteen priests and five bishops.   It is unlikely that many of those whose class was not recorded were prominent, that at least half the victims were drawn from the ranks of the agricultural poor is therefore likely to be an understatement.   Possible reasons for this class-structure include the emigration of many rich or important Protestants, and the fact that there is some indication that it was the extremists who suffered, poor men and women with Anabaptist views, who caught the eye of authority both by the fervour with which they expressed their opinions and also by the extreme nature of the opinions themselves.

The geographical distribution of the victims also shows a clear-cut pattern: London sixty-seven; Kent fifty-eight; Essex thirty-nine; Sussex twenty-three; Suffolk eighteen; Norfolk fourteen; Middlesex eleven.   Almost 80 per cent came from the south-east, while in the north of England there was only one burning.   The proximity to the continent, from which protestant influences radiated, together with the greater efficiency of government agents near London, probably account for this distribution.

The positive achievements of the reign lie in the fields of financial administration.   In the years from 1540 to 1553 the financial structure built up by Henry VII and Thomas Cromwell had been seriously weakened.   Mary's government retrenched and recovered to such effect that income from the old sources increased once more and the system passed, unchanged and undestroyed, to Elizabeth.

Mary's councillors faced the same financial problem which

had bedevilled Edward's reign—rising prices eroding a fixed income. The financial machinery was overhauled by Paulet, the Courts of First Fruits and Augmentations being absorbed into the Exchequer, which at the same time adopted some of the new financial methods. No further debasement took place, but neither was any attempt made to call in the base money. The sale of Crown lands was checked, and those that remained were exploited more efficiently, so that the income from these lands again reached £70,000 a year. On the other hand, the surrender by Mary of the Crown's right to first-fruits and tenths seriously depleted the royal income. Expenditure was cut down; 'it must be considered that the Queen's expenses be so moderated as the crown be able to bear it . . . and for this cause all such superfluous new charges as have of late crept in are to be taken away'.

In Ireland expenditure was reduced from £40,000 in 1553 to £17,000 in 1556. Officials and courtiers found it less easy to feather their own nests, grants to the latter group being reduced from £20,000 to £6,000 a year. The most valuable and realistic measure was a revision of the Book of Rates, since it brought the Crown's most important and flexible source of income, the revenue from the customs, into line with the rising prices. The revised Book was issued in 1558 and in it the dues were increased by about 75 per cent. The income from the customs dues, which had been £25,000 in 1553, rose to about £80,000 a year at the beginning of the next reign.

The worst financial abuses had been avoided, improvements had been set on foot which would increase the Crown's income in the years to come, but the full effect of these reforms would take time to make themselves fully felt. Meanwhile the government was forced to follow Henry VIII's example and borrow on the Antwerp money market at a high rate of interest —12 per cent to 14 per cent—and in 1557 and 1558 it resorted to the illegal expedient of demanding forced loans at home. Parliament had to be asked for subsidies in 1555 and 1558. Nevertheless, the situation was very much better than it had been five years earlier. In 1557 both France and Spain went bankrupt. England did not.

Indeed, the country as a whole prospered. The price rise had the effect of encouraging traders, and merchants began to reach out towards more distant markets. The first of the great

companies of modern times, the Muscovy Company, was
founded in 1555 to trade with Russia; a treaty with that country
was signed in the following year, and in 1557 the Company's
representative, Anthony Jenkinson, reached Bokhara in central
Asia.   Meanwhile other Englishmen voyaged for the first time
to Guinea in Africa and to Mexico in the New World.   The
pattern of later Elizabethan expansion was already taking
shape.

Yet the importance of Mary's reign lies in the Queen's
failures rather than in her successes.   The loss of Calais and the
fires of Smithfield fed political animosity and religious disgust.
Spain and Catholicism were to become during the next forty
years the enemies of England, and Mary's reputation was linked
with that enmity.   In the growth of this reputation Foxe's
Book of Martyrs (see p. 233) played its part.   Yet Mary I's
character is more complex than that of 'Bloody Mary'.   Rigid
towards heretics, she was lenient towards traitors, tolerant
towards her sister Elizabeth.   Like all the Tudors, she possessed
more than her share of bravery.   She had remained firm in the
face of her father's changes of mood, she had acted decisively
in 1553.   During her reign she did what she could for her little
army, raising the soldiers' pay from 6*d.* to 8*d.* a day and leaving
money in her will to establish a place in London for destitute
men-at-arms.

Mary and Cardinal Pole died within a few hours of each
other towards the end of 1558:

> Both displayed the tragedy of the doctrinaire called to
> practical leadership, yet lacking that instinct towards human
> beings, that sense of the possible in a real world, which have
> always proved more useful in English affairs than high
> principles and strict logic based on narrow premises.[1]

Already men spoke of Elizabeth as 'a jolly liberal dame' and
she inherited much goodwill funded in her sister's failures.
In March 1558 Simon Renard had written:

> It must not be forgotten that all the plots and disorders
> that have troubled England during the past four years have
> aimed at placing its government in Elizabeth's hands. . . .

The gentry and the protestants, the exiles and the Commons, all
alike looked towards the new reign with hope and Elizabeth

---

[1] A. G. Dickens, *The English Reformation*, Batsford, p. 282.

kept the support of these groups throughout her reign, though she did not always satisfy those hopes.

Extracts

I. *John Hales, in* A Discourse of the Common Weal of this Realm of England, *discusses the causes of the great dearth:*

HUSBANDMAN: Marry for these inclosures do undo us all, for they make us pay dearer for our land that we occupy, and causes that we can have no land in manor to put to tillage; all is taken up for pastures, either for sheep or for grazing of cattle. I have known of late a dozen ploughs within less compass than six miles about me laid down within these seven years, and where forty persons had their livings, now one man and his shepherd hath all. Which thing is not the least cause of these uproars, for by these inclosures men do lack livings and be idle; and therefore for very necessity they are desirous of a change, . . . Moreover all things are so dear that by their daily labour they are not able to live.

CAPPER: I have well experience thereof, for I am fain to give my journeymen twopence a day more than I was wont to do, and yet they say they cannot sufficiently live thereon . . . and by reason of such dearth as ye speak of, we that are artificers can keep few or no apprentices like as we were wont to do. Therefore the city, which was heretofore well inhabited and wealthy, (as ye know every one of you,) is fallen for lack of occupiers to great desolation and poverty.

MERCHANT: So the most part of all the towns of England, London excepted; . . . And albeit there be many things laid down that to fore times were occasions of much expenses, as stage plays, interludes, May games, wakes, revels, wagers at shooting, wrestling, running, . . . and many such other things, yet I perceive we be never the wealthier but rather the poorer; . . . for there is such a general dearth of all things as I never knew the like, not only of things growing within this realm, but also of all other merchandise that we buy beyond the seas. . . . [yet] I never saw more plenty of corn, grass, and cattle of all sorts than we have at this present, thanked be Our Lord. If these inclosures were the cause thereof, or any other thing else, it were pity but it were removed.

KNIGHT: . . . I confess there is a wonderful dearth of all things; and that do I, and all men of my sort, feel most grief in, which have no wares to sell, or occupation to live by, but only our lands . . . for as much as all things are dearer than they were, so much do you raise the price of your wares and occupations that you sell again; but we have nothing to sell, whereby we might advance the price thereof, to countervalue those things that we must buy again.

HUSBANDMAN: Yes, you raise the price of your lands, and you take farms also and pastures into your hands, which was wont to be poor men's livings, such as I am, and gentlemen ought to live only upon their lands.

MERCHANT and CAPPER: On my soul, ye say truth, . . . it was never merry with poor craftsmen since gentlemen became graziers; . . .

HUSBANDMAN: Yea, those sheep is the cause of all these mischiefs, for they have driven husbandry out of the country, by the which was increased before all kind of victual, and now altogether sheep, sheep. It was far better when there was not only sheep enough, but also oxen, kine, swine, pigs, geese and capons, eggs, butter and cheese, yea, and bread corn and malt corn enough besides, and all together reared upon the same land.

II. i. *Cranmer, addressing the Council, defends the practice of kneeling to receive the sacrament, 1552:*

Your lordships are wise, but is it wisdom to alter without Parliament what has been concluded by Parliament at the bidding of vain glorious and unquiet spirits, who would still find faults if the Book were altered every year? They say that kneeling is not commanded in Scripture, and what is not commanded is unlawful. There is the root of the errors of the sects! If that be true, have no more trouble in setting forth an order in religion, or indeed in common policy. If kneeling be not expressly enjoined in Holy Scripture, neither is standing or sitting. Let them lie down on the ground, and eat their meat like Turks or Tartars.

ii. *The death of Cranmer at Oxford, 1556:*

And when the wood was kindled, and the fire began to burn near him, stretching out his arm, he put his right hand into the flame, which he held so steadfast and immovable (saving that once with the same hand he wiped his face) that all men might see his hand burned before his body was touched. His body did so abide the burning of the flame, with such constancy and steadfastness, that standing always in one place, without moving his body, he seemed to move no more than the stake to which he was bound: his eyes were lifted up unto heaven, and often times he repeated his 'unworthy right hand,' so long as his voice would suffer him: and using often the words of Stephen, Lord Jesus receive my spirit; in the greatness of the flame he gave up the ghost.

FURTHER READING

W. C. Richardson, *Some Financial Expedients of Henry VIII*, Ec.H.R., VII, 1954

H. Chapman, *The Last Tudor King*, Cape, 1958

H. F. M. Prescott, *Mary Tudor*, Eyre and Spottiswoode, 1952

D. M. Loades, *Two Tudor Conspiracies*, C.U.P., 1965

S. T. Bindoff, *Ket's Rebellion*, H.A. Pamphlet G 12, 1949

E. C. S. Gibson, ed., *The First and Second Prayer Books of Edward VI*, Dent, 1910

R. B. Outhwaite, *The Trials of Foreign Borrowing: the English Crown and the Antwerp Money Market in the Mid-Sixteenth Century*, Ec.H.R., XIX, 1966

A. Fletcher, *Tudor Rebellions*, Longmans, 1968

VII · THE ELIZABETHAN SETTLEMENT

Introduction

ON 17 November Elizabeth I, then twenty-five years old, came to the throne. The Venetian ambassador described her as:

> A lady of great elegance both of body and mind, although her face may rather be called pleasing than beautiful; she is tall and well-made; her complexion fine though rather sallow; her eyes, and above all her hands, which she takes care not to conceal, are of superior beauty.

The new Queen's early life had given to her character two outstanding features—culture and caution. She had received the usual intensive sixteenth-century education. Her tutors, drawn from the Cambridge circle of radical humanists, had an apt pupil. Roger Ascham, the greatest of them, wrote that she could speak French and Italian fluently, Latin well, and Greek moderately. In 1562 he was daily reading Latin and Greek with her. This was not academic learning only, in old age Elizabeth was still capable of delivering impromptu speeches in Latin to visiting ambassadors.

Caution she had taught herself. Her mother had been executed when she was two years old; for the next nine years she had been in and out of her father's temperamental favour; during Edward's reign the Admiral Thomas Seymour, Somerset's brother, had tried to acquire her for himself—and had been executed; in 1554 Wyatt's rebellion had led to her imprisonment in the Tower. Throughout her life Elizabeth had lived in the shadow of destruction, and the experience had taught her not to commit herself if possible and, when action was inevitable, to move with extreme prudence and as short a distance as was practicable. They were lessons that she never forgot.

In later years Holinshed could write:

> After all the stormy, tempestuous and blustering windy weather of Queen Mary was overblown, the darksome clouds of discomfort dispersed, the palpable fogs and mist of the most intolerant misery consumed, and the dashing showers of persecution overpast: it pleased God to send England a

calm and quiet season a clear and lovely sunshine, a quitset [release] from former broils of a turbulent estate, and a world of blessings by good Queen Elizabeth.

But this is the historian's hindsight. In 1558 the accession of another queen appeared only to add to England's existing difficulties. The precedents, the reigns of Matilda and Mary, were discouraging. Of course, Elizabeth would marry, but whom? Any choice posed problems. If her husband were an Englishman he would create jealousies and counter-loyalties, whilst her sister's reign had underlined the dangers of a foreign marriage.

The heir to the throne was the king of France's daughter-in-law, Mary Stuart—indeed by canon law she was the rightful Queen already. Henri II proclaimed her title and quartered the leopards of England with the lilies of France. Immediately Philip II hurried to the defence of Elizabeth's right to the throne. He had no wish to see a French bloc stretching from the Shetlands to the Pyrenees and controlling the Channel route to the Netherlands. In this rivalry between France and Spain Elizabeth perhaps already perceived the clue that was to guide her through the maze of marital and political dangers.

Besides the question of the Queen's marriage there were plenty of other difficulties facing Elizabeth and her advisers:

The queen poor;[1] the realm exhausted; the nobility poor and decayed; want of good captains and soldiers; The people out of order; Justice not executed. All things dear. Excess in meat, drink and apparel. Divisions among ourselves. Wars with France and Scotland. The French king bestriding the realm, having one foot in Calais and the other in Scotland. Steadfast enmity but not steadfast friendship abroad.

These were the terms in which a memorandum *The Distresses of the Commonwealth* (written by Armagil Waad) summarized the condition of the state. It was not the view of Englishmen only. Feria, the Spanish ambassador, called England 'the sick man of Europe'.

Elizabeth had inherited the Tudor eye for the right servant. She kept ten of Mary's twenty-six councillors (and eight of these had served Edward VI as well), but within three days of her accession she had appointed Sir William Cecil as Secretary.

[1] Mary had left debts of about £200,000.

He remained her chief adviser until his death forty years later. It was a close partnership, so close that historians are still uncertain as to the relative contributions of its two members, though there is no doubt that the Queen was the dominant partner.

Cecil's father was a Northamptonshire squire and minor court official. His family were rising men who had moved from the Welsh marches a generation earlier. Born in 1520, William Cecil was educated at Cambridge and Gray's Inn, sat in parliament in 1543, was Somerset's private secretary and then, as one of Northumberland's two Secretaries of State, became the engine of daily administration. Under Mary he survived, though he lost the Secretaryship. He remained close to the centre of power, for the Queen found it convenient to employ him on government business, and he also administered the Princess Elizabeth's lands and sat in the parliament of 1555. To him the new Queen now said:

> This judgement I have of you, that you will not be corrupted by any manner of gift and that you will be faithful to the state; and that without respect of my private will you will give me that counsel which you think best and if you shall know anything necessary to be declared to me of secrecy you shall show it to myself only, and assure yourself I will not fail to keep taciturnity therein.

She was not to be disappointed.

Like Elizabeth, Cecil belonged to the growing group of *politique* statesmen in Europe, men who put political expediency before inflexible *a priori* principles, who had—as Sir William Paulet said of himself—more of the willow than the oak in their character. Feria recognized something of this perhaps when he wrote to Philip that Cecil was 'said to be a prudent and virtuous man albeit a heretic'. He developed into a statesman who will stand comparison with William the Silent, with Richelieu or with Bismarck.

The Religious Settlement

The first of Elizabeth's parliaments met in January 1559, its business the settlement of urgent political and religious matters. The queen's claim to the throne rested on Henry VIII's third Succession Act (1543) and on the terms of that king's will. However, in view of the French attitude and of her own position in canon law, parliament immediately passed a brief act recognizing her title to the throne.

In a country where the church was a part of the state machinery and in an age when religious nonconformity was also political treason, a religious settlement was a matter of urgency. In less than thirty years the people of England had experienced five distinct forms of religion. This was clearly a process that could not be repeated indefinitely. The temper of her advisers, the political and diplomatic climate, the volcanic nature of Pope Paul IV, above all the descent and character of the daughter of Henry VIII and Anne Boleyn—together these factors made a continuance of Mary's Catholic policy out of the question.

Elizabeth herself would probably have liked to return to the position at the close of her father's reign; she certainly told Feria that she was 'resolved to restore her religion as her father left it'. She was not anxious to be under either the Pope at Rome or 'the Pope and Emperor of Geneva'. Yet, a *politique* not a *dévote*, she was prepared to settle for what was possible. If she could not carry the Marian bishops with her she would have to rely on protestant opinion of one shade or another.

During her sister's reign about 800 people, one-third of them clergy or those intended for the ministry, had fled the country. Amongst the 472 Marian exiles whose background is known to us, there were 166 gentry, 119 students, 67 clergy, 40 merchants, and 32 artisans. These refugees—largely drawn not from the ranks of the poor, but from the educated, opinionated gentry and middle classes—established themselves at Emden, Wesel, Frankfurt, Strassburg, Zurich, Basle, Geneva and Aarau. The Lutheran states were inhospitable, and the exiles found themselves under the influence of Zwinglians and Calvinists. To a large extent they preserved the Anglicanism they had known at the end of Edward's reign, but there were some interesting developments. For instance, Bishop Ponet, Cranmer's chaplain and an exile under Mary, wrote the first English defence of tyrannicide in 1556, a politico-religious treatise which based the origin of authority in the community and not in the king, to whom authority had merely been delegated. An influential work was the production of the Geneva Bible, with its highly political notes, which went through seventy editions by 1640. It was at this time also that the metrical version of the

M

psalms (including both the words and music of the well-known Old Hundredth, *All people that on earth do dwell*) made its appearance.

These were the sort of people, travelled, well-informed, radical, who now came hurrying back and by their busy pressure helped to force the Queen towards a more extreme settlement than she had first intended. The Marian exiles from Geneva did not arrive in time to influence opinion, but those from other parts of Europe played a large part in moulding the opposition to the Queen's intentions. The government's original plan seems to have been to introduce very moderate reforms by stages. The first step would have comprised an act of supremacy including a clause permitting communion in both kinds to the laity. This would indeed have been a return to the situation as it had been in 1547, but the Commons, about a quarter of whom were strongly opposed to the government's cautious policy, altered this bill in the committee stage to such an extent that it was no longer acceptable either to the lords or to the Queen and Elizabeth found herself dependent on a Commons and clergy who desired a much more 'puritan' settlement than the one she had proposed to introduce.

Deadlock seemed likely and the Queen made arrangements to dissolve parliament. Then something, almost certainly the news that France and Spain had finally concluded Peace at Cateau-Cambrésis, made her change her mind. Consultations were held, parliament was recalled after Easter, and a settlement was quickly agreed upon, consisting of an Act of Supremacy and an Act of Uniformity.

Elizabeth was a woman. The Commons might speak of the queen as their 'Deborah' but many of them did not believe that a woman could be head of the church and instead the new Act of Supremacy declared her 'the only Supreme Governor of this realm . . . as well in all spiritual or ecclesiastical things or causes as temporal'. This small verbal adjustment carried profound implications. Elizabeth's position was not that of her father. He had ruled the Church from within, she must rule it from without, and in partnership with Parliament. The Act also repealed Mary's heresy laws, and made provision for the administration of communion in both kinds.

The Act of Uniformity took as its basis the Second Prayer Book of Edward VI (1552) but made certain changes, all of them in a conservative direction. Attacks on the Pope were removed. The 'Black Rubric' was omitted. The communion service combined the words of administration of the 1549 book 'The body of our Lord Jesus Christ' which implied the Real Presence, with those of the Second Book 'Take and eat this in remembrance' which asserted no more than a commemorative practice. Finally, and this was to cause the most trouble in the future, it ordered that the ornaments in the church and the vestments of the priest should be those in use in 1548—vestments and ornaments obnoxious to the radical reformers. Nevertheless the Queen had made much greater concessions to her puritan subjects than she had originally intended—or than they had made to her. A state-imposed compromise, and one that was to prove remarkably successful, it was for all that an unintentional triumph, born of the clash between the Queen and the Commons, achieved by Elizabeth not as part of a subtly-conceived policy, a deliberate attempt to create a *via media*, but as the accidental consequence of her ability to trim her sails to the winds of political pressure.

The new church was as yet unopposed by the Catholics, unaffected by the Genevans still hurrying back from exile, almost completely uninfluenced by the Lutherans. To that extent it was pure English—the Duchess of Suffolk, a Marian exile, wrote to Cecil, that 'Christ's plain coat without seam is fairer than all the joggs of Germany'—but its creators had shown a fine eclecticism. The country acquired a church governed by the queen in parliament, catholic in liturgy and organization, protestant in intention and ambiguous in its communion service.

The settlement proved generally acceptable. When the oath of supremacy was administered, the majority of the clergy conformed. Many were quiet, luke-warm men, untouched by the new enthusiasm for reform, catholic or protestant, and often ignorant of the issues involved—in the diocese of Worcester, for instance, only 19 per cent were graduates. In many cases the oath was not administered at all; the Dean of Durham asserted in 1566 that 'many papists enjoy liberty and livings who have neither sworn obedience to the Queen nor yet do any part of their duty towards their miserable flocks'. In the end only about 300 of the lesser clergy, out of a total of over 8,000, lost their livings.

With the higher clergy the case was different. All but one of the Marian bishops refused the oath. They were deprived of their sees, some of which were filled by Edwardian bishops, others by new men. Elizabeth's former tutor, Edmund Grindal, an ardent reformer, was made bishop of London, while as Archbishop of Canterbury the Queen appointed Matthew Parker (1560–75). Parker provided a valuable element of continuity. He had been a member of the circle of humanist reformers at Cambridge known in the twenties as 'Little Germany'; he had worked with Cranmer, and he had remained in England during Mary's reign. Doctrinally, he was a moderate protestant. Parker was not anxious to exchange Cambridge for the hurly-burly of political religion but, once having done so, he played an active and important part in working out the detailed pattern of the new church. In 1563 he succeeded in obtaining the acceptance by convocation of the Thirty-Nine Articles, based on Cranmer's Forty-Two. In the same year Bishop Jewel, encouraged by Parker, produced his *Apology*, a defence of the new church that held the field until the appearance of Hooker's *Ecclesiastical Polity* in the nineties.

The settlement, originally seen as an uneasy armistice between contending forces, endured and, by the mere fact of that endurance, acquired prestige, cohesion and permanence. The prayer book proved itself capable of acceptance by a wide range of opinions and survived four centuries almost unaltered. By the end of her reign Elizabeth's church had become part of the established order and its followers were boasting that 'The Church of England hath ever kept a mean between the meretricious gaudiness of Rome and the squalid sluttery of fanatic conventicles.'

The Problems of Marriage, France and Scotland

At the close of 1558 England's position in Europe was very weak. She was still involved in the Habsburg-Valois war. France, the traditional enemy, appeared to control Scotland. Spain was an ally, but an ally that clearly hoped to swallow up its junior partner. In the background the slow ground-swell of the Counter-Reformation was taking shape, with more than a hint of a political-religious crusade against weak protestant countries.

Nevertheless, the situation was not quite as black as it seemed.

Neither France nor Spain wished to see England under a rival's control; there was thus a hope that they might be played off against one another. Scotland, as always, was divided between rival groups of jealous lords. Self-interest might weaken the crusading unity of the Counter-Reformation, while in France and in the Spanish Netherlands there were signs of religious dissent which could lead to civil war.

None of this was entirely obvious to contemporaries nor is it likely that it was at first clear to the Queen herself. Elizabeth's nature helped her. Time was the essence of the matter. William Thomas, clerk to Edward VI's council, had advised that when England was weak 'our extremest shift is to work by policy' and Elizabeth was by temperament inclined to put off making decisions. Procrastination was for her an element of statecraft: 'only a woman' Lytton Strachey has written, 'could have shuffled so shamelessly'. She was, like her grandfather, a pragmatist, an opportunist determined to use every favourable circumstance and ally, while committing herself to none:

She was loyal to treaties only so long as they served her purpose, and broke them unscrupulously, in spirit if not in letter, when they threatened to hamper her freedom of movement. A master of prevarication and deceit, when occasion drove her to it, she was adept at finding subterfuges for actions of doubtful legality, and always had emergency exits at hand when strategic retreats became necessary. Watchfulness and flexibility were the very essence of her system; for each situation, as it arose, had to be examined afresh in the light of England's vital needs and policy modified or redirected accordingly.[1]

Feria summed up his impressions of the queen as follows:

She is a very vain woman but a very acute one. She evidently has great admiration for the King her father and his way of doing things. I greatly fear that in religion she will not go right, as I perceive her inclined to govern by men who are held to be heretics. . . . She is much attached to the people and is very confident that they are all on her side, which is indeed true; indeed she gave me to understand that the people had placed her where she now is. On this point she will acknowledge no obligations either to your Majesty

[1] J. B. Black, *The Reign of Elizabeth*, O.U.P., 2nd ed. 1959, p. 333.

[Philip II] or to her nobles. . . . She seems to me incomparably more feared than her sister, and gives her orders and has her way absolutely, as her father did. . . . After all, everything depends on the husband she chooses. . . .

The marriage, Feria saw, was as much a matter of foreign as of domestic policy. The fact that she was unmarried was, indeed, the strongest card in Elizabeth's hand—but only so long as it was not played. While she was single, each country might hope to win her hand and with it control of England. The Commons never understood this, and as early as February 1559 they made a 'request to her Highness for marriage'. The Queen replied with the first of those ambiguous statements in the making of which she was already an adept, concluding 'yet may my issue grow out of kind and become perhaps ungracious. And in the end, this shall be for me sufficient, that a marble stone shall declare that a Queen, having reigned such a time, lived and died a virgin.' There for the moment, the matter was to rest. It still rested there forty-five years later.

The bankruptcy of France and Spain in 1557 soon brought the long Habsburg-Valois struggle to an end. The Peace of Cateau-Cambrésis was signed in April 1559. France gave up her claims in Italy, but kept the cities of Metz, Toul and Verdun beyond her eastern frontier. Spain was left in control of Italy and Philip was to marry Henri II's daughter, Elizabeth de Valois. (Elizabeth Tudor had put aside, politely, his offer of marriage to her.) The French were to hold Calais for eight years and then to return it or to pay England half a million crowns.

At a tournament held to celebrate the Franco-Spanish marriage, Henri II died of an accidental lance-thrust. The new king was Francis II and his wife was Mary Stuart. Seventeen years old, Mary was Queen of Scots in her own right, Queen of France by marriage, and heir to the English throne by virtue of her descent from Henry VII's daughter Margaret. Mary's mother, Mary of Guise, had ruled in Edinburgh since 1550, and now the two countries were united. The French king was indeed 'bestriding the realm' and with regard to English reactions Feria wrote: 'It is incredible the fear these people are in of the French on the Scottish border.'

The fear was short-lived. Nine years later Scotland was

allied to England, Mary Stuart was an exile in Elizabeth's power, and France was divided by civil war. The events which produced this astounding reversal of fortune were an intricate web of political, religious and personal discords.

In May 1559 John Knox (1505–72) returned to Scotland. He had served nineteen months in the French galleys for his part in the anti-Catholic rising of 1547: on his release he had preached before Edward VI, and he had refused an offer of the see of Rochester. Since then, except for one short visit (1555–6), he had been an exile from Scotland, living at Frankfurt and Geneva.

Intolerant, bold, irascible, Knox was an uncompromising fighter, one of the four great Calvinist theologians of the sixteenth century. His speech was uncompromising. In 1549 he had addressed the Council of the North on the subject of the Mass: 'All service invented by the brain of man in the religion of God, without his express command, is idolatry. The mass is invented by the brain of man without the command of God; therefore it is idolatry.' In 1552 he had described the Second Prayer Book as 'impure, unclean and imperfect'. In 1558 he had published his *First Blast of the Trumpet Against the Monstrous Regiment of Women*—a blast directed against Mary Tudor, Mary Stuart and Mary of Guise. They were Catholics but, more important, they were women and women should not rule. It was unfortunate that Elizabeth was now Queen of England, and Knox admitted that the *Blast* 'hath blown from me all my friends in England'.

The Scotland to which Knox returned was already in arms against the French regent, Mary of Guise. Two years earlier the protestant Scottish Lords of the Congregation had formed an association and signed a Covenant. Encouraged by Knox and led by the earl of Arran, the protestant claimant to the throne, they now attacked the French garrisons. They would not have succeeded without English help.

Elizabeth, it will be clear, had nothing in common with Knox, and she strongly disapproved of rebels, but principles gave way to policy. Sir Nicholas Throckmorton had written from Paris to Cecil: 'I doubt not but you do consider how much it standeth the Queen's Majesty upon to nourish and entertain the garboyle [tumult] in Scotland'. A defensive treaty was signed at Berwick (1560). Soon English ships under Sir

William Winter blocked the Firth of Forth, while an army under Lord Grey de Wilton besieged Edinburgh. In 1560 Mary of Guise died, and Cecil (who had gone to Scotland) was able to conclude the Treaty of Edinburgh. French troops were to be withdrawn and Mary Stuart was to renounce her claim to the English throne. For the time being government was securely in the hands of the protestant lords and ministers—men such as Maitland of Lethington and John Knox.

Elizabeth's intervention had cost her at least £250,000 but it was money well spent. The old alliance with France was broken, and protestantism was established. Different as they were, Knox and Elizabeth each owed something to the other: she had helped to establish Calvinism in Scotland, and he had made more secure the Anglican settlement.

A few months later, in December 1560, Francis II died. Power passed into the hands of the queen-mother, Catherine de Médicis, who was anxious to break the power of the Guises in France. Mary was half-Guise and she soon (1561) found herself on her way back to Scotland. She was still only eighteen and unfitted both by her religion and her character to deal with the situation which she found there: a Catholic in a Presbyterian environment, she was intelligent, emotional, self-centred and completely lacked her cousin Elizabeth's calm detachment. She could be charming, but she failed to charm Knox, who 'espied such craft as I have not found in such age'. In 1564 she married Henry Lord Darnley, the grandson of Margaret Tudor and therefore with a claim to the English succession, a claim made stronger in English law by the fact that he had been born in England. In 1566 Mary gave birth to a son, the future James I of England. Neither the marriage nor the birth pleased Elizabeth, and it brought from the Commons a renewed demand that she herself should marry.

Elizabeth was still inclined both by temperament and by considerations of policy to keep the question of her own marriage unanswered. In late 1559 and early 1560 a number of candidates had been considered: the protestant earl of Arran; the Habsburg Archduke Charles, son of the Emperor Ferdinand and nephew of Philip II; Eric, king of Sweden, and even the duke of Saxony. Cecil had written drily, 'Here is great resort of wooers and controversy among lovers', and nothing had been decided.

Later that year it appeared that the Queen had fallen in love with Robert Dudley, a son of Northumberland's, handsome, thoughtless and already married. The court held its breath. Soon Dudley's wife was found dead in circumstances nicely balanced between murder, suicide and accident. (Modern opinion inclines towards the last of these.) Elizabeth's common sense began to reassert itself. Dudley was created earl of Leicester, but became no more than the leading court favourite.

In the autumn of 1562 Elizabeth caught smallpox and nearly died. When parliament met in 1563 the members, alarmed both by Dudley and the smallpox, once again pressed the queen to marry and to name her successor. Setting aside Mary Stuart, the most likely claimants were Lady Catherine Grey and the Earl of Huntingdon. Lady Catherine was the sister of Lady Jane Grey and was descended from Henry VII's daughter Mary, while the Earl was descended from Edward IV's brother Clarence, and the Council was said to be divided on the respective merits of their claims. The Lord Keeper read to the Commons the Queen's reply to their petition. Elizabeth, as usual, promised nothing. With regard to her marriage she answered that 'a silent thought may serve' and touching the succession: 'I hope I shall die in quiet with *nunc dimittis*, which cannot be without I see some glimpse of your following surety after my gravèd bones.'

The same parliament met again in three years time. Alarmed by Mary's marriage and the birth of her son, it at once returned to the attack. Elizabeth retorted that, when she married, her critics would be 'as ready to mislike him with whom I shall marry, as they are now to move it'. The succession was none of their business—'A strange thing that the foot should direct the head in so weighty a cause;' she knew, as they did not, the danger of being next in line, 'I stood in danger of my life, my sister was so incensed against me: I did differ from her in religion, and I was sought for divers ways. And so shall never be my successor.' Neither fear nor pressure would move her.

Her success in Scotland perhaps played its part in stampeding Elizabeth into her first—and her only major—error in foreign policy. Religious tensions in France had brought the country to civil war. Three groups of nobles expressed their political ambitions and rivalries in terms of religious antagonism. The most powerful was that of the Guises of Lorraine, half-German, richer than the king himself, and ultra-catholic.   The Bourbon family, strong in the south and next in line of succession to the throne, were Huguenots.   The Montmorencis were *politiques*. Lesser nobles attached themselves to one or other of these three main groups, while Catherine de Médicis attempted to play off one against another, and to build up the strength of the crown in opposition to them all.

In 1562 the duc de Guise, coming on a Huguenot congregation at Vassy, 'mingled their blood with their sacrifices'.   The first of the French wars of religion had begun.   They were to continue intermittently[1] until 1598.   The Huguenots appealed to Elizabeth, and it seemed a good idea to help them and perhaps create in France a situation similar to the one in Scotland.   From Flanders her adviser Sir Thomas Gresham had already written: 'Now is the time (they say here) to recover those pieces we have lost of late in France, or better pieces', and the Spanish ambassador, De Quadra, commented sourly: 'This woman desires to make use of religion in order to excite rebellion in the whole world.'   Neither his fears nor Gresham's hopes were to be realized.

Negotiations opened with the Huguenots and, by the secret Treaty of Richmond, Havre would be held by 3,000 English and eventually exchanged for Calais, while a further 3,000 English would help the Huguenot prince of Condé, and 140,000 crowns would be lent to the rebels.   The intervention was a failure. Condé, defeated by the royal forces, soon joined with them to expel the foreigner.   An English force was driven out of Dieppe, and Havre was strongly besieged.   The English commander, the earl of Warwick, wrote of his men 'They fight like Hectors, labour like slaves, are worse fed than peasants, and are poorer than common beggars', and after six months he was forced in 1563 to surrender.   Peace came officially with the Treaty of Troyes in 1564.

Calais was forfeited and English attempts to recover their lost French empire came to an end.   Soon Spain would replace France as the 'natural' enemy.   Meanwhile Elizabeth had learnt a lesson.   Ever afterwards she was cautious—over-cautious, her advisers lamented—of involving herself in foreign commitments.

[1] For reference, the dates are: 1562–3; 1567–8; 1568–70; 1572–3; 1574–6; 1577; 1580; 1585–9; 1589–98.

Three years later, in Scotland, fortune worked for Elizabeth. Distaste for Darnley had led Mary into a close, though probably innocent, relationship with her Italian Secretary, Riccio. In March 1566, shortly before the birth of her son James, Darnley murdered the Italian. Mary waited. At the end of 1566 her husband caught smallpox. In February 1567 while he was recovering at Kirk o' Field just outside Edinburgh, he was murdered, and the house blown up by a group of lords led by the protestant Earl of Bothwell. It is uncertain whether or not Mary knew the details beforehand, but she was in love with Bothwell, of whom it was reported that she would 'go with him to the world's end', and in April she allowed him to take her north to Dunbar where they were married according to protestant rites. Neither Catholic nor Calvinist now had any further use for the Queen. In June she was captured, forced to abdicate, and imprisoned at Loch Leven. Bothwell fled to Scandinavia. Within a year Mary had escaped, but she was defeated again at Langside, and in May 1568 she crossed the border to Carlisle and appealed to the Queen of England. It was, for Elizabeth, the end of the Scottish menace in one form and the beginning of quite a different sort of threat. Next year Cecil was writing, 'The Queen of Scots is and shall always be a dangerous person to your estate'.

Mary was a queen and a cousin. Elizabeth had no sympathy for rebels, and Cecil had in earlier days written of the situation north of the Border, 'it is against God's law to aid any subjects against their natural princes'. Yet what was to be done with Mary? To attempt to restore her to Scotland would be difficult and expensive, would lose England her new friends there, and might yet in the end fail. To send her to Europe, perhaps to France, would be to place a valuable piece in the hands of England's old enemies. The French King might once again bestride the realm. To keep Mary in England was the easiest course and the one that was finally adopted, for it fell in with Elizabeth's characteristic inclination to do nothing, but for too many years Mary proved a menace to the Queen—a risk that Cecil had recognized from the start. Analysing the disadvantages of each course of action he wrote of the danger that Elizabeth's enemies would find in Mary a focus of discontent and '. . . no man can think but such a sweet bait would make concord betwixt them all.' In the light of later events, it can be seen that Elizabeth's best course of action might possibly have been to let Mary go discredited to France. By keeping Mary prisoner Elizabeth lost a portion of her own freedom, and lived for over eighteen years under the intermittent threat of plots to release Mary Stuart and place her on the throne of England.[1]

Economic Decisions

Armagil Waad's memorandum had listed a number of economic 'distresses'. Tudor government was always at its weakest when attempting to legislate on these matters—indeed, governments in all ages find such legislation the most difficult. Nevertheless, important decisions were taken.

Sir Thomas Gresham (c. 1519–79) was the Queen's economic adviser. His father, who came of a Norfolk family, had been employed by Henry VIII, had made a fortune trading in the Low Countries, and had been Lord Mayor in 1537. Sir Thomas operated in Antwerp as a member of the Mercer's Company. During the economic crisis of 1551 he was employed by the government and during the next two years made no fewer than forty journeys to the Netherlands on government business. He was dismissed by Mary, but had to be re-appointed. To Elizabeth he was indispensable, haggling with the Antwerp money lenders, buying arms there for the new government, operating a private intelligence service, advising the Queen how to handle the debased coinage. In 1567 he began the construction of the Royal Exchange, modelled on that at Antwerp, and in his will he made provision for the foundation of Gresham College.[2]

The debased coinage was called in. During the autumn of 1560 a proclamation was circulated establishing the real values of the base silver coins, which were then to be exchanged at these values for new coins of standard weight and fineness. By the following April £700,000 of the old money had been called in, melted down and recoined. The whole operation was carried out with surprising smoothness—and not the least remarkable feature is the fact that the Crown made a net profit of perhaps £45,000.

[1] In Scotland itself a series of Anglophil regents (Murray, Mar and Morton) maintained the understanding with England, though the Marian party were only expelled from Edinburgh Castle, with English help, in 1573.

[2] See p. 342.

In the parliament of 1563 laws were passed to encourage shipping by the establishment of a 'fish-day' on Wednesdays, and to check the export of corn when the price rose above ten shillings a quarter. A new Poor Law introduced the principle of a compulsory assessment by J.P.s for those who would not give voluntarily.

Bulkiest, and most important, was the Statute of Apprentices. This was a summary and extension in scope of many earlier acts, an attempt by the government to maintain social stability and security. The final product was not entirely a government measure, but a combined operation in which the members of the Commons played a large part, amending and expanding. There is evidence that the clauses dealing with apprenticeship may have been introduced by business men in the Commons. It can be read as an act protecting the poor against exploitation, or as a determined attempt to keep these people in their place. It is both, for the two aims were not mutually exclusive. Labourers and artificers were to stay in the areas and carry on the work to which they had been born. Apprenticeship was to be strictly enforced for the full seven-year period. Wages were to be assessed by J.P.s and the assessments were to vary in time and place, so as to 'yield to the hired person, both in time of scarcity and in time of plenty, a convenient proportion of wages'.

Conclusion

Almost every problem facing the queen at her accession had now been tackled. Much had been achieved in the first five years. When preparing for the parliament of 1563 Cecil showed himself already well-satisfied with the progress that had been made. He prepared a memorandum of the government's achievements:

1559 The religion of Christ restored. Foreign authority rejected . . . 1560 The French at the request of the Scots, partly by force, partly by agreement sent back to France, and Scotland set free from the servitude of the Pope. 1561 the debased copper and brass coinage replaced by gold and silver. England, formerly unarmed, supplied more abundantly than any other country with arms, munitions and artillery. 1562 The tottering Church of Christ in France succoured. . . .

In 1563 economic strains and stresses were reduced, while by

1566 the new church settlement had demonstrated its power of survival, and the struggle to modify it was entering a new, parliamentary phase. In 1568 the flight of Mary marked the end of the ancient danger from Scotland.

EXTRACT

Gresham's proposals to the Queen at her accession:

Finally, and it please your Majesty to restore this your realm into such estate, as heretofore it hath been: First, your Highness hath none other ways but, when time and opportunity serveth, to bring your brass money into fine, of XI ounces fine. And so gold after the rate. Secondly, not to restore the Steelyard to their usurped privileges. Thirdly, to grant as few licences as you can. Fourthly, to come in as small debt as you can beyond seas. Fifthly, to keep your credit; and specially with your own merchants; for it is they must stand by you at all events in your necessity. . . .

By your Majesty's most humble and faithful obedient subject,

Thomas Gresham, Mercer

(J. W. Burgon, *Life and Times of Sir Thomas Gresham*, 1839, Vol. I, p. 234.)

FURTHER READING

J. B. Black, *The Reign of Elizabeth* , O.U.P., 2nd ed., 1959
J. Hurstfield, *Elizabeth I and the Unity of England*, E.U.P., 1960
— *The Elizabethan Nation*, B.B.C., 1964
J. E. Neale, *Queen Elizabeth I*, Cape, 1934
— *The Age of Catherine de Medici and Essays in Elizabethan History*, Cape, 1963
C. Read, *Mr. Secretary Cecil and Queen Elizabeth*, Cape, 1955
— *Lord Burghley and Queen Elizabeth*, Cape, 1960
A. L. Rowse, *The England of Elizabeth*, Macmillan, 1950
W. MacCaffrey, *The Shaping of the Elizabethan Regime*, Cape, 1969

VIII · FOREIGN AFFAIRS AND THE GROWING CONFLICT, 1568–85

Introduction

OVER the centuries England's relations with Europe have swung between violent entanglement in the affairs of the continent and an equally extreme isolation. During the greater part of Elizabeth's reign the country was greatly involved in the European scene.

That scene was one of turmoil. The forces of national feeling, Spanish might, overseas trade, Catholic Counter-Reformation and militant Calvinism were all linked in a complex pattern of shifting power. These forces involved England, the Netherlands, France and Spain in war. From 1562 France was plunged into a series of civil wars, partly religious and partly political, which developed after 1589 into a national war against Spain that was not ended until 1598. Spain was locked in combat with her possessions in the Netherlands, a combat partly religious and partly national that lasted from 1572 to 1609. Finally, England and Spain were at war from 1585 to 1604, fighting on the seas, in Ireland, in France, in the Netherlands and even, briefly, in Spain itself.

Mary, Queen of Scots

For Elizabeth, foreign affairs began at home. To hold Mary in captivity was at the same time a security and a risk. It simplified Elizabeth's foreign problems in one way and complicated them in another.

The Scottish Queen had been in England less than eighteen months when the potential danger of her presence there was made clear. Early in 1569 a plot, or rather a number of plots, developed. Cecil was to be disgraced; Mary was to be freed, restored to Scotland, recognized as Elizabeth's successor, and wedded to Thomas Howard, Duke of Norfolk. Various forces were at work. The Spanish ambassador, de Spes, had a hand in the matter, but the plots were at least in part a home-grown protest, made by the heads of the old order against the leaders of the new. This protest was, politically, against the growing

WESTERN EUROPE ABOUT 1560

bureaucratic powers of the government; in matters of religion it was against the new state protestant church; socially it represented the opposition of the north to the new pressures, industrial, agricultural, and commercial, of the south. These were to a large extent the same resentments as those that had powered the Pilgrimage of Grace thirty years earlier.

In the spring a half-hearted attempt to discredit Cecil in the Council failed. In the summer news of Norfolk's marital plans reached the queen's ears, and she summoned the Duke to London. Norfolk was the premier peer in England and owned large estates in Sussex and in Norfolk, where he lived like a sovereign. To him Leicester and Cecil were *nouveaux riches* upstarts. Yet Norfolk was himself a conceited, feeble, middle-aged temporizer and when summoned by Elizabeth, he came quietly to court, and was lodged in the Tower.

The other conspirators were made of sterner stuff. Mary, as usual, was sanguine. 'Tell the Spanish ambassador', she wrote, 'that if his master will help me, I shall be queen of England in three months, and Mass shall be said all over the country.' Meanwhile in the troubled feudal north to which Elizabeth never went and where the memory of the Pilgrimage of Grace was still green, the Earls of Westmorland and Northumberland, seeing Howard as a symbol of their lost power and Mary as the instrument by which they might regain it, called out their men.

Sussex had already reported 'an intended stir of the people in the north part of Yorkshire.' From York he had written that he was having difficulty in raising troops for the royal army; 'Except it be a few protestants and some well affected to me, every man seeks to bring as small a force as he can of horsemen and the footmen find fault with the weather and besides speak very broadly.' Yet victory proved unexpectedly easy. When Sussex moved north the earls fled to Scotland, leaving their 7,000 followers to their fate. The leaderless men put up little resistance, and the government harshly restored order. Eight hundred men were executed, and sentences of exile and confiscation were imposed which destroyed northern feudalism and left the area economically depressed for many years.

Norfolk did not learn by experience. Released from the Tower he was at once involved in another plot. The aims of the Ridolfi Plot (1571) were broadly similar to those of the

N

Northern Rising, except that this time Mary was to replace Elizabeth on the throne. The plans were prepared by Ridolfi, a Florentine merchant-banker living in London. It was hoped that Alva might land men. Too many people knew what was intended, and soon Cecil had heard it all. Norfolk was rearrested and sentenced to death. Elizabeth delayed his execution, but parliament was pressing for Mary's death as well (the bishop of London set at the top of a list of things to be done, 'Forthwith to cut off the Scottish Queen's head') and in June 1572 Norfolk went to the scaffold. His death marked the final triumph of the Tudors over the reactionary aristocracy.

For the next eleven years Mary was moved from castle to castle in the north and the midlands. Then in 1583 came a third plot. By chance Walsingham uncovered the activities of Francis Throckmorton, a young Catholic gentleman serving as go-between for Mary and the Spanish ambassador, Mendoza. Throckmorton was taken and, under torture, confessed. Mendoza was ordered to leave the country, which he did early in 1584, protesting that he 'was born to conquer, not to subvert, kingdoms'. It was twenty years before there was another Spanish ambassador in London.

Once again parliament pressed for Mary's execution. 'I would,' burst out one member, 'have her hopeless to reign and headless to live.' The assassination of William the Silent in the summer of 1584 underlined the danger to Elizabeth. Three months later the Council drew up the Bond of Association. Those who signed it pledged themselves, in the event of an attempt on the Queen's life, to prevent the accession of anyone in whose interest the attempt had been made, and also to pursue that person to the death. Mary, though not named, was clearly aimed at. In 1585 the main provisions of this extraordinary agreement were embodied in an Act for the Queen's Surety.

Mary was now more strictly guarded and eventually lodged at Chartley in south Derbyshire. There the final plot was uncovered in 1586. Anthony Babington, a romantic young Catholic, unintentionally incriminated Mary. Their correspondence was smuggled in and out of the manor in beer barrels— which were tapped by Walsingham's agents—and Mary was persuaded to give her specific approval to a plot that included the assassination of Elizabeth. Babington was executed. In

October a special commission tried Mary and found her guilty. Parliament, which had been called in the same month, demanded 'that Jezebel may live no longer to persecute the prophets of God'. Elizabeth temporized: 'If I should say I would not do it, I should peradventure say that which I did not think or otherwise than it might be. If I should say I would do it, it were not fit in this place, nor at this time, although I did mean it. Wherefore I must desire you to hold yourselves satisfied with this answer answerless.' At last, early in 1587, the Queen signed the death warrant. Then she would not allow it to be sent. Eventually the council dispatched it without telling her, and Mary was executed on 7 February 1587. Elizabeth was furious, or pretended to be. The wretched Secretary of State, Davison, was sent to the Tower and fined 10,000 marks—but a year later he was released, the fine remitted, and his salary restored. In fact Elizabeth was no doubt both relieved and angry. Her Councillors had disobeyed her and she herself had never become reconciled to the execution of a Queen, yet that execution had resolved the impossible situation which had existed ever since Mary had fled to England eighteen years earlier. The new catholic claimant was a remote Spanish princess, in whose interests romantic young Englishmen were hardly likely to plot.

The European reaction was unfavourable, especially in France and Scotland. The former country remembered Mary's French connections and a flood of writings attacked Elizabeth, 'this singular bastard and shameless harlot'. In the north the Border with Scotland was closed for a time, but the Government had concluded the Treaty of Berwick in 1586, by which King James received a pension of £4,000 a year from England, and after a formal protest that cold King in due course professed himself satisfied.

France

The years around 1570 form a watershed in English foreign policy. The Bull and the Ridolfi Plot on the one hand, the seizure of the Spanish payships and the voyages of Hawkins on the other (see p. 186) marked the first stages in the drift to war and led to the ending of the old Spanish alliance that had been for so long a normal feature of English foreign policy. A natural consequence was a coming together of the traditional enemies, England and France, the beginning of an uneasy friendship which nevertheless became the rule rather than the exception for the next hundred years.

Circumstances drew Elizabeth and Catherine de Médicis towards agreement. Both feared Spain, both were by temperament *politique*. The years from 1570 to 1572 saw the ascendancy in France of the Huguenot Gaspard de Coligny. Walsingham was sent to Paris and soon plans were being made for the marriage of Elizabeth to Catherine's son Henri, Duke of Anjou. Cecil regarded the scheme as an insurance policy. If it took place, 'The Pope's malice with his bulls and excommunications . . . would be suspended and vanish in smoke'. It proved an empty political gesture. Henri was well known for a fanatical Catholic and as for Elizabeth, Leicester wrote to Walsingham: 'I am persuaded that her Majesty's heart is nothing inclined to marry at all.'

The scheme was quietly dropped, but the more substantial aim of a defensive league was achieved by the Treaty of Blois, signed in April 1572. Four months later the French Huguenots in Paris were cut down in the massacre of St. Bartholomew, and Walsingham wrote of the Catholics, 'I think it less peril to live with them as enemies than friends'. The treaty was apparently in ruins. Yet, in spite of religious tension and a temporary *rapprochement* with Spain, it was renewed in 1575. Neither France nor England could afford to neglect the other's offers of friendship.

Fresh religious wars tore France from 1572 to 1577. Henri succeeded to the French crown and Catherine's fourth son, the Duke of Alençon, became heir to the throne. He was a man of *politique* outlook, and it seemed possible that he might lead France into open war against Spain in the hope of seizing Spanish Flanders. From 1578 to 1584 he was 'protector' of the Netherlands; French soldiers fought there and French ships sailed against the Azores.

One aspect of this activity was the project for a marriage between Elizabeth and Alençon, a project first broached in the middle seventies and now actively canvassed in 1579 and again in 1581. It was another diplomatic move, pure farce really. The Queen was forty-five, Alençon was squat and pockmarked. Walsingham, as usual, disapproved: 'The gentleman sure is void of any good favour, besides the blemish of smallpox.'

Alençon's friend Simier was sceptical. He would not believe it, he said, 'until the curtain was drawn, the candles out, and Monsieur fairly in bed'. The marriage was unpopular in England. In 1579 the Puritan John Stubbs published *The Discovery of a Gaping Gulf whereinto England is like to be swallowed by another French marriage if the Lord forbid not the banns by letting her Majesty see the Sin and Punishment thereof*. He described Alençon as 'the old serpent himself in the form of a man come a second time to seduce the English Eve and to ruin the English paradise'. Stubbs lost his right hand as a punishment—and waved his hat with his left, crying 'long live the Queen'. The whole episode is characteristic of the complex character of Elizabethan national and religious feeling.

Alençon died in the Netherlands in 1584. Next year the French civil wars of religion broke out once more, and when in 1589 England and France at last joined forces, they were both already at war with Spain.

Spain

It is easy to antedate the final change in England's attitude to Spain. The men of Wyatt's rebellion, it is true, had cried out against the Spanish, but that had been mere insular prejudice. As late as 1575 England was still formally allied to Spain. In the deterioration of Anglo-Spanish relations three phases can be distinguished, a period of crisis from 1567 to 1572 followed by a temporary concord during the three years 1573–5, which in turn gave place to increasingly sharp encounters during the next ten years.

The Spanish friendship, a natural counterbalance to the traditional hostility of France, was an ancient one or it would not have survived for as long as it did. Now religious, economic and political differences were each in their various ways driving a wedge between the two countries. The Counter-Reformation was moving into its political phase. English opinion supported the growing crisis in the Netherlands and was alarmed by the arrival there of a large Spanish army under the Duke of Alva in 1567. It enjoyed the spectacle of that Spanish power being subsequently weakened, while at the same time thousands of immigrant Flemings strengthened the economic structure of England. On the other hand Spanish ambassadors encouraged Catholic dissidents in England. One of them, De Quadra, complained that 'Not a prisoner is arrested for State reasons without his being asked whether he had any conversation with me.'

To politico-religious antagonism was added economic rivalry. England was beginning to trespass on Spain's

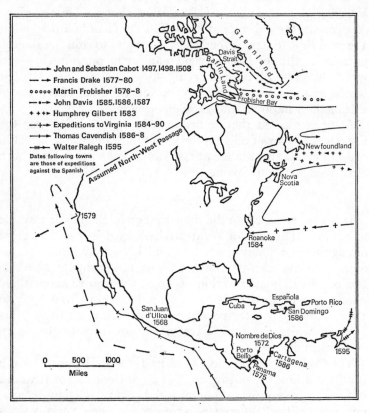

Legend within map:
John and Sebastian Cabot 1497, 1498, 1508
Francis Drake 1577–80
Martin Frobisher 1576–8
John Davis 1585, 1586, 1587
Humphrey Gilbert 1583
Expeditions to Virginia 1584–90
Thomas Cavendish 1586–8
Walter Ralegh 1595
Dates following towns are those of expeditions against the Spanish

Assumed North-West Passage
1579
Greenland
Davis Strait
Baffin Land
Frobisher Bay
Newfoundland
Nova Scotia
Roanoke 1584
Cuba
Española
Porto Rico
San Domingo 1586
San Juan d'Ulloa 1568
Nombre de Dios 1572
Porto Bello
Cartagena 1586
Panama 1575
1595

0 500 1000
Miles

THE NEW WORLD

Caribbean preserves. In 1562 and again in 1564 John Hawkins took slaves to Spanish America and brought back cargoes of gold, pearls, sugar and fish—making a profit of 60 per cent. Spanish colonists might be ready to trade, their government was not. A third expedition (1567–8) found the Spanish authorities waiting for them. At San Juan d'Ulloa, Hawkins was trapped and four of his seven ships were lost.   In 1572 Drake, who had been present at San Juan, led his own expedition against Nombre de Dios, striking at the land passage that was one of the weak points on the Spanish treasure-routes.   With the help of the Indians the town was surprised and sacked, but the triumph could not be repeated, as Oxenham and Barker discovered in 1575 and 1576.

There were pinpricks in other areas: piracy in the Channel, continual complaints about the treatment of English sailors in Spanish ports, a brisk economic tussle in the Netherlands (1563–4) with currency restrictions on both sides.   Economic rivalry, political ambitions and religious differences magnified each incident.

The crisis years 1568–73 saw the first major clash.   The news of the attack on Hawkins' ships reached England in September 1568.   In December Spanish ships carrying £85,000 from Genoese merchant-bankers to Alva's troops in the Netherlands put in to English ports.   Elizabeth took the money as a loan. This high-handed action strengthened her, hurt the Spanish and helped the Netherlanders.   Moreover, since the money did not become Spanish property until it reached its destination, it was not an act of war.   The Spanish retaliated. English trade was stopped and an embargo put on English property in the Netherlands.   De Spes gave encouragement to the Northern Rising and the Ridolfi plotters.   The Merchant Adventurers moved their staple to Hamburg, but neither merchants nor manufacturers could afford the trade war.   In 1573 economic relations with the Spanish Netherlands were restored, and next year reparations were fixed by the Treaty of Bristol.   The Spanish agreed to expel English refugees from the Netherlands while Elizabeth promised to close her ports to the Dutch rebels.   English merchants might trade with Antwerp and might practice their religion privately, and in return England engaged not to help William the Silent.

During the next four years there was something of a pause, and then the march to war continued again with increasing rapidity.   Papal forces, encouraged by Spain, landed in Ireland in 1579 and in the following year the first of the Jesuit missionaries set foot in England.   On the English side, Drake's circumnavigation of the world between 1577 and 1580 gave rise to a storm of Spanish protests.   In recent years raids on the Caribbean had found the Spanish well prepared, and it was a natural reaction to consider the possibilities of attacking the Pacific coast instead. In November 1577 Drake led three ships and one hundred and sixty men on an expedition, financed by shareholders who included the Queen, to raid the Pacific ports and then perhaps seize the isthmus or return by way of the North-West Passage, which was optimistically believed to open on to the Pacific in the neighbourhood of latitude forty north.

The ships passed through the Magellan Straits in the fast time of sixteen days, but then struck persistent northerlies. Drake in the *Golden Hind* was blown south of Cape Horn and the other ships were lost. It was not till November 1578 that he was able to sail north again. He raided the open ports of South America without difficulty, and ensured a profit for the expedition when he took a carrack-load of silver from the Spanish *Cacafuego*, but though he sailed to about latitude fifty north, he found no passage back. To retrace his steps would be dangerous so, after refitting in the neighbourhood of San Francisco and claiming the area for the Queen, Drake made instead for the Moluccas. He reached those islands in July 1579 and there he bought a cargo of cloves and made a sort of trade treaty with the Sultan of Ternate. The *Golden Hind* ran on the rocks and the cloves had to be jettisoned, but beyond that point the voyage home, by way of the Cape of Good Hope, was comparatively uneventful. Drake tied up at Plymouth in September 1580. As he stepped ashore he asked 'Is the Queen alive?'

The Queen, very much alive, was moving cautiously towards a more active policy. At about this time she wrote: 'We think it good for the King of Spain to be impeached both in Portugal and his Islands and also in the Low Countries, whereto we shall be ready to give such indirect assistance as shall not at once be a cause of war.'

The Netherlands

It was in the Netherlands that the unofficial struggle between Spain and England turned at last into official war. In 1569 William the Silent had licensed privateers to prey on Spanish shipping. In 1572 these 'Beggars of the Sea' were forbidden to use English ports in which to victual and refit, as had been their custom:

No manner of victual from henceforth shall pass to be carried to the sea for the victualling or relief of the fleet now serving the Prince of Orange.

The Beggars therefore seized Brill off the Dutch coast and, six days later, took the much more important town of Flushing. The States of Holland and Zeeland rose against the Spanish and the revolt of the Netherlands had begun.

Elizabeth's attitude to the States was complex.   As rebellious subjects she disapproved of them; as a thorn in Spain's side she was secretly pleased by their efforts.   As an area of enormous economic importance to England, it was essential to keep the English interests alive there; but as a dangerous foreign entanglement, open intervention in their affairs was undesirable.   French help for the States was to be encouraged on the grounds that it embroiled the Queen's enemies, actual and potential; on the other hand, French intervention might result in the area falling into French hands—a frightful consequence to be avoided at all costs.   Balancing these delicately conflicting considerations, Elizabeth and Cecil decided that they wished to see the Netherlands reconciled with Spain, but enjoying their old liberties and local independence.   Cecil thus summed up the matter early in 1578: 'Necessary for England that the State of the Low Countries should continue in their ancient government, without either subduing it to the Spanish nation or joining it to the Crown of France.   Profitable to have the State continue as it hath done whereby England may continue both peace and intercourse.'

This proved not to be possible.   Within a month of the seizure of Brill English volunteers were preparing to cross to the Low Countries.   Roger Williams (who fought on both sides) wrote: 'At this time there was a fair muster of Londoners before the Queen's Majesty at Greenwich.   Amongst the Londoners were divers captains and soldiers who had served, some in Scotland, some in Ireland, others in France.   And having nothing to do, with the contenance of some great men who favoured the cause and the small helps of the deputies of Flushing, Captain Thomas Morgan levied a fair company of three hundred strong; amongst whom were divers officers which had commanded before, with many gentlemen, at the least above one hundred, amongst which myself was one.'   From then on there were always volunteers, at first under Sir

Humphrey Gilbert, later under Sir John Norris, serving in the Netherlands.

In 1579 the Walloon south made peace with Spain. The seven northern States formed the Union of Utrecht, binding themselves to continue the struggle 'as one province'. The Union was inspired by William the Silent, who was outlawed by Philip in the following year. The States then issued an Act of Abjuration (1581) in which they declared that when a ruler ceases to defend his people from oppression and violence 'then he is no longer a prince but a tyrant, and they may not only disallow his authority, but legally proceed to the choice of another prince for their defence.' This they proceeded to do, offering supreme power to Alençon, an offer which helps to explain Elizabeth's courtship of the duke.

Alençon, perhaps fortunately for England, proved weak and treacherous. In 1583 he was persuaded by his advisers to attempt a *coup d'état* and seize the northern States. He failed, the French were discredited, and for the next eighteen months William was the real ruler in the north. Alençon died in May 1584, but in the following July William the Silent was assassinated. Once more there was a power vacuum in the Netherlands, and this time Elizabeth would have to fill it if the States were not to be in great danger of falling again under Spanish control. The Council discussed the matter in October: 'The arguments were very many on either side, on the one part to show the great peril and danger to her Majesty and her realm if the King of Spain should recover Holland and Zeeland as he had the other countries for lack of succour in seasonable time, either by the French King or the Queen's Majesty. And on the other side many difficulties were remembered to depend upon the succouring of them by her Majesty.'

Negotiations with the Dutch opened in November and there followed nine months of hard bargaining. Burghley had made it clear that the Queen would not accept the sovereignty of the States; she would help to a limited extent with men and money—but every penny must be repaid, and meanwhile she must have towns to hold as guarantees. Meanwhile the Spanish pressure increased, Brussels fell in February 1585 and Antwerp in August. Next month the Treaty of Greenwich was signed, and open war with Spain had come at last. There was not to be peace again until after the Queen's death.

The Queen's Forces

On land the Queen's forces were limited, both in quality and quantity. The feudal levy was out of date, mercenaries were expensive to hire and often unreliable, volunteers proved enthusiastic but unprofessional. Henry VII had established the yeomen of the guard; Henry VIII had created the Honourable Artillery Company. Neither was suitable for warfare on the grand scale. There remained the militia, regulated by the acts passed in 1549 and—the more important—in 1558. These made provision for the holding of musters throughout the country and laid down the scale of equipment which those summoned must provide, based on their position in society and their wealth. In normal times these musters were held four times a year. The unit of administration was the county; the officials involved were the J.P., the sheriff, and the lord-lieutenant. The commission of the lord-lieutenant enabled him to call up men in his area, to array, test and arm them, to lead them against the foe, to administer martial law, and in general 'to repress, subdue, slay, kill and put to execution of death these enemies by all ways and means'. In the years after 1587 between one-third and one-half of the Council were lords-lieutenant. The lord-lieutenant was normally in charge of a group of counties and during the war years his office became very important indeed, but the prime mover was the J.P. and, in this as in other matters, much depended on his efficiency or corruptibility.[1] The final organization was based on the Commission of 1573. Men between the ages of sixteen and sixty were liable to be mustered. Legally they might not be required to serve overseas, but in practice they were sent abroad. Not all those mustered were called up. In the 1575 muster 183,000 men were called in 37 counties, of whom about 12,000 were selected for special training (the 'trained bands'), while a further 63,000 were equipped but not trained and the remainder were not used. Organization developed in a haphazard, pragmatic way. About the year 1572 the regiment began to appear as a unit designed to fill the gap between the company under the command of a captain, and the general. At the head of the regiment was the colonel and under his

---

[1] The joys and difficulties of recruitment have been described by Shakespeare in *Henry IV Part II*, Act III, sc. ii.

control were something between 750 and 1,000 men, divided into seven or eight companies.

The company contained five types of soldier, one of which was non-existent. For instance, in the French campaign of 1589, it was laid down that a company should be composed of 50 pikemen, 15 musketeers, 15 calivermen (the caliver was a light gun with a shorter range but a more rapid fire-power than a musket), 10 halberdiers and 10 'dead pays'—soldiers who had never formed part of the army but whose pay was designed to supplement that of the captain and other gentlemen.[1] The firearm had already conquered the longbow and it was in process of eclipsing the pike; a decade later, in 1601, a company contained 64 firearms to 36 other weapons.

The contemporary Robert Barret described the ideal soldier as follows:

> . . . the eyes, quick, lively and piercing; the head and countenance upright; the breast broad and strong; the shoulders large; the arms long; the fingers strong and sinewy; the belly thin; the ribs large; the thigh big; the leg full; and the foot lean. . . .

It was an optimistic picture.

There was no regular uniform, though on the whole one levy from one county would be dressed at least approximately alike. For overseas service troops were provided with clothing twice a year. The summer kit for a soldier in the Netherlands consisted—in theory—of a canvas doublet lined with white linen; a pair of breeches of Kentish broadcloth, linen-lined; two shirts and collars of linen; two pairs of leather shoes; two pairs of woollen stockings; and a hat. In addition each soldier carried the equipment suitable to his work. Thus the archer had his longbow (a good quality one cost 6s. 8d., compared with 40s. for a musket) and arrows; a steel cap; a jerkin of overlapping metal plates; a shooting-glove and a leather bracer to protect his bow arm; a sword not more than a yard long; and a dagger about a foot long.

The archer, though, was already obsolescent. Military methods developed in the Dutch campaigns were changing the pattern of war. Drillbooks appeared, very complicated affairs. It required approximately 160 words of command to carry out the manœuvre, 'Shoulder your pikes and march', from the

---

[1] Sometimes 'dead pay' referred to the pay of soldiers who *had* died on service.

initial order, 'all the pikers of the front rank falling back with their right feet almost a foot behind their left' to the triumphant conclusion 'and so they must all with great silence and with a grave soldierlike grace, march'. The application of mathematics to warfare led to the appearance of textbooks like that of Thomas Digges, *An Arithmeticall Warlike Treatise named Stratiocos* (1571), which contained such questions as

If 500 pioneers can, in ten hours, cast up 400 rods of trench, I demand how many labourers, will be able with a like trench in three hours to entrench a camp of 2,300 rods compass?

The answer provided was $9,416\frac{2}{3}$ pioneers!

What did this growing, changing organism achieve? Part of the answer is contained in Chapter IX. Strategic decisions were taken by the Queen on the advice of her Council, and for them she must bear the final responsibility. At the lower levels, those of everyday recruitment and administration, the army was riddled with 'deceits and strategems' which, as always, were borne ultimately on the shoulders of the common soldier, and it is hardly surprising that the desertion rate ran at about 25 per cent. Yet those who served and survived received small thanks:

In the time of wars, they spare not in their country's behalf, to forsake their wife, children, father, mother, brother, sister, to leave their friends, and only betake themselves against their enemies: contented to yield themselves to continual watch, ward, fasting, hunger, thirst, cold, heat, travail, toil, over hills, woods, deserts, wading through rivers, where many sometimes lose their lives by the way, lying in the field, in rain, wind, frost and snow, adventuring against the enemy, the lack of limbs, the loss of life, making their bodies a fence and a bulwark against the shot of the cannon; but the wars being once finished, and that there is no need of them, how be they rewarded, how be they cherished, what account is there made of them, what other things gain they than slander, misreport, false impositions, hatred and despite! (Barnaby Rich, *Allarme to England, foreshewing what perilles are procured where the people live without regarde of martiall lawe,* 1578.)

When all the obstacles are taken into account, the size of the English land forces is surprising. It has been estimated that the numbers of men sent abroad (not all at the same time) was:

naval expeditions, 17,000; the Netherlands, 20,000; France, 20,000; Ireland, 25,000.

The raising of a naval force presented fewer problems. A survey in 1577 found that there were 135 merchantmen of 100 tons and over in port, of which 44 were in the Thames estuary, 14 at Newcastle, 10 at Hull, 8 at Bristol and 6 at Plymouth. Merchant ships with sailors already trained and expert in the craft of seamanship could be used in warfare and three-quarters of the ships that fought the Armada were of this type, though the pattern of the man-of-war was becoming more specialised. In addition there was the royal navy. Elizabeth inherited 22 ships of 100 tons or over and bequeathed 29 to her successor, James I. The oar-propelled galley and the tubby merchantman or carrack with a proportion of length to beam of only one to two, were neither of them suitable for northern seas and Atlantic storms. The galleon was an Italian development, but its construction was taken up with most enthusiasm by those countries with an oceanic seaboard. This new ship was narrower, its length about three times its beam, and carried more sails. By the seventies the English were making their own improvements to this basic type. The leading spirits were Hawkins, created Treasurer of the Navy in 1577, and Drake. A few big ships of 800 to 1,000 tons were built, but the middle-sized galleons of about 500 tons, ships such as *Revenge*,[1] were the most efficient. These ships were quick to manoeuvre and were armed with the culverin, which was smaller, faster to fire, and had a longer range than the heavy cannon. The smallest ships were the pinnaces, fast ocean-going scouts of which the navy had eighteen by 1588. Sir Walter Ralegh described other improvements:

> . . . in my own time the shape of our English ships hath been greatly bettered. It is not long since the striking of the top-mast (a wonderful ease to great ships both at sea and har-bour) hath been devised, together with the chain-pump, which takes up twice as much water as the ordinary did.

Hawkins greatly cut down waste and corruption to such an extent that the cost of upkeep was actually reduced from £10,000 a year to £6,000. New and efficient, the English

---

[1] *Revenge*'s proportions were 92 feet by 32 feet.

navy was nevertheless, like its contemporaries, handicapped in certain fundamental ways. Storms would always scatter a fleet, nor could ships be kept at sea for more than about eight weeks without refitting.

Living conditions were bad, sanitation non-existent, water soon foul and food notoriously bad. Naval rations were theoretically a pound of biscuit, a gallon of beer, and two pounds of salt beef a day for three days each week; for three days the beef was replaced by two ounces of butter, four ounces of cheese and four ounces of dried and salted fish, and on the seventh day the crew should have received instead a pound of bacon and a pound of peas. In practice the victuallers were unscrupulously dishonest and Hakluyt regarded them as 'Many times the only overthrowers of the voyage; for the company thinking themselves to be stored with four or six months victuals, upon survey they find their bread, beef, or drink short, yea perhaps all, and so are forced to seek home. . . .'

In consequence many more men died of disease than ever suffered at the hands of the enemy. Richard Hawkins thought that scurvy alone, 'the plague of the seas', had accounted for ten thousand deaths in twenty years and it is certainly true that English losses in the Armada campaign were about one hundred men killed in action and several thousand killed by disease.

Fighting ships were commanded by a Captain, originally a landsman who left the working of the ship to the Master, but by the end of the reign himself experienced in navigation. Other officers included the Mates, the Boatswain (responsible for the sailors and the rigging), the Coxswain, Steward, Purser, and four Quarter Masters. The monthly wages in the Queen's ships ranged from 10s for a seaman to £2 1s. 8d. for the Master. The total number of seamen in the navy was probably never more than about twenty thousand.

Naval tactics were changing as the shape of ships altered and the efficiency of guns increased. Hawkins' streamlined ships carried improved sails and rigging. The effect of his improvements was that the English ships lay lower in the water than those of the Spanish, were on the whole faster, and were more manoeuvreable. In particular, they could sail nearer to the wind.

Henry VIII had had portholes cut in the side of his ships

close to the waterline, from which heavier guns might fire in unison. By so doing he made possible the broadside. At the time of the Armada both English and Spanish ships had gun ports. The Spanish intention was to fire at the English masts and sails, thus immobilizing the ships, while the English tended to fire at the hulls of their opponents. Philip II wrote to Medina Sidonia:

> It must be borne in mind that the enemy's object will be to fight at long distance, in consequence of his advantage in artillery. . . . The aim of our men, on the contrary, must be to bring him to close quarters and grapple with him. For your information a statement is sent to you describing the way in which the enemy employs his artillery, in order to deliver his fire low, and sink his opponent's ships.

The Spanish ships were equipped with a larger number of cannon than the English and could deliver a broadside of perhaps twice the weight, but the English had the advantage in the matter of range, carrying about three times as many of the long-range culverins as the Spanish.

Privateering, too, played its part in the war against Spain and developed in extent and importance until Thomas Nashe could write in 1599 that it was 'a common traffic'. Ports from London south, and west to Bristol, were mainly involved, but as the years went by the proportion of larger ships grew and the dominance of London became more marked.[1]

FURTHER READING

C. G. Cruickshank, *Elizabeth's Army*, O.U.P., 1966
J. A. Williamson, *The Age of Drake*, Black, 1946
— *Hawkins of Plymouth*, Black, 1949

[1] See p. 302 below.

IX · ENGLAND AT WAR
1585–1604

Introduction

THE menace of war had hung over Elizabeth's head for twenty-seven years. In 1585 the thread snapped, and for the last eighteen years of her reign England was at war—the longest encounter between the end of the Hundred Years' War (1453) and the final wars against Louis XIV (1689).

There were three areas of conflict. The first was at home, where there were several perils. Until her execution in 1587 Mary, Queen of Scots, remained a focus for discontent (see pp. 179–82). There was always the threat of a foreign invasion—a threat that did not end with the defeat of the Armada. Finally, there was Ireland, the Achilles' heel of Elizabeth's dominions, where men and money drained away and where even the Spaniards obtained eventually a temporary foothold.

The second area was that of the high seas, where actions took place that ranged in scope from isolated privateering through commercial piracy to full-scale naval expeditions and in scope from the narrow Channel to the round world itself.

Thirdly, on the continent English land forces were engaged—with very varying degrees of success—in the Netherlands (1585–1604) and in France (1589–95).

The total effort involved, although quite small compared with Spain's exertions against her various enemies, represented a great strain on England's resources. It cost a lot of money. Elizabeth was forced to borrow abroad and to sell crown lands at home in order to finance her efforts, while every one of the six parliaments called during the war years was required to vote subsidies.

England was weak in manpower. Her population was probably smaller than that of the United Provinces and certainly less than half that of Spain itself and there was no standing army. She suffered from her customary lack of great commanders on land, while at sea the best captains were dead by the time the war was half over (Grenville, 1591; Frobisher, 1594; Drake and Hawkins, 1595).

The First Stage of the War, 1585–8

William the Silent had been assassinated in July 1584, and in December of the same year France had entered the most critical period of her civil wars when the Catholic League concluded the Treaty of Joinville with Philip II by which Henri of Navarre was to be excluded from the succession and Philip was to pay a monthly subsidy to the League. Soon an eighth civil war began in France. That country would be in no position henceforth to support the revolt in the Netherlands and the time had clearly come for England to intervene there.

In August 1585 the Spanish took Antwerp. Gilbert Talbot, writing to his uncle the Earl of Shrewsbury, perceptively commented: '. . . it is thought that her Majesty shall be forced of very necessity to send some great person with great forces presently for the defence of Holland and Zeeland, or else they will, out of hand, follow Antwerp'. The Dutch and English agreed on terms. By the Treaty of Greenwich (1585) Elizabeth accepted a partial interest in their fate. She agreed to provide a force of men in return for the ports of Flushing and Brill, which were to be held in pawn by her until her expenses were repaid. By the end of the year Leicester was in the Netherlands at the head of an army of six thousand foot and a thousand horse.

The campaign was a failure. Leicester accepted from the States the title of 'Governor and Captain-General', for which he was roundly censured by the Queen, wasted his resources to the tune of £236,000 a year, and quarrelled with his most experienced captain, Sir John Norris. He did, however, succeed in defending the eastern flank of the States against the offensive of the Spanish commander, the Prince of Parma. After eleven months he returned to England. Next year the Earl went back with a fresh force of five thousand men and another £30,000. He quarrelled again with Norris and also with William's son, Maurice of Nassau; he failed to relieve Sluys; Deventer, the key to the eastern flank, was betrayed to the enemy; and in November 1587 the Queen recalled him once more, this time for good.

It was not only in the Netherlands that Spain and England came to grips in 1585. In May Philip ordered the seizure of all English vessels then in Spanish harbours. In retaliation

Elizabeth allowed Drake to sail with nearly thirty ships and over two thousand men, financed by a joint-stock company to which the Queen herself contributed £1,000. His aim was to catch the treasure fleet at the Azores or, failing that, to raid the Caribbean. Drake calmly completed his fitting out in the Spanish port of Vigo. He missed the treasure fleet, put in at the Cape Verde Islands, and then made for the West Indies. There he sacked San Domingo and Cartagena. The expedition returned having failed to make a profit, but having exerted considerable political pressure. Spain's credit had been damaged and the rate of interest at which she could borrow was raised by the Italian bankers, while valuable stores and equipment had also to be diverted from Europe to the defence of the Spanish Main. The Caribbean voyage (1585-6) had perhaps helped the Dutch rebels more than Leicester's expedition had done.

Philip decided that the Enterprise of England, the *Empresa*, must be put in hand. Schemes for an invasion had been in the air for a decade. The acquisition of Portugal in 1580 had given Spain for the first time a suitable Atlantic base from which to launch her fleet, and had added to that fleet ten first-class Portuguese galleons. English actions in the New World and in the Netherlands had made the matter urgent, while the execution of Mary was soon to remove any doubts that Spain herself might not enjoy the profit from a successful invasion. All things pointed to the same conclusion. The war should be carried into the enemy's camp. Santa Cruz, admiral-designate, wrote to the King: 'It will be no small advantage to your Majesty that the game should be played out on the English table, just as she has tried to make Flanders and France the arena.' Then there were setbacks: the original plan of a direct invasion proved too expensive; British control of the Baltic route and Drake's Caribbean raid created difficulties of respectively, supply and credit.

Meanwhile Elizabeth, thanks to Walsingham's intelligence system, knew fairly accurately how Spanish schemes were developing. In 1587 two counter-measures were taken; one proved a failure, the other a success. In the Netherlands Leicester's second expedition achieved little. In the summer Drake was sent to strike at the Spanish preparations. He caught Cadiz unawares and burnt thirty ships there. Then he established a base at Sagres in Portugal and for two months harried the Spanish shipping. Finally he sailed to the Azores and captured a carrack, the cargo of which (£140,000) more than covered the cost of his activities. It was a faultless operation which further weakened Philip's prestige and delayed the *Empresa*. The delay was significant. When at last the Armada sailed the staves of its water barrels were rotten, for the seasoned ones had been destroyed, and its admiral, Medina Sidonia, was a last-minute replacement for Santa Cruz, who had died in the spring of 1588.

. In the Armada campaign there was not much to choose between the two fleets. Each consisted of about fifty powerful ships and eighty smaller ones. In general the Spanish ships were less manœuverable, they were lumbered with soldiers, and their guns had a shorter range than those of the English. The tactical skill with which they kept their formation as they sailed up the Channel was considerable, but Medina Sidonia suffered a serious strategic handicap. He was forbidden to try to capture an English port. His instructions were to rendezvous with Parma and to convoy the latter's army, embarked in barges, from the Netherlands to England. Then he would guard Parma's communications. The plan was economical and not impossible to execute, but it had serious drawbacks. It was too inflexible; it was too slow, there could be no element of surprise; it assumed exact co-ordination between the movements of Parma and those of the fleet; it depended on finding a suitable port in the Netherlands. Flushing, the best, was in English hands. Philip hoped to use Dunkirk and Nieuport, but neither of these was an adequate deep-water port.

Throughout the campaign the pattern of events was largely determined by the weather. In May the Spanish fleet set sail, met heavy winds, and was forced to put into Corunna and refit. In March Drake had urged the Queen 'to seek God's enemies and Her Majesty's wherever they may be found . . . for that with fifty sail of shipping we shall do more good upon their own coast than a great many more will do here at home', and three times during the summer the English fleet, now assembled at Plymouth under the command of Lord Howard of Effingham, Lord High Admiral (1585–1619), put to sea only to be blown back to harbour. At last, on 19 July, the Armada was sighted off the Lizard.   The two fleets remained in touch for a fortnight, until the English turned for home after following the enemy as far as the Firth of Forth.   During most of this time the average speed of the antagonists was not more than about three knots.   From this slow-motion engagement six actions stand out.

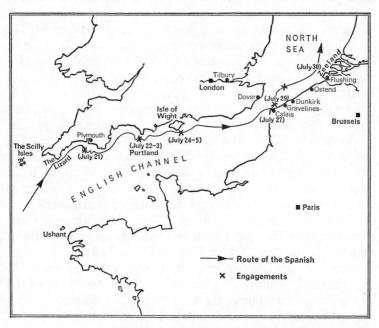

THE ARMADA CAMPAIGN

The Armada, sailing before a crisp south-west wind, had at first the weather-gauge.   The wind that drove it forward penned the English in their harbour to leeward.   It was essential to remove this tactical advantage before the Spanish were in sight.   Fortunately the tide was ebbing from Plymouth Sound that evening and with its aid all through the night the English fleet was warped out of the Sound.   Next morning Howard had fifty-four ships off the Eddystone and as the Armada came up he slipped to windward and took the weather-gauge.   It was a piece of efficient seamanship of some importance, for the wind blew from the west for the next nine days.

If English skill had won the first point, Spanish discipline scored the next two. It was not Medina Sidonia's business to fight, but to take his fleet intact to a port within reach of Parma's army, and this he achieved. By 21 July he had formed his fleet into a great crescent with its wings pointing back towards the English. It was a powerful defensive pattern, for to attack the centre was impossible, and the most powerful ships guarded the wings. The Spanish held this formation, very expertly, for seven days as they sailed east up the Channel. They moved, an impressive floating army, slowly but steadily towards their uncertain rendezvous, while the English fleet nimbly pounced on stragglers and continually harassed the enemy. General but indecisive actions took place off Portland (July 22–3) and again off the Isle of Wight (July 24–5), but these failed to halt the Spanish progress and not one Spanish ship had yet been sunk by English gunfire.

The fourth action took place at Calais. Medina Sidonia had still to find a port in which to harbour his fleet. On 27 July he ran out his anchors in Calais Roads, only thirty miles from Dunkirk where Parma should be waiting. He wrote to the Duke: 'I am anchored here, two leagues from Calais with the enemy's fleet on my flank. They can cannonade me whenever they like, and I shall be unable to do much harm in return. If you can send me forty or fifty flyboats of your fleet I can, with their help, defend myself here until you are ready to come out.' Meanwhile Howard, offshore, had been joined by the thirty-five ships under Lord Henry Seymour which had been guarding the Dover-Dunkirk narrows.

During the night of 28 July the English prepared eight fireships of from 90 to 200 tons. These were gutted, filled with everything inflammable, their guns double-shotted. Then they were sent drifting on the tide into the Spanish fleet. The Spanish had suffered in 1585 from 'the hellburner of Antwerp', a ship filled with explosives, a floating bomb which had had a fallout a mile in diameter. Now they slipped or cut their cables and stood out to sea, their formation lost. It was the turning-point.

Next morning the two fleets engaged in battle off Gravelines, halfway between Calais and Dunkirk. The fighting lasted eight hours. At least fifty Spanish ships were committed and eight were lost as the English, still with the wind at their backs, forced the enemy inexorably towards the Flemish sandbanks.

That night Howard wrote to Walsingham, 'Their force is wonderful great and strong; and yet we pluck their feathers little and little.' On the night of 30 July the wind backed from northwest to west-south-west and the Spanish fleet was able to stand away from the Zeeland Sands. The Spanish thought it a miracle, but it drove them north towards Scotland, the English still in pursuit. Drake wrote: 'We have the army of Spain before us and mind with the grace of God to wrestle a pull with him. There was never anything pleased me better than the seeing of the enemy flying with a southerly wind northward. I doubt not, ere it be long, so to handle the matter with the Duke of Sidonia as he shall wish himself at St. Mary Port among his orange trees.'

Off the Firth of Forth the English, short of food and ammunition, turned back, leaving the Spanish fleet to sail before the storm round the north of Scotland. By the time it got back to Spain the Armada had lost about fifty ships, including twenty-five first-rate vessels. The largest group of these were those which sank off the Irish coast or ran on the rocks there.

Throughout England preparations had been made for an invasion: the county musters had been raised; the beacons prepared; the army encamped at Tilbury under the command of Leicester. Foreigners were at a discount, the protestant Petruccio Ubaldini wrote ruefully, 'It is easier to find flocks of white crows than one Englishman (and let him believe what he will about religion) who loves a foreigner.' On 9 August the Queen visited Tilbury and spoke to the army:

My loving people, we have been persuaded by some that are careful for our safety, to take heed how we commit ourselves to armed multitudes, for fear of treachery. But I assure you, I do not desire to live to distrust my faithful and loving people. Let tyrants fear. I have always so behaved myself that, under God, I have placed my chiefest strength and safeguard in the loyal hearts and good will of my subjects; and therefore I am come amongst you as you see, at this time, not for my recreation and disport, but being resolved, in the midst and heat of the battle, to live or die amongst you all, and to lay down for my God and for my kingdom and for my people, my honour and my blood, even in the dust. I know I have the body of a weak and feeble woman, but I have the heart and stomach of a king, and of a king of England too, and think it foul scorn that Parma or

Spain or any prince of Europe should dare to invade the borders of my realm; to which, rather than dishonour shall grow by me, I myself will take up arms, I myself will be your general, judge, and rewarder of every one of your virtues in the field.

'Incredible it is,' wrote Camden, 'how much she encouraged the hearts of her captains and soldiers by her speech to them.'

The Armada had been destroyed by superior naval skill, by the shortcomings of the Spanish plan, by the weather. One feels that, though the Spanish had not come very near to victory, Howard might—as might Jellicoe—have lost the war in an afternoon, and that the success of the fireships played an important part in the Spanish failure. It had proved a decisive victory, yet what exactly had been decided? England was saved, but triumph at sea did not bring peace. There was a long haul ahead, for the country was only a sixth of the way through the struggle and later Armadas sailed, though none came as near success as the first had done. The immediate importance of the defeat lay in its effect on the minds of men. The English were confirmed in their belief in their own superiority; those parts of Europe that were opposed to Spain took heart. Perhaps, men thought, there was some truth in the view that Spanish power was more apparent than real, that Spain was 'a colossus stuffed with clouts'. Cecil and Elizabeth were masters of the art of propaganda and the failure of Spain was shown as a triumph for protestantism. At St. Paul's there was a service of thanksgiving: *Afflavit Deus et dissipati sunt*— God blew and they were scattered. Elizabeth condemned the Spanish plan to James of Scotland as a 'tyrannical, proud and brainsick attempt', while Cecil produced a pamphlet for European consumption: *A Pack of Spanish Lies sent abroad in the world, . . . Now ripped up, unfolded, and by just examination condemned . . .* In parallel columns were printed, first Spanish statements, then the facts. The Spanish had claimed that the English lost sixty-two ships. Cecil replied that on the contrary the English had

. . . chased the Spanish as a brace of greyhounds would a herd of deer. The Spanish ships were beaten, spoiled, burnt, sunk, some in the main seas afore Dunkirk, some afore Flushing and the rest chased away . . . until they were chased out of all the English seas, and forced then to run a violent course about Scotland and Ireland . . . Why durst any report that twenty-two English ships were sunk and forty taken when in truth there was not one sunk or taken.

The importance of the English victory lay in the blow to Spain's reputation and in the consequent encouragement given to Spain's enemies.

The Second Stage of the War, 1589–1604

The dispatch of the Armada and its defeat was in certain ways the peak of the war between England and Spain, yet that war had barely begun. Neither country was to achieve such heights again. Each did something to encourage the rebellious subjects of the other—Spain in England and Ireland, Elizabeth in the Netherlands—and both tried to tip in their own favour the balance of forces in a divided France. The countries in which they intervened directly were decisively affected, while the protagonists themselves drew nearer, not to victory, but to bankruptcy.

In France the death of Catherine de Médicis and the assassination of the duc de Guise and Henri III (1589) had simplified the complex situation in the country. The Huguenot Henri of Navarre had now the clearest title to the throne. The Catholic League however put forward the claims of Philip or, alternatively, of his children by the French princess Elizabeth de Valois. Spanish forces occupied parts of southern Brittany and Elizabeth I at once sent men and money to help Henri (1589). The English contribution was considerable in scale, but limited in achievement. Five expeditions were dispatched, £380,000 was spent, some 20,000 men were involved (of whom about half never returned), but action was limited to opposing the Spanish in Brittany and the League in Normandy, and to garrisoning Dieppe and other ports on the Channel coast in order to ensure that they did not fall into the hands of Spain. Henri received large subsidies from Elizabeth, 'such aids as never any king hath done the like to any other'. The king won decisive victories at Arques (1589) and at Ivry (1590) and then in 1593 he took the critical step of becoming a Catholic. In the following year he entered Paris. By the treaty of Greenwich (1596) England, France and the United Provinces formed a Triple League against Spain, but two

years later France withdrew from the war, making peace with
Spain by the Treaty of Vervins (1598).

After the defeat of the Armada English forces garrisoned
Brill and Flushing, and successfully held Bergen-op-Zoom,
which controlled one of the mouths of the Scheldt.   Yet Spanish
ambitions in the north were finally defeated by the United
Provinces themselves rather than by English troops, though
English men and money helped to keep the resistance going.

There was continual friction between English and Dutch.
In 1589 the cautious Walsingham wrote: 'I wish our fortune and
theirs were not so strictly tied as it is, so as we cannot well untie
without great hazard,' and next year Burghley complained,
'No enemy can more displeasure [us] than they do by their daily
trade to Spain.   In very truth her Majesty is herewith tempted
greatly both to repent herself of aiding them and to attempt how
to be quit of them.'

Two Netherlanders were primarily responsible for the success
of the United Provinces.   Oldenbarneveldt, the Advocate of
Holland, disposed of the wealth and influence of that province,
which was equal in amount to that of the other six put together,
while Maurice of Nassau, the elected Stadtholder and Captain-
General, cleared the Spanish from the north in a series of
campaigns which began with a success at Breda in 1590 and
culminated in a brilliant victory at Turnhout in 1597.   By that
date the Spanish had lost any chance which they might once
have had of regaining the northern provinces, and though the
war dragged on until the Twelve Years' Truce of 1609, Maurice
found it impossible to make any great impression south of the
great rivers.

The English troops were commanded by Sir Francis Vere,
a cool, foxy, tough professional.   His men fought alongside
those of Maurice and played their part in the victories of
Turnhout and Nieuport (1600) and in the defence of Ostend
(1603).   In 1598 Elizabeth concluded a second treaty with
the United Provinces by which they agreed to pay the cost of
the English force.   Six years later, in 1604, James I made
peace with Spain.   England refused to recognize the Dutch
as rebels and reserved the right to continue trading with them,
while she also obtained the privilege of trading freely with the
Spanish possessions in Europe.

Legend:
- Ecclesiastical Territories
- Boundary of the Spanish Netherlands in 1559
- The United Provinces Southern Boundary in 1579

THE NETHERLANDS

English support had played its part in stiffening Dutch resistance during the critical years between the assassination of William and the emergence of Maurice. Intervention had proved a heavy drain on Elizabeth's resources, costing altogether over £1,500,000, but in the end England had successfully maintained her economic and political interests in the area.

England supported Dutch rebels; Spain attempted to support Irish ones and to turn Ireland into an English Netherlands. Events there were often decided by the special nature of the area (see p. 28). The island was not a foreign country, it was a foreign society, so strange to English eyes that in the early seventeenth century a retired lord deputy could write: '. . . before these last wars it was as inaccessible to strangers as the Kingdom of China.'

Ireland was the home of a Celtic community in decline. The question was not how were the Irish to be protestantized, or colonized, but how they were to be turned into civilized Tudors. It was a question which the Elizabethans were not equipped to answer. Here was a country where time had stood still, a society like that of the Dark Ages in Britain. The Irishman lived 'together with his beast in one house, in one room, in one bed'. The peoples' reactions were those of the Iceland of the sagas. Edmund Spenser described how, 'At the execution of a notable traitor at Limerick, I saw an old woman, which was his foster-mother, take up his head whilst he was quartered and suck up all the blood that ran thereout, saying that the earth was not worthy to drink it. . . .'

A religious division was added to the older differences. The Catholic church was in a state of decay but soon, under the stimulus of the Counter-Reformation and in reaction against foreign English pressures, it recovered and came to be identified with the national determination to maintain Irish independence.

Sixteenth-century Englishmen, themselves living in a country where life had become notably more suave in the last generation, could find no point of contact with such people. Their attempt to subdue Ireland took three forms; the suppression of rebellion, the extension of direct government control, and the encouragement of individuals prepared to 'plant' the country with English colonists.

In 1558 Ireland consisted of four main parts. The Pale had been enlarged under Mary by the addition of two new counties, King's County and Queen's County, carved out of the tribal lands to the west. From this area the government derived a paltry revenue of £5,000 a year. To the south the land was controlled by the Earl of Ormonde (Butler), a lord who was comparatively loyal. The south-west was dominated by the earl of Desmond (Fitzgerald) and was a permanent centre of disaffection. Connaught and Ulster were even more inaccessible and savage. In Ulster the great chieftains were the earls of Tyrconnel (O'Donnell) and Tyrone (O'Neill).

From the government's point of view, the easiest course of

action would have been to leave Ireland alone. Various factors made this impossible. The Tudor break with Rome and the Spanish war involved England in the attempted conquest of the country. Then, too, the Elizabethan desire for order was affronted by the Irish muddle, while the Elizabethan lust for profit from settlement, colony or trade hoped to find an outlet in the Irish plantations. The outcome was that Ireland, which had been ungoverned and heathen, became unwillingly English in government and ardently Catholic in religion—a combination that was in later centuries to prove disastrous.

The Irish were well-equipped to carry on guerrilla warfare. The terrain could conceal the war-band, and the Irish mantle—'a fit house for an outlaw, a meet bed for a rebel, and an apt cloak for a thief' Spenser called it—could hide the individual. In many parts malaria, to which the local inhabitants were accustomed, killed the stranger. With these advantages, Irish unity might have spelt English defeat, but ancient feuds made that impossible, the Irish being 'great traitors to one another', as a Spanish ambassador observed.

By the middle of the reign it could be said 'there is no land in the world of so continual war within himself, nor of so great shedding of Christian blood, nor of so great robbing, spoiling, preying and burning, nor of so great wrongful extortion continually, as Ireland.' The consequences were, for the Irish, terrible. An English observer described the effects of starvation on the people, 'They looked like anatomies of death; they did eat the dead carrion and one another soon after, insomuch as the very carcasses they spared not to scrape out of their graves; . . .' The detailed story is greatly complex, but four rebellions demand mention; those of O'Neill (1559–66), Fitzgerald (1569–72 and 1579–83), and—the most dangerous— that of Tyrone (1594–1603).

The first grew out of a disputed succession to the earldom of Tyrone in Ulster. Sean O'Neill, a great, savage man, was successful at first, but when, encouraged by this success, he began to look to France and Rome for help against the English, the Lord Deputy Sir Henry Sidney combined with O'Neill's old enemy Hugh O'Donnell to defeat him. O'Neill was killed by the Antrim Scots and his son, Hugh O'Neill, who had been taken to England in 1562, was brought up at the English court.

Soon there was trouble in the south.   The Lord Deputy had
begun an attempt to anglicize and plant the area and this led
to a rebellion headed by James Fitzgerald.   He appealed
unsuccessfully to Spain for help.   Defeated in 1572, Fitzgerald left the island in 1575, and went to Rome.   In 1577 he
attempted to return with a force of eighty Spaniards and
Portuguese, but got no farther than St. Malo.   Next year with
the help of Gregory XIII a larger expedition was equipped
and placed under the command of the English exile, Sir
Thomas Stukeley.   Instead, at Lisbon, Stukeley diverted the
force to Sebastian of Portugal, who was preparing to sail
against the Moors.   In 1579 Fitzgerald tried again.   This
time the expedition, which included papal representatives,
reached Ireland and seized Smerwick on the Dingle peninsula.
Fitzgerald himself was killed, but a relief force of Italians and
Spaniards arrived in 1580 and held the area until the end of
the year when they were defeated and put to death by Lord
Grey de Wilton.   The affair had cost Elizabeth over £250,000.
It was the end of the only military effort attempted by the
Papacy itself.

Hugh O'Neill had been in England from 1562 to 1576.   He
had grown up a serious, cautious, intelligent leader, who knew
the minds and methods of the English.   When he returned to
Ireland he moved almost imperceptibly from loyalty to
rebellion.   In 1595 he possessed a large and—by Irish ·stan-
dards—very well-trained army of 6,000 men.   For two years
he was barely held in check by old Sir John Norris, who died at
the close of 1597.   Next year an English force was cut to pieces
at the battle of the Yellow Ford on the Blackwater River in
Ulster.   It was a triumph for the classic tactics of guerrilla
fighters—never to meet the enemy in open country but instead
to ambush columns on the march and strike hard whilst they
were changing formation to meet the attack.   At the Yellow
Ford the English lost 1,300 men, one in four of their total
force.   It was the worst defeat ever experienced by the English
in Ireland and the south and west rose when the news reached
those parts, while in London Elizabeth stormed at the thought
that 'a bare bush kern' should have humiliated her.   The
Venetian ambassador wrote home that Ireland was the
Englishman's grave, a sentiment that was to be often heard in
later centuries.

Something must be done if England were not to lose the island. In 1599 Essex was made Lord-Lieutenant and dispatched at the head of 16,000 men. It was the largest and most expensive expedition yet sent, but the choice of Essex as leader was unfortunate. He had no patience and no modesty.

The Pale in 1500

The Pale under Elizabeth

Annexed for plantation under Mary

Tyrconnel (O'Donnell)

ULSTER

Clandeboy

Ards Peninsula

Tyrone (O'Neill)

Yellow Ford

CONNAUGHT

Dublin

LEINSTER

Ormond (Butler)

Smerwick

MUNSTER

Desmond (Fitzgerald)

Waterford

Kinsale

0   40   80

Miles

TUDOR IRELAND

Instead of advancing into Ulster he peacocked his way through Munster. When, urged on by letters from the Queen, he at last met Tyrone he was blarneyed into signing an immediate truce. 'You and the traitor spoke half an hour together without anybody's hearing;' wrote Elizabeth, adding 'To trust this traitor upon oath is to trust a devil upon his religion. . . .' Meanwhile disease was cutting down the English army. Essex hurried back to London to defend himself, with nothing to show but wasted time and vanished money. He had spent

£300,000 in seven months, almost twice the cost of defeating the Armada. It was the end of his career (see p. 360).

Charles Blount, Lord Mountjoy, was sent out in Essex' place. His appointment proved to be the turning-point in the struggle. He was in every way a contrast to Essex, being cautious, systematic and tenacious. By 1600 Mountjoy was breaking the rebellion. He fought small actions, built little blockhouses and, undramatically but step by step, drove Tyrone back until he was able to split Ulster in two. Success came in the nick of time, for in 1601 a force of 4,000 Spaniards, trained men, occupied Kinsale near Cork. Three years earlier they might have tipped the balance. Now it was too late. Within five months they were compelled to surrender, and in 1603 Tyrone gave himself up unconditionally. By then Elizabeth was dead. James I pardoned the old Earl, but when, in 1607, O'Neill and O'Donnell were ordered to come to England, they fled instead to Rome. The flight of the Earls marked the end of a chapter in Anglo-Irish relations. It left Ulster open to plantation by the protestant Scots, a plantation that was to have a permanent effect on later Irish history.

During Elizabeth's reign efforts had been made to plant Ireland with colonists, and also to assimilate its legal and social structure to that of England. Between 1569 and 1585 Government officials struggled to establish English rule in Connaught and Munster. Following Thomas Cromwell's earlier plan, it was decided that the chiefs were to surrender their lands and receive them back as tenants-in-chief of the crown. English sheriffs and justices of the peace were to be introduced, roads and bridges were to be built, Irish national dress was forbidden, Irish bards were put in the stocks until they found other employment. Ireland was to be modelled on England, willy-nilly. In general, the attempt was unsuccessful.

Unsuccessful too, were the efforts to establish pockets of English colonists. Four main attempts were made, by Humphrey Gilbert, Richard Grenville and other west country adventurers in Leinster and Munster (1568–70), by Thomas Smith in the Ards district of Ulster (1572–3), by the first earl of Essex at Clandeboye in Ulster (1573–5) and, most ambitious of all, by Sir Walter Ralegh in Munster, after Desmond had been beheaded in 1583. None of the plantations was successful. The English wanted to be landlords not exiles, and they aroused the natural opposition of the Irish—the connection of the plantations with the rebellions in Munster being particularly clear.

Did Spain miss the opportunity to turn Ireland into an English Netherlands? One feels that she did not. Although the pattern was in some ways similar—national feeling aroused by social, economic and religious grievances—there were yet important differences. The Netherlands were rich, well organized and well able to take care of themselves. The Irish were poor, uncivilized and fatally disunited. It was geographically easy for France and England to support the Dutch, but it was extremely difficult for Spain to land a large expedition on the coasts of Ireland. It could be done, as Kinsale showed, but the effort did not take place until after Philip's death. Not for nothing was that monarch known as 'the Prudent'.

At sea during the period from 1589 to 1603 efforts were made by both England and Spain which were far greater than those involved in the Enterprise of England and its defeat—and the costs were correspondingly enormous. Yet neither side was able to repeat their achievements of earlier times, the golden expeditions of Drake, the hair-breadth failure of the first Armada.

In 1589 an ambitious operation was planned in London. A counter-Armada was to sail and destroy the forty or so Spanish vessels sheltering in Santander, San Sebastian, and other Biscayan ports. The expedition was to be led by Drake and Norris and to be financed as a joint stock expedition. Two further targets were added to the original plan. The commanders were to take on board Don Antonio, the Portuguese pretender, and create a new Netherlands in Portugal. They were also to attack the Azores and perhaps seize one of the islands. None of these aims was achieved: failure was due to divided command and divided objectives.

Corunna was plundered, and the Spanish sank the one Armada galleon there, to prevent her falling into English hands. At Lisbon Norris and Drake failed to use their forces in efficient combination. The suburbs were reached overland, but that was all. On the way back the expedition, its numbers depleted by dysentry, raided Vigo and then sailed for the Azores.

P

Gales beat them off. Honour might be satisfied—Norris pointed out that 'if the enemy had done as much upon us, his party would have made bonfires in most parts of Christendom' —but in every other way the expedition illustrated the weaknesses of English methods. Lack of simplicity in planning, absence of co-ordination in execution, amateur financing and manning, inadequate understanding of the importance of supply and of hygiene—all contributed to neutralize English valour and seamanship.

In 1591 a Spanish fleet, which had been dispatched to convoy the treasure *flota* to Spain, attacked Lord Thomas Howard's squadron, then waiting at Flores for the same treasure-fleet. There Sir Richard Grenville with *Revenge* fought his famous single-handed action, but the real importance of the episode was that it marked the first success for Spain's new strategy, that of establishing a system of convoys between the West Indies and Spain, with a strongly fortified half way house at Terceira in the Azores. In 1592 the English scored a solitary success when the *Madre de Dios*, a Portuguese galleon from the East Indies, was captured off Flores and brought into Plymouth. There it was ransacked. The Queen made perhaps £90,000 as a return on her investment of £3,000, but a great part of the cargo, valued at £800,000, disappeared in spite of Sir Robert Cecil's efforts: 'Everyone I met within seven miles of Exeter that either had anything in a cloak, bag or malle which did but smell of the prizes either of Dartmouth or Plymouth (for I could well smell them also such had been the spoils of ambergris and musk among them) I did (though he had little about him) return him with me to the town of Exeter.'

The year 1595 saw another full-scale expedition. This time it sailed to the Caribbean and was led by Drake and Hawkins. Cities were sacked but little treasure was taken, for the Spanish were prepared. Hawkins fell ill and died off Porto Rico, Drake contracted dysentery and was buried at sea off Porto Bello 'somewhat to the east of the castle of St. Philip'. The expedition returned in 1596 having lost money and commanders.

In 1596 the best equipped of all the forces that left England achieved a great success when Essex, Howard, Ralegh and Vere landed in southern Spain. Their fleet comprised about 50 warships and 6,000 men (including the poet John Donne).

Cadiz was taken and held for a fortnight, land and sea forces for once meshing accurately, while the Spanish were forced to sink the *flota* then in harbour. For the third time in half a century Spain was compelled to repudiate its debts in national bankruptcy. Next year the same commanders sailed for the Azores and narrowly failed to intercept the *flota*, which slipped past them into Terceira.

The Spanish, for their part, planned further Armadas. In 1593 Burghley addressed the Lords on the danger:

First, the King of Spain since he hath usurped upon the Kingdom of Portugal, hath thereby grown mighty by gaining the East Indies. He is . . . now greater than any Christian prince hath been . . . the King of Spain maketh these his mighty wars not purposely to burn a town . . . but to conquer all France, all England and Ireland.

And for proof hereof, first for France, he hath invaded Brittany . . . , he hath at his commandment all the best parts of Brittany towards England, so as he is become as a frontier enemy to all the west parts of England, and by his commandment of Havre, he hath enlarged his frontiers now against all the south parts of England as Sussex, Hampshire, the Isle of Wight. . . . none ought to think, because he was disappointed of his intention for the conquest of England by his huge navy, therefore he will put that disgrace up and leave with that loss. It is certain he hath the last two years . . . made a number of ships of war, as near as he can to the mould and quantity of the English navy, finding by experience his monstrous great ships not mete for the Narrow Seas.

In 1595 four Spanish ships reached Cornwall and in 1596 and 1597 fleets were dispatched against England and Ireland, only to be turned back by the equinoctial gales. In 1596 Burghley was making every preparation against a possible invasion, from the holding in readiness of the country levies to such points of detail as the removal of millstones and windmill sails should the enemy make a landing. In 1601 the Spanish, as we have seen, did reach Kinsale, but both sides were in fact trying to conduct campaigns of combined operations and invasions that were still to prove beyond naval competence two hundred years later.

The triumphs came in other ways. Spain adopted vigorous and successful defensive measures: the fortification of strongpoints in the West Indies and the Azores; the use of convoys;

the development of new and faster types of ship, such as the *avisos* or scouts. On the English side it was perhaps the activities of the privateers that did most damage. Privateering had intensified after Spain's seizure of English shipping in the spring of 1585 and soon anything between one hundred and two hundred ships of all sizes from thirty to three hundred tons were sailing each year against the Spanish. They were usually ordinary merchantmen, carrying a privateer's licence, a few guns and a larger crew. The men were drawn from the ranks of professional sailors, the largest group coming from the Thames estuary. For them it was a gamble; a contemporary noted: 'As for the business of pillage, there is nothing that more bewitcheth them, nor anything wherein they promise to them-selves so loudly nor delight in more mainly.'

The backers, too, were gamblers—amateur, professional or merchant. It was the last class who were the most successful and by the end of the war privateering was dominated by a small group of London merchants. They combined respect-able business with privateering, sending their ships on normal trade routes to the Mediterranean or West Africa but hoping to pick up a prize or two as well if they were lucky. They were notably successful in intercepting the sugar cargoes from Brazil—in 1591 a Spanish spy reported 'that English booty in West Indian produce is so great that sugar is cheaper in London than it is in Lisbon or the Indies themselves'.[1] The stimulus given to English shipping interests may easily have been the most important positive consequence of the war at sea.

EXTRACTS

I. *Thomas Nashe (1567–1601) writes, satirically, of the new voyages and the new sailors:*

Voyages of purchase or reprisals, which are now grown a common traffic, swallow up and consume more sailors and mariners than they breed, and lightly not a slop of a rope-hauler they send forth to the Queen's ships but he is first broken to the sea in the herring-man's skiff or cock-boat, where having learned to brook all waters, and drink as he can out of a tarry can, and eat poor John out of sooty platters, when he may get it, without butter or mustard, there is no ho with him, but,

---

[1] K. R. Andrews, *Elizabethan Privateering*, C.U.P., 1965, p. 208. See also pp 196 and 302.

once heartened thus, he will needs be a man of war, or a tobacco taker, and wear a silver whistle. Some of these for their haughty climbing come home with wooden legs, and some with none, but leave body and all behind. Those that escape to bring news tell of nothing but eating tallow and young blackamores, of five and five to a rat in every mess and the shipboy to the tail, of stopping their noses when they drank stinking water that came out of the pump of the ship, and cutting a greasy buff jerkin in tripes and broiling it for their dinners. Divers Indian adventures have been seasoned with direr mishaps, not having for eight days' space the quantity of a candle's-end among eight score to grease their lips with; and landing in the end to seek food, by the cannibal savages they have been circumvented and forced to yield their bodies to feed them. (Thomas Nashe, *Lenten Stuffe*, 1599.)

II. *Sir Henry Sidney, Lord Deputy of Ireland (1565–7, 1568–71, 1575–8), reports to the Queen on the state of Munster and Connaught in 1567:*

. . . as I never was in a more pleasant country in all my life, so never saw I a more waste and desolate land, no, not in the confines of other countries where actual war hath continually been kept by the greatest princes of Christendom. And there heard I such lamentable cries and doleful complaints made by that small remain of poor people which yet are left. Who, hardly escaping the fury of the sword and fire of their outrageous neighbours, or the famine with the same, which their extortious lords hath driven them unto, either by taking their goods from them, or by spending the same by their extort taking of coign purveyance and livery, make demonstration of the miserable estate of that country. Besides this, such horrible and lamentable spectacles there are to behold as the burning of villages, the ruin of churches, the wasting of such as have been good towns and castles; yea, the view of the bones and skulls of the dead subjects, who, partly by murder, partly by famine, have died in the fields; as, in truth, any Christian with dry eyes could behold. . . .

I found the like of the whole country of Limerick and the county of Thomond (through which I travelled) as well for desolation, waste and ruins of the country, as also for the lack of reverence to your name, obedience to your laws and evil disposition of the people. . . . From thence I went to your Highness' town of Galway, the state whereof I found rather to resemble a town of war, frontiering upon an enemy, than a civil town in a country under one sovereign.   They watch their walls nightly and guard their gates daily with armed men. (*Sydney Papers* (*Letters and Memorials*), ed. A. Collins, London 1746.)

FURTHER READING

M. Lewis, *The Spanish Armada*, Batsford, 1960
G. Mattingley, *The Defeat of the Spanish Armada*, Cape, 1959
A. L. Rowse, *The Expansion of Elizabethan England*, Macmillan, 1955

X · RELIGIOUS PRESSURES

Introduction

FROM 1529 to 1689 politics and religion were intertwined more closely than they had ever been in the past or were ever to be in the future. Religious creeds were statements also of political demands, while political thoughts and ambitions found natural expression in terms of religious enthusiasm.

In this matter England was still part of western Europe; throughout the area religious nonconformity implied political opposition and potential treason. Religious unity, on the other hand, ensured national strength. In 1571 Edwin Sandys, a former Marian exile, and then Bishop of London, preaching to members of Parliament in Westminster Abbey, outlined the conventional theory:

> This liberty, that men may openly profess diversity of religion, must needs be dangerous to the Commonwealth. . . . One God, one King, one faith, one profession, is fit for one Monarchy and Commonwealth. Division weakeneth: Concord strengtheneth. . . . Let conformity and unity in religion be provided for; and it shall be as a wall of defence unto this realm.

It followed that religious toleration was regarded as not only morally indefensible but also as politically disastrous. Yet gradually the *politique* ruler (the word itself implied recognition of a possible division between religious and political allegiances) faced with opposition from powerful religious minorities found it expedient to grant a measure of religious toleration, or to attempt at least a limited compromise.

The Elizabethan settlement had been one such compromise adopted unwillingly and accidentally by the Queen in reaction to pressure from below. As the years went by its very ambiguity became a source of strength. Given the desire to avoid controversy, it could be made to embrace all shades of opinion from the Anglo-Catholic to the Puritan. Given the desire to agree to differ—but that desire was just what religious enthusiasts could not, by definition, be expected to feel. The church came

under fire from the extremists on either wing.   On the one
hand, as the Counter-Reformation grew in strength so it
became harder for an English Catholic to distinguish between
theological resistance and political disobedience.   On the
other hand, the Puritan clergy had only accepted the 1559
settlement as a half-way house on the journey towards the new
Jerusalem.   The government, for its part, found both groups
in the end intolerable.   In the last years of the reign (1590)
Cecil made a memorandum

> To have care that all papists . . . be restrained . . . also is the
> care to be taken to suppress all the turbulent Precisians
> [Puritans] who do seek violently to change the external
> government of the church.

The Puritan Pressure

Of the two threats outlined above, that from the religious
radicals was much the stronger.   They did not, at this stage,
propose to break away, but to take over the new church from
within.   Their loyalty was unquestionable, though their
attitude to Elizabeth herself was ambivalent.   She was their
Judith, who had destroyed the Catholic settlement, but she was
also their affliction, refusing to let England walk in the paths of
righteousness.   The 1563 parliament contained twenty-four
Marian exiles who, together with like-minded enthusiasts, made
up what a contemporary termed a 'puritan choir' of about
forty-three members, mainly representatives of the boroughs.[1]

In 1566, during the second session of this parliament, there
was an open clash over clerical vestments, 'the rags of Rome'.
To clarify the meaning of the rubric, Parker issued his *Advertisements*.   They made no concessions and did not at all satisfy the
radicals.   In London thirty-seven clergy refused to conform,
and in parliament the 'choir' launched an attack.   The clergy
were deprived of their livings, the attack failed.   But the
religious debate had become also a debate on parliamentary
privilege, on the right to discuss the church settlement, and
soon the word 'Puritan'—it was used in France as early as
1564, and the first recorded occurrence in England was in
1572—became itself a party label.

What was a Puritan?   He was one who wished to *purify* the
church from all remaining traces of what he considered to be

---

[1] Throughout, reference should also be made to Chapter XI.

Popery. He laid great stress on an absolute moral standard, on the individual's social conscience, on zeal, and on the minister—provided one did not call him a priest or a bishop. His object, at first, was not to leave the church but to convert it. There were many types of Puritans, but these characteristics may serve to define, at least approximately, the general boundaries of Elizabethan Puritanism, its common tone of voice.

The issue of Parker's *Advertisements* had, as one of its consequences, the increased use by the bishops of their disciplinary authority, and so a further result was that the Puritan attack shifted from vestments to episcopacy—'bishops must be unlorded'. Nonconformity was becoming presbyterian. The spokesman of the new movement was Thomas Cartwright, Lady Margaret Professor of Divinity at Cambridge. His Calvinism had been made clear in his lectures on the Acts of the Apostles. He quarrelled with Whitgift, the Master of his college, lost his professorship, and withdrew to Geneva. Cartwright returned to England in 1572 and played his part in the new attack, the most determined attempt to take by force the citadel of the established Church. The attack had opened in 1571 with Strickland's bill to reform the prayer-book (see p. 245). The campaign manager was a London minister, John Field, who was mainly responsible for the appearance next year of an *Admonition to Parliament*, which urged members to introduce the Calvinist régime into England. A vigorous pamphlet war followed. A tract accompanying the *Admonition* described the Prayer Book as 'an imperfect book, culled and picked out of that Popish dunghill, the Mass-book, full of abominations'. Vestments came under fire; 'Copes, caps, surplices, tippets and such like baggage . . . are as the garments of the idol, . . .' Clergy were 'men-leasing mongrels and own belly-filling pastors, vainglorious prelates, refusers of reformation, and maliciously and wilfully blind bishops.'

Cartwright was more restrained. His *Second Admonition* was a reasoned statement of the movement's position. The New Testament, he wrote, contained a clear description of the only acceptable system of church government, a system that bore little relationship to the Elizabethan one, but was similar to that introduced by Calvin at Geneva. In 1574, he was once more forced to leave England. In that year another Calvinist,

Walter Travers, provided in his *Discipline* the essential basis of the presbyterian programme.

Three years later Matthew Parker died and was succeeded as Archbishop by Elizabeth's old tutor, Edmund Grindal (1576). Grindal was a Puritan who had in 1566 said of the settlement, 'We . . . contended long and earnestly for the removal of those things that have occasioned the present dispute; but as we were unable to prevail, either with the Queen or the Parliament, we judged it best, after a consultation on the subject, not to desert our churches for the sake of a few ceremonies'. His appointment brought into the arena a new development, 'prophesyings'. In many parts of south-east England informal meetings of clergy and laity had for some time been held to study the Scriptures—meetings which took their name from I Corinthians, xiv: 'He that prophesieth speaketh . . . to edification, and exhortation, and comfort. . . .' The first of these probably took place at Northampton as early as 1571 and by 1576 they had become obnoxious to the Queen on two grounds; first, because laymen and clergy took part together, thus blurring the distinction between priest and congregation, and secondly, because exposition often led to criticism of the doctrines and structure of the existing settlement.

Grindal immediately issued regulations to control—but nevertheless to allow—'prophesyings' and 'exercises'. The Queen ordered their suppression; Grindal refused to obey her, saying, 'Bear with me, I beseech you, Madam, if I choose rather to offend your earthly majesty than to offend the heavenly majesty of God'. The Archbishop went on to remind the Queen that she was mortal 'and although you are a mighty Prince, yet remember that He which dwelleth in Heaven is mightier'. As a result he was suspended from the exercise of his authority (1577) and continued in disgrace until his death in 1583.

The Queen did not make the same mistake twice. As Grindal's successor she chose John Whitgift (1583–1604), a firm supporter of the established order. Doctrinally Calvinist, he was nevertheless a rigid opponent of the Puritans. He spoke unequivocally to them:

> The question is not whether many things maintained in your platform of discipline were fitly used in the apostles' time or may now be well used in sundry reformed churches; but

whether, when there is a settled order in doctrine and discipline established by law, it may stand with godly and Christian wisdom to attempt so great an alteration as this platform must needs bring in, with disobedience to the queen and law and injunctions of the church, and offence to many consciences.

To maintain this 'settled order' Whitgift issued six articles by which all the clergy were compelled to take an *ex officio* oath accepting without qualification the royal supremacy, the prayer-book, and the Thirty-Nine Articles. About two hundred refused to do so and left the Church.

From 1559 onwards the Crown had appointed *ad hoc* commissions to enforce the state religious policy—commissions that derived their authority partly from the royal prerogative and partly from the 1559 Act of Supremacy. Now the Court of High Commission became established as a regular Court to impose discipline and uniformity. As an instrument supporting Whitgift's authority there was some truth in its opponents' claim that it behaved like an English Inquisition, especially in the years after 1587, when Richard Bancroft became its most forceful member. It is difficult, though, to see what other means the government might have adopted, since they could not rely on the uniform support of either parliament or the J.P.s.[1] The Court soon came to deal also with appeals from private suitors in all matters affecting the Church except those where property was involved.

The situation appeared to demand strong measures. Calvinism was in the fifteen eighties an active force in England. Its main weapon was what was known as the 'classical' movement—a name derived from the Latin *classis*, a group. These groups were organized in a pyramidal structure of secret synods after the Genevan pattern. The movement flourished from 1582 to 1589. In the former year a *classis* was started at Dedham in Essex and soon the Church in many areas was permeated by the familiar cell-like administrative anatomy of Calvinism, and provincial and national synods were held at centres such as Oxford, Cambridge and London. The movement was weakened, however, by a fatal division between those who were only tepidly opposed to the existing settlement and those who wished to launch a full-scale attack upon it.

[1] See also p. 269.

In 1585 the Queen addressed Whitgift and three of her bishops on the need for uniformity of doctrine.

> . . . you suffer many ministers to preach what they list and to minister the sacraments according to their own fancies, some one way, some another, to the breach of unity: yes, and some of them so curious in searching matters above their capacity as they preach they know not what—that there is no Hell but a torment of conscience. Nay, I have heard there be six preachers in one diocese the which do preach six sundry ways. I wish such men to be brought to conformity and unity: that they preach all one truth; and that such as be found not worthy to preach, be compelled to read homilies. . . .

Whitgift agreed, but added that it was not possible to place learned men in each of thirteen thousand parishes. Elizabeth replied that all she required were honest, sober men who could read well. Meanwhile John Field expressed the Puritan reaction to Whitgift: 'The peace of the Church is at an end if he be not curbed.'

As preparations went forward in 1586 for the calling of Parliament the Puritans began a political campaign. Pamphlets were distributed: 'Let cathedral churches be utterly destroyed' said one, for they were dens 'where the time and place of God's service, preaching and prayer is most filthily abused: in piping with organs; in singing, ringing and trolling of the Psalms from one side of the choir to the other, with squeaking of chanting choristers. . . .', and the clergy were 'Dumb dogs, unskilful, sacrificing priests, destroying drones, or rather, caterpillars of the Word'. The Puritan choir in Parliament must be strengthened. One Puritan wrote to John Field: 'I hope you have not let slip this notable opportunity of furthering the cause of religion by noting out all the places of government in the land for which burgesses for the Parliament are to be chosen, and using all the best means you can possibly for . . . procuring the best gentlemen for those places, by whose wisdom and zeal God's causes may be preferred'. When parliament did meet, Sir Anthony Cope introduced a Bill and a Book which together were designed to set up a Presbyterian Church, but the Queen sent for the Bill and Book, and Cope was soon in the Tower (see p. 248).

The campaign in Parliament ended in failure—indeed, that

Parliament was soon dissolved—but it continued in the countryside. In 1588 and 1589 there appeared the seven Martin Marprelate tracts, scurrilous but amusing attacks on the established Church: the author is unknown, but the most likely candidates seem to be Job Throckmorton, Puritan member for Warwick in the 1586–7 parliament, or John Penry, who later became a Brownist. The following extract suggests their tone:

Is it any marvel that we have so many swine, dumb dogs, non-residents, with their journeymen the hedge priests, so many lewd livers, as thieves, murderers, adulterers, drunkards, cormorants, rascals, so many ignorant and atheistical dolts, so many covetous Bps. in our ministry, and so many and so monstrous corruptions in our Church, and yet likely to have no redress; seeing our impudent, shameless, and wainscot-faced bishops, like beasts, contrary to knowledge of all men against their own consciences, dare in the ears of her Majesty affirm all to be well where there is nothing but sores and blisters . . .

Puritan preachers were more elegant in their language, but equally threatening in their attitude. A Northampton minister made the following suggestion to his congregation: 'How say you if we devise a way whereby to shake off all the antichristian yoke and government of bishops, and . . . jointly together erect the [Presbyterian] discipline and government all in one day . . .?' No wonder the authorities were alarmed. The Earl of Hertford warned 'As they shoot at bishops now, so will they do at the nobility also, if they be suffered.'

The eighties were the high water mark of Puritan protest in the reign. During the nineties the Presbyterian movement as a revolutionary force came to an end. The bishops had won; the clergy conformed, the synods no longer met. There were several reasons for this decline in activity: the Puritans were themselves split into rival groups; with every year that passed the new church became increasingly the old-established Church; the great patrons at court were dead—Leicester in 1588 and Walsingham in 1590; the firm policy of Whitgift and Bancroft encouraged conformity, while the bitter taste of failure disheartened many of their opponents.

In parliament the last manifestation was the introduction by James Morice (see p. 250) in 1593 of two bills attacking the *ex officio* oath, the Whitgift articles, and the jurisdiction of the

Court of High Commission. Shall we, he asked, 'yield our bodies to be burned, our consciences to be ransacked, and our inheritance to be disposed at the pleasure of our prelates; and not so much as once open our mouths to the contrary?' Morice appeared before the Council and was punished.

In the same parliament the government introduced an Act Against Seditious Sectaries (1593) which transferred some of the business of repression from the bishops to the common law courts. Failure to conform would be punished by imprisonment for three months, continued refusal would lead to exile, and unlicensed return from exile would be punishable by death.

The presbyterian attack had been defeated. The Presbyterians themselves survived, but as members of a minority movement which at the end of the reign comprised between 280 and 350 ministers (105 of whom had university degrees) and perhaps something between 50,000 and 100,000 lay members.

The act of 1593 was directed not only against the presbyterians but even more against a second group of dissenters, the Separatists, often known as Brownists or Independents. These were opposed to the close connection between church and state which was a feature of both the anglican and presbyterian churches, regarding it as unscriptural. In their ministers the Separatists looked for inspiration rather than learning, in their services they were non-hierarchic and non-ritualist, and in the voluntary, 'gathered', congregation they found the basis for their organization. One of their leaders, Robert Browne, wrote that 'the Kingdom of God was not to be begun by whole parishes, but rather of the worthiest, were they never so few'. Individual congregations elected their own ministers and sought their own way to heaven without reference to any superior authority.

The separatist movement had first appeared in the sixties, then had been lost to view, and had reappeared at Norwich in 1581. The leading figures were Robert Browne, Robert Harrison, and Henry Barrow. In 1582 persecution drove the Brownists to Middelburg in Holland. Browne himself eventually returned to England and became a country parson (1591–1633). Barrow was imprisoned in 1587 and hanged in 1593 for seditious writings. His followers moved to Amsterdam, and it was their descendants who were later to sail in the *Mayflower* to America.

These groups, small in numbers (in 1593 Ralegh thought that there were perhaps ten or twelve thousand Brownists in the country), obscure in origin, and usually helpless in the face of persecution, resembled the first squirrel-like mammals in the age of the great reptiles—they were the unconsidered fore-runners of the seventeenth-century Independents who won the Civil War, executed the king, and set up a joint republic of England, Scotland and Ireland.

Meanwhile the presbyterian and separatist movements had both been broken, but Puritanism in the broadest sense of the term survived within the Church, laying its own special emphasis on the Sabbath, on discipline and on preaching.

The Catholic Pressure

The Catholic pressure presents a different, and more puzzling, pattern. Potentially the Catholic threat must have been most dangerous in the first decade of the reign. Yet these are precisely the years when the government was able to dis-regard the Catholics, while they dwindled in numbers and in influence. In 1558 the majority of the population had been brought up in the old religion, yet by 1570 it seems likely that there was left a hard core of not more than about 150,000 Catholics.

One reason for this decline was the lack of support from the continent. Philip II had, for political reasons, persuaded the Papacy to delay the publication of the Bull declaring the Queen excommunicate. No priests arrived from the outside world. A new generation grew to maturity, a generation that had learnt to conform and to equate catholicism with political and social disabilities. Later (1665) Fuller suggested these reasons for Catholic dismay: 'The old store of Papists in England began now very much to diminish and decay; insomuch that the Romanists perceived they could not spend at this rate out of the main stock, but it would quickly make them bankrupt. Prisons consumed many, age more of their priests; and they had no place in England whence to recruit themselves.'

In consequence, when the Catholic political and religious threat to the established Church became apparent in the seventies, it revealed itself as of much smaller proportions than might have been expected. Nevertheless that decade and the next witnessed a limited Catholic counter-attack.

Mary's presence in England (1568), the rising of the Northern Earls (1569) and the Bull of Excommunication (1570) together revived the Catholic problem. The Bull *Regnans in Excelsis*, issued by Pius V, excommunicated Elizabeth, absolved Englishmen from the oath of allegiance, and ordered them to depose her:

> Elizabeth, the pretended Queen of England, the servant of wickedness . . . having seized on the kingdom and monstrously usurped the place of Supreme Head of the Church in all England. . . .   We do out of the fullness of our Apostolic power declare the aforesaid Elizabeth as being a heretic. . . . We do declare her to be deprived of her pretended title to the kingdom aforesaid, and of all dominion, dignity, and privilege whatsoever; and also the nobility, subjects, and people of the said kingdom, and all others who have in any sort sworn unto her, to be for ever absolved from any such oath, . . .   And we do command and charge all and every noblemen, subjects, people, and others aforesaid that they presume not to obey her. . . .

The Bull had effects quite other than those intended. The English Catholics had shot their bolt the year before, and foreign rulers showed no intention of coming to their aid now. The English Protestants,. on the other hand, were encouraged by the Pope's action to close their ranks 'lest', as one of them observed, 'we all go together and row in the galleys of Spain'. The government itself reacted promptly, and the Act Against Bulls from Rome was passed in 1571, by which it was made treason to question the Queen's title to the throne, or to affirm that she was a heretic.

The 'monster Bull' had roared to little effect, more practical help came in other ways.   In 1568 an English exile, William Allen, set up a college at Douai in southern Flanders to which English Catholics might send their sons.   There the pupils, aged fourteen to twenty-five, received a first-class education of the up-to-date Jesuit type.   Other colleges were started in Rome (1575–8), and in Spain at Valladolid (1589) and Seville (1592) by Persons.   The English College at Douai began a translation of the New Testament (completed in 1582 at Rheims to which place the College had moved in 1578) and of the Old Testament, completed in 1609.   Students placed themselves at God's disposal and a number of them became priests. They vowed: 'I am ready and shall always be ready to receive Holy orders, in His own good time, and I shall return to England for the salvation of souls. . . .' The first of these seminary priests reached England in 1574 and by 1580 there were at least a hundred of them. They were, for the most part, not concerned with political propaganda, but the act of 1571 had made them traitors willy-nilly and the first execution (that of Cuthbert Mayne) took place in 1577.

Meanwhile a different Catholic influence had begun to make itself felt in England. Gregory XIII (1572–85) was an active, political Pope; optimistic and ingenuous, he has also been called unscrupulous. This combination of qualities led him to lend his support to a succession of uncoordinated, impractical schemes for the recovery of England; the dispatch of expeditions to southern Ireland (1578–80),[1] plans for the Queen's assassination, and the Jesuit mission to England.

Extremists, whether catholic or protestant, held that tyrannicide was justified and there is evidence that Gregory knew at least something of the plots against Elizabeth. In 1580 the cardinal of Como, Gregory's secretary of State, wrote to the papal nuncio in Madrid as follows:

> Since that guilty woman of England rules over two such noble kingdoms of Christendom and is cause of so much injury to the Catholic faith, and loss of so many million souls, there is no doubt that whosoever sends her out of the world with the pious intention of doing Gods service, not only does not sin but gains merit, especially having regard to the sentence pronounced against her by Pius V of holy memory. And so if these English nobles decide actually to undertake so glorious a work, your lordship can assure them that they do not commit any sin.

The invasion of Ireland and the plots against the Queen worked against the success of Gregory's third project, the Jesuit mission. Allen had persuaded the Pope to allow the Jesuits to take part in the English Mission. In 1580 the first two Jesuit priests, Edmund Campion and Robert Persons entered the country. In character they well symbolized the two aspects of the Counter-Reformation; Campion was a sincere, pacific, saintly figure, Persons a more political priest. Within a year of their arrival, Campion was dead and Persons

---

[1] For details, see p. 210.

back on the continent, but other Jesuits continued to come over.
Campion had written:

> I cannot long escape the hands of the heretics; the enemies
> have so many eyes, so many tongues, so many scouts and
> crafts.   I am in apparel to myself very ridiculous: I often
> change it, and my name also.   I read letters sometimes
> myself that in the first front tell news that Campion is taken,
> which, noised in every place where I come, so filleth my ears
> with the sound thereof, that fear itself hath taken away all
> fear.

In the next century Fuller described the same situation from
the protestant point of view:

> Now began priests and Jesuits to flock faster into England
> than ever before; having exchange of clothes, and names, and
> professions.   He who on Sunday was a priest or Jesuit was
> on Monday a merchant, on Tuesday a soldier, on Wednesday
> a courtier, etc., and with the shears of equivocation (con-
> stantly carried about him) he could cut himself into any
> shape he pleased. . . .   These distilled traitorous principles
> into all people wheresoever they came, and endeavoured to
> render them disaffected to her Majesty; maintaining that she
> neither had nor ought to have any dominion over her subjects
> whilst she persisted in a heretical distance from the Church
> of Rome.[1]

In 1580 Gregory had assured Catholics that the Bull against
Elizabeth was not binding on them 'while things remain as they
are', but this was not sufficient to save the priests.   They could
always be accused, under the basic treason law of 1352, of
adhering to the Queen's enemies.   On the scaffold Campion
declared, 'If you esteem my religion treason, then I am guilty,
as for other treason I never committed any, God is my judge'.
A bystander retorted, 'In your Catholicism all treason is
contained'.   In that brief encounter is contained the essence
of the argument.

The government reacted at once to the Jesuit mission with
the statute of 1581 Against Reconciliation to Rome.   This
extended the definition of treason to cover those who withdrew
the Queen's subjects from their allegiance and those who
allowed themselves to be so withdrawn; it also raised the fines
for recusancy from 1s. a week to £20 a month.   Two later acts

---

[1] Fuller, *The Church History of Britain*, Vol. iii, p. 20 (1837 edition).

carried the attack further. In 1585 the Act Against Jesuits and Seminary Priests gave them forty days to leave the country, after which they would automatically become guilty of treason. Finally, in 1593 the Act Against Popish Recusants forbade them to move more than five miles from their homes.

The persecution was sharp, but limited. One hundred and eighty-seven priests suffered death for treason, one hundred and ten of them after 1588, and another sixty died in prison.

Those who suffered, said Burghley, did so, not because they believed in transubstantiation or upheld the Mass, but because they were traitors and sedition-mongers. But the catholic priests, on whom fell the burden and heat of the day, were just as convinced that they were martyrs for their faith. Therein lies the profound pathos of this terrible time. . . . In fact, all the conditions incidental to a reign of terror prevailed. The innocent suffered with the guilty . . . in extracting information, with the help of torture, and with the hideous penalty for treason lurking in the background, if the government introduced a system of judicial inquiry as bad as that practised by the Spanish Inquisition, which it professed to abhor. . . . The fairest criticism that can be passed is to say that both parties to the conflict were the victims of a tragic dilemma, from which there seems to have been no escape but by the shedding of blood on the one side, and by self-sacrifice on the other.[1]

With Cardinal Allen's death at Rome in 1594 quarrels broke out between the Jesuits, militant supporters of Spain, and the secular priests, anxious only for the spiritual welfare of their flocks. Archbishop Whitgift was growing old and Richard Bancroft, appointed Bishop of London in 1597, was from then on virtually in charge of the Church. It was part of Bancroft's policy to exploit these differences between Catholics by reducing the pressure, and in 1603 he was successful in persuading thirteen secular priests to pledge their loyalty to the Queen in matters temporal, while reserving their obedience to the Catholic church in spiritual matters. By that time any attempt to make converts on a large scale, or to overthrow the established church, was clearly out of the question. The old Catholics, loyal to Crown and Pope, probably numbered something between 100,000 and 150,000—much the same figure as a generation earlier.

[1] J. B. Black, *The Reign of Elizabeth*, O.U.P. 1959, pp. 185-7.

The Church Established

Catholic and Puritan had alike failed in their attacks on the Church of England, but their pressures had affected its evolution. The Church had become more rigid, both in doctrine and discipline, but it remained flexible enough—its enemies said vague enough—to include within its ranks a wide spectrum of opinions, and it now seemed unlikely that it would adopt any specific continental pattern. In spite of frequent attempts to bring its affairs within parliamentary control (see Chapter XI) it remained firmly under the sway of the Royal Supremacy, exercised in administrative matters through the bishops and in legislative matters through a muzzled parliament, and with the Court of High Commission as its active watchdog.

The new Church had by the end of the reign acquired a distinctive character of its own. The acquisition was the result of various factors, not least the Church's survival during the storms of forty years. It had inherited from the first half of the century congregations with strong anti-clerical prejudices. It had also inherited clergy who were, in Dr. Elton's words, 'a mixed lot', though during the reign the proportion of graduate clergy increased. The nature of the original settlement had been such that, though the form of service might be identical in every parish, the production of the service could vary greatly, while the doctrine expounded in the sermon was often at variance with both liturgy and ceremonial. In London it was remarked that '. . . the pulpit spake pure Canterbury in the morning and Geneva in the afternoon'.

The morning preacher referred to was Richard Hooker. If Whitgift gave the Church its operational efficiency, Hooker gave it its intellectual foundation. He was born near Exeter about 1554, became an Oxford don, and then rector of Boscombe in Hampshire. The greater part of his work, *Of the Laws of Ecclesiastical Policy*, appeared between the years 1594 and 1597. In it he provided a philosophical justification, based on Catholic and Renaissance learning, for the Church of England. Church and State were, he argued, two aspects of the same body. He denied the puritan view that the Bible was the only law of God; God had also provided man with reason by which to interpret the Bible and, where Scripture was silent, to frame laws for the government and life of the Church. Where the

Bible 'appointeth no certainty, the use of the people of God or
the ordinances of our fathers must serve' for

> All things cannot be of ancient continuance which are
> expedient and needful for the ordering of spiritual affairs;
> but the Church, being a body which dieth not, hath always
> power, as occasion requireth, no less to ordain that which
> never was than to ratify what hath been before. . . .

In these matters Hooker's view was the traditional Catholic one,
owing much to Aquinas.

Hooker's work was philosophical, not propagandist. 'My
meaning,' he wrote, 'is not to provoke any, but to satisfy all
tender consciences.'   He ended by producing the greatest piece
of sustained reasoning and classical prose in Elizabeth's reign,
an attempt to explain man in his entirety:

> Man doth seek a triple perfection: first a sensual, consisting
> in those things which very life itself requireth either as neces-
> sary supplements, or as beauties and ornaments thereof;
> then an intellectual, consisting in those things which none
> underneath man is either capable of or acquainted with;
> lastly, a spiritual and divine, consisting in those things
> whereunto we tend by supernatural means here, but cannot
> here attain unto. . . .

Very different in attitude, but equally valuable to the new
church, was John Foxe's *Acts and Monuments*, commonly known
as 'Foxe's Book of Martyrs'.   Foxe, born in Lincolnshire in
1516 and educated at Oxford, fled to Europe during the
Marian persecution.   He returned in 1559 and died in 1587.
By that date his book, first published in 1563, had gone through
four editions.   Hooker had provided a philosophical foundation for the Church, Foxe provided an emotional one, a
martyrology to set against the catholic martyrology.   Hooker
was all-embracing, intellectual and aloof, Foxe was puritan,
simple, writing in words that could be understood by all,
passionately committed.   His work soon came second only to
the Bible in distribution and influence.   His style illustrates
the other pole of Elizabethan writing, that of direct narrative.
Here is part of his description of the death of Rowland Taylor,
Vicar of Hadleigh:

> Then cried his wife, 'Rowland, Rowland, where art thou?'—
> for it was a very dark morning, that the one could not see
> the other.   Dr. Taylor answered, 'Dear wife, I am here,'

and stayed.   The sheriff's men would have led him forth,
but the sheriff said, 'Stay a little, masters, I pray you, and
let him speak with his wife.' . . .   Coming within a two mile
of Hadleigh he desired to light off his horse, which done he
leaped and set a frisk or twain, as men commonly do in
dancing.   'Why, master Doctor,' quoth the sheriff, 'How do
you now?'   He answered, 'Well God be praised, master
Sheriff, never better; for now I know I am almost at home.
I lack not past two stiles to go over, and I am at my father's
house.'

What was the final outcome of almost a century of religious
change?   A state Church had been firmly established, and
already that Church had begun to acquire the stability and
traditions which would help it to endure for four hundred years.
The powers of the state had been greatly increased by its control
of that Church.   The survival of relatively small but extremely
strong pockets of resistance, both Catholic and Puritan, was to
have important consequences in the next century.

In more material ways the English Reformation, though it
had not greatly affected capitalist theory and practice, had
certainly accentuated economic developments that were already
taking place.   Sixteenth-century land-hunger had found some
satisfaction in the dispersal of church lands, and the consequent
changes in land-ownership and social wealth had in their turn
affected the economy.   The Reformation had also provided
a new source of investment.   The aristocracy (among them the
Earl of Leicester) and the gentry had succeeded the monastic
houses as the proprietors of many livings, and the buying and
selling of these 'impropriated'[1] livings became a normal feature
of the economic scene.   In 1603 the bishops estimated that, out
of 9,284 livings, 3,849 had been impropriated.   It was good
business to pay the vicar as little as possible.   Thus a poor
clergy was created—or perpetuated—and at the same time the
new Church was firmly bound into the new social system.

EXTRACTS

I.   *Father Edmund Campion defends himself against the charge of
treason, 1581:*
The only thing that we have now to say is that if our religion
do make us traitors we are worthy to be condemned; but

[1] To impropriate means, in this connection, to annex or place in lay hands
church tithes or property.

otherwise are and have been true subjects as ever the Queen had. In condemning us you condemn all your own ancestors —all the ancient priests, bishops and kings—all that was once the glory of England, the island of saints and the most devoted child of the see of Peter. For what have we taught, however you may qualify it with the odious name of treason, that they did not uniformly teach? To be condemned with these old lights—not of England only, but of the world—by their degenerate descendants is both gladness and glory to us. God lives; posterity will live; their judgement is not so liable to corruption as that of those who are now going to sentence us to death.

II. *The interrogation of Father John Gerard:*
We went to the torture-room in a kind of solemn procession, the attendants walking ahead with lighted candles.

The chamber was underground and dark, particularly near the entrance. It was a vast place and every device and instrument of human torture was there. They pointed out some of them to me and said I would try them all. Then they asked me again whether I would confess.

'I cannot,' I said.

I fell on my knees for a moment's prayer. Then they took me to a big upright pillar, one of the wooden posts which held the roof of this huge underground chamber. Driven into the top of it were iron staples for supporting heavy weights. Then they put my wrists into iron gauntlets and ordered me to climb two or three wicker steps. My arms were then lifted up and an iron bar was passed through the rings of the second gauntlet. This done they fastened the bar with a pin to prevent it slipping, and then removing the wicker steps, one by one from under my feet, they left me hanging by my hands and arms fastened above my head. The tips of my toes, however, still touched the ground, and they had to dig away the earth from under them. ...

Hanging like this I began to pray. The gentlemen standing around asked me whether I was willing to confess now.

'I cannot and I will not,' I answered.

(*The Autobiography of John Gerard*, trans. P. Caraman, Longmans, Green, 1951, p. 107. Copyright U.S.A. 1952 by Pellegrini & Cudahy under the title *The Autobiography of a Hunted Priest*. By permission of Farrar, Straus & Giroux, Inc.)

III. *Henry Barrow defends himself before the Council:*
BURGHLEY: 'Why are you in prison?'
BARROW: 'I am now in prison, my lord, upon the statute made for recusants.'

BURGHLEY: 'Why will you not come to the church?'

BARROW: 'My whole desire is to come to the church of God.'

BURGHLEY: 'Thou art a fantastical fellow, I perceive, but why not to our churches?'

BARROW: 'The causes are many and great, my Lord, and it were too long to show them in particular. But briefly, my Lord, I cannot come to your churches because all the wicked and profane of the land are received into the body of your churches. Again, you have a false and anti-Christian ministry set over your churches, neither worship you God aright, but after an idolatrous and superstitious manner. And not your church is governed by the word of God but by Romish courts.'

BURGHLEY: 'Indeed, I perceive you have a delight to be an author of this new religion.'

FURTHER READING

V. J. K. Brook, *Whitgift and the English Church*, E.U.P., 1957

H. G. Alexander, *Religion in England 1558–1662*, University of London Press, 1968

P. McGrath, *Papists and Puritans under Elizabeth I*, Blandford, 1967

XI · PARLIAMENT, 1559–1601

Structure and Privileges

ALTHOUGH parliamentary liberty was not born, fully grown, in Elizabeth's reign, it was during these years that it reached at least adolescence. For the first time members appeared, consistently and continuously, on the political stage. If it was not yet a framer of policy, the House of Commons was nevertheless usually claiming that it ought to be.

The clash between the Queen's interpretation, which was the conventional one, of the function of the Commons and their own view of their role was the clearer for the fact that it took place in full view of all. In almost every session the pattern was the same. The Commons would assert their right to privileges which they had never possessed and would frame bills and resolutions which they already knew ran counter to the Queen's wishes. Elizabeth, for her part, would lecture them on their duties and their limited rights, and would scold them for their temerity.

Yet there was no head-on collision, as there had been in Wolsey's time or as there was to be so often in the next century. The aims of Queen and Commons were essentially the same. The Commons might be critics, but they were loyal critics. They might wish that they controlled the country, but as yet they could hardly hope to do so. They might think the Queen misguided and her policies misapplied but—with the important exception of the Church settlement—they did not consciously desire to change radically the existing order of things.

Their criticism and their loyalty sprang, to some extent, from the fact that the most articulate members shared a common social and intellectual background. During the reign there was no alteration in the county representation, where ninety gentlemen represented the shires, but important changes took place in the borough representation. The two members for Calais lost (in the literal sense of the word) their seats, but borough representation increased. Sixty-two new seats were created between 1558 and 1586. This was only the final stage in a process that had during the century increased the size of the House by 50 per cent, the total numbers, including county members, rising from 296 to 462. Under Henry VIII thirty-one members, representing the boroughs and shires of Wales and Cheshire, had taken their seats, and there were thirty-four additional members in Edward VI's reign and another twenty-five under Mary I.

The newly-enfranchised boroughs were of all types. Many were rising towns, but some were rotten from the start. The increase in the number of borough members was the result of royal action but it was not, as was once thought, an attempt by the Crown to control the Commons. On the contrary, the pressure came from below, from the boroughs themselves and from landed interests anxious for the prestige of a seat in the Commons. An increasingly large number of boroughs were represented in parliament by country gentlemen though, constitutionally, boroughs should only have been represented by those who lived in them. If the law had been strictly applied, this would have resulted in a house composed of one-fifth (90) gentry representing the counties, and four-fifths (372) burgesses representing the boroughs. In fact by the end of the century the proportions were almost exactly reversed. Four-fifths of the members were country gentlemen and the majority of these were representing boroughs. 'Elizabeth's later parliaments contained four gentlemen to every townsman. The country gentleman and his cousin, the lawyer, had captured the House of Commons. It is a fact of quite fundamental importance in our history.'[1]

The townsman was glad to be represented by someone who would pay his own expenses and who might not be too much overawed by the City and the Court. The gentleman was anxious to enjoy the reputation and the possibilities of preferment that membership would provide. It was not a new development; as early as 1422 a quarter of the borough seats had been held by non-residents, and gentlemen had been relatively numerous in the parliaments of Edward IV. In 1529 the first borough representative to be elected Speaker was a gentleman, Sir Humphrey Wingfield, and in the later years of Henry VIII's reign the country gentlemen flooded in, exerting pressure on the monarch to create new boroughs and pressure on the townsmen to accept non-resident members, so

[1] J. E. Neale, *Elizabeth I and her Parliaments, 1559–1581*, Cape, 1953, p. 148.

that by Elizabeth's time the Commons were dominated by the landed gentry, the most important section of Tudor society. Soon the new pattern was accepted as the normal one, so that in the early seventeenth century the earl of Arundel was able loftily to inform a borough that '. . . it hath been a usage of long continuance for most towns to make choice of such foreigners as were fit and worthy'.

An analysis of the Commons of 1584 reveals the following social structure:

Country gentlemen	240
Royal officials	75
Lawyers	53
Burgesses	53
Miscellaneous	39

Ninety of the members had been to Oxford or Cambridge and to the Inns of Court, seventy-four had been to the Inns only, fifty-five had been to a university only, so that two hundred and nineteen had had an intellectual training of one sort or another.[1]

The urge to sit in parliament made for continuity. A member who had got control of a seat might be expected to want to keep it. In the parliament of 1584 only one hundred and nine of the members were newcomers, and during the reign as a whole two-thirds of the M.P.s were usually old hands. (The proportion was not so very different in the eighteenth century when, as Namier has shown, in a parliament of 558 members one might expect to find about 150 new members.)

Elizabeth faced, in consequence, parliaments composed of members who were better educated, more vocal, more independent, better versed in parliamentary procedure and therefore more difficult to handle, than they could possibly have been if the towns had been represented solely by local townsmen. It is perhaps significant that in the last seventeen years of her reign the Queen created no new boroughs.

The Spanish ambassador, de Silva, warned the Queen as early as 1566 that what her parliaments wanted was liberty, and that, if rulers did not look after their own interests and combine together, it was easy to see how the licence that these people had taken would end.

[1] J. E. Neale, *The Elizabethan House of Commons*, Cape, 1949, pp. 302–9.

To what extent did Elizabeth make use of parliament? While noting the growing power of the members it is important to remember also the intermittent nature of that power. During the reign ten parliaments were summoned. They held thirteen sessions, the members sitting for a total of thirty-five months, an average of only about three weeks for each year of the reign. The longest interval without a parliament was during the years of comparative peace and quiet from 1576 to 1581.

In the Queen's eyes it was the duty of her parliament to vote subsidies to cover extraordinary expenditure, to pass the Queen's laws, and to show a united front to the country's enemies. In addition there was the practical convenience of being able to speak, directly or through her ministers, to over four hundred men of substance drawn from all parts of England and Wales who might then go home, there to expound her policies and enforce her laws. The initiation of public legislation was the business of her council, who might discuss policy, after which the councillor M.P.s must steer the bills safely through the House.

The Queen was in this, as in so much else, a traditionalist. For their part the Commons accepted this view of their functions as far as it went—but it did not, in their eyes go far enough. Members had long presented private bills. During the present reign there was a growing tendency for them to introduce private bills dealing with matters which the Queen considered were the preserve of her prerogative, and moreover to hold up the voting of subsidies until private bills had been dealt with—redress of grievances before supply. It was an elegant form of blackmail, though the Commons perhaps did not see it in quite that light. What they did come to feel was that parliament existed for their convenience at least as much as for the Queen's. Thus one member grumpily protested in 1601 that 'the granting of the subsidy seemed to be the alpha and omega of this parliament' and clearly felt that he was making a valid complaint.

In 1604, at the very beginning of James I's reign, a Commons Committee asserted that 'The prerogatives of princes may easily, and do daily, grow; the privileges of the subject are for the most part at an everlasting stand', but it was in fact their own privileges that had grown and become firmly established

during the sixteenth century. In the *Apology* the committee
went on to claim three rights: freedom of election, freedom from
arrest; and freedom of speech 'without check and control-
ment'. . . . continuing, 'we stand not in place to speak or do
things pleasing. . . .' and concluding, 'the voice of the people
in the things of their knowledge, is said to be as the voice of
God.' This—though it represented a minority opinion which
proved not acceptable to the whole House—was placing the
Divine Right of Parliament over against the Divine Right of
Kings with a vengeance.

Parliamentary privileges had their origin in earlier centuries
but the sixteenth saw their great extension. At the beginning
of every parliament the Speaker claimed freedom of access
to the Crown. Nominated by the Crown, the Tudor Speaker
was theoretically the servant of the Commons, but in practice
he was a valuable instrument in the Crown's management of
the House. He had long claimed freedom of access for himself;
by 1559 he was also requesting it for the whole House.

Freedom from arrest for M.P.s and their servants was an
ancient privilege. In the sixteenth century the Commons
obtained the important additional right of enforcing this freedom
through the action of their own officials, and not through the
ordinary machinery of the law (1543, Ferrers' Case).

Subsidiary privileges included the recognition of the Commons' claim to be a court of record (a body with powers to
keep records valid as legal evidence, to order the attendance
of the officers of other courts, and to take decisions affecting
individuals); to decide disputed elections—a privilege not
finally recognized till 1604 in Goodwin's Case, though after
1586 it became usual to commit all election disputes to a
standing committee, appointed at the beginning of each new
parliament: to act against those, whether members or non-
members, who had offended against the Commons.

The basic privilege, claimed by the House but only partially
acknowledged by the Crown, the major source of conflict
between Elizabeth and her essentially loyal Commons, was that
of freedom of speech. A limited freedom the Crown
recognized; the Speaker's traditional petition included a request
that the House 'might have liberty and freedom of speech in
whatsoever they treated of or had occasion to propound and
debate in the House'. That limited freedom might even be of

value to the Crown, as when it enabled Henry VIII to inform
the Pope that 'The discussions in the English Parliament are
free and unrestricted; the Crown has no power to limit their
debates or to control the votes of members. They determine
everything for themselves, as the interests of the commonwealth require.'

In 1523 Sir Thomas More had, as Speaker, requested 'licence
and pardon, freely, without doubt of your dreadful displeasure,
every man to discharge his conscience and boldly in every thing
incident among us to declare his advice: . . .' Clearly there
must be limits to this claim and it was over these limits that
there was disagreement in Elizabeth's reign. Originally the
dispute was not about an abstract freedom, but about the
topics over which this freedom might be exercised, yet in
practice differences between the Queen and her members over
religion and over foreign affairs led inevitably to protests from
individual members on points of constitutional principle, to
conflicts not about the practical details of policy but about the
theoretical question of fundamental rights.

Elizabeth's view—and there is no doubt that the weight of
precedent and of logic was on her side—was that M.P.s were
free to speak on the bill before them, but were not to introduce
bills or to debate matters that were, literally, none of their
business. The excluded matters can be briefly defined as all
those affairs of state in which the royal prerogative was involved.
This definition included all questions touching Elizabeth
personally (in practice, her marriage and the succession), and all
questions touching her office as Queen and Supreme Governor
(religion, foreign policy and the regulation of trade).

The clearest statement of the royal attitude to parliamentary
freedom of speech is contained in the address delivered by the
Lord Keeper, Sir John Puckering, in 1593:

> . . . her Majesty granteth you liberal but not licentious
> speech; liberty, therefore, but with due limitation. For
> even as there can be no good consultation where all freedom
> of advice is barred, so will there be no good conclusion where
> every man may speak what he listeth, . . . For liberty of
> speech, her Majesty commandeth me to tell you that to say
> yes or no to bills, God forbid that any man should be
> restrained, or afraid to answer according to his best liking,
> with some short declaration of his reason therein, and therein

to have a free voice—which is the very true liberty of the House: not, as some suppose, to speak there of all causes as him listeth, and to frame a form of religion or a state of government, as to their idle brain shall seem meetest. She saith, no king fit for his state will suffer such absurdities.

Elizabeth and her Parliaments

To appreciate the interplay of the Queen's prerogative and the Commons' privilege; of royal need, royal graciousness, and royal rebuke; of loyal support and factional manœuvre; in short, of the whole complex relationship between Elizabeth and her subjects, between the existing order and that of the future—to understand all this it is necessary, having established the general pattern, to consider briefly the detailed story of Elizabeth's parliaments. As far as possible the same order has been followed in describing each assembly: the reasons for its calling; the most important laws enacted; debates and bills initiated by private members and the ensuing conflicts; the Queen's reactions.

The parliament of 1559 was called to deal with the problems facing Elizabeth at her accession (see Chapter VII). The most important acts passed were those of Supremacy and Uniformity. Before getting down to business, the Commons had requested the Queen to marry and had received in return the first of those ambiguous, magnetic replies of which Elizabeth was an artist. Its work done, parliament was dissolved.

A new parliament was not called for four years. When it met in 1563 the main reason for its summoning was the need for money to cover the costs of the help given to the Scots and of the expedition to France. Two important government bills were enacted, the first Elizabethan Poor Law and the Statute of Apprentices. Less welcome to the Queen were renewed petitions that she should marry and establish the succession to the throne. Once more she gave the members no direct answer, and parliament was prorogued after three months.

It remained prorogued for three and a half years and was then recalled in 1566 for a second session. Once again, the Queen's prime need was for money, the expenses of the French war had still not been covered. Many of the Commons were clearly determined that debate should precede supply; they discussed the perennial topics of marriage and succession, while they held up the granting of supplies. The Queen summoned a committee of the House and personally delivered a speech to its members:

> As for my own part, I care not for death; for all men are mortal. And though I be a woman, yet I have as good a courage, answerable to my place, as ever my father had. I am your appointed Queen. I will never be by violence constrained to do anything. I thank God I am endued with such qualities that if I were turned out of the realm in my petticoat, I were able to live in any place in Christendom.

Meanwhile it was, she concluded, not convenient to discuss the succession to the throne.

This time the magic did not work. One of the puritan choir, Paul Wentworth, put a critical question to the House; 'Whether her Highness's commandment, forbidding the Lower House to speak or treat any more of the succession and of any of their excuses in that behalf, be a breach of the liberty of the free speech of the House, or not?' The Queen returned a soft answer, remitted part of the subsidy asked for, and herself addressed parliament at the end of the session:

> As to liberties, who is so simple that doubts whether a Prince that is head of all the body may not command the feet not to stray when they would slip? God forbid that your liberty should make my bondage, or that your lawful liberties should anyways have been infringed. . . . Let this my discipline stand you in stead of sorer strokes, never to tempt too far a Prince's patience; and let my comfort pluck up our dismayed spirit, and cause you think that, in hope your following behaviours shall make amends for past actions, you return with your Prince's grace: . . .

Four years elapsed before, in 1571, the third parliament of the reign was summoned. This parliament was the first in which no Catholic sat, since all members were required to take the Oath of Supremacy. The reasons for its calling were partly financial and partly political. The cost of suppressing the Northern Rising had to be met, and legislation was required to deal with the rebels and also to reply to the Bull of Excommunication. The most important Act was the one against Bulls from Rome.

In this parliament Peter Wentworth, brother of Paul and the most redoubtable of the Queen's parliamentary opponents, made his *début*.   Wentworth was born in 1524 of Yorkshire stock and educated at the Inns of Court.   He was connected by marriage with other members of the Puritan group, since his first wife was a cousin of Catherine Parr, his second a sister of Francis Walsingham, and his daughter married the Puritan member William Strickland.   Now in his mid-forties, Wentworth entered parliament as member for Lillingstone-Lovell, near Buckingham.   Later, Wentworth recalled an event of 1571. Strickland had introduced a motion to bring in a Puritan religious settlement and to reform the 1559 Prayer book, removing offensive ceremonies and vestments.   This had led to a meeting between a deputation and Archbishop Parker.   The Archbishop had said, 'You will refer yourselves wholly to us therein.'   To which Wentworth had stoutly replied: 'No, by the faith I bear to God! we will pass nothing before we understand what it is, for that were but to make you Popes.   Make you Popes who list, for we will make you none.'

At the close of the session Sir Nicholas Bacon, the Lord Keeper, delivered the Queen's closing speech and condemned a minority of members 'for their audacious, arrogant and presumptious folly, thus by frivolous and superfluous speech spending the time and meddling with matters neither pertaining unto them nor within the capacity of their understanding'.

The uncovering of the Ridolfi Plot led within a year to the summoning of a fourth parliament (1572).   In it the members bayed for Mary's blood; 'cut off her head and make no more ado about her,' 'Mary Stuart, called Queen of Scots, is a traitor', 'Let the Queen, therefore, while she hath such an enemy in hand, execute her, lest hereafter herself come to be executed by her', 'The examples of the Old Testament be not few for the putting of wicked kings to death.'   There was difference of expression, but unanimity of opinion.   The Queen refused to take action; she neither accepted nor rejected a bill to bar Mary from the succession, but the prorogation of parliament effectively destroyed it.

This parliament was recalled four years later, its business to vote money.   The usual subsidy together with two fifteenths and tenths was granted almost without comment, and the session would have been a quiet one, had it not been for Peter Wentworth's great outburst, which he had been preparing since the last session:

R

... two things do very great hurt in this place, of the which I mean to speak. The one is a rumour that runneth about the House, and this is: 'Take heed what you do. The Queen's Majesty liketh not of such a matter: whosoever preferreth it, she will be much offended with him.' Or the contrary: 'Her Majesty liketh of such a matter: whosoever speaketh against it, she will be much offended with him.' The other is: sometimes a message is brought into the House, either of commanding or inhibiting, very injurious unto the freedom of speech and consultation. I would to God, Mr. Speaker, that these two were buried in Hell: I mean rumours and messages.

For these 'violent and wicked words' the Commons themselves committed Wentworth to the Tower. After a month the Queen graciously released him and sent him back to the House, 'absolutely persuaded that his speech proceeded of abundance of zeal towards her'.

Parliament was again prorogued and five years later (1581) it held its third and last session. It was recalled partly to vote money, partly to face the Catholic threat—the arrival of Jesuit priests in England and of Papal and Spanish troops in Ireland. Its business concluded, the longest-lived of Elizabeth's parliaments was dissolved.

The later parliaments of the reign met under conditions of war, or approaching war. They faced a different type of problem, one of supply rather than of consolidation. The Queen was in her fifties and time had settled the question of her marriage. On the other hand, Mary was still alive and over the succession there still hung what Professor Neale has termed an 'awful mark of interrogation'. In the past the major clashes had taken place over religious matters. The Marian émigrés and the Puritan divines, working through like-minded gentlemen and patrons in the Lower House, had schooled that House in the elements of parliamentary manœuvring, and their attack was by no means over. During the eighties it reached new heights, in conjunction with the 'classical' movement, but by this time there were other sources of friction as well.

The international situation was grave: Jesuits were busy in England and Scotland; Philip II had plans for the Enterprise, the overthrow of protestantism; in 1583 Walsingham uncovered

Throckmorton's Plot; in 1584 William the Silent was assassinated, and the Council reacted by drawing up the Bond of Association. The reign of Elizabeth was moving towards its climax.

In November 1584 a new parliament met. Its composition was unusually young and unusually new. Its official business was to provide for the Queen's safety, to take steps to prevent a constitutional vacuum should she die, and to frame legislation against the Jesuits and seminary priests. In addition, the Commons intended to do something about Mary, Queen of Scots, and the Bond of Association was embodied in an Act.

Then there came the question of a subsidy. Sir Walter Mildmay, Chancellor of the Exchequer, disarmingly admitted that members might be surprised that the government was asking for more:

> This I myself would likewise marvel at, if two things did not move me, which I think will move you also; one the costliness of the wars and the great increase of prices of all things in this age, far surmounting the times before; and the other, the easiness of the taxation of the subsidies, . . . If I should tell you how meanly the great possessors in the country and the best aldermen and citizens of London and the rich men of the realm are rated, you would marvel at it. . . . Thereby a very great deal less than is given to her Majesty is paid into her coffers: . . .

It was a perceptive synopsis of the revenue problem.

The 'classical' movement was now at its height and extensive lobbying helped to link the vote of money with a demand for religious changes. The members knew quite well what they were doing; it was a good move, said one, 'for that her Majesty, expecting a benevolence from them, would the sooner yield to their lawful and necessary petitions'. But the Queen vetoed two bills dealing with religion and, proroguing parliament, herself addressed the members:

> I see many overbold with God Almighty. . . . The presumption is so great, as I may not suffer it. Yet mind I not hereby to animate Romanists. . . ., nor tolerate new fangledness. I mean to guide them both by God's holy true rule. In both parts be perils. And of the latter, I must pronounce them dangerous to a kingly rule; to have every man, according to his own censure, to make a doom of the validity and

privity of his Prince's government, with a common veil and cover of God's word, whose followers must not be judged but by private man's exposition. God defend you from such a ruler that so evil will guide you.

The exposure of the Babington Plot and the consequent approach of Mary's trial led Elizabeth's councillors to request a new parliament. The 1584 parliament was dissolved and the sixth parliament of the reign met, late in 1586. The members were informed that the Queen required neither new laws nor a subsidy, but that 'The cause was rare and extraordinary', the fate of the Queen of Scots. In the course of the debates which followed, Job Throckmorton, Puritan member for Warwick, made a strong attack on Mary:

> If I should term her the daughter of sedition, the mother of rebellion, the nurse of impiety, the handmaid of iniquity, the sister of unshamefastness; or if I should tell you that which you know already—that she is Scottish of nation, French of education, Papist of profession, a Guisan of blood, a Spaniard in practice, a libertine in life; as all this were not to flatter her, so yet this were nothing near to describe her.

Later the two Houses told the Queen that they were resolved that Mary should die. Elizabeth replied in a speech which was later revised and printed. It was her apologia: 'What will they not now say, when it shall be spread that for the safety of her life a maiden Queen could be content to spill the blood of her own kinswoman?' After all, her subjects had to risk death for her: 'I am not so void as not to see mine own peril; nor yet so ignorant as not to know it were in nature a foolish course to cherish a sword to cut mine own throat; nor so careless as not to weigh that my life daily is in hazard. But this I do consider, that many a man would put his life in danger for the safeguard of a King. I do not say that so will I; but I pray you think that I have thought upon it.' The Queen's dignity counterpointed the Commons' indignation.

Yet all was not sweet accord during this parliament's life. After Mary's execution, Hatton, Mildmay and other councillors put pressure on the Queen, encouraging the Commons to vote an extra subsidy if Elizabeth would accept the sovereignty of the Netherlands, while at the same time the presbyterian group renewed their demand for religious changes. Anthony Cope introduced a Bill to sweep away the whole existing government and liturgy of the Church, together with a Book which was the Genevan Prayer-Book. The Queen sent for the Bill and Book. Her action led to another protest from Peter Wentworth 'for I am fully persuaded that God cannot be honoured, neither yet our noble Prince or Commonweal preserved or maintained, without free speech. . . .' Wentworth, Cope and three other Members were sent to the Tower by the Council.

There were long debates on foreign policy. A parliamentary diarist noted that Job Throckmorton 'spoke very sharply of princes': Charles IX of France was anatomized; 'Mark what king it was, it was the same king that wept to the Admiral Coligny overnight, and gave him up to the butchery to be cut in pieces in the morning'; Catherine was no better but she 'hath not many (thanks be to God) left of her loins to pester the earth with'; the Pope was 'that man described in the Apocalypse —I mean that man of sin, that beast with the mark in his forehead—'; Philip II was worse; 'his religion idolatrous, his life some think licentious, his marriage we all know incestuous, great uncle to his own children'. As for the French, 'A Frenchman unreformed is as vile a man as lives, and no villainy can make him blush. . . . Whither, then, shall we cast our eye? Northward towards the young imp of Scotland? Alas! it is a cold coast (ye know) and he that should set up his rest upon so young and wavering a head might happen find cold comfort. . . .' Fortunately, the outlook was not entirely black, the Netherlands' offer of sovereignty was, Throckmorton said, 'an evident sign that the Lord hath yet once more vowed himself to be English. . . .'

Elizabeth, however, had no intention of accepting that sovereignty, nor did she relish attacks on the French and Scots. Throckmorton was committed to the Tower, and in March this important parliament, which had seen the defeat of the Puritan campaign and the execution of Mary, was dissolved.

In 1589 a seventh parliament was summoned, its main object being to pay for the defeat of the Armada. The Lord Chancellor, Sir Christopher Hatton, opened with a stirring account of the situation. The King of Spain was not so strong as appearances might suggest: 'Though the Spaniard hath under him many kingdoms and countries, yet is he thereby drawn, we know not to what exceeding charges.' God was on England's side, 'Their bulls He hath caused to gore themselves, and given us of late a most notable victory.' There must, though, be no relaxation:

> Our enemies make great preparation to assail us by sea: our navy must be made fit to encounter them. They have great strength to invade us by land: a correspondency of force must be had to withstand them. They are caring for means to continue their offence: we must likewise consider of good means to continue our defence. Our duties towards God, her Majesty, and our country doth require all this at your hands.

Two subsidies were asked for and voted, but in other matters the Commons were less co-operative, criticizing abuses of the royal prerogative of purveyance—which the Queen promised should be looked into—and attempting yet again to make ecclesiastical changes. Elizabeth dissolved this parliament as soon as she conveniently could.

Four years passed before another parliament assembled in 1593. The need for revenue, and problems of internal security prompted the calling of this parliament. Elizabeth's foreign commitments had proved increasingly expensive and she had been compelled to realize capital assets, selling crown lands. The Queen spoke graciously to the Commons through their Speaker-elect, Sir Edward Coke:

> And though (she saith) you may have a wiser prince—for I must use her own words—she dare avow, you shall never have one more careful of your safeties, nor to give more even stroke among her subjects, without regard of person more than matter. And of such mind she beseecheth God ever send your prince.

Acts against sectaries and recusants were eventually passed, but meanwhile James Morice had attacked Whitgift's religious administration. Morice introduced two bills, couched as petitions, the first against the High Commission *ex officio* oath, the other against unlawful imprisonment. Whitgift hastened to inform the Queen of the political dangers of the presbyterian attitude, 'In the end, your Majesty will find that those which now impugn the ecclesiastical jurisdiction will endeavour also to impair the temporal and to bring even kings and princes under their censure.' Elizabeth had already taken action. Morice appeared before the Council and was placed under a mild form of house arrest for eight weeks. On his release Burghley reminded him that religion was part of the Queen's prerogative and that 'If it pleased her to reform it, it was well: if not, we were to pray to God to move her heart thereunto, and so to leave the matter to God and her Majesty.'

The debate on the subsidies produced a financial analysis from the Chancellor of the Exchequer, Sir John Fortescue. Could Henri IV have held out against the League 'had not her Majesty assisted him with her men and money, which hath cost her above £100,000?' The defence of the Netherlands consumed £150,000 a year. On her accession, there had been a debt of £4,000,000 and the navy had been decayed:

> ... yet all this she hath discharged, and, thanks be to God, is nothing indebted. And now she is able to match on sea any Prince in Europe; which the Spaniards found when they came to invade us. ... She hath with her ships compassed the world, whereby this land is made famous throughout all places. She found all iron pieces in her navy: now she hath furnished them with artillery of brass, so that one of her ships is not a subject's but rather a petty king's wealth. ... In her building she hath consumed little or nothing; in her pleasures, not much. ... As for these subsidies which are granted nowadays to her Majesty, they are less by half they were in the time of her father, King Henry VIII. And although her Majesty had borrowed money of her subjects, besides her subsidies, yet had she truly repaid it and answered everyone fully.

At the same time Burghley told the Lords that since 1589 the Queen had spent £1,030,000 out of her own treasure. Parliament responded nobly, voting three subsidies to be collected over the next four years, though Francis Bacon warned the government that 'In histories it is to be observed that of all nations the English care not to be subject, base and taxable.'

Peter Wentworth had intended to raise the question of the succession in this Parliament. He was 'a pre-meditative type of man; of slow, deliberate pace and corresponding courage',[1] and he had been brooding on the matter for some time. In 1587 he had composed *A Pithie Exhortation to Her Majesty for establishing her successor to the crown*. Later the tract had come into the hands of the Council and he had been imprisoned for

[1] J. E. Neale, *Elizabeth I and her Parliaments, 1584-1601*, Cape 1957, p. 251.

about six months during the winter of 1591–2. The Queen now heard that he planned to debate the subject in the Commons. Early in 1593 Wentworth was summoned before the Council and then sent to the Tower, where he remained until his death in 1597. He composed his own appropriate epitaph:

> Sith I have said and done my best,
> Meekly, with prayer, God grant me rest.

During this parliament Elizabeth imprisoned or sequestered seven Members, yet it was on the whole a tractable assembly. At its dissolution the Queen herself addressed the Commons:

> Many wiser princes than myself you have had, but, only excepted—whom in the duty of a child I must regard, and to whom I must acknowledge myself far shallow—I may truly say, none whose love and care can be greater, ... You have heard in the beginning of this Parliament, some doubt of danger: more than I would have you to fear. Doubt only should be, if not prevented; and fear, if not provided for. For mine own part, I protest I never feared, and what fear was, my heart never knew. . . . I would not have you returning into the country to strike a fear into the minds of any of my people.... For even our enemies hold our nature resolute and valiant: which, though they will not outwardly show, they inwardly know. . . . Now must I give you all as great thanks as ever prince gave to loving subjects, assuring you that my care for you hath, and shall, exceed all my other cares of worldly causes, whatsoever.

The Churchillian eloquence no doubt eased the pain of giving.

The ninth parliament of the reign met in the autumn of 1597. The subsidies granted four years earlier were coming to an end, while war expenditure had increased, and the government had even levied a forced loan. Bad harvests, plague and the impressment of men for service overseas had all helped to produce a feeling of discontent in the country; economic and social legislation might ease the situation, and the great acts of this parliament were of that type, for the punishment of sturdy beggars, for erecting hospitals for the poor, and—most important of all—the great Elizabethan Poor Law.

The Commons initiated a debate on the matter of monopolies. These were licences granted by the Queen's letters patent to individuals and were originally concerned, like modern patents, with new manufacturing processes. They proved a convenient way of rewarding royal officials and court favourites and soon they were also issued to cover the manufacture of established products such as paper, salt and starch. The patentee might manufacture the product himself or, more commonly, might insist that tradesmen paid him for licences to carry on their businesses. It was this development which was now attacked, for there was no redress in the Common Law courts nor by statute, since monopolies were an expression of the royal prerogative and, as Francis Bacon reminded the Commons in 1601, 'we ought not to deal, to judge or meddle, with her Majesty's prerogative. . . .' Monopolies had been denounced as early as 1571. The attack was decorous in 1597. A committee prepared a petition to be delivered to the Queen by the Speaker. Elizabeth promised that all the patents should be examined 'to abide the trial and true touchstone of the law'.

A treble subsidy was voted. During the debate, Francis Bacon, using an appropriately scientific simile, made the very modern point that money voted in taxes returned eventually to the taxpayer: 'Sure I am that the treasure that cometh from you to her Majesty is but as a vapour which riseth from the earth and gathereth into a cloud and stayeth not there long, but upon the same earth it falleth again. And what if some drops of this do fall upon France or Flanders? It is like a sweet odour of honour and reputation to our nation throughout the world.'

The last parliament of the reign met in the autumn of 1601, its main purpose—as usual—to vote money, which was largely required to pay for the Irish wars. By now Burghley was dead, as was Essex, and Robert Cecil was the dominant Councillor. There was a growing tendency for patrons to control little groups of M.P.s and Cecil secured the nomination to at least fourteen seats, six of his employees and secretaries sitting in the House. Similarly, Archbishop Whitgift nominated perhaps another half-dozen members.

Yet it was not an altogether tractable parliament. Half the members were old hands who remembered the monopolies debate. Although the Queen had repealed some patents, new ones had been granted and the total number had increased. The Commons returned to the attack. William Hakewill, a

lawyer, asked sarcastically if bread were not on the list:
'"Bread?" quoth one; "Bread?" quoth another. "This voice
seems strange", quoth a third. "No," quoth Mr. Hakewill,
"but if order be not taken for these, bread will be there before
the next Parliament".' Robert Cecil did what he could, 'I had
rather all the patents were burnt than her Majesty should lose
the hearts of so many subjects, as is pretended she will.' A
committee was set up. The opposition used the new technique
of lobbying, crowding the stairs with a mob who claimed they
were being 'spoiled, imprisoned and robbed by monopolists',
while in the streets men shouted 'God prosper those that further
the overthrow of these monopolies. God send the prerogative
touch not our liberty.' Next day the house insisted on deferring
the subsidy bill until the committee had reported on monopolies.
These were noisy interruptions. Cecil spoke again; 'I have
been, though unworthy, a Member of this House in six or seven
parliaments, yet never did I see the House in so great confusion. . . . What an indignity is it then to the Prince, and
injury to the subject, that when any is discussing this point he
should be coughed and cried down? This is more fit for a
grammar school than a Court of Parliament.'

The Queen now used the political skill of forty-three years.
Cecil's speech had been delivered on Tuesday, 24 November.
On Wednesday the Speaker reported that she had graciously
agreed that the abuses should be removed immediately. On
Thursday Cecil told the House that she would not receive their
thanks until she had carried out her promise. By Saturday the
royal proclamation concerning monopolies had been printed
and every member had a copy. Finally, on the following
Monday afternoon the Queen addressed the members in the
Council Chamber at Whitehall, making her greatest 'golden'
speech:

> . . . I do assure you there is no prince that loves his subjects
> better, or whose love can countervail our love. There is
> no jewel, be it of never so rich a price, which I set before
> this jewel: I mean your love. For I do esteem it more than
> any treasure or riches; for that we know how to price, but
> love and thanks I count unvaluable. And though God hath
> raised me high, yet this I count the glory of my crown, that
> I have reigned with your loves. . . . Of myself I must say
> this: I never was any greedy, scraping grasper, nor a strait,

fast-holding Prince, nor yet a waster. My heart was never
set on any worldly goods, but only for my subjects' good. . . .
The Queen desired the members, who had been kneeling, to
stand and then continued speaking. When she heard of the
oppressive monopolies, she said, she could not rest until she
had reformed them. Then came the carefully prepared
peroration:

> I know the title of a King is a glorious title; but assure your-
> self that the shining glory of princely authority hath not so
> dazzled the eyes of our understanding, but that we well know
> and remember that we also are to yield an account of our
> actions before the great Judge. To be a King and wear a
> crown is a thing more glorious to them that see it, than it is
> pleasant to them that bear it. For myself, I was never so
> much enticed with the glorious name of a King or the royal
> authority, of a Queen, as delighted that God hath made me
> His instrument to maintain His truth and glory, and to
> defend this Kingdom (as I said) from peril, dishonour,
> tyranny and oppression.
>   There will never Queen sit in my seat with more zeal to my
> country, more care for my subjects, and that will sooner with
> willingness venture her life for your good and safety, than
> myself. For it is my desire to live nor reign no longer than
> my life and reign shall be for your good. And though you
> have had and may have many princes more mighty and wise
> sitting in this seat, yet you never had nor shall have any that
> will be more careful and loving.

The Queen took up this theme again in her dissolution
speech, three weeks later. 'This testimony I would have you
carry hence for the world to know: that your Sovereign is more
careful of your conservation than of herself, and will daily
crave God that they that wish you best may never wish in
vain.'

It was the last word in the long love-hate relationship
between Elizabeth and her parliaments, a relationship that
had produced important constitutional developments: the
extension of More's claim for freedom of speech (1523) into a
claim to oppose any bill or motion; the planning, management and general enlargement of parliamentary techniques
which had been a consequence of the Puritan campaigns; the
employment by the Crown of a whole range of devices for
presenting the royal point of view, and of obtaining subsidies

without giving way to demands for the redress of grievances before the granting of supply.

In the next reign parliamentary procedure continued to evolve, but there was not a corresponding development of royal finesse; instead, especially after Robert Cecil's death in 1612, there was a disastrous failure to understand the necessity for a tactful firmness in handling this valuable but increasingly independent instrument of government. The consequences of the Elizabethan development of parliament and of the Stuart failure to control that development were, by the middle of the seventeenth century, revolutionary.

FURTHER READING

W. A. Barker, *Religion and Politics 1559–1642*, H.A., Aids for Teachers No. 29 1957

J. E. Neale, *The Elizabethan House of Commons*, Cape, 1949

— *Elizabeth I and her Parliaments 1559–81*, Cape, 1953

— *Elizabeth I and her Parliaments 1584–1601*, Cape, 1957

W. Notestein, *The Winning of the Initiative by the House of Commons*, Raleigh Lecture, O.U.P., 1924

R. K. Gilkes, *The Tudor Parliament*, University of London Press, 1969

XII · ELIZABETHAN ADMINISTRATION AND TUDOR POLITICAL THOUGHT

Introduction

THE sixteenth century was in many parts of western Europe a period of important political developments not only in practice but also in theory. In England the changes were—at least superficially—less startling than on the continent, and in political thought there was remarkably little originality. Writers tended to compile what were in effect handbooks of existing practice rather than to consider the theoretical basis of that practice.

It would be dangerous to underestimate the changes that in fact took place. By 1603 Elizabethan England had more in common with the England of 1685 than it had with the England of Edward IV's day. The Elizabethan age, like its Queen, was conservative, but if there was nothing very new, it has been observed, there was nevertheless much that was recent. The national Church, the sovereign state, the new bureaucracy—all those offices that had been created or at least, to use Dr. Elton's words, 'given a new twist' in the earlier years of the century were somehow found to be compatible with an almost medieval respect for an unchanging political and social structure based on natural degree and order. Men find it quite easy to carry two contradictory sets of ideas in their minds at the same time, and the Elizabethans were no exception. It was usually unnecessary for them to define the limits of political rights and of the royal prerogative and they continued, as their ancestors had done, to assume, consciously or unconsciously, that there was a law of nature built by God into the universal order, a law that was above man-made law. Yet at the same time within the actual structure of their government, they were inclined to give increased weight to the conception of the supremacy of statute law, the representative of security in an insecure age. And so two potential sources of conflict were created, that between parliament and the Crown and that between the dictates of the natural order and the regulations of parliamentary statutes. The Elizabethans could disregard these, but their appearance would pose intractable problems for the men of the seventeenth century.

Central Administration[1]

Within the area of central administration Elizabeth's reign saw no revolutionary developments and the general pattern remained much as it had been at mid-century. The Crown was still the unchallenged ruler of England. Elizabeth's sex set her apart from her officials and this must have helped in practice to support the conception that, in the words of her successor, James, 'a subject and a sovereign are clean different things'. The Queen was content to assume this without talking about it at great length. She touched regularly for the Queen's Evil. She reminded parliament, with magnificent simplicity, 'I am your anointed Queen', combining in five words the religious and political foundations of her right to rule. The vast majority accepted that right.

The Queen's instrument of government was, as in earlier reigns, the Council, and the business it transacted remained very varied. It covered the greatest matters of state, such as the preparations made to meet the Armada, or the perennial question of what to do with Mary Stuart. It also included the most microscopic matters—a man's debts, the discovery of Catholic vestments near Reading, a multitude of private land disputes. In general terms its duty was to preserve the established order, to settle or quell disorder whether national or individual. As formerly, the Council often operated through the Star Chamber where it heard cases of riots (almost any form of disagreement might come under this head) and supervised the enforcement of proclamations. The Court sat in public, and a contemporary noted that spectators would flock to it 'when causes of weight are there heard. . . .' It was now perhaps at the height of its popularity. Its loss of public support in the next century was due more to a change in the climate of opinion than to a change in its actions—though it is true that it always tended to become, as Maitland has said, 'a court of politicians enforcing a policy, not a court of judges administering the law'. During at least the greater part of Elizabeth's reign this tendency was curbed. The members of the Council discussed, advised, and implemented, but the

[1] See also Chapter XVI.

decisions were hers. Her Council was relatively small, numbering from twelve to eighteen, and the key men were even fewer—Leicester, Walsingham and Cecil.

During Elizabeth's reign Cecil[1] was continuously in office, first as Secretary of State (1558–72) and then as Lord High Treasurer (1572–98). Historians have argued and will probably always argue over the relative parts played by the Queen and her chief minister in the government of England. In fact, the relationship was symbiotic, a partnership that worked with increasing smoothness as the years went by. There were minor crises of confidence in 1560 and again in the years 1568–72, but Cecil was never in any real danger of losing Elizabeth's trust. His civil service mentality put a brake on her impulsiveness, while her quicksilver imagination prevented him from being hobbled by precedent. Yet in their approach to problems the two were basically very similar; cautious, hard-working, *politique*. There is however no doubt that the partnership remained one of mistress and servant. When there was disagreement, as over religious matters, or when the Queen did not wish to act, as in the matter of Mary Stuart, it was the Queen's will that prevailed and Cecil was left to lament the wrong decision, the indetermination.

The potential powers of the Secretary were great, and Cecil used them to the full, restoring to the office all its former authority, but the ambiguity of those powers held its own dangers. The Secretary's position was at one and the same time that of minister, bureaucrat and courtier. A later Secretary wrote:

> Only a secretary hath no warrant or commission in matters of his own greatest peril but the virtue and word of his sovereign. For such is the multiplicity of occasions and the variable motions and intent of foreign princes, and their daily practices, and in so many points and places as secretaries can never have any commission so large and universal to assure them.

The successful Secretary must combine empirical judgement and official methods, the qualities of a company chairman and a sensitive psychologist. Robert Beale, Clerk to the Privy Council, wrote in 1592 of the techniques required:

---

[1] For Cecil's earlier life, see p. 164.

Favour not secret or Cabinet Councils which do but cause jealousy and envy. . . .   When there shall be any unpleasant matter to be imparted to her Majesty from the Council, or other matters to be done of great importance, let not the burden be laid on you alone. . . .   Burden not yourself with too many clerks or servants, as Sir Francis Walsingham did. Let your secret services be known to a few; the lord treasurer Burghley, being secretary, had not above two or three. . . . A secretary must have a special cabinet whereof he is himself to keep the key, for his signets, ciphers and secret intelligences, distinguishing the boxes or tills rather by letters than by the names of the countries. . . .

Have in a little paper note of such things as you are to propound to her Majesty and divide it into titles of public and private suits. . . .

Learn before your access her Majesty's disposition by some of the privy chamber, with whom you must keep credit, for that will stand you in much stead. . . .

When her Highness is angry or not well disposed, trouble her not with any matter which you desire to have done, unless extreme necessity urge it.

When her Majesty signeth it shall be good to entertain her with some relation or speech whereat she may take some pleasure.

In 1600 John Herbert was appointed second Secretary, his main sphere of work being foreign affairs, and he has left a memorandum of his duties. These included responsibility for foreign treaties and ambassadors, the work of the Councils of the Marches and of the North, Ireland, the expenses of intervention in the Low Countries and in France, the order of the Council-book and Muster-book, foreign correspondence, and the interpretation of intelligence reports from abroad.

In 1561 Cecil was appointed Master of the Court of Wards, an important office which gave him great powers of patronage and sources of income—in the last three years of his Mastership he made over £3,000. In 1571 the Queen created him Baron of Burghley, the only one of her officials whom that cautious woman ennobled. In 1572 he became Lord Treasurer on the death of William Paulet, Marquess of Winchester, the man responsible for Mary I's financial reforms, who had held office since 1550—having, as he observed, more of the willow than the oak in his nature. As Lord Treasurer, Cecil was Elizabeth's chief minister, supreme and powerful, a link in the chain that binds earlier Treasurers, feudal officials such as the dukes of Norfolk, to eighteenth-century ministers like Walpole and Pitt. Yet it was not wealth or office that was the foundation of Lord Burghley's power, but the confidence of the Queen, which he never lost. Throughout the reign he played Ariel to the Queen's Prospero—and Elizabeth recognized the fact, calling him her 'spirit' and boasting that 'no prince in Europe had such a counsellor as she had of him'.

To describe Burghley's work would be to re-write the history of the reign. The details of his career must be pieced together from that history. One point, though, deserves emphasis. Historians have seen Cecil as the pursuer of a deliberate economic policy, and he has even been called the only true mercantilist. Burghley's economic actions do exhibit state paternalism, but their congruence does not imply a carefully thought-out mercantilist policy; it springs rather from the fact that they are the consistent expression of an economic nationalism inspired by social conservatism and fear of war.

Burghley was an Eminent Victorian born before his time. It is apparent in his probity, his religious scruples (which must nevertheless give place when necessary to the good of the country), in a certain coolness in personal relationships—even in his buildings, Victorian in their ostentatious extravagance. His political testament was brief: when dying, he echoed his aim of a generation earlier, 'I have no affection to be of a party, but for the Queen's Majesty.' In 1592 Bacon, then a perceptive young contemporary, described the old Lord Burghley as

> never no violent or transported man in matters of state, but ever respective and moderate; . . . he was never no vindictive man in his particular, no breaker of necks, no heavy enemy, but ever placable and mild; . . . ever real and certain . . . ever civil familiar and good . . . ever a true reporter of her Majesty of every man's deserts and abilities; . . . and lastly, though he somewhat be envied without just cause whilst he liveth, yet he shall be deeply wanted when he is gone.

Sir Francis Walsingham (c. 1536–1590), Elizabeth's expert on foreign affairs was, next to Cecil, Elizabeth's principal minister and like Cecil he was a representative of the new men. In the fifteenth century his family had been London tradesmen. In the sixteenth they were country gentry in Kent, and his father was a barrister. Sir Francis went to Cambridge, travelled abroad, became a protestant, and went into exile in Mary's reign, reading law at Padua and meeting other refugees in the Empire and in Switzerland. On Elizabeth's accession he returned to England, a cosmopolitan Renaissance gentleman and a Puritan. In 1570 he was appointed the Queen's ambassador in Paris. As already noted, he observed with little enthusiasm the prospect of the Anjou marriage and with horror the business of St. Bartholomew's day. In 1573 he became the principal Secretary of State, a position which he held until his death in 1590. He attached himself more closely to Leicester than to his old patron Cecil, for the latter, he thought, was inclined to put the interests of England before those of the reformed religion. As early as 1571 he had stated his view of the priorities, 'I wish God's glory and next the Queen's safety'. Reform in religion must come from the state, not the individual: 'I would have all reformation done by the public authority. It were very dangerous that every man's private zeal should carry sufficient authority of reforming things amiss.'

Walsingham was well-informed on foreign affairs, receiving reports from 13 places in France, 9 in Germany, 7 in the Spanish Netherlands and 3 in the United Provinces, 5 in Spain and 3 in the remote Ottoman Empire. He was, not surprisingly, a rigid opponent of the Catholics, a relentless hunter of Mary, 'that devilish woman', and an inflexible enemy of Philip II (who, hearing of his death, noted 'good news' in the margin of the report).

There was another side to Sir Francis, that of the European intellectual. It coloured his careful, devious thoughts—James I called him 'a very Machiavel'—but it also made him a patron of Renaissance culture. He gave support to Spenser and helped to finance the voyages of Frobisher and Drake. To him Hakluyt dedicated the first edition of his *Voyages*, and at Oxford Walsingham endowed a chair of international law.

The financial administration had been reorganized in Mary's first year, and two men supervised its operation during the next half-century, Paulet and Cecil. The task which both men faced was to make the medieval structure strong enough to bear the weight of modern expenditure. It was a work that occupied a considerable part of Burghley's time and energy.

The general pattern of Crown revenue and expenditure is well-defined, though all the details will never be exactly known, for accountancy was rudimentary and officials were cheerfully inaccurate. The figures available should therefore not be regarded as exact statements of account, but rather as illustrations of the relative importance of the different elements in the Crown's financial position.

In outline the situation is crystal clear. Elizabeth faced a growing and, within her own terms of reference, insoluble financial problem. The purchasing power of her ordinary revenue was being rapidly reduced by the price rise, while the Crown's expenditure was climbing to alarming heights in consequence of increasing, and apparently inescapable, foreign commitments arising out of the struggle with Spain. Higher prices and the cost of war combined to create a gap between revenue and expenditure which could be only partially bridged by such extreme actions as the sale of crown lands or the voting by parliament of double and even treble subsidies.

The ordinary revenue was still drawn from the sources described on pages 21–3. During the reign it rose from about £200,000 to about £300,000—an increase that nevertheless did not keep pace with the rise in prices. Crown lands provided £60,000, customs dues £50,000 to £80,000,[1] profits from the Court of Wards averaged just under £15,000.

Peacetime expenditure fluctuated between £125,000 and £150,000 and in the years of peace Elizabeth was able to build up a reserve, which was nevertheless soon lost in the gulf of war. In 1584 it totalled £300,000; by 1590 it was exhausted. Taking the forty-five years of the reign as a whole, the Crown's total ordinary revenue was in the region of £10,500,000, while its total expenditure was about £15,000,000. The gap was partially bridged by extraordinary means: twenty parliamentary subsidies[2] were voted, twelve of them in the last fifteen years of the reign, and in the ten years, 1593–1602, £1,092,000 was actually collected; crown lands were sold to the value of almost a further million pounds (£876,332). There remained debts which had to be met by borrowing. The practice of raising

[1] During the middle years of the reign the customs were farmed to Mr. 'Customer' Smythe, who was at one time paying £30,000 a year for the privilege, and still making a handsome profit for himself.

[2] A subsidy bill normally consisted of one subsidy (c. £100,000) and two-fifteenths and tenths (c. £60,000).

high-interest loans in Antwerp ended in 1574, and in the preceding twelve years Gresham had raised only £95,000 in that manner.   Between 1575 and 1603 £461,000 was borrowed, a great part of it interest-free from the Corporation of London.[1] At her death Elizabeth left to her successor outstanding debts of about a third of a million.

The greater part of the additional expenditure went on foreign wars and internal rebellions, expenses incurred particularly in the years after 1585.   The cost of aiding the Netherlands rose each year: 1585 £23,000; 1586 £100,000; 1587 £175,000.   Sir Walter Mildmay, the Chancellor of the Exchequer, told the Commons that the Queen had spent £1,000,000 during the years 1589–93.

		Approximate expenditure
Scotland	1560	£178,000
France	1562–3	£245,000
Northern Rising and raid into Scotland	1569–70	£93,000
Netherlands	1585–1603	£1,500,000
Armada	1588	£160,000
Operations against Spain	1589–1603	£180,000
France	1588–97	£380,000
Ireland	1567, 1579–81, 1595–1603	£1,900,000

The figures speak for themselves, particularly the ruinously heavy cost of the Irish campaigns.   The unforeseen consequence of Elizabeth's military expenditure was to make parliamentary grants a regular part of the Crown's income.

In the constitutional structure the Court of Wards played a significant part.   Under Elizabeth seventy to ninety wardships were sold each year, bringing to the Crown a total of about £650,000 during her reign.   Wards 'sold like an ox' brought 'the ruin of every man's family once in three descents'.   A peak had been reached in Mary's reign,[2] Elizabeth receiving perhaps one-third of the market value of the wardships, while the

[1] R. B. Outhwaite, *The Trials of Foreign Borrowing*, Ec.H.R., XIX, 1966.
[2] In 1542–3 the profit from wardship had been £5,452; the average for Edward's reign was £11,027, for Mary's reign £15,423, for Elizabeth's reign £14,700; see J. Hurstfield, *The Queen's Wards*, Longmans, Green, 1958.

remainder went to her servants. As Master of the Wards Cecil saw clearly that this feudal fiscalism served two purposes: it was a traditional form of indirect taxation, providing the Crown with a useful income; it was also a means of supplementing the inadequate salaries of her officials, without having recourse to parliament, and of binding them by patronage to the existing order. 'The general history of the Court of Wards ran parallel with that of the prerogative courts: dynamism under Henry VIII, conservatism, sliding into abuse through patronage under Elizabeth, roaring corruption under James I, reassertion under Charles I, angry abolition by his enemies in the 1640s,' (H. R. Trevor-Roper).[1]

Throughout the hierarchy of law courts the administration of justice was little altered. The legal profession continued to grow in power. In Elizabeth's reign for the first time all the Chancellors were drawn from the ranks of the judges. At the other end of the scale the lawyer—or at least the gentleman with a legal education—was becoming increasingly often an active member of parliament, while the number of lawyers in the country rose by two-thirds between the closing years of the reign and the sixteen thirties. The common law courts continued as before and—also as before—Chancery continued to grow at their expense. The prerogative courts were still the backbone of administration, whether they sat in the capital or in the provinces. The Queen's eye for the right man and her conservative love of the well-established can be seen in the length of tenure of some of her administrators: the Council of Wales was controlled by Sir Henry Sidney from 1559 to 1586, while that of the North was headed by the Earl of Huntingdon from 1572 to 1595.

The chief development was the appearance as a regular body of the Court of High Commission. The new Court had evolved gradually. Wolsey had exercised his legatine power through commissions, and Thomas Cromwell's vicegerency had rested on a general commission from the Supreme Head, King Henry. Commissions to enforce the state's religious settlement had been issued on an *ad hoc* basis during the next thirty years. In the seventies the term 'High Commission' began to appear, and from about 1580 the Court sat pretty regularly in London, a legal weapon in Whitgift's firm hands.

[1] From a review in *The New Statesman*, 3 January, 1959, of *The Queen's Wards*.

The Court's activities came under fire, for different reasons, from both the Puritans and the common lawyers. Burghley himself was not altogether happy with its methods. 'I think the inquisitors of Spain', he said, 'use not so many questions to comprehend and trap their preys.' Yet in many ways the High Commission was popular, providing cheap and speedy law for private suitors in a host of cases with which it was competent to deal. It was an instrument of the Crown's ecclesiastical powers very similar to the secular Star Chamber in advantages, in methods, and in the possibility of abuse.

In 1591 the question of the Court's legal position was finally established when a Puritan clergyman, Cawdrey, brought an action in Queen's Bench. Cawdrey had refused to take the *ex officio* oath and had consequently been deprived of his living by the Court. The common law judges decided against him, finding that the Crown might make such a Commission 'by the ancient prerogative and law of England'. The Court of High Commission, like the other prerogative courts, remained a power in the land until its abolition by the Long Parliament of 1641.

Local Administration

There were three main instruments of local government in the sixteenth century: the feudal, shire and hundred courts; the royal officials; and the local men commissioned by the government. The courts were by this time of little importance, their only notable activity being the election by the shire court (presided over by the sheriff) of two knights to represent the shire in parliament.

Originally the chief royal officials had been the sheriff, the escheator, and the coroner. To these were added during the sixteenth century the receivers of royal revenue such as the feodaries of the Court of Wards, and—the most important development—the lords-lieutenant and their deputies. The sheriff, once the key man, became increasingly the figurehead that he is today, his office a troublesome and expensive decoration.

The lord-lieutenant was one of the few original creations of the Tudors—and even he did not spring fully-formed from the head of a single ruler. Henry VIII had appointed men to supervise the levying of musters when necessity required, and then in 1550 Northumberland began the custom of sending lieutenants to the shires regularly each year. By the end of Elizabeth's reign the country had been divided into districts each under the control of the lord-lieutenant, usually a local man who was also a courtier. He in turn appointed deputies for each shire who did most of the detailed work, and under them came *their* subordinates, the provost-marshals. As usual the officials' duties multiplied. They raised contingents for overseas service, but they also supervised the levying of taxes, the enforcement of the recusancy laws and the administration of economic legislation, until at length they grew to be in many ways the administrative heads of their areas responsible directly to the Privy Council. In maritime counties there was a vice-admiral, who was responsible for administering naval and commercial matters arising out of such affairs as piracy, salvage, embargoes and empressment.

By far the most important group of officials was that of local men commissioned by the Government. Their commissions were of several types: *ad hoc* general commissions, such as those which dealt with the dissolution of the smaller monasteries; *ad hoc* special commissions to enquire into cases brought before the various conciliar courts; standing commissions, such as the commissions of sewers, which dealt with marshes, waterways and drainage. Of all these by far the most important was the commission of the peace.

The administrative duties of the justices of the peace increased until by the end of Elizabeth's reign they had become, for all practical purposes, the local government of England. Lambarde complained that 'stacks of Statutes' were loaded on their shoulders; more recently they have been called 'the Tudor maids-of-all-work'. Lambarde's *Eirenarcha* (1581) required over 600 pages to describe fully their responsibilities, listing 309 statutes, of which 133 were earlier than 1485, 60 were made between 1485 and 1547, 39 between 1547 and 1558, and 77 under Elizabeth.

The first and still the most important of these duties was judicial, the enforcement of the law. This the justices achieved by summary jurisdiction, in petty sessions, and in the full-scale quarter sessions held in January, in the week after Easter, in July and in September. The importance of the work carried out at these quarter sessions, as compared with the assizes, can be assessed from such figures as these, which refer to Devon in 1598: quarter sessions, 166 prisoners, 39 criminals hanged; assizes, 221 prisoners, 35 criminals hanged.   Since the majority of the J.P.s were amateurs, certain of them who had official or legal experience were specifically named of whom (*quorum*) at least one must always be present.   To this *quorum* of experts was added a clerk of the peace to assist the justices.

The J.P.s fixed wages and prices, inspected weights and measures, licensed ale-houses, supervised the upkeep of roads and bridges, and punished poachers; they concerned themselves with weeding out 'enchantments, sorceries and arts magic', suppressed the playing of football, redeemed English sailors from the Barbary pirates and maintained the old sumptuary laws.   The most important of their new duties were those involved in the enforcement of the poor laws, the recusancy laws, and the Statute of Apprentices.

With an increase in duties came an increase in numbers from an average under ten per shire to forty or fifty.   Naturally there were wide local variations—Kent had eighty justices, Rutland fifteen.   Though they were unpaid and in some ways overworked, there was never any lack of candidates.   Social conscience, love of interference, local prestige, the knowledge that this was the first step on the ladder to Court favour—all played a part in ensuring an adequate supply of J.P.s.

In 1565 Sir Thomas Smith wrote of these amateur officials in his *De Republica Anglorum*

The justices of the peace be those in whom at this time for the repressing of robbers, thieves and vagabonds, of privy complots and conspiracies, of riots and violences, and all other misdemeanours in the commonwealth the prince putteth his special trust. . . .   Each of them hath authority . . . a few lines signed with his hand is enough. . . .

There was never in any commonwealth devised a more wise, a more dulce and gentle, nor a more certain way to rule the people, whereby they are kept always as it were in a bridle of good order, and sooner looked unto that they should not offend, than punished when they have offended. . . .

In practice the system had both advantages and drawbacks. It was cheap and it kept the government in touch with the provinces, but it depended on the efficiency and goodwill of volunteers who could hardly be coerced. Justices Shallow and Slender (*Henry IV, Part II*) are a comment on possible types of inefficiency. Self-interest meant that the laws against enclosures were not enforced, and that the collection of the recusancy fines was patchy—in parts of Lancashire, for instance, Catholics went unmolested—while the raising of troops, the enforcement of the poor laws and the assessment of wages varied both in time and place. In 1571 Sir Nicholas Bacon, then Lord Keeper, had some hard things to say about a minority of the J.P.s:

> Is it not, trow you, a monstrous disguising to have . . . him that should by his oath and duty set forth justice and right, against his oath offer injury and wrong: . . . to have him that is specially chosen . . . to appease all brabbling and controversies, to be a sower and maintainer of strife and sedition . . .; leading and swaying of juries according to his will, acquitting some for gain, indicting others for malice, bearing with him as his servant or friend, overthrowing the other as his enemy, procuring all questmongers to be of his livery. . . . ?

In October 1587 the Judges of Assize reported on the J.P.s of Devon and Cornwall. Three had been removed for lack of dignity: one 'a weak brain not able to bear drink', another 'a man ridiculous to all men for his folly'. Seven were to be investigated, including 'an old fornicator', 'a furious maintainer of factions', and 'Humphry Specott: in times past a great Papist, now in the other extreme, a server of the time, extreme, covetous, corrupt, and a great maintainer of stentons and factions.'

In 1601 an M.P. attacked the venality of J.P.s: 'A justice of the peace is a living creature, yet for half a dozen chickens will dispense with a whole dozen of penal statues. So unless you offer sacrifices to the idol-justices, of sheep and oxen, they know you not. If a warrant comes from the Lords of the Council to levy a hundred men, he will levy two hundred and what with chopping in and choosing out he'll gain a hundred pounds by the bargain.' These were the dark, often overlooked, sides of a system which normally worked with surprising success.

The basis of local government was the ecclesiastical parish, taken over by Thomas Cromwell as a civil unit. The parson had his place in the administration of poor relief and in the enforcement of the recusancy laws. The churchwardens were the executive parish officials in these matters. There was the parish constable, unpaid and usually only holding his office for one year. In theory he was to prevent breaches of the peace, swearing, unlawful games and Sabbath-breaking, and to get rid of rogues, vagabonds and strolling players. Here, too, there might be a wide gap between theory and practice. Dull, Dogberry and Verges had their counterparts in reality. When, in August 1586, the constables were out in many places, on the watch for the Babington conspirators, Burghley wrote as follows to Walsingham:

> Sir, As I came from London homeword in my coach, I saw at every town's end the number of ten or twelve standing with long staves, and until I came to Enfield I thought no other of them but that they had stayed for avoiding of the rain, or to drink at some alehouse, for so they did stand under pentices at alehouses. But at Enfield finding a dozen in a plump, when there was no rain, I bethought myself that they were appointed as watchmen, for the apprehending of such as are missing. And thereupon I called some of them to me apart and asked them wherefore they stood there. And one of them answered 'To take three young men.' And demanding how they should know the persons, one answered with these words, 'Marry, my lord, by intelligence, of their favour.' 'What mean you by that?' quoth I. 'Marry,' said they, 'one of the parties hath a hooked nose.' 'And have you,' quoth I, 'no other mark?' 'No' saith they. And then I asked who appointed them. And they answered one Banks, a head constable, whom I willed to be sent to me. Surely, sir, whosoever had the charge from you hath used the matter negligently. For these watchmen stand so openly in plumps as no suspected person will come near them; and if they be no better instructed but to find three persons by one of them having a hooked nose, they may miss thereof. And thus I thought good to advertise you, that the Justices that had the charge, as I think, may use the matter more circumspectly.

Political Thought

Namier has observed that for sixteenth-century man religion was only another name for nationalism, and the converse is equally true. For many, nationalism was another name for religion. The political debate concerning the powers of the sovereign and—either openly or by implication—the rights of the subject was couched almost entirely in theological terms. Religious creeds were at the same time expressions of belief and also political ideologies.

Did the Tudors in general, and in particular Elizabeth I, believe in the divine right of kings? In one sense the question has no meaning. To the sixteenth-century political philosopher all right was 'divine', part of God's order which had established every element in the universe, from the angels to the rocks, in its proper place—a place that involved both rights and obligations divinely ordained. This was the pattern, the 'Great Chain of Being', and only by breaking this pattern could one forfeit one's divine rights.[1] Obligations and rights were reciprocal. Thus in *The Tree of Commonwealth* Dudley wrote:

> For as subjects are bound to their prince of their allegiance, to love, dread, serve and obey him, or else to be punished by him, as straightly is the Prince bound to God to maintain and support as far as in him is or lieth, the commonwealth of his subjects. . . . And God hath ordained their Prince to protect them, and they to obey their Prince.

And in the mid-century Robert Crowley believed that all would be well if only 'the possessioners would consider themselves to be but stewards and not lords of their possessions'.

As far as the state was concerned, the theory rested securely on the words of St. Paul, 'The powers that be are ordained of God'. In England the Reformation, by uniting under one ruler State and Church, laid an increased emphasis on the religious duty of political submission. Rebellion was a sin, moreover it weakened the state and opened a door to the foreigner. In his *Obedience of a Christian Man*, 1528, Tyndale wrote: 'He that judgeth the king, judgeth God; . . . The king is, in this world, without law, and may at his lust do right or wrong and shall give accounts but to God only'. *The Bishops' Book* of 1537, in its gloss on the words 'Our Father', commented: 'If our Sovereign Lord the King would say to any of us, Take me for your father and so call me, what joy in heart, what comfort, what confidence would we conceive of so favourable and gracious words.' The implications are clear. The Homily of 1547 was sweepingly condemnatory of the rebel: 'He that nameth rebellion nameth not one only and singular sin, but the whole puddle of sins against god and man. . . .' In 1549 Cranmer wrote: 'Though the magistrates be evil and very tyrants against the commonwealth yet the subjects must obey in all wordly things' and the Homily of 1571 stated specifically that those who disobey the prince 'disobey God and procure their own damnation'. In the sixteenth-century secular state the divine rights to which the medieval ruler had been entitled by the duties imposed on him in the order of things were in danger of becoming the Divine Right of Absolute Monarchy.

Yet in England Divine Right failed to establish itself. Various factors, religious, political, legal worked against it. Since it was the duty of the ruler to defend the Christian religion, his divine right to govern depended on his accomplishment of that duty. But what was the Christian religion? In earlier centuries there could have been only one conventional answer to that question, but in the sixteenth century the unity of Christendom was shattered and half a dozen major variations contended for the individual's soul and for his temporal support. In England attacks on the established political order came from the religious minorities. The Elizabethan Prayer Book was in the old tradition when it declared God to be *the only Ruler of princes*, but Catholic and Puritan were prepared to struggle for liberty of conscience[1] and in that struggle some at least became convinced that the subject had a duty to overthrow any prince who was leading his people to universal damnation by upholding the wrong religion.

In 1594 the Jesuit, Robert Persons, wrote: 'I affirm and hold that for any man to give his help, consent or assistance toward the making of a king, whom he judgeth or believeth to be faulty in religion . . . is a most grievous sin to him that doth it, of what side soever the truth may be.' The various shades of Puritan opinion spoke with the same voice as the Jesuit did. In 1592 the Calvinist John Penry rebuked the Queen in an unpublished petition: 'The practice of your government sheweth, that if you could have ruled without the gospel, it would have been to be feared, whether the gospel should be established or not.' Protestantism had placed her where she was, he said, yet 'now that you are established in your throne, and that by the gospel, ye have suffered that gospel to reach

---

[1] Something of the Catholic and Puritan protest can be found in Chapters X and XI.

no further than the end of your sceptre'. Brown, the Independent, wrote in 1582: 'The Magistrate's commandment must not be a rule unto me of this and that duty, but as I see it agree with the Word of God.' Across the Border, John Knox, forthright as ever, proclaimed: 'It is blasphemy to say that God hath commanded kings to be obeyed when they command impiety.'

Catholic and Puritan spoke in the same tone, yet neither was concerned with toleration, the aim of each was to establish the liberty of their own conscience when in a minority, to set up the 'true religion' when in power. For instance Anthony, Lord Montague, in the parliament of 1563 held that, 'naturally no man can or ought to be constrained to take for certain that that he holdeth to be uncertain'—but Viscount Montague was a Catholic, desperately defending the faith of an oppressed minority. In power his Church spoke with a different voice, the voice of authority.

That voice—the voice of the established majority—was the voice of Whitgift asking; 'Is it meet that every man should have his own fancy and live as him list?', or, more politically, the voice of Thomas Bilson, later Bishop of Worcester, declaring in 1585 that: 'Princes must either not meddle with matters of religion at all or else of necessity they must command and afterwards punish if their commandment be despised.' State and church were two aspects of a single section of God's order: Whitgift in 1574 wrote: 'I perceive no such distinction of the commonwealth and the Church that they should be counted as it were two several bodies governed with divers laws and divers magistrates.' Toleration and a measure of political freedom were the products, but only the accidental products, of the struggle against a national state and a national church.

At the same time the traditional link between state and church was growing weaker, as the *politique* solution to the wars of religion became more and more common. Machiavelli may not have directly influenced the new attitude, but he had expressed it. He had broken the theoretical link between morality and political activity and had described the conduct in practice of princes and statesmen. By so doing he had made easier the birth of the secular state. His reward had been to become a political smear-word: Protestants and Catholics called one another Machiavellian; Puritans declared that parliament contained 'the politic Matchevils of England', and ancient tricks newly revealed provided the Elizabethan and Jacobean dramatists with a mainspring for their plots: 'The Machiavellian villain strutted the stage in innumerable guises, committing every conceivable crime, revelling in villainous strategem to the horrified enjoyment of audiences and the profit of theatrical entrepreneurs.'[1]   Soon all that would be *du vieux temps*: in 1612 the first book in English was printed that wholeheartedly approved of Machiavelli.

Religious dissent and *politique* disengagement were two solvents of the established order, parliamentary reactions to the powers of the Crown were a third.   Something of that can be found in Chapter XI, and here one further example must suffice. In 1593 James Morice opened his attack on the established Church with a fine description of the Crown under the Law:

> Behold with us the sovereign authority of one, an absolute Prince, great in majesty, ruling and reigning, yet guided and directed by principles and precepts of reason, which we term the law: no Spartan king, or Venetian duke, but free from account and coercion of any, either equal or superior, yet firmly bound to the Commonwealth by the faithful oath of a Christian prince; bearing alone the sharp sword of justice and correction, yet tempered with mercy and compassion; requiring tax and tribute of the people, yet not causeless, nor without common assent.   We, again, the subjects of this kingdom, are born and brought up in due obedience, but far from servitude and bondage; subject to lawful authority and commandment, but freed from licentious will and tyranny; enjoying by limits of law and justice our lives, lands, goods and liberties in great peace and security.

It is a political statement that anticipates the great constitutional debates of the next century.

In 1583 Sir Thomas Smith's *De Republica Anglorum*, which attempted to describe not the theoretical constitution but the practice of government, was published posthumously.   Sir Thomas had lectured at Cambridge and at Padua, had been ambassador in Paris in 1562 and a Secretary of State from 1572 until his death in 1577.   In a famous passage he describes Parliament:

[1] F. Raab, *The English Face of Machiavelli*, Routledge and Kegan Paul, 1964, the whole of which is relevant.

The most high and absolute power of the realm consisteth in the Parliament. The assent to a bill is the prince's and the whole realm's deed: whereupon justly no man can complain but must accommodate himself to find it good and obey it. . . . The Parliament abrogateth old laws, maketh new, giveth order for things past and for things hereafter to be followed, changeth rights and possessions of private men, legitimatiseth bastards, establisheth forms of religion, altereth weights and measures, giveth forms of succession to the Crown, defineth doubtful rights whereof is no law already made, appointeth subsidies, tallies, taxes and impositions, giveth most free pardons and absolutions, restoreth in blood and name as the highest court, condemneth or absolveth them whom the prince will put to that trial. . . . For every Englishman is intended to be there present, either in person or by procuration and attorneys, of what preeminence, state, dignity or quality soever he be, from the prince (be he king or queen) to the lowest person in England. And the consent of the parliament is taken to be every man's consent.

Clearly Sir Thomas Smith is describing parliament as he had seen it in action, without direct reference to abstract political theory. He depicts what writers on the subject call a 'mixed' constitution. As long as the various elements of which parliament is composed know their place and keep it, that body can fit, if a little uneasily, into the Great Chain of Being. That it would continue to do so in the future was a large assumption: in 1566 the Queen had reminded the Commons of their relative degrees, saying 'who is so simple that doubts whether a Prince that is head of all the body may not command the feet not to stray when they would slip?' In the next century this would no longer prove an acceptable rebuke.

A fourth factor in the destruction of the established political order was the victory in England of the common law. In the medieval world the ruler was under God, under the natural law. His powers were also limited by the powers of the Church and by feudal liberties, he was very much only the first among equals. The rise of the nation-state had seen throughout Europe a great extension in the power of the ruler. In particular, the adoption in many parts of western Europe of Roman law had strengthened that power. Roman law was not adopted in England, where since the twelfth century one common law had developed. Was the king above or below this common law? That question, too, was to be worked out in the next century, but already some political thinkers had no doubt of the answer. Hooker, characteristically moderate, nevertheless wrote:

> Though no manner of person or cause be unsubject to the King's power, yet so is the power of the king over all and in all limited, that unto all his proceedings the law itself is a rule. The axioms of our regal government are these: *lex facit regem*; the king's grant of any favour made contrary to the law is void; *rex nihil potest nisi quod jure potest*.

The idea of a natural law, before and above man-made law, survived and acquired a new lease of life. In *A Treatise of Monarchy* Fulke Greville wrote:

> There was a time before the times of story
> When nature reigned, in stead of laws or art,

and Hooker considered that

> Laws human must be made according to the general laws of nature, and without contradiction into any positive law in Scripture. Otherwise they are ill made.

—a cautious statement which nevertheless looks forward to John Locke and the contractual theory of government. And that theory was in essence the old structure of rights and obligations, removed from its theological foundation and re-erected on a legal base.

Religious protest, the secularization of political thought, parliamentary privilege, the undying common law, the concept of natural law—each in its own way was preventing the erection of an absolute monarchy in England. These factors were at the same time destroying the medieval world order. Ralegh in 1614 was still able to describe the conventional view of Order in words which differ little from those of Elyot (see p. 32) written eighty years earlier:

> ... that infinite wisdom of God, which hath distinguished his angels by degrees, which hath given greater and less light and beauty to heavenly bodies, which hath made differences between beasts and birds, created the eagle and the fly, the cedar and the shrub, and among stones given the fairest tincture to the ruby and the quickest light to the diamond, hath also ordained kings, dukes or leaders of the people, magistrates, judges, and other degrees among men.

And ten years before Ralegh, Shakespeare had described in
Troilus and Cressida the chaos that would follow the destruction
of established Order:

> Oh, when degree is shak'd,
> Which is the ladder to all high designs,
> The enterprise is sick.   How could communities,
> Degrees in schools and brotherhoods in cities,
> Peaceful commerce from dividable shores,
> The primogenitive and due of birth,
> Prerogative of age, crowns sceptres laurels,
> But by degree stand in authentic place?
> Take but degree away, untune that string,
> And hark, what discord follows. . . .

But though Ralegh might analyse Order and Shakespeare's
Ulysses might warn men against the consequences of its dissolution they were already describing what was past.   In 1610,
between the first production of *Troilus* and the publication of
Ralegh's *History of the World*, John Donne had written:

> And new Philosophy calls all in doubt,
> The element of fire is quite put out;
> The Sun is lost, and th' earth, and no man's wit
> Can well direct him where to look for it.
> And freely men confess that this world's spent,
> When in the Planets, and the Firmament
> They seek so many new; then see that this
> Is crumbled out again to his Atomies.
> 'Tis all in pieces, all coherence gone;
> All just supply, and all Relation:
> Prince, Subject, Father, Son, are things forgot; . . .

Economic change, scientific exploration, religious enquiry—
these developments of the later Tudor period helped in the
next century to make impossible the survival of the old
philosophy on which, among other things, the Tudor method
of government had been securely based.

Extracts

I.   *Sir Thomas More laments a new type of government* (*1516*):
Therefore when I consider and weigh in my mind all these
commonwealths, which nowadays anywhere do flourish, so
God help me, I can perceive nothing but a certain conspiracy
of rich men procuring their own commodities under the name
and title of the commonwealth.   They invent and devise all

T

means and crafts, first how to keep safely, without fear of losing, that they have unjustly gathered together, and next how to hire and abuse the work and labour of the poor for as little money as may be. These devices, when the rich men have decreed to be kept and observed under colour of the community, that is to say, also of the poor people, then they be made laws. (*Utopia*, p. 112.)

II. *Sir John Fortescue (mid-fifteenth century) outlines the world order:*

In this order hot things are in harmony with cold; dry with moist; heavy with light; great with little; high with low. In this order angel is set over angel, rank upon rank in the King-dom of Heaven; man is set over man, beast over beast, bird over bird, and fish over fish, on the earth, in the air, and in the sea; so that there is no worm that crawls upon the ground, no bird that flies on high, no fish that swims in the depths, which the chain of this order binds not in most harmonious concord. God created as many different kinds of things as he did creatures, so that there is no creature which does not differ in some respect from all other creatures, and by which it is in some respect superior or inferior to all the rest. So that from the highest angel down to the lowest of his kind there is absolutely not found an angel that has not a superior and inferior; nor from man down to the meanest worm is there any creature which is not in some respect superior to one creature and inferior to another. So that there is nothing which the bond of order does not embrace. And since God has thus regulated all creatures, it is impious to think that he left unregulated the human race, which he made the highest of all earthly creatures. (Sir John Fortescue, *Works*; ed. Lord Clermont, London 1869, Vol. I, p. 322.)

III. *Certain Sermons or Homilies, appointed by the King's Majesty to be declared and read by all Parsons, Vicars, or curates every Sunday in their Churches where they have Cure (1547):*

The Homily on Obedience:

Almighty God hath created and appointed all things in heaven, earth and waters in a most excellent and perfect order. In heaven he hath appointed distinct orders and states of archangels and angels. In the earth he has assigned kings, princes, with other governors under them, all in good and necessary order. The water above is kept and raineth down in due time and season. The sun, moon, stars, rainbow, thunder, lightning, clouds, and all birds of the air, do keep their order. The earth, trees, seeds, plants, herbs, and corn, grass and all manner of beasts keep them in their order. All the parts of the whole year, as winter, summer, months, nights and days, continue in their order. All kinds of fishes in the sea, rivers and waters, with all fountains, springs, yea, the seas themselves keep their comely course and order. And man himself, also, hath all his parts, both within and without, as soul, heart, mind, memory, understanding, reason, speech, with all and singular corporal members of his body, in a profitable, necessary and pleasant order. Every degree of people, in their vocation, calling and office, has appointed to them their duty and order. Some are in high degree, some in low; some kings and princes, some inferiors and subjects, priests and laymen, masters and servants, fathers and children, husbands and wives, rich and poor, and every one hath need of other, so that in all things is to be lauded and praised the goodly order of God, without the which no house, no city, no common wealth, can continue and endure. For where there is no right order there reigneth all abuse, carnal liberty, enormity, sin and bablonical confusion. Take aways kings, princes, rulers, magistrates, judges, and such states of God's order, no man shall ride or go by the highway unrobbed, no man shall sleep in his own house or bed unkilled, no man shall keep his wife, children and possessions in quietness; all things shall be common and there must needs follow all mischief and utter destruction, both of souls, bodies, goods and commonwealths. . . . God has sent us his high gift, our most dear sovereign lord, King Edward VI, with godly, wise and honourable council, with other superiors and inferiors, in a beautiful order. Wherefore let us subjects do our bounden duty. . . .: let us all obey, even from the bottom of our hearts, all their godly proceedings, laws, statutes, proclamations and injunctions. . . . Let us mark well and remember that the high power and authority of kings, with their making of laws, judgments and officers, are the ordinances not of man but of God. . . . We may not resist, nor in any wise hurt, an anointed king which is God's lieutenant, vicegerent and highest minister in that country where he is king. . . . Yet let us believe undoubtedly, good Christian people, that we may not obey kings, magistrates or any other (though they be our own fathers) if they would command us to do anything contrary to God's commandments. In such a case we ought to say with the Apostles: we must rather obey God than man. But nevertheless in that case we may not in any wise resist violently or

rebel against rulers or make any insurrection, sedition or
tumults, either by force of arms or otherwise, against the
anointed of the Lord or any of his appointed officers.   But we
must in such cases patiently suffer all wrongs or injuries, referring the judgment of our cause only to God. . . .   Let us
all therefore fear the most detestable vice of rebellion, ever
knowing and remembering that he that resisteth common
authority resisteth God and His ordinance, as it may be proved
by many other more places of Holy Scripture. . . .

IV.   *The Homily against Disobedience and wilful Rebellion*
(*1571*):
How horrible a sin against God and man rebellion is cannot
possibly be expressed according unto the greatness thereof.
For he that nameth rebellion nameth not a singular or one only
sin, as is theft robbery murder and such like, but he nameth
the whole puddle and sink of all sins against God and man,
against his prince his country his countrymen his parents his
children his kinsfolks his friends and against all men universally;
all sins, I say, against God and all men heaped together nameth
he that nameth rebellion. . . .   What shall we say of those
subjects?   May we call them by the name of subjects who
neither be thankful nor make any prayer to God for so gracious
a sovereign, but also themselves take armour wickedly, assemble
companies and bands of rebels, to break the public peace so
long continued and to make not war but rebellion, to endanger
the person of such a gracious sovereign, to hazard the estate of
their country for whose defence they should be ready to spend
their lives, and bring Englishmen to rob spoil destroy and burn
in England Englishmen, to kill and murder their own neighbours and kinsfolk, their own countrymen, to do all evil and
mischief, yea and more than foreign enemies would or could
do—what shall we say of these men, who use themselves thus
rebelliously against their gracious sovereign, who, if God for
their wickedness had given them an heathen tyrant to reign
over them, were by God's word bound to obey him and to pray
for him? . . .   Turn over and read the histories of all nations;
look over the chronicles of our own country; call to mind so
many rebellions of old time and some yet fresh in memory;
ye shall not find that God ever prospered any rebellion against
their natural and lawful prince, but contrariwise that the rebels
were overthrown and slain and such as were taken prisoners
dreadfully executed.   Consider the great and noble families
of dukes marquises earls and other lords, whose names ye shall
read in our chronicles, now clean extinguished and gone: and

seek out the causes of the decay, you shall find that not lack of issue and heirs male hath so much wrought that decay and waste of noble blood and houses as hath rebellion.

Now as I have showed before that pestilence and famine, so is it yet more evident that all the calamities miseries and mischiefs of war be more grievous and do more follow rebellion than any other war, as being far worse than all others wars. For not only those ordinary and usual mischiefs and miseries of other wars do follow rebellion, as corn and other things necessary to man's use to be spoiled, houses villages towns cities to be taken sacked burned and destroyed, not only many very wealthy men but whole countries to be impoverished and utterly beggared, many thousands of men to be slain and murdered, women and maids to be violated and deflowered: which things when they are done by foreign enemies we do much mourn, as we have great causes; yet are all these miseries without any wickedness wrought by any of our own countrymen. But when these mischiefs are wrought in rebellion by them that should be friends, by countrymen, by kinsmen, by those that should defend their country and their countrymen from such miseries, the misery is nothing so great as is the mischief and wickedness when the subjects unnaturally do rebel against their prince, whose honour and life they should defend, though it were with the loss of their own lives: countrymen to disturb the public peace and quietness of their country, for defence of whose quietness they should spend their lives; the brother to seek and often to work the death of his brother, the son of the father; the father to seek or procure the death of his sons . . . and so finally to make their country, thus by their mischief weakened, ready to be a pray and spoil to all outward enemies that will invade it, to the utter and perpetual captivity slavery and destruction of all their countrymen their children their friends their kinsfolks left alive, whom by their wicked rebellion they procure to be delivered into the hands of foreign enemies, as far as in them doth lie.

(Extracts III and IV are from *Homilies appointed to be read in Churches*, ed. J. Griffiths, O.U.P., 1859.)

FURTHER READING

J. W. Allen, *Political Thought in the Sixteenth Century*, Methuen, 1928
J. Hurstfield, *The Queen's Wards*, Longmans, Green, 1958
C. Morris, *Political Thought in England from Tyndale to Hooker*, O.U.P., 1953
A. G. R. Smith, *The Government of Elizabethan England*, Arnold, 1967
E. M. W. Tillyard, *The Elizabethan World Picture*, Chatto and Windus, 1943

XIII · ECONOMIC CHANGE I

Introduction

CHANGES in agriculture, changes in industry, changes in society
—all were bound up together in a common economic acceleration. Whether or not one describes aspects of this acceleration
as an 'agricultural revolution', an 'industrial revolution', and
so on, is a matter of debate among economic historians, but it
is largely a debate over emphasis. No one denies that, compared with earlier centuries, the sixteenth was a period of
exceptionally rapid development, which decisively altered
the economic and social structure of the country.

Characteristic of the period are a rise in population and
in prices, to some extent linked, which in turn stimulated
the more efficient use of land, primitive industrial improvements, and a rather more sophisticated expansion in overseas
trading methods. In the process some classes—or perhaps it
would be wiser to say a majority of the members of some
classes—benefited at the expense of their neighbours.

The Price Rise

At some point before the end of the fifteenth century the
fall in prices came to an end and was succeeded by about 150
years of rising prices. This prolonged phase of inflation is the
most important single development in the period. Other,
more obvious, changes, such as the growth in parliamentary
strength, would not have taken the form they did had it not
been for the great price rise and the inflation of profits. The
consequent accumulation of capital was the power behind
Elizabethan expansion in every sphere.

Between 1500 and 1540 prices rose by about 50 per cent,
between 1540 and 1557 they doubled again, and during the
remainder of the century they continued to rise, though less
spectacularly, apart from an alarming jerk upwards in the
nineties. By the end of the century prices were four or five times
as high as they had been in 1500. It was the sharpest inflation
that the country was to experience before the twentieth century
and a society still emerging from medieval conditions was quite

unable to control the changes involved or to discover their causes.

In one respect the modern historian is little better off than sixteenth-century man for though he can trace the consequences of this staggering rise in prices he too is still uncertain

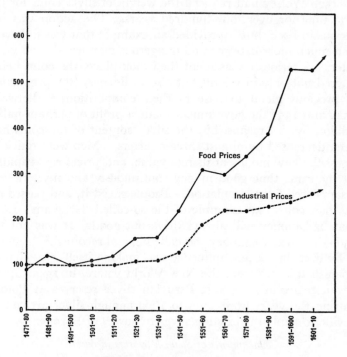

THE GREAT INFLATION

Based on Y. S. Brenner, *The Inflation of Prices in England, 1551-1650*, Ec.H.R., XV, 2, 1962, page 270 and on the references given there.

as to the full explanation. A provisional answer to the question 'What caused the great price rise?' would include the following early influences, the effects of which overlapped one another both in space and time: the rise in population during the century, so that demand for food pressed upon supply; greater silver production from the mines of Germany and Bohemia, which may have helped to produce the first rise in prices at the end of the fifteenth century, and the increased use of credit facilities such as bills of exchange; the rise in government expenditure during the period; the great sales of monastic lands, which accelerated the circulation of money—all the above would help to force up prices, and all had begun to take effect by 1540.

A slightly later factor was the debasement of the coinage. In 1526 Wolsey had reduced the weight of silver coins for the first time for over four hundred years. The action was not serious in itself, but it provided an example that was followed, in a much more extreme and dangerous manner, sixteen years later. A serious debasement then took place, the coins being altered not only in weight but also in fineness (the proportion of precious metal to base in their composition).[1] Between 1542 and 1551 the government made a profit of perhaps half a million by this means, but the silver content of the coins had been decreased by almost three-quarters. Men were quick to assess the new money at its real value, and prices rose rapidly. At the same time good money continuously and mysteriously disappeared from circulation. People saved it, and passed on the bad coins—an example of the so-called 'Gresham's Law' that bad money will always drive out good. It was not till 1560 that the base money was called in and recoined.[2]

By that time a new influence was making itself felt—that of Spanish treasure from the New World where, in 1545, Spain began to exploit the vast Peruvian silver reserves at Potosi. During the years from 1503 to 1660 enough silver arrived at Seville to triple the existing silver resources of Europe:

Total imports of Spanish treasure in ducats

period	total
1531–1535	1,980,277
1541–1545	5,944,806
1551–1555	11,838,637
1561–1565	13,449,043
1571–1575	14,287,931
1581–1585	35,249,534
1591–1595	42,221,835
1601–1605	29,283,994

This increase in the volume of silver would certainly cause inflation in Europe and, while historians do not at the moment

[1] For Henry VIII's debasement, see pp. 132–3; for that of Edward VI's reign, see p. 144.

[2] For Elizabeth's recoinage, see p. 176.

regard the influx of Spanish silver as the mainspring of the English price rise, it must have played a considerable part in maintaining that rise in the second half of the century. Silver, 'the common drudge 'tween man and man',[1] was dispersed by the Spanish armies operating in the Low countries and in France, and through the trading centres of Amsterdam, Antwerp, London and Rouen. Besides helping to raise prices, this flow of money stimulated economic changes. Industry was able to adjust itself to these changes much more rapidly than agriculture.

It seems probable that the years 1560–80 were ones of relative security for the ordinary man, the rate of population growth lessened, the gap between prices and wages narrowed, 'rents almost stagnated and both nominal and real wages rose again'.[2] Then, in consequence of these better times, the rate of population growth increased once more and this, combined with war, plague and bad harvests, ushered in a second period of hard times towards the end of the reign.

None of this was clear to contemporaries, who normally sought the explanation of what they called 'the great dearth' in the greed of every class but their own (as men usually do for any economic fact which they do not understand). In their attempts to explain the price rise they were handicapped by their continued acceptance—at least in theory—of the medieval doctrine of the just price. This laid down that for every transaction there existed a just price, one which would ensure a reasonable, fixed profit to all those involved in the sale. In times of plenty the price might fall a little and in times of shortage it demonstrably rose, but these would be temporary fluctuations about the normal figure. If prices rose continuously men were taking more than their just profit. The blame must be laid on forestallers, engrossers, and regraters, men who cornered the market in order to sell at monopoly prices, on usurers who made barren money to breed, on enclosers and rack-renters, on artisans who demanded higher wages.

It was not until the second half of the sixteenth century that the theory of a just price began to be replaced by the suggestion

---

[1] Shakespeare, *The Merchant of Venice*, III, 2. Between 1558 and 1600 about £5,150,000 was coined, four-fifths of which was in silver.

[2] Y. S. Brenner, *The Inflation of Prices in England, 1551–1650*, Ec.H.R. XV, 1962 and Y. S. Brenner, *The Inflation of Prices in Early Sixteenth-Century England*, Ec.H.R. XIV, 1961.

that prices might depend on increased demand or on the relation between the amount of money in circulation and the supply of goods available. In Spain this connection was mentioned almost casually by a Spanish priest, Francisco Lopez de Gomara, at some date before 1558. In France Jean Bodin stated it independently in 1568 when he wrote: 'I find that the scarcity we are witnessing springs from three causes. The chief and almost the only one (which no one has yet touched on) is the abundance of gold and silver, which in this kingdom today is greater than at any time in the last four centuries.' At that time no Englishman had made similar comments.

The Land

The price rise and the growth in population intensified the more efficient commercial exploitation of land (which had, of course, begun in earlier centuries) by the use of improved agricultural techniques, by concentration on the most profitable products, and by the enclosure of land and the redistribution or elimination of strips, either for arable or pasture.

Improved techniques were described by such writers as Sir Anthony Fitzherbert, Barnaby Googe, and Thomas Tusser. Fitzherbert (?1470–1538) wrote in *The Book of Husbandry* (?1523) of the value of mixed farming:

> The most general living that husbands [farmers] can have is by ploughing and sowing of their corn and rearing or heeding of their cattle; and not the one without the other. Then is the plough the most necessary instrument that a husband can occupy.

In 1577 Barnaby Googe (1540–94) produced his translation, *The Four Books of Husbandry*, which described, amongst other matters, advanced Dutch farming practice including a reaping machine, the planting of turnips to provide winter food for livestock, marling, the use of horses rather than oxen, the development of new crops such as hops (first introduced in the late fifteenth century),[1] improved drainage (the Essex marshes were brought into use during Elizabeth's reign), and the restoration of soil fertility by planned manuring and allowing land to lie fallow—all of them techniques that depended on individual initiative and hence, usually, on enclosure.

---

[1] Googe optimistically hoped to grow apricots and olives as well.

Efficient farming, any departure from conventional routine, any large transfer from arable to pasture, the landlord's need to increase his income in order to meet the inflation—each encouraged the consolidation of holdings and the enclosure of common and waste. What is surprising is not that there were enclosures but that there were not more of them. Among agricultural writers the chorus of approval was general. Thomas Tusser[1] (c. 1524–80) in his *A Hundred Good Points of Husbandry* (1557) grew lyrical over the advantages of land enclosed and farmed individually (several) over land in open fields (champion):

> More plenty of mutton and beef,
> Corn, butter and cheese of the best,
> More wealth anywhere (to be brief)
> More people, more handsome and prest, [alert]
> Where find ye (go search any coast)
> Than there where enclosures are most?

and

> Good land that is several, crops may have three,
> In champion country it may not so be, ...

In short

> The country enclosed I praise,
> T'other delighteth not me, ...

Contemporaries extended the term *enclosure* (see also Chapter II) indiscriminately to refer to the four great changes: the consolidation of strips into compact packets which could then be fenced; the eviction of tenants in order that the landlord might farm the land himself or let it to a tenant-farmer; the conversion of arable to pasture; the extinction by the landlord of tenants' rights over the common and the waste. Writers usually distinguished, however, between 'good' and 'bad' enclosures. Good enclosures were for arable, resulted in increased production and took place with the minimum of eviction. Bad enclosures were for pasture and led to depopulation, which was undesirable since it produced vagabonds and left the country empty and open to the foreigner.

In the *Discourse of the Common Weal* the Knight observes 'that countries where most enclosures be are most wealthy', and the

---

[1] It is interesting that Googe was a Lincolnshire man and Tusser farmed in Suffolk, both areas in the van of agricultural progress in the eighteenth century.

Doctor accepts this, explaining that he is opposed only to 'such enclosures as turneth commonly arable fields into pastures; and violent enclosures . . .', though he considers that 'there is more lucre by grazing to the occupier alone than is in tillage of twenty, . . .' John Hales, the probable author of the

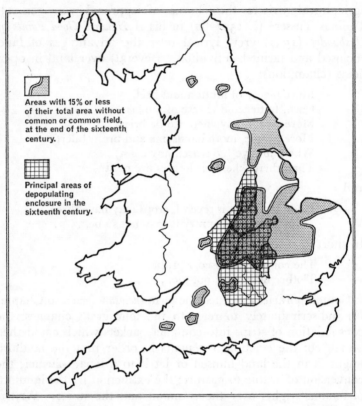

Areas with 15% or less of their total area without common or common field, at the end of the sixteenth century.

Principal areas of depopulating enclosure in the sixteenth century.

SIXTEENTH-CENTURY ENCLOSURES

Sixteenth-century enclosure appears to have been most intense in the Midlands. Nevertheless, much of this area was still unenclosed in 1600.

Discourse, in his instructions in 1548 to the jurors concerned with investigating enclosures carefully defined bad enclosure:

It is not taken where a man doth enclose and hedge in his own proper ground, . . . For such inclosure is very beneficial to the commonwealth . . .: but it is meant, thereby, when any man hath taken away and enclosed any other men's commons, or hath pulled down houses of husbandry, and converted lands from tillage to pasture.

Between 1489 and 1597 eleven acts against enclosure were passed, including those of 1489–90 (see p. 39), 1515, 1533, 1536, 1549 and 1597, and government enquiries were made in 1517, 1548, 1565 and 1607. The long sequence, and the content of their preambles, indicate that they were ineffective. Towards the end of the century Robert Cecil was still supporting the traditional view that 'The balancing of the misery of the people and the decay of the realm's strength with some trifling abridgement to gentlemen hath no proportion', but in 1608 the first act to assist enclosure—a portent—was passed.

The extent of the enclosures seems to have been exaggerated by contemporary and near-contemporary accounts, and the speed and extent of agricultural change certainly varied greatly both in space and time. In the counties most affected, such as Leicestershire or Northamptonshire, perhaps 3 per cent of the total area was enclosed during the period—a very small figure indeed, though in certain areas it might represent up to 30 per cent of the arable. The pace of enclosure appears to have been greatest in the years from 1450 to 1520, and again at the end of the century. The cloth boom played its part in the earlier phase, but by the end of Edward VI's reign the cloth trade was suffering from depression, and the later enclosures were usually for increased arable farming. Finally, to complete a complex and often puzzling picture, it must be remembered that enclosure would only take place on land that was suitable, notably in the Midlands, where large-scale conversion could most surely be made to pay, while it did not figure largely in heavily wooded areas or in the fertile fenland, where there was already a very satisfactory balance between corn and grassland.

Where depopulating enclosure did take place, what was the machinery by which it was achieved? The price rise enriched those who were producing goods which they could sell at a profit, such as food or wool, but it impoverished those whose income was derived from land in the form of fixed rents. Such men must either become producers, increasing if possible the acreage they themselves farmed and when profitable turning it over to sheep, or else they must become rack-renters, raising their rents whenever leases fell in.   An analysis of the social status of 585 enclosers in six midland counties shows that lords of manors were responsible for 61 per cent of the recorded enclosed acreage, farmers and lessees for 26·4 per cent, freeholders and copyholders for 12·4 per cent.[1]

Much depended, clearly, on the terms by which tenants held their land.   At the top of the scale, the freeholder was safe.   At the bottom the serf was almost extinct.   Between these limits there existed three main classes of villager: the tenant-at-will, the customary tenant, and the copyholder.   The tenant-at-will was completely vulnerable, he held his land only so long as his lord pleased.   The rights of the customary tenant depended on the customs of his manor as defined in the manorial court roll. The copyholder—in theory, at least—possessed a copy of his rights and obligations which he might produce as evidence in the king's courts.   (A copyholder was originally a man who had converted his tenure from one of villeinage, under which he held by service, to one under which he held by rent.)   If he had an 'estate of inheritance' his heir would succeed without hindrance, but if the manorial custom provided only a life interest, or laid down that the lord might impose an arbitrary fine on inheritance, then the heir could easily be forced out. Generalizing, one may say that most tenancies were customary or copyhold, often with a variable fine of inheritance, that lords were anxious where possible to alter copyhold tenancies to leasehold ones, and that, except for a lull in the period 1560–80, there is little doubt that rents rose rapidly.   The interesting question is, did they outpace prices?   Existing evidence suggests that rents had doubled by 1530, and trebled again between that date and 1609.   If this is a correct picture, rents at the end of the century were in pace with prices.

The price rise encouraged landlords to raise their rents whenever and wherever possible, to sell land if they were hard hit, to buy land if they had the cash and the opportunity to do so.   It was a land-hungry society and the market was partially satisfied from three sources—the lands of the monasteries and chantries, those of impoverished aristocrats, and those of a Crown ultimately unable to make ends meet.   This fluid land market combined with the rise in population and the inflation

---

[1] See Ec.H.R., III, 1950, for a review by Christopher Hill of V. E. Semeonov, *Enclosures and Peasant Revolts in England in the Sixteenth Century*, Moscow-Leningrad, 1949.

to accelerate changes in agricultural practice and in social structure—changes which seemed to contemporaries more startling, revolutionary and widespread than they in fact were.

Enclosure, rack-renting, the eviction of peasants or their transformation into landless day-labourers, a large increase in the number of leasehold tenant-farmers, an unusual volume of unemployment, a lust for land both as a badge of social respectability and as a source of profit—traces of all these phenomena can be found in earlier centuries, but taken together on a sixteenth-century scale they none the less represented the greatest upheaval in agricultural life and practice that England had yet experienced, and to that extent contemporary amazement was completely justified. There was hardship, but in the long run food production increased and agriculture flourished both in the newly enclosed areas and in those where farming practice had changed more gradually, such as the vale of Taunton which Camden described as 'most delectable on every side with green meadows, flourishing with pleasant gardens and orchards and replenished with fair manor houses, . . .' There is evidence that the weight of the best-kept stock almost doubled during the century and that yields per acre of arable rose from eight to sixteen bushels.

Industry

Increased demand at home, the opening up of new markets abroad as old-established trading monopolies such as that of Venice in the Levant came to an end, the state's encouragement of home production and a spatter of new inventions all combined to produce a small-scale, but significant, industrial revolution and a rather greater expansion of overseas trade between the years 1575 and 1625.

At home the chief productive industries remained the traditional medieval ones of house building, shipbuilding, and weaving. Building, by its nature, remained a local industry, the style varying from region to region, the organization in the hands of thousands of individuals. The most important changes were the increased glazing of windows and the widespread use of brick. The latter had been known in the eleventh century, but by the end of the next century had ceased to be employed, on any significant scale. (Little Wenham Hall in Suffolk was built of brick c. 1260–80.) In the fifteenth century architecture in brick includes Tattershall Castle in Lincolnshire, begun *c.* 1434, and Eton (1442–52). The bricks for these buildings were imported from Flanders, but Kirby Muxloe Castle (1480–4) was constructed from bricks made on the spot. In the sixteenth century bricks were employed in increasingly large numbers but, like glazed windows, only the well-to-do could at first afford them.

Growing prosperity, however, increased the numbers of those who could hope to make improvements and between about 1570 and 1640 there took place what Professor Hoskins has christened 'the great rebuilding'. During these years thousands of houses in those areas where stone was the normal building material were modernized, and in other areas thousands of less solidly constructed houses were completely rebuilt. Modernization usually took the form of the construction of a ceiling in the hall to make a bedroom upstairs, of the erection of partitions to break up the larger rooms, and of the insertion of a staircase, a fireplace and glazed windows. By 1500 great houses often had glazed windows, but in the ordinary 'middle-class' house, glass appears in wills and inventories in the eighties, a sign that it was still regarded as a valuable moveable. Soon after 1600 it disappears from these documents—it has become a regular fixture.

The clothing industry remained the great example of production organized on a large scale for both home consumption and export. The thirties and forties were a boom period: exports practically trebled between 1500 and 1550, in the years 1534–9 they averaged 102,647 cloths a year, and in 1550 they reached their highest point, 132,000. Then they fell dramatically, a fall at least partly due to unsettled conditions in the Frankfurt area; in 1551 exports were 112,000 cloths and in 1552 only 82,000. After a period of difficulty, made more acute by the trouble in the Netherlands, exports settled down in the last years of the century at about three-quarters of the peak figure. Even at that level cloth remained far and away the country's most valuable export.

The traditional English cloth was the broadcloth, made from a short-staple wool, warm and heavy, monotonous in design, suited to the climate of north, central and eastern Europe. The new urban civilization demanded lighter cloths, 'bays' and 'says', serges and calicoes, known collectively as the 'new draperies'. These had been developed first on the continent, but by the second half of the century they were well-established in Suffolk and Essex, with Colchester as one of the chief centres of production. These cloths were made from a

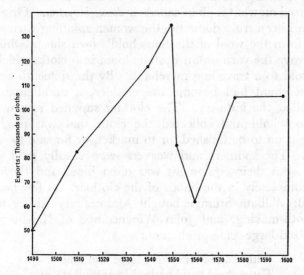

Exports: Thousands of cloths

THE CLOTH TRADE IN THE SIXTEENTH CENTURY

After 1540 the figures are for London only, which then handled the bulk of the export trade. The information for individual years presents difficulties; there is no doubt, however, that the general picture of a mid-century boom and slump followed by more stable conditions at a lower level is roughly correct.

long-staple wool, were light in weight, various in pattern, and ideal for export to warmer lands.

There is some evidence that sheep kept on permanent pasture, one of the consequences of enclosures, produced a heavy, coarse wool not suitable for the new cloths.

. . . the sheep to receive that gift of fineness and goodness thereof must needs feed off the layers of the earth like as in old time when the earth was wrought and opened by tillage. . . .[1]

[1] See P. J. Bowden, *Wool Supply and the Woollen Industry*, Ec.H.R., IX, 1956.

U

There were three main centres of cloth production: the western counties of Somerset, Gloucestershire and Wiltshire, specializing in broadcloths and, adjoining them, Berkshire, the centre of kerseys: the East Anglian area weaving worsteds: and Yorkshire, producing mainly cheap, coarse cloths.

The clothing industry, whatever its final product, was still organized on what is often called *the domestic system*. Originally this had been truly domestic, the women spinning yarn downstairs from the wool of the household's own sheep, while the men wove the yarn on an upstairs loom into cloth, which was then sold to a travelling merchant. By the sixteenth century the merchant had become the clothier, a middleman who controlled the industry. The clothier supplied raw wool to the household and collected the cloth that was produced, taking it on to be finished, or to market, or for sale to wholesalers. The spinners and weavers were usually paid piece-rates, even their equipment was often hired and they were thus completely in the hands of the clothier. A few factories existed; William Stumpe bought Malmesbury Abbey to use for cloth-making, and John Winchcombe of Newbury also organized large-scale production:

> Within one room being large and long
> There stood two hundred looms full strong;
> Two hundred men the truth is so
> Wrought at these looms all in a row.

These, though, were colourful and dramatic exceptions, a sign of things to come. Most cloth continued to be woven in cottages and to that extent the system was still 'domestic'. In the finishing stages, however, water-driven machinery was being used to an increasing extent. Fulling-mills were comparatively widespread, and other machines included the gig-mill for knapping cloth, a mechanical knitting-machine and the Dutch loom for the making of ribbons.

Coal had long been mined and burned on the spot, but it was only in the sixteenth century that large-scale mining began. Production quadrupled between 1541–50 and 1551–60. The north-east coalfield was the main area of development, its production rising from nearly 33,000 tons in 1564 to about 252,000 tons in 1609. In 1606 Newcastle was shipping 'sea-coal' to London at the rate of 74,000 tons a year. Where water transport was not available, coal was not consumed far from the coal-fields, but near to the mines it was being used on an increasingly large scale as an industrial fuel—in Cheshire, Tynemouth and Wearmouth for the manufacture of salt, in other areas for soap-boiling, brewing, dyeing, the making of glass and the refining of sugar. All these projects involved large injections of labour and capital. One saltworks in the north-east required an investment of £4,000 and employed 300 men.

One industry in which coal was not used was the production of iron. The technical problems involved in smelting iron by coal were not solved till the eighteenth century.[1] The iron industry, based mainly on Sussex and on the Forest of Dean, relied on timber for its fuel. The growth in the use of firearms had led to the increased mining of iron and of other minerals, including lead and calamine (zinc ore) on the Mendips, and copper, necessary for the production of bronze and brass in Cumberland. Cornish tin-mining expanded in response to the increased demand for pewter and brass. Saltpetre was refined for use in the making of gunpowder. (The first gunpowder factory had been set up in 1554 and in 1561 a German received a licence to manufacture saltpetre.) Alum was manufactured for the dyeing of cloth. All these developments were as yet scattered and relatively small-scale, but the industrialization of England had begun.

Industrial expansion was stimulated by the influx of foreign craftsmen, in the second half of the century usually religious refugees, and also by government encouragement. This took many forms. Licences were issued to aliens to introduce new industrial techniques—to cut metal plates, to draw metal thread, to crush seeds for oil, to drain the fens, and so on. One of the most important was that given to the Mines Royal Company and to the Mineral and Battery Works in 1568. The former was given a monopoly of the right to mine for copper and precious metals in the north and west, the latter was empowered to mine for calamine and to make brass. The copper mines were developed between the years 1565 and 1579 with the help of German miners under Daniel Höchstetter, and German money. In the latter year the German financiers withdrew and the mines were taken over by Mr. 'Customer'

[1] In 1709 by Abraham Darby.

Smythe who not only made them pay but also transferred some of the German technicians to Cornwall to develop the tin mines there. As the easier deposits were worked out, mining moved westwards, and placer-mining gave place to shaft mining. Increased production meant harder conditions of work. Carew described the life of the Cornish tin-miners in his *Survey of Cornwall* (begun in the eighties though not published till 1602): 'the loose earth is propped by frames of timber-work as they go, and yet now and then falling down, either presseth the poor workmen to death, or stoppeth them from returning. . . In most places their toil is so extreme as they cannot endure it above four hours in a day, . . .' He then went on to complain that the miners' holidays were too long. The need of the landlord to increase his income, in a time of rising prices, was another factor that encouraged intensive mining. It has been estimated that 22 per cent of the Elizabethan aristocratic families were involved, in one way or another, in the production of iron alone.

In the iron industry the most important technical development was the introduction of the blast furnace. This led both to increased production and to a different form of organization. The furnace was known in the fifteenth century, but its adoption in England took place in Henry VIII's reign—the first cast-iron cannon were probably produced in Sussex at Buxted in 1543. By the end of the century there were upwards of a hundred forges and iron mills at work in the Weald, the Tudor Black Country. The yield of a late medieval bloomery, in which the impurities were hammered out of the iron by hand and which might easily be operated as a family enterprise, was about twenty to thirty tons a year. The yield from a sixteenth-century blast furnace could be two hundred tons of pig-iron which would ultimately yield about one hundred and thirty tons of purer bar iron. Such an enterprise might require £1,000 capital and involved detailed organization, and control of ironworking passed into the hands of the landowner and the City merchant. Increased production also meant the extended felling of wood for fuel—it required two tons of charcoal for every ton of iron ore, and within the next hundred years supplies began to run out.

The new industrial developments took place in the countryside. In the extractive industries the reason for this is obvious: in the days before cheap power was available, heavy industries could only develop where the raw materials were situated. Light industries, on the other hand, tended to establish themselves in fresh areas in order to avoid the monopoly control which the gilds usually exercised in the existing towns.

Changes in the gilds had begun long before the sixteenth century, which on the whole saw these changes carried to their logical conclusion. The craft gilds had in earlier centuries established recognized standards, enforced regular apprenticeship, looked after the welfare of their members and shared out a limited market among them. They had never, however, been democratic, and it had always been natural that the owners of capital, whether in the form of money, machinery or markets, should control the gilds in their own interests, often at the expense of the working craftsman. Towns, especially London, came to be dominated by gilds of wholesale merchants and industrial employers.

In the Tudor period the distribution of economic power changed with increasing rapidity: the overseas merchant—the mercer, haberdasher, vintner—profited from the expansion of trade, the appearance of new markets, and the inflation of prices; the man working for a local market—the shoemaker or the mason—held his own; the wholesale industrialist—the clothier for instance—grew in wealth; the wage-earner became, in terms of real wages, poorer.

The gilds reflected these changes. Within the companies the masters often formed a self-perpetuating oligarchy. High entrance fees, costly dinners, over-elaborate time-consuming masterpieces all helped to prevent the poor apprentice from becoming a member of the magic circle. In the larger towns, notably London, the organization that dominated the scene was the livery company. The twelve companies in London were in theory concerned with separate trades, but in practice their members were no longer manufacturers, they had become merchants and financiers who controlled every aspect of city life.

Ninety per cent or more of the population still lived in the countryside and got their living from the land, but the surplus of births over deaths was probably as high as 10 per cent a year. This increase in population, unemployment in the countryside, the rise of new industries and the expansion of old ones all combined to increase the number and size of the towns. London, always head and shoulders above the rest, moved into a class of its own as its population increased five-fold. In 1590 an unsuccessful attempt was made to limit its size. By 1603 there were about 300,000 people in the area and men were complaining that the London bakers and brewers 'do daily come down into the country and very greedily do buy great quantities of corn and grain. . . .' The City had become a great financial centre, stimulated by the opening of the Royal Exchange in 1571, its merchants' financial sinews strengthened by inflation, by privateering, by a growing volume of native-borne imports, by the profitable organization of agriculture, mining and metallurgy and by a very low rate of taxation. In the next reign Bristol merchants were to complain to James I that it seemed 'as if God had no sons to whom He gave the benefit of the earth but in London'.

Provincial towns (with a population not a tenth that of London) included Norwich, York, Bristol, Newcastle, Exeter, Coventry and Ipswich. Of these, Exeter had increased very rapidly, its economic power stimulated and symbolized by the construction of the Topsham-Exeter Canal (1564–7).

The more successful the gild was in regulating and monopolizing trade in the old towns, the more the new industries tended to avoid these and to establish themselves in large villages where there were no gilds, like Birmingham and Wolverhampton, or in the countryside. The centres of the cloth-trade, in particular, began to move from the old corporate towns to fresh centres where there was cheaper labour, abundant waterpower and freedom from excessive control. Examples of such new centres are Halifax and Manchester in the north, Lavenham in East Anglia, and Malmesbury in the west. Broadcloths produced in small settlements in the south-west were exported through old-established Exeter and were largely responsible for its growth in size and prosperity. Similarly the new draperies developed in many East Anglian villages, and there were 4,000 Flemings, who had introduced the new cloths, in old-established Norwich by 1572. In Yorkshire expansion was rapid: some idea of its pace can be deduced from the fact that Leeds and Wakefield, which together produced

500 cloths a year in Edward VI's time, were making ten times that number by the end of Elizabeth's reign. In Lancashire the production of cotton fustians was well established by 1610.

The government legislated, ineffectively, in an attempt to prevent the decay of towns through the movement of cloth-working to the countryside. The York act of 1542, for instance, described how 'Of late, evil-disposed persons, not expert apprentices, withdrawing from York into the country do daily make coverings (not of good stuff) to the great impoverishing of the said city' and went on to order that no one should make coverings for sale unless he lived in the city.

Overseas Trade

The great cloth-trading company was that of the Merchant Adventurers, a company based on London whose three or four thousand members were the great exporters of the first half of the century. After 1550 matters began to go wrong for the Adventurers. The cloth boom collapsed, and this was followed by the troubles in the Netherlands, which eventually drove the Adventurers from their base at Antwerp. The company won its long struggle against the Hanse merchants when the latter finally lost their privileges in 1558, and in 1564 the Adventurers at last received a royal charter giving them a monopoly of the export of white cloth to Europe. Their political difficulties, a declining market, and these legislative victories combined to make the Adventurers in the second half of the century a conservative body, restrictive and cautious, but they remained a powerful group useful to the government in the provision of short-term loans, and cloth worth between £1,000,000 and £1,500,000 a year was still shipped to the company's markets at Hamburg, Emden, Stade and eventually Middelburg.

The Adventurers were a regulated company. That is to say, each member traded as an individual, his activities controlled by the company's regulations, his position strengthened by their privileges, but buying his own cloths and selling them as a personal venture. In this type of company commercial expertise was clearly essential. In the second half of the century a quite different form of trading association began to appear, the joint-stock company. Here no specialized knowledge was required, those who were not merchants might risk their money in a common venture, at first established for each voyage, at the end of which the profits were divided in proportion to the amount of capital invested.

It was generally agreed that trade without the control exercised by monopoly companies would be, as the secretary of the Merchant Adventurers expressed it, 'a private, irregular and straggling trade' and a number of new companies, both regulated and joint-stock, were established in the second half of the century, though the benefits from them were not fully felt until the reigns of James I and Charles I. These new companies included the Muscovy (joint-stock) in 1555; the Eastland (regulated) in 1579, set up to trade with the Baltic; the Levant (regulated) operating from 1581 in the eastern Mediterranean; the Barbary Company (regulated) formed by the Earl of Leicester to trade with Morocco (1585); and the great East India Company (joint-stock), which received its charter on the last day of 1600. Temporary companies were often set up for specific ventures, as for instance Hawkins' slaving voyages, Drake's expedition of 1577–80, and the attempts made in the eighties to plant a colony in Virginia.

The most striking change in the nature of England's overseas trade was the creation of these new trading companies. The foundations of English overseas enterprise were laid in Elizabeth's reign, though the great bulk of investment occurred in the thirty years after 1600. The London merchant dominated the scene, but something in the region of one in four of the investors in the new companies was noble or gentle. About half of the latter came up to London to sit in Parliament and then found the opportunity to invest in a company.[1]

Yet the keynote is not change but continuity. The sheep and its products remain supreme:

exports of cloth
as %, by value, of total exports

1564–5	78

and, similarly, London continues to tower above other ports, handling nine-tenths of these exports. Imports also passed mainly through London but they were more various:

[1] For a slightly later period (1606–30) the Virginia Company provides the following figures: 1,600 members, including 478 gentry, of whom 275 sat in Parliament. T. K. Rabb, *Investment in English Overseas Enterprise, 1575–1630*, Ec.H.R., XIX, 1966.

	%, by value, of
1559-90	total imports
Linen and canvas	17
Oil, woad, madder and alum	13
Wine (largely French claret and Spanish sack)	10
Oriental products	10
Manufactured metal goods	6
Luxury cloths (from Italy)	6

Thus England exported a single product—cloth—obtaining in exchange a number of products, some of which she was herself unable to produce for climatic reasons, while others were sophisticated manufactures which presumably found a market among the increasingly comfortable middle and upper classes. On cloth depended the balance of trade.

English shipping had decayed during the years between 1530 and 1560. Most of the overseas trade was carried in foreign-owned vessels, while a quarter of the exports and two-fifths of the imports were in the hands of alien merchants. Virtually all the exports and two-thirds of the imports passed to Antwerp, 'the warehouse of the world'. Most of the remaining overseas trade was carried on with Spain, and with the French ports of Rouen, La Rochelle and Bordeaux.

At the end of the reign London was still dominant, paying 80 per cent of the nation's customs dues, and cloth was still king, though the rise of the 'new draperies' had led to a shift in the type of cloth exported, as the old coarse white cloth lost ground to the lighter kerseys and the finer 'bays and says'. The ruin of Antwerp had forced English exporters to find new entrepôts, but the final destination of the cloth remained little changed, the Merchant Adventurers sending 71 per cent to west Germany and the Netherlands. Next in importance came the Eastland Company, exporting only 11½ per cent. Half of England's imports came from France and from the Netherlands, in approximately equal proportions. Economic necessity thus combined with military strategy to determine Elizabeth's attitude to these countries during the war years.

The most significant performance during the reign was the building of an ocean-going fleet. During the seventies the number of English ships of over 100 tons probably doubled and by 1603 the majority of large ships using the port of London were English. This revival was partly a consequence of the collapse of the Antwerp market, partly due to a government subsidy, and partly the result of the opening-up of the oceanic trade routes. London nevertheless failed to take over the role of Antwerp, which passed instead to Amsterdam.[1]

The raiding of the Spanish trade routes had economic and social, as well as military, importance. Everyone was eager to make a fortune. Amateur adventurers such as the Earl of Cumberland tried to get out of debt by gambling at sea and usually ended worse off than they had been before. Professional sailors did rather better, but the men who made privateering pay were London merchants like Sir Thomas Myddleton, shrewd operators who lent money to the amateurs and to the professionals, and also themselves fitted out expeditions in which trade and plunder went hand in hand.

The most regular types of prizes were the ships in cargo from Pernambuco, carrying wood, hides, cotton and above all sugar. Profits seem to have averaged as much as £100,000 a year, a concentration of gain in the hands of precisely those men most likely to use it as capital to finance other enterprises at home in England. In the early seventeenth century the Venetians reported that

> Nothing is thought to have enriched the English more or done so much to allow many individuals to amass the wealth they are known to possess as the wars with the Spaniards in the time of Queen Elizabeth. All were permitted to go privateering and they plundered not only Spaniards but all others indifferently, so that they enriched themselves by a constant stream of booty.[2]

Overseas Expansion

England came late into the European movement overseas. The trails were blazed by Spain and Portugal. At first English energy was absorbed commercially by the cloth trade, politically by the lure of French possessions and the danger of Scottish aggression, domestically by disorder in the fifteenth century followed in the sixteenth by the break with Rome and the diplomatic dangers which that break involved. In the first half of the century there had been little activity after the abortive

---

[1] L. Stone, *Elizabethan Overseas Trade*, Ec.H.R., II, 1949, p. 30.
[2] V. K. R. Andrews, *Elizabethan Privateering*, C.U.P., 1964, especially pp. 128–9.

expeditions of John and Sebastian Cabot (see p. 42) except for the trading voyages to Brazil made in the decade 1530–40 by William Hawkins.

Matters were different in the second half of the sixteenth century. The cloth trade declined, the political pattern altered, England was in many ways withdrawn from Europe. At the same time the naval struggle with Spain and the material economic expansion at home made it natural that the country should now look overseas for victory, trade and wealth.

The fifties saw voyages made by Thomas Wyndham to the Atlantic coast of Barbary (1551, 1552) and to Benin (1553). The first voyage that broke new ground, however was that of Chancellor and Willoughby in search of a North-East Passage to Asia in (1553–4). Willoughby was lost and died on the coast of Lapland, but Chancellor reached Moscow and in 1555 the Muscovy Company was set up to trade with Russia, exchanging cloth for oil, tallow, hides, tar, timber, hemp and wax—raw materials many of which were useful in ship-building. The Muscovy Company provided the springboard for the overland journeys of its representative, Anthony Jenkinson, who travelled in 1557 to Bokhara and in 1561–4 to Persia. The eastern route to Asia, though, whether by land or by sea, proved impracticable and, after Pet and Jackman had in 1580 failed to enter the Kara Sea, the effort to get through was abandoned.

A second line of expansion was that in search of a North-West Passage to Asia. In this direction the key figure was Sir Humphrey Gilbert who argued in his *Discourse to Prove a North-west Passage* 'that there lieth a great sea between it [North America], Cathaia, and Greenland, by the which any man of our country that will give the attempt, may with small danger pass to Cathaia, the Moluccae, India, and all the other places in the east, in much shorter time than the Spaniard or the Portugal doth'. It was a plausible, attractive argument. Martin Frobisher made three voyages (1576–8) in search of the Passage, finding instead Frobisher Bay and Hudson Bay, observing the Esquimaux, 'anthropophagi, or devourers of men's flesh', and bringing back a cargo of fool's gold (iron pyrites) which, Camden says, was eventually used to mend a road at Dartford. Ten years later John Davis made three voyages (1585–8), in the course of which he reached 73° north in Davis

Strait, and came home declaring 'the passage is most probable, the execution easy'. Davis had found the right route, but he was wrong about the ease with which it might be followed. In the course of his voyage round the world Drake searched for, but could not find, the fabled western outlet of the North-West Passage. The failure of these various attempts to find a new route to Asia combined with the Spanish war to produce a temporary slackening in the pace of exploration.

Another line of attempted expansion was along routes already opened, but in the hands of England's enemies. In 1583 the newly-formed Levant Company sent an expedition east under John Newbery and Ralph Fitch. Travelling down the Euphrates to Basra past the as-yet-undiscovered oil-fields of the Middle East they observed 'a strange thing to see: a mouth that doth continually throw forth against the air boiling pitch with a filthy smoke: which pitch doth run abroad into a great field which is always full thereof. The Moors say it is the mouth of Hell'. Next they crossed the Indian Ocean to Goa, and travelled across India to Agra, where they presented the Great Mogul with letters from Queen Elizabeth. Fitch continued east, following the Ganges to Bengal, and then going on to Burma and Malacca. He finally got safely back to England nine years after he had set out. In 1586–8 Cavendish repeated Drake's feat of sailing round the world. In 1591 London merchants sent three ships under James Lancaster by the Cape of Good Hope route to Ceylon and Malacca. Only a handful of men returned in 1594, but the voyage had shown the possibilities of this route and in April 1601 Lancaster and Davis led the first expedition of the new East India Company, five ships out of Torbay bound for Java. A year earlier Will Adams had become the first Englishman to reach Japan, where he taught the Shogun mathematics.

A third aspect of the English expansion was the attempt at colonization, essentially a movement of the eighties, before the war diverted men's attention in other directions. Apart from the obvious economic reasons for colonization, there was also a belief that England was becoming overpopulated. The men behind the movement to set up colonies consisted of an active group, the Gilberts, their half-cousin Ralegh and their full cousin Grenville, and what might be called a propaganda group, headed by John Dee[1] and both the elder and younger Hakluyt.

Between 1578 and 1590 there was continuous pressure. In the former year Gilbert sent out his first expedition, which failed to cross the Atlantic; next year a sixteen-tonner reached America. In 1582 Hakluyt published his first work, the *Divers Voyages*:

> I marvel not a little that since the first discovery of America (which is now full fourscore and ten years) after so great conquest and plantings of Spaniards and Portingales there, that we of England could never have the grace to set fast footing in such fertile and temperate places as are left as yet unpossessed by them. But again when I consider that there is a time for all men, and see the Portingales' time to be out of date and that the nakedness of the Spaniards and their long-hidden secrets are now at length espied. . . . I conceive great hope that the time approacheth and now is that we of England may share and part stakes (if we will ourselves) both with the Spaniard and the Portingale in part of America and other regions as yet undiscovered.

In that same year Gilbert led an expedition of about 260 men including 'shipwrights, masons, carpenters, smiths and such-like requisites to such an action; also mineral men and refiners'. It is significant that one of the objects of the expedition was to settle 'needy people . . . which now trouble the commonwealth'. Gilbert formally annexed St. Johns, Newfoundland, but was drowned in the little 10-ton *Squirrel* on the homeward voyage.

In 1584 Ralegh equipped an expedition to the southern part of the coast. It reached North Carolina and found the Indians there 'most gentle, loving and faithful, void of all guile and treason, and such as live after the manner of the golden age'. Next year a larger expedition, organized by Ralegh and led by Grenville, settled colonists on Roanoke Island. They remained a year, and John White made accurate maps and drawings of the area. Then Drake, fresh from his West Indies campaign, visited the colony and offered, as supplies from England were overdue, to bring the settlers home. A fortnight later Grenville arrived. Finding the colony deserted, he left a further fifteen men with supplies for two years. In 1587 Ralegh sent out a third expedition, which found no

[1] See p. 345.

settlers; they had been killed by the Indians. This time one hundred and seventeen colonists were left behind. In 1590 three ships were sent. They found the site abandoned, and returned home. The next attempt—a successful one—did not take place till 1607.

In 1595 Ralegh himself sailed to a third area of possible settlement, the Caribbean, led a force up the Orinoco and made friendly contact with the natives, but left no settlers.

Though they ended in failure, these expeditions paved the way for the successes of the next century. Bacon, in his essay *Of Plantations*, emphasized two lessons:

> It is a shameful and unblest thing to take the scum of the people and wicked condemned men to be the people with whom you plant, and not only so, but it spoileth the plantation: for they will ever live like rogues, and not fall to work, but be lazy, and do mischief, and spend victuals, and be quickly weary, . . . Planting of countries is like planting of woods; for you must make account to lose almost twenty years' profit, and expect recompence at the end.

FURTHER READING

P. J. Bowden, *The Wool Trade in Tudor and Stuart England*, Macmillan, 1962

Y. S. Brenner, *The Inflation of Prices in Early Sixteenth Century England*, Ec.H.R., XIV, 1961

— *The Inflation of Prices in England, 1551–1650*, Ec.H.R., XV, 1962

H. C. Darby, ed., *An Historical Geography of England before 1800*, Chapter IX, 'Leland's England', Chapter X, 'Camden's England', C.U.P., 1936

J. Hampden, ed., Richard Hakluyt: *Voyages and Documents*, O.U.P., 1958

G. N. Clark, *The Wealth of England*, O.U.P., 1946

E. Lamond, ed., *A Discourse of the Common Weal of this Realm of England*, C.U.P., 2nd ed. 1929

E. V. Morgan, *The Study of Prices and the Value of Money*, H.A. Aids for Students of History, No. 53, 1952

J. U. Nef, *The Progress of Technology and the Growth of Large Scale Industry in Great Britain, 1540–1640*, Ec.H.R., V, 1934

P. Ramsey, *Tudor Economic Problems*, Gollancz, 1963

R. H. Tawney, *The Agrarian Problem in the Sixteenth Century*, Longmans, Green, 1912

— and E. Power, ed., *Tudor Economic Documents*, 3 vols, Longmans, Green, 1925

J. Thirsk, *Tudor Enclosures*, H.A. Pamphlet No. 41, 1959

R. B. Outhwaite, *Inflation in Tudor and Early Stuart England*, Macmillan, 1968

XIV · ECONOMIC CHANGE II

Poor Relief

THE empirical nature of Tudor economic legislation—what has been called its reluctant paternalism—can be seen particularly clearly in the development of the Tudor Poor Law. During the period sixteen laws were passed dealing specifically with the problem of the poor, ranging from the legislation of Henry VII to the great Elizabethan Poor Laws of 1599 and 1601. Those in authority gradually came to accept the fact that repression was not possible, that some able-bodied poor were unable to find work, and that a policy of alleviation, using methods which often had been evolved in the first instance by town corporations, was the best solution to the problem. As in so much else the Tudor legislation made no organic break with that of earlier centuries. In particular, as early as 1388 an act had ordered that the impotent poor were to return to the towns where they were born and that beggars in transit must carry a form of passport.

Henry VII's act of 1495 provided for the punishment of vagabonds, who were to be held in the stocks for three days and then sent back to the hundred where they had last lived. In 1501 the responsibility for the enforcement of these conditions was placed on the shoulders of the Justices of the Peace.

An act of 1531, while declaring that the cause of unemployment was idleness 'the mother and root of all vices', nevertheless made the important distinction between the able-bodied poor 'whole and mighty in body' who were to be whipped and sent home, and the 'aged, poor and impotent persons' who were to be given licence to beg. In 1536 poor relief was made the responsibility of the parish, which was ordered to support the impotent poor by 'voluntary and charitable alms', so that 'none of them of very necessity shall be compelled to wander idly and go openly in begging'. This was the main line of development. An aberration was the savage act of 1547. This attempted to deal by force with the situation; vagabonds were to be branded and enslaved for two years, if they attempted to escape they were to be enslaved for life, and after a second attempt they were to be executed. The act was repealed in 1550, and in 1552 every town and parish was ordered to appoint two collectors who were to organize voluntary weekly collections

The first half of the century had been occupied by a variety of experiments, the second half saw a fairly orderly progression towards the final solution. In 1563 compulsion replaced voluntary almsgiving. The J.P.s were to levy a rate from those who would not contribute voluntarily. In 1572 'overseers of the poor' were appointed, and in 1576 the J.P.s were empowered to build two 'houses of correction' in each county where the able-bodied poor could be provided with work and made to do it.

The Elizabethan Poor Law reached its ultimate form in the Act of 1598 (amended and confirmed in 1601 and finally made permanent in 1640), which remained in force until 1834. A national compulsory poor rate was established; children were to be apprenticed, girls until twenty-one, boys until twenty-four. Begging was forbidden. Justices were to appoint parish overseers, whose duty it was to raise the poor rate, buy with it stocks of material, and manage the workhouses. The impotent poor were to be looked after in almshouses. The vagabond was to be whipped, and then sent back to his birth-place, or failing that to the place where he last lived, there to be made to work. He must carry a sort of passport of the following type:

> A.B., a sturdy rogue, of tall stature, red-haired and bearded, about the age of 30 years and having a wart near under his right eye, born (as he confesseth) at East Tilbury in Essex, was taken begging at Shorne in this county of Kent the 10 March, 1598, and was then there lawfully whipped therefor, and he is appointed to go to East Tilbury aforesaid the direct way by Gravesend, over the River Thames; for which he is allowed one whole day and no more, at his peril.

Local experiments had often anticipated national legislation. Thus in London the distinction between a poor man and a beggar was made in 1524, the compulsory collection of alms was adopted in 1547, and by 1557 Bridewell, the prototype of all workhouses, had been established to deal with the sturdy beggar by the method of punishment and compulsory work. St. Thomas's and St. Bartholomew's for the sick, Christ's for the children and Bedlam (St. Mary of Bethlehem) for the insane

completed the picture. Ipswich had set up a hospital by
1569, and in 1570 Norwich had taken a census of its poor, had
ordered away non-residents and had divided those who were
left into the three categories of the young, the impotent and the
sturdy. At Chester the following regulations were made in
1539:

> ... the number and names of all indigent and needy mendi-
> cant people shall be searched, known and written, and there-
> upon divided into xv parts, and every of them assigned to
> what ward they shall resort and beg within the said city, and
> in no other place within the same, and their names to be
> written in a bill and set up in every man's house within every
> ward for knowledge to whom they shall give their alms and
> to no other. . . . And further it is ordered that all manner
> of idle persons, being able to labour abiding within the said
> city and not admitted to live by alms within the said city,
> shall every workday in the morning in the time of winter
> at vi of the clock, and in time of summer at iiii of the clock,
> resort and come unto the high cross of the said city, and there
> to offer themselves to be hired to labour for their living
> according to the king's laws and his statutes provided for
> labourers; . . .

Behind both national and local activity, various motives
were at work. Fear of social disorder was powerful. The
peasant revolts on the continent were spectres haunting the
Tudors. Rural unrest was still prevalent. Closely coupled
with fear of disorder was its opposite, admiration for order.
There was a strong element of paternalism in Tudor attempts to
deal with the poor, and social conscience, too, played its part.
There is still some debate as to whether the scale of private giving
rose or fell during the sixteenth century. On the whole it seems
likely that the level fell after about 1540, but that what was given
was now more often invested in charitable trusts, almshouses and
educational endowments instead of, as formerly, being distributed as gifts or devoted to religious ends.[1] It is possible that
the poor law machinery operated intermittently, in those areas

---

[1] In a series of studies Professor Jordan has analysed sixteenth-century charity,
but has not allowed for the rise in the cost of living. Professor Stone has written
that 'the scale of giving . . . in fact falls catastrophically and almost continuously
from 1510 to 1600', and again, 'the proportion of their wealth given away by the
greater merchants of London was at its peak (29·4 per cent) between 1480 and
1540. . . . it would seem that the scale of giving never approached the pre-Reform-
ation figure. What changed was that the charitable bequests were now invested

and at those times when circumstances demanded it, rather in the manner of a fire extinguisher, and that, taking the reign as a whole, private donors accounted for much larger sums than those raised by the parishes.

The pressure of unemployment was lessened by public law and private charity, but it was only removed by the passage of time. Elizabethan and Jacobean writers alike described the continuing presence of the poor. 'They lie in the streets,' wrote Philip Stubbs (1583), 'in dirt as commonly is seen . . . and are permitted to die like dogs or beasts without any mercy or compassion shown them at all.' Twenty years later, in 1608 Thomas Dekker anatomized a 'Rogue' in his *Bell-Man of London: A Discovery of all the idle Vagabonds in England: their Conditions: their laws amongst themselves: their degrees and orders: their meetings, and their manners of living, (both men and women).*

> A *Rogue* is known to all men by his name, but not to all men by his conditions; no puritan can dissemble more than he, for he will speak in a lamentable tune and crawl along the streets, (supporting his body by a staff) as if there were not life enough in him to put strength into his legs: his head shall be bound about with linen, loathsome to behold; and as filthy in colour, as the complexion of his face; his apparel is all tattered, his bosom naked, and most commonly no shirt on: not that they are driven to this misery by mere want, but that if they had better clothes given them, they would rather sell them to some of their own fraternity than wear them, and wander up and down in that piteous manner, only to move people to compassion, and to be relieved with money, which being gotten, at night is spent as merrily and as lewdly, as in the day it was won by counterfeit villainy. Another sect there be of these, and they are called *Sturdy Rogues*: these walk from county to county under colour of travelling to their friends or to find out some kinsman, or else to deliver a letter to one gentleman or other, whose name he will have fairly endorsed on paper folded up for that purpose, and handsomely sealed: other use this shift to carry a Certificate or passport about them, with the hand or seal of some Justice to it, . . . all these writings are but counterfeit, they having amongst them (of their own *Rank*), that can write and read, who are their secretaries in this business.

as permanent capital, not dispersed in immediate largesse, and that the objectives of charity had now taken on a much more secular tone.' *v.* History, 152 (1959), p. 260, and the E.H.R., 303 (1942), p. 328.

The Attitude of the Government

The sixteenth century saw a massive increase in the extent of government interference in social and economic affairs. About two hundred and fifty laws were passed—some concerned local or private interests, of course—and to these must be added a large number of proclamations. Legislation was widespread but it was often ineffective, though the motives which inspired it were practical rather than theoretical.

The largest group of acts is concerned with the regulation of industry and the maintenance of fixed standards of production, matters that would once have been the province of the gilds. Forty-four acts deal with woollens and worsteds, and a further fifteen with the leather industry. Many of these acts are extremely detailed. Thus in 1552 the exact length, breadth and weight of twenty-three different types of cloth was clearly defined. Standard quality was a matter of great importance to the merchant, and the passing of this act was a consequence of the slump in cloth exports, which the Merchant Adventurers attributed to the production of sub-standard cloths. Another series of acts was intended to encourage the cloth-finishing industry by restricting the export of unfinished cloths. The first of these acts was passed in 1487 and the government was still legislating, clearly ineffectually, in 1566, when an act laid down the rule that one finished cloth must be exported for every nine unfinished ones, though this provision, like the earlier acts, was evaded by the Merchant Adventurers. A third group of textile acts was designed to protect the declining worsted industry of East Anglia. Once again the acts do not seem to have been effective and the area was saved from unemployment not by government legislation, but by the establishment there of the new draperies.

The most important single act was perhaps the Statute of Apprentices (1563) described in Chapter VII. Yet this act was largely conservative and restrictive, and the innovations that it contained were introduced, not by the government, but by the commons.

Legislation concerning usury showed a change of attitude about the middle of the century. The acts of 1487 and 1495 had attempted to eliminate loop-holes in the existing laws. Then in 1545 interest of up to 10 per cent was legalized. This act was repealed in 1552, but in 1571 the rate of 10 per cent was once more allowed. Both the act of 1545 and that of 1571 were introduced by the government in order to depress the unofficial rate of interest prevailing among merchants so that it might itself borrow at the new lower rate.

The price rise was uncontrollable. Acts intended to hold down prices in the interests of the consumer proved quite ineffective, while the grant of monopolies was merely a method of rewarding government servants and loyal courtiers, and tended to raise prices and lower standards.

Government attempts to regulate the national economy and direct its movements according to a preconceived plan will not be found in the above-mentioned acts so much as in the long series of laws and proclamations dealing with shipping and overseas activities. 'To sell to others yearly more in value than we buy from them' seemed a common-sense point of view and it was expressed long before the seventeenth-century bullionists made the doctrine fashionable. The fifteenth-century *Libel of English Policy* demanded a ban on foreign luxuries such as 'apes and japes and marmosets'; the mid-sixteenth-century *Discourse of the Commonweal* proposed to protect English trade from foreign competition; an anonymous Elizabethan argued:

> . . . if England would spend less of foreign commodities than the home commodities will pay for, then the remain must of necessity be returned of silver or gold; but if otherwise, then it will fare in England in short time as it doth with a man of great yearly living, that spendeth more yearly than his own revenue, and spendeth of the stock besides. . . .

and Burghley himself held that: 'It is manifest that nothing robbeth the realm of England but when more merchandize is brought into the realm than is carried forth.'

Treasure must not be allowed to leave the country in excessive quantities and various devices were employed in the attempt to achieve this end. The import of specified foreign manufactures was banned from time to time, as for instance in 1553 when the importation of caps was forbidden. Throughout the century there was a stream of acts and proclamations forbidding the export of grain, notably in the difficult years 1547–50 and 1595–7.[1] The Book of Rates was revised in 1558. In it 1,100 commodities were enumerated, of which only 67

[1] V. Ponko, *N. S. B. Gras and Elizabethan Corn Policy*, Ec.H.R., XVII 1964.

were described as exports.   The rates were not touched again till 1604.[1]

During the period a series of what would later have been called Navigation Acts were passed.   In the late fourteenth century an attempt had been made to ensure that English merchants employed English ships; Henry VII's acts of 1485 and 1489 were intended to regulate the French trade in this way, and in 1539 it was decreed that foreigners should pay the lower rate of customs applicable to English merchants—provided they used English shipping.   Protestantism implied the rejection of fasting and hence the possibility of a serious fall in the consumption of fish, which in turn might weaken shipping.   Successive governments therefore introduced 'political' fasting in Lent, on Fridays, and in addition on Wednesday, by the acts of 1548, 1563 and 1603.   Shipping certainly increased, but it is doubtful to what extent the increase was due to these remarkable acts.

The laws which attempted to prevent or to undo enclosures were unenforced and perhaps unenforceable.   On the other hand the sixteen acts which dealt with the poor represent the most determined attack that the government made on any specific economic problem and in them by a process of trial and error a practical solution was worked out.   Yet, as already mentioned, there remains uncertainty as to whether the Poor Laws were regularly enforced or were essentially reserve measures, the intermittent operation of which depended on the efficiency of the local J.P.s, the scale of private charity, and the onset of local or national periods of dearth.

Tudor economic legislation was perhaps ineffective, but it was certainly extensive.   What were the motives behind the erection of this stack of statutes?   Conservatism, concern for the national security, paternalism, all played their part.   Moreover these motives reacted one with another, so that in any single statute one can usually discover all three impulses at work.   Even radical provisions turn out, on closer inspection, to be designed to preserve the *status quo*.   In this, as in so much else, Elizabeth's reign may be regarded as imposing a brake on further change.

Security against the foreigner naturally loomed large in

[1] T. S. Willan, *A Tudor Book of Rates*, Manchester U.P., 1962.

councillors' minds. Shipping must be encouraged, bullion must be amassed, war materials must not be exported. One reason for deploring enclosures was that depopulation might open the coasts to the enemy. 'Whoever commands the sea commands the trade, whoever commands the trade commands the riches of the world, and consequently the world itself,' wrote Ralegh. National security also implied the preservation of internal order. If no sixteenth-century rebellion was purely economic in origin it is also true that there was no rising—with the possible exception of Wyatt's rebellion—without its economic aspect.

Paternalism was implicit in Tudor political thought, which maintained that one of the duties of government was to preserve due rank, to keep each class in its appointed place and there to protect it against the pressure of other classes. In opposition to the traditional patterns of society and its philosophy there were now set the new forces of unemployment, inflation and enclosures, forces which presented to officials an unholy trinity of outstanding and apparently insoluble social problems. Tudor economic legislation was based on hope, faith and charity rather than on economic theory, and any consistency in Burghley's economic activities sprang from the mental climate, from a base line of commonly shared assumptions and difficulties, not from some early form of theoretical mercantilism.

Changes in Society

The aristocracy as a class seems to have experienced three major changes of fortune during the period of Yorkist and Tudor rule. Between 1471 and 1530 the old medieval baronage declined in both status and opportunity. Rulers on the whole did little more than recruit a limited number of new members to the lower ranks of the peerage, the total remaining much what it had been a hundred years earlier. Between 1485 and 1547 forty-three titles became extinct, thirty from natural causes and thirteen from attainder. During the same period thirty-nine families were raised to the peerage, twenty-five for administrative services. During Elizabeth's reign Cecil was the only man ennobled for his services and the number of peers at the time of her death was much the same (59) as it had been in 1509, though the turn-over during the century had been rapid.

In less than twenty years, between about 1538 when the monastic lands began to come on the market and 1554 when the golden fountain dried up, there lies the formative period of the Tudor aristocracy. If we are looking for 'new men' it is here that we shall find them. Officials and favourites, together with a number of the old nobility, made their fortunes, taking full advantage of the great land market. In the dramatic words of Burke 'The lion having sucked the blood of his prey threw the offal carcase to the jackal in waiting'. Among the jackals who fattened on the monastic carcase were the earls of Bedford (Tavistock, Woburn and Thorney), Pembroke (Wilton), Rutland (Beverley, Rievaulx and Belvoir), Cumberland (Bolton), Worcester (Tintern) and Shrewsbury (Worksop).

During the second half of the century the pattern of aristocratic fortune changed once more as the nobility, old and new alike, experienced hard times. Mary and Elizabeth were cautious in their creation of peerages. People who earlier might have expected to have been ennobled were now passed over. The land market contracted again, until the great sale of crown lands in the last decade of the century. Thirdly, the inflation slashed incomes derived mainly from land rents, as were those of most lords. So much is beyond dispute.

An analysis[1] of the occupation of manors in seven counties in 1561 gives the following pattern of distribution:

	%
Gentry	67·1
Peers	13·1
Crown	9·5
Spiritual	7·2

How did these noble landowners face the crisis in their affairs? Aristocratic expenditure was rocketing, and it was not entirely due to the price rise. The state service expected of a lord was costly and though there were prizes to be won (perhaps a quarter of the aristocracy benefited from their connections with government) it was a lottery in which the majority inevitably drew blanks. Litigation soaked up income, and it was an age notoriously fond of going to law. The conspicuous waste necessary to keep up social appearances was doubly necessary if one was in the Queen's favour—the laying-out

[1] R. H. Tawney, *The Rise of the Gentry: A Postscript*, Ec.H.R., VII, 1954.

of money on clothes, hospitality, plate and jewels, buildings, even on funerals (the Marquess of Northampton lay unburied for weeks while money was raised for his funeral)—and could easily prove ruinous.

Professor Stone has shown that the aristocracy were in serious financial straits, and that it was at least partly their own fault:

> To the inevitable changes wrought by the eccentricities of human reproductive capacity were added in the late sixteenth century exceptional temptations and compulsions to overspend on conspicuous consumption, royal service, or marriage portions, exceptional need for adaptability in estate management, novel opportunities and exceptional dangers in large-scale borrowing.[1]

Whatever the reasons, it is clear that the landed gentleman faced a serious crisis in the period 1580–1610, and was forced to search for new sources of income. Competent administration of estates and the renewal of leases for short, seven-year periods when the old ones fell in could make land-owning pay, but one could make a larger initial profit on long leases, and to sell land was easier than to improve it; 'A seller I have been all the days of my life', Sir Fulke Greville admitted. Records suggest that peers may have disposed of as much as a quarter of their property.[2]

Some engaged, directly or indirectly, in the new industrial developments. Mines were enthusiastically sunk to such depths that the primitive pumps could no longer keep pace with the water that came in, and aristocrats invested heavily in ironworking. Other men adopted more eccentric solutions; they fought against the Turk, took up the profession of Barbary pirate, or lived with their mothers-in-law. The earl of Cumberland became an amateur privateer—and lost by it.[3] Despair might even lead to rebellion: Essex in 1601 received some support among bankrupt gentlemen.

---

[1] L. Stone, *Social Change and Revolution in England, 1540–1640*, Longmans, Green, 1965, where it is quoted from his *The Crisis of the Aristocracy, 1559–1641*, O.U.P., 1965, which contains Professor Stone's most recent conclusion in the matter.

[2] In a selected area, on 31 December 1558, 63 families held an average of 54 manors each, while on 31 December 1602, 57 families held an average of 39 manors each. Professor Stone writes: 'There is overwhelming evidence that the holdings of the surviving peers of 1558 had fallen by about a quarter by 1602 . . .'

[3] See p. 302.

The minority who found a niche at court might recoup the expenses involved in getting there, and the necessity to do so helps to account for the growth of governmental graft and patronage in the last decade of the century.[1] The success of the few and the comparative failure of the many certainly played its part in the tendency that always existed, and which became pronounced in the seventeenth century, for two cultures to develop—those of the Court and of the Country, opposed politically, psychologically and morally.

Pressing into the areas vacated by those of the nobility and landed gentlemen who failed to maintain their position were the new gentry, a group composed of successful landed men, of merchants, traders and officials who had prospered and who, buying land, bought with it security and respectability—in general, those rising men whom Sir Thomas Smith described as 'gentlemen of the first head'.

So much is generally accepted, but beyond this, there is disagreement among historians. In 1941 R. H. Tawney coined the phrase *the rise of the gentry* to cover what he believed was a decisive change in the ownership of property, due mainly to the old-fashioned landowners' inability to adapt their methods of estate management to the problems posed by inflation. Since that date the phrase has been attacked, defended, and redefined in a protracted academic free-for-all. At present the evidence suggests that the aristocracy recovered some of their lost ground in the seventeenth century, that many 'mere gentry' declined and that those who rose were on the one hand the hard-working yeomanry and on the other the courtiers, court lawyers and monopoly merchants, men who were 'in' at Court or in the City.[2]

The new merchant and the new wealth certainly caught the attention of contemporaries. As early as 1528–31 the Venetian Lodovico Falier was contrasting the poverty of the Welsh and the Cornish with the wealth of the Englishman, whom he describes as 'mercantile, rich, affable and noble'. In 1559 an English memorandum contained the complaint that 'Merchants have grown so cunning in the trade of corrupting and find it so

[1] See pp. 355–6.
[2] See, throughout, L. Stone, *Social Change and Revolution in England, 1540–1640*, Longmans, Green, 1965, and especially pp. xi–xiv.

sweet, that since [1509] there could never be won any good
law or order which touched their liberty or state, but they
stayed it, either in the Commons, or higher House of Parliament, or else by the prince himself.'   A little later the Spanish
ambassador Mendoza said of the English that 'Profit to them
was like nutriment to savage beasts'.

No doubt these traits were not limited to the sixteenth
century, but there is also no doubt that the opportunities for
great gain were enlarged, and the Puritan Philip Stubbes
anatomized the resulting emphasis on birth in the higher ranks
of society, 'every man crying with open mouth I am a gentleman, I am worshipful, I am Honourable, I am noble, and I
cannot tell what: my father was this, my father was that; . . .'
while John Norden criticizes the 'waspish ambition and wolvish
emulation' of the country gentlemen.   Amidst all this hubbub
the writer Robert Greene (c. 1560–92) may perhaps be allowed
to have the last word: 'What is gentry if wealth be wanting, but
base servile beggary?'

England was becoming a mercantile community and
middle-class men with money to spare were beginning to
realize that the investment of money could be as profitable
as agriculture or commerce.   The expansion of opportunities
for the investment of capital took place at much the same time
that the break with Rome occurred.   Political and economic
thought became secularized, and religious nonconformity
was paralleled by economic individualism.   It is debatable
whether there was a connection between the two developments.
In *Religion and the Rise of Capitalism* R. H. Tawney assembled
evidence to demonstrate that there was.   Critics of the theory
pointed out that money-lending and banking were not confined to protestant countries, that not all protestant countries
became at once commercial centres—Scotland for instance
was undeveloped—and that both Luther and Calvin denounced
usury.   Nevertheless the protestant emphasis on the individual, on the religious importance of work well done, on
the idea that, for some at least, prosperity was a possible
indication of God's favour—all this provided a climate of
opinion in which new commercial techniques might flourish.

The man in the street was, as usual, conservative in these
matters.   He regarded the usurer as 'a great taker of advan-

tage' and considered that the man who lived 'upon his usury as the husbandman doth upon husbandry ought to be thrust out of the society of men'. The new ethic, though, had come to stay, symbolized by such men as Sir Horatio Palavicino from Genoa who at the time of his death in 1600 was worth £100,000 in capital created from his myriad activities in the new world of finance. In 1572 Thomas Wilson had described that new world in *A Discourse upon Usury*: 'by all laws a man may take as much for his own wares as he can get . . . and a bargain is a bargain, let men say what they list'. At St. Paul's Cross when the preacher attacked usury a City financier retorted, 'Tush, Tush, Scripture is Scripture, but for all the scripture, a man must live by his own, and I tell you my money is my plough.'

Even at the base of the social pyramid there were signs of change, or of the desire for change. The Separatists in the nineties were persecuted at least in part because they were suspected of a leaning towards the Christian communism of the extreme Anabaptists. Cecil noted that the new textile workers were 'of worse condition to be quietly governed than the husbandmen'. During the famine riots of 1596 the men involved declared, 'They must not starve, they will not starve' and perhaps it was this outburst that an M.P. had in mind when he said, in the following year, that if the poor were 'privy to their own strength and liberty allowed them by the law' they would be as 'untamed as wild beasts'. The social tensions between Court and Country, merchant and aristocrat, rich and poor, were to find expression in the Civil War of the next century.

EXTRACTS

I. *An anonymous writer describes the geographical advantages of London:*

This realm hath only three principal rivers, whereon a royal city may well be situated. Trent on the north, Severn in the south-west, and Thames in the south-east, of which the Thames both for the straight course in length reachest farthest into the belly of the land, and for the breadth and stillness of the water is most navigable up and down the stream; by reason whereof London, standing almost in the middle of that course, is more commodiously served with provision of necessaries than any town standing upon the other two rivers can be, and doth also more easily communicate to the rest of the realm the commodities of her own intercourse and traffic. The river openeth indifferently upon France and Flanders, our mightiest neighbours, to whose doings we ought to have a bent eye and special regard: and this city standeth thereon in such convenient distance from the sea, as it is not only near enough for intelligence of those princes, and for the resistance of their attempts, but also sufficiently removed from the fear of any sudden dangers that may be offered by them; whereas for the prince of this realm to dwell upon Trent were to turn his back or blind side to his most dangerous borderers; and for him to rest and dwell upon Severn were to be shut up in a cumbersome corner, which openeth but upon Ireland only, a place of much less importance. Neither could London be pitched so commodiously upon any other part of the same river of Thames as where it now standeth; for it if were removed more to the west it should lose the benefit of the ebbing and flowing, and if it were seated more towards the east it should be nearer to danger of the enemy, and further both from the good air and from doing good to the inner parts of the realm; neither may I omit that none other place is so plentifully watered with springs as London is. And whereas amongst other things, corn and cattle, hay and fuel, be of great necessity; of which cattle may be driven from afar, and corn may easily be transported. But hay and fuel being of greater bulk and burthen must be at hand; only London, by the benefit of this situation and river may be served therewith. (Composed *c.* 1578; printed in the *Survey of London*, by John Stow.)

II.   *William Camden describes the iron industry of Sussex:*

This county is full of iron mines, all over it; for the casting of which there are furnaces up and down the country, and abundance of wood is yearly spent; many streams are drawn into one channel, and a great deal of meadow-ground is turned into ponds and pools for the driving of mills by the flashes, which, beating with hammers upon the iron, fill the neighbourhood round about it, night and day, with continual noise. But the iron, wrought here, is not everywhere of the same goodness, yet generally more brittle than the Spanish, whether it be from its nature, or tincture and temper. Nevertheless, the proprietors of the mines, by casting of cannon and other things, make them turn to good account; but whether the nation is in any way advantaged by them is a doubt which the next Age will be better able to resolve. Neither does this county want glass-houses: but the glass (by reason of the matter or making I know not which) is not so transparent and clear and therefore is only used by the ordinary sort of people. (W. Camden, *Britannia*, 1586.)

III. *Richard Hakluyt, suggests a method of colonizing America:*
Yea, if we would behold with the eye of pity how all our prisons are pestered and filled with able men to serve their country which for small robberies are daily hanged up in great numbers, even twenty at a clap out of one jail (as was seen at the last assizes at Rochester) we would hasten and further every man to his power the deducting of some colonies of our superfluous people into those temperate and fertile parts of America, which, being within six weeks sailing of England, are yet unpossessed by any Christians, and seem to offer themselves unto us, stretching nearer unto her Majesty's dominions than to any other part of Europe. (R. Hakluyt: *Divers Voyages Touching the Discovery of America*; 1582; ed. J. W. Jones, Hakluyt Society, Vol. vii, 1850.)

IV. *William Harrison describes three economic grievances 1586–7:*
. . . they speak also of three things that are grown to be very grievous unto them, to wit the enhancing of rents, lately mentioned; the daily oppression of copyholders, whose lords seek to bring their poor tenants almost into plain servitude and misery, daily devising new means, and seeking up all the old, how to cut them shorter and shorter, doubling, trebling, and now and then seven times increasing their fines; driving them also for every trifle to lose and forfeit their tenures (by whom the greatest part of the realm does stand and is maintained) to the end they may fleece them yet more, which is a lamentable hearing.   The third thing they talk of is usury, a trade brought in by the Jews, now perfectly practised almost by every christian, and so commonly that he is accounted but for a fool that does lend his money for nothing . . . men of great port and countenance are so far from suffering their farmers to have any gain at all, that they themselves become graziers, butchers, tanners, sheepmasters, woodmen and *denique quod non* thereby to enrich themselves, and bring all the wealth of the country into their own hands, . . . (*Description of England*, New Shakespeare Society, 1908.)

V. *Thomas Wilson (c. 1560–1629) describes the social structure of England in 1600:*
It cannot be denied but the common people are very rich, albeit they be much decayed from the states they were wont

to have, for the gentlemen which were wont to addict themselves to wars are now for the most part grown to become good
husbands and know as well how to improve their lands to the
uttermost as the farmer or countryman, so that they take their
farms into their hands as the leases expire and either till themselves or else let them out to those who will give most; whereby
the yeomanry of England is decayed and become servants to
gentlemen, which were wont to be the glory of the country
and good neighbourhood and hospitality. . . .

Notwithstanding this that the great yeomanry is decayed, yet
by this means the commonalty is increased, twenty now perhaps
with their labour aad diligence living well and wealthily of
that land which our great yeoman held before. . . .   Of these
yeomen of the richest sort which are able to lend the Queen
money (as they do ordinarily upon her letters called privy
seals whensoever she has any wars defensive or offensive or
any other enterprise) there are accounted to be about 10,000
in country villages, besides citizens.   There are, moreover, of
yeomen of meaner ability which are called Freeholders, . . . and
are accounted to be worth each of them in all their substance
and stock betwixt £300 and £500, more or less; of these, I say,
there are reckoned to be in England and Wales about the
number of 80,000, . . .

The rest are copyholders and cottagers, as they call them,
who hold some land and tenements of some other lord which is
parcel of the demesne of his seigniory or manor, at the will of
the Lord, and these are some of them men of as great ability
as any of the rest; and some poor, and live chiefly upon country
labour, working by the day for meat and drink and some small
wages. . . .

. . . in Norwich I have known in my time twenty-four
aldermen which were esteemed to be worth £20,000 apiece,
some much more, and the better sort of citizens the half; but
if we should speak of London and some other maritime places,
we should find it much exceeding this rate.   It is well known
that at this time there are in London some merchants worth
£100,000 and he is not accounted rich that cannot reach to
£50,000 or near it. . . .

. . . Earls some day decay, some increase according to the
course of the world, but that which I have noted by perusing . . .
is that still the total sum grows much to one reckoning, and that
is to £100,000 rent yearly, accounting them all in gross. . . .   If
a man would proportion this amongst nineteen Earls and a
Marquis, it would be no great matter, to every one £5,000 rent,
but as some exceed that so many come short of it.

The thirty-nine Barons and two Viscounts do not much exceed this sum, their revenue, is reckoned together to amount of £120,000 yearly.

The Bishops' revenues amount to about £22,500 yearly altogether, whereof three of them, viz. Canterbury, Winchester and Ely, receive rent per annum betwixt £2,000 and 3,000, the rest betwixt £1,000 and 500 and some less. . . .

There are accounted to be in England about the number of 500 knights. . . . These for the most part are men living betwixt £1,000 and £2,000 yearly, and many of them equal the best barons and come not much behind many Earls. . . .

Those which we call esquires are gentlemen whose ancestors are, or have been, knights, or else they are the heirs and eldest of their houses, and of some competent quantity of revenue fit to be called to office and authority in their county where they live; of these there are esteemed to be in England, as I have seen by the book of musters of every several shire, to the number of 16,000 or thereabouts, whereof there are of them in Commissions of the peace about 1,400 . . . these are men in living betwixt £1,000 and £500 rent.   Especially about London and the counties adjoining, where there lands are set to the highest, he is not counted of any great reckoning unless he be betwixt 1,000 marks or £1,000, but northward and far off a gentleman of good reputation may be content with £300 and £400 yearly. . . .

. . . lawyers by the ruins of neighbours' contentions are grown so great that no other sort dare meddle with them; their number is so great now that, to say the truth, they can scarcely live one by another, the practice being drawn into a few hands of those which are most renowned, and all the rest live by pettifogging, seeking means to set their neighbours at variance whereby they may gain on both sides. . . .   there being no province, city, town, nor scarce village free from them, unless the Isle of Anglesey, which boast they never had lawyers nor foxes. (*The State of England*, ed. F. J. Fisher, *Cam. Soc.* LII, 1936.)

VI.   *Richard Hakluyt praises the expansion of England:*
. . . in this most famous and peerless government of her most excellent Majesty, her subjects through the special assistance and blessing of God, in searching the most opposite corners and quarters of the world, and to speak plainly, in compassing the vast globe of the earth more than once, have excelled all the nations and people of the earth.   For, which of the kings of this land before her Majesty, had their banners ever seen in the Caspian Sea? which of them hath ever dealt with the Emperor of Persia, as her Majesty hath done, and obtained for her

merchants large and loving privileges? who ever saw, before this regiment, an English leger [resident ambassador] in the stately porch of the Grand Signor at Constantinople? who ever found English consuls and agents at Tripolis, in Syria, at Aleppo, at Babylon, at Balsara, and which is more, who ever heard of Englishmen at Goa before now? what English ships did heretofore ever anchor in the mighty river of Plate? pass and repass the unpassable (in former opinion) straits of Magellan, range along the coast of Chile, Peru and all the backside of Nova Hispania further than any Christian ever passed, traverse the mighty breadth of the South Sea, land upon the Luzones in despite of the enemy, enter into alliance, amity and traffic with the princes of the Moluccas and the Isle of Java, double the famous Cape of Bona Speranza, arrive at the Isle of Santa Helena, and last of all return home most richly laden with the commodities of China, as the subjects of this now flourishing monarchy have done? (Richard Hakluyt, *Principal Navigations*, epistle dedicatory, 1589.)

VII.   *Nicholas Breton praises the English merchant:*
A worthy merchant is the heir of adventure, whose hopes hang much upon wind.   Upon a wooden horse he rides through the world, and in a merry gale he makes a path through the seas. He is a discoverer of countries and a finder out of commodities, resolute in his attempts and royal in his expenses.   He is the life of traffic and the maintainer of trade, the sailor's master and the soldier's friend.   He is the exercise of the exchange, the honour of credit, the observation of time and the understanding of thrift.   His study is number, his care his accounts, his comfort his conscience, and his wealth his good name.   He fears not Scylla and sails close by Charybdis, and having beaten out a storm, rides at rest in a harbour.   By his sea gain he makes his land purchase, and by the knowledge of trade finds the key of treasure.   Out of his travels he makes his discourses, and from his eye-observations brings the models of architecture. He plants the earth with foreign fruits, and knows at home what is good abroad.   He is neat in apparel, modest in demeanour, dainty in diet and civil in his carriage.   In sum, he is the pillar of a city, the enricher of a country, the furnisher of a court, and the worthy servant of a king.   (Nicholas Breton (*c*. 1551–*c*. 1623), *The Good and the Badde*, 1616.)

FURTHER READING

L. Stone, *Social Change and Revolution in England, 1540–1640*, Longmans, Green, 1965
R. H. Tawney, *Religion and the Rise of Capitalism*, Murray, 1926

XV · THE ARTISTIC AND INTELLECTUAL SCENE

The New Learning

RENAISSANCE influences were felt in England, piecemeal and often at second-hand, over the best part of two hundred years. The developments in the plastic arts that were taking place in such centres as Florence, Assisi and Siena were almost unknown to fourteenth-century England, though faint echoes reached the country by way of France. In literature, on the other hand, there was a much closer connection. The legends of gods and heroes, the tenets of astrology, and the stories of Boccaccio (1313–75) were available in England and provided material for Chaucer (*c.* 1340–1400), Gower (*Confessio Amantis*, 1390–93), and Lydgate (*Troy Book, c.* 1450). Old texts in the new 'humanist' script had found a market in England by the third quarter of the fifteenth century. John Shirwood, bishop of Durham, knew Greek and Latin and built up an important private collection of texts, which included (1464) a copy of Pliny's *De Viris Illustribus* in the new script.

Printing accelerated the spread of the new learning. Caxton's career illustrates the close interconnections of trade, patronage, classical learning and the new technique. He had been Governor of the English Nation at Bruges, an association of merchants who dealt not only in wool but also in spices and manuscripts. In 1471 he saw one of the new printing presses at Cologne. Four years later he printed at Bruges his first book—an English version of the French *Tale of Troy*. Next year (1476) he set up his press at Westminster. The first book printed was the *Sayings of the Philosophers*, which had been translated from the French by Lord Rivers, brother-in-law of the King, who gave Caxton his support. Before his death Caxton had printed nearly one hundred books. Of those which have survived 45 per cent are religious, 29 per cent literary (including works by Chaucer, Gower, Lydgate, Boethius, Cicero, Aesop), and 12 per cent official publications. By 1510 the press had abandoned Caxton's black-letter type for one based on Italian script.

By the close of Henry VII's reign humanist learning was well-established in southern England.[1]   At the King's court the humanist Bernard André was appointed King's Librarian (1492) and Latin Secretary (1495), and has some claim to be regarded as England's first poet laureate.   Grocyn (c. 1446–1519) and Linacre (c. 1460–1524) had travelled in Italy and were teaching Greek at Oxford, and a few years later in 1518 the latter founded the Royal College of Physicians.   Colet (1467–1519) had lectured in Greek at Oxford in 1496, and in 1510 established St. Paul's School, where he made specific provision for the teaching of Greek.   The great Erasmus (c. 1466–1536) came to England for six months in 1499 and became a friend of Colet and of Thomas More.   In 1509 he paid a second visit and remained till 1514, lecturing on Greek at Cambridge.

English humanism, inspired in part directly from Italy and in part indirectly through the example, conversation and teaching of Erasmus, had a strongly Platonic flavour and, perhaps in consequence, it tended to turn to the didactic, the educational.   The universities of Oxford and Cambridge were endowed with new foundations: at Cambridge, Jesus College (1496), Christ's College (1505), St. John's College (1511), Magdalene (1542); Trinity (1546), Emmanuel (1584) and Sidney Sussex (1596); at Oxford, Brasenose (1509), Corpus Christi (1517), Cardinal (1525) re-endowed as Christ Church (1546), Trinity (1554), St. John's (1555) and Jesus (1571). Regius Professorships were endowed at Oxford and Cambridge in theology, medicine, civil law, Hebrew and Greek.

The most remarkable product of English humanism was Thomas More's *Utopia* (1517).   Here More described an imaginary commonwealth in which all goods were held in common; men and women wore the same clothes; there was religious 'toleration; meals were taken in common; all must work; all must be trained to fight; euthanasia was practised; women might become priests.   *Utopia* is so different from the principles by which More as a sincere Catholic regulated his own life that men have ever since discussed the difference. Some think, like Tyndale, that More 'knew the truth and forsook it', but it seems more probable that the book was an

[1] In Scotland the first book—a Chaucer—was printed in 1508.

intellectual exercise, an inventive demonstration of the practical application of Renaissance theorizing, a mixture of satire and paradox. It remains a disturbing book, with undertones of melancholy realism.

Architecture

Renaissance influence on architecture appears in ornament and detail, classical motifs grafted on to an essentially English base, and in this form it continued to make its impact throughout the century. The neutral tone of Tudor architecture made it particularly appropriate as a setting for ornament whose interest was intrinsic and not dependent on its surroundings.

The fan-work tracery of the English perpendicular style reached its climax in St. George's Chapel, Windsor (1473–1519), Henry VII's Chapel, Westminster (1503–19), Bath Abbey (1499–1536) and King's College Chapel, Cambridge (vault, c. 1512). Yet Henry VII's tomb at Westminster is pure Italian Renaissance, the work of Pietro Torrigiano, and when Henry VIII had the wooden screen built in King's College Chapel (1532–6) he chose for it the work of North Italian craftsmen, classical in structure and detail—though there is a certain northern heaviness about the final product

Very few large secular buildings have survived from the period up to 1540. Royal palaces were built or rebuilt under the supervision of the state department known as the King's Works. This department played an important part in diffusing new styles and techniques through southern England. The palaces include Richmond (1501), Whitehall (rebuilt 1530–36), St. James's (1532–40) and Nonsuch, Surrey (c. 1538–c. 1555) but except at St. James's very little survives. Richmond was a mixture of palace and castle, based on French examples and built of brick with a strong emphasis on the gatehouse. Nonsuch was the most original, a fantastic erection probably intended to rival Francis I's château at Chambord; it introduced to England strap-work and the use on a large scale of plaster decoration.

Wolsey's Hampton Court (1514–40) is native in style, but the gateways are decorated with terracotta medallions containing the heads of Roman emperors (c. 1521) and are the work of an Italian, Giovanni da Maiano. Similarly, the walls of Wolsey's closet are panelled in the traditional English linenfold pattern, but the ceiling of the same room is decorated with gilded stucco ornament of the Italian type. When the palace passed into the King's hands, the roof of the Great Hall (1536–40) was English in its style of construction, but was worked over with Italian detail. Layer Marney Towers in Essex (*c.* 1520–5) has a Gothic gatehouse, but the large perpendicular window has Renaissance ornament on the mullions.

These examples are typical of the general pattern of contact between English architecture and the Renaissance. In most buildings there is Renaissance detail, in none are structure and detail one integrated whole. The Renaissance influence is everywhere in evidence, but no school of Renaissance architects developed, and there was no break in the evolution of a traditional English style.

Compton Wynyates in Warwickshire neatly illustrates contemporary social and architectural trends. In 1510 Sir William Compton received permission to enclose two thousand acres of land. In this new park he built himself a manor house, using bricks from the nearby castle of Fulbrook, a castle which had itself been built a century earlier by the duke of Bedford when he created a deserted village by emparking the original settlement and church. Sir William's new house embodied no startling stylistic innovations, but only a decently modern blend of Tudor-Gothic detail.

In architecture the forties and fifties were—as in so much else —a period of change. The patrons were no longer the Crown or the great ecclesiastics, but the lay intelligentsia, which derived its power and its money from office, its members often being connected in one way or another with the Protector Somerset. The latter's own palace, Somerset House (*c.* 1549), was the most important single building of the period, being perhaps the first conscious attempt to build an English house entirely designed within the classical framework. The way was now prepared for the impressive country houses of the last part of the century. The prototypes of these can be found in one or two provincial manor houses. Barrington Court (1514–48) in Somerset is in appearance a typical 'Elizabethan' manor-house, its ground plan consisting of an open court, made up of a hall block with central porch, and two wings, the whole composing an E-shaped pattern. Another early house, Hengrave Hall in Surrey, where building began about 1525, is organized around a central court. These two houses fore-shadow the two main types of later plans.

In the last quarter of the sixteenth century the 'prodigy houses' of Elizabeth's reign were built, great buildings erected by the ministers and courtiers of the Queen. Their aim was single and simple—to impress by splendour, by conspicuous waste. These houses—in any other European country they would have been called palaces—were designed to overshadow their neighbours, to advertise to the world that their owners had succeeded, and to house the Queen when she deigned to recognize that success by allowing herself to be entertained in them during one or other of her royal progresses through England south of the Pennines. Of their respective houses (Theobalds and Holdenby) Burghley, who had in eleven years spent an average of £1,000 *per annum* on building, wrote to Sir Christopher Hatton, 'God send us long to enjoy Her, for whom we both meant to exceed our purses in these'. The motives that prompted their erection and the air of tasteless opulence that sometimes resulted are reminiscent of the houses built by nineteenth-century dukes and industrialists—with one impor-tant qualification, the Elizabethan houses were original, the Victorian ones were imitative.

Classical influences became more pervasive, more direct, easier to recognize, but they continued to be a matter of decorative design, not a method of building. Decked out with an eclectic pattern of continental ornamentation, there is an obvious parallel between the buildings themselves and the English courtier adorned with a variety of foreign fashions, who 'bought his doublet in Italy, his round hose in France, his bonnet in Germany, and his behaviour every where'.[1]

Italian detail came to England through the works of such men as John Shute, who had been sent to Italy by Northumber-land and who later composed *The First and Chief Grounds of Architecture* (1563) which he based on the writings of Vitruvius. By the end of the reign these influences had been absorbed, sifted, and transformed into a native idiom. Certain elements, such as the pilaster, Flemish-transformed strapwork, and Italian grotesqueries then became the hallmark of Jacobean architecture. By 1612 Henry Peacham could describe 'the antique' as 'an unnatural or disorderly composition for delight's

[1] *The Merchant of Venice*, I, ii.

sakes, of men, birds, fishes, flowers, etc., without (as we say) Rhyme or Reason, for the greater vanity you show in your invention, the more you please'. It was a definition that would have profoundly shocked the fifteenth-century Italian rediscoverers of the classical style.

Longleat in Wiltshire is the first important example of Elizabethan architecture and probably the greatest, representing the brief 'High Renaissance' of English architecture. It was built for Sir John Thynne, who had superintended the building of Somerset House, by William Spicer and then rebuilt after a disastrous fire. On the second occasion Robert Smythson (c. 1536–1614) was employed as mason-designer. Longleat (1568–80) is symmetrical in plan, coherent in design, restrained and refined in detail. Earlier buildings, for reasons of defence or tradition, had usually turned inward on themselves. Longleat is an outward-looking house, reflecting self-confidence, security and ostentation—all of them characteristics of the Elizabethan period. More self-assertive is Kirby Hall, Northants, begun for Sir Humphry Stafford in 1570, which has been described as 'an amazing mixture of sophistication and bucolic ignorance'. The chief mason was Thomas Thorpe (d. 1596) who designed a columned porch with giant pilasters for 'the first Elizabethan house to display in spectacular measure the influence of the Renaissance in architecture'.[1]

Other houses followed, each embodying its owner's private dream, his individual romance. The greatest of the other prodigy houses are Burghley House, Northants, begun in 1556 but the main part, with its 360 foot-long front, built in 1577–84, an international building which depended for its construction on German workmen, Flemish designs, and French books such as Philibert de l'Orme's *Nouvelles Inventions* (1561); nearby Holdenby House built for Christopher Hatton, Elizabeth's Lord Chanceller; Wollaton House, 1580–8, another of Smythson's works, built round a great central hall for Sir Francis Willoughby, Sheriff of Nottingham; Bess of Hardwick's Hall in Derbyshire, 1590–7, also designed by Smythson, of which it was remarked that there was 'more glass than wall'; Montacute, Somerset, built (1588–1601) for Edward Phelips, a successful lawyer and a Master of the Rolls, a provincial house which quietly absorbed the now traditional continental influences.

[1] J. Summerson: *Elizabethan Architecture*, B.B.C., 1965.

Each house is different, yet each could only have been built in the Elizabethan age.

Of Smythson at Wollaton his biographer has written:

He was no more than an ignorant local mason, with no intellectual training; yet how far he was from being swamped, as many local masons were, by influences he could not control and did not understand. Instead, from the late Gothic of the Midlands and West Country, from his own Longleat, from the great layouts of France, from Serlio, from the extravagances of the Low Countries, he selected, adapted, and integrated until in the end he produced what his client required: a building that was at once a magnifico, every bit as resplendent and ornamented as the most expensive Elizabethan courtier; an original, one of those 'ingeniose devices' which the age pursued with such enthusiasm, in literature and the arts; and a fantasy, an early expression of a new romantic urge, which was to show itself in many ways, from Philip Sidney throwing off his cuisses at the battle of Zutphen to Lord Pembroke and his friends dining at Ludlow in the dress and with the names of the knights of the Round Table.[1]

The lust to build was not confined to the extremely rich. The new influences were also apparent in college architecture, such as parts of Trinity and the Gate of Virtue at Caius (c. 1567), in provincial guildhalls like those of Guildford and Leominster and the portico at Exeter (1592-5), in Sir Thomas Gresham's Royal Exchange (1566-70), the work of a Flemish architect, Henri de Pass. Less obvious today than these institutional buildings, is the great rebuilding of the smaller country houses and farms:

All over England, except in the four most northerly counties, we find abundant visual evidence of a great age of rebuilding in the two generations between about 1570 and 1640. The wave of country house building, from Henry VIII's time onwards, is well enough known . . .; but what is less well known, though it is very evident when one's attention is drawn to it, is the remarkable surge of rebuilding and new building among all social classes except the poorest, in town and country alike.[2]

[1] M. Girouard, *Robert Smythson and the Architecture of the Elizabethan Era*, Country Life, 1966.

[2] W. G. Hoskins; *The Making of the English Landscape*, Hodder and Stoughton, 1955, p. 119.

Painting and Music

In 1506 Castiglione was sent on a diplomatic errand to England by the duke of Urbino, Guido da Montefeltro, who had been created a Knight of the Garter. Castiglione brought with him as a present for Henry VII a picture of St. George in which the Saint wore the Garter. The picture had been specially painted by Raphael and it was the first Italian painting by an important artist to reach England. It remained, though, an isolated incident.

The chief link with advanced European practice was Hans Holbein the Younger (c. 1497–1543). Holbein was born in Augsburg, one of the cities through which Italian influence entered Germany, and he lived for a time in France, observing artistic fashions at the court of Francis I. From 1526 to 1528, and again from 1532 until his death from the plague in 1543, he worked in England as a fashionable portrait painter. Holbein's aim was not to reveal his own character but that of his sitter; his portraits are exact maps of what he observed and are thus of particular value to the historian. They range from that of Henry VIII straddling the Privy Chamber at Whitehall (1537), through those of hard-faced courtiers like Sir Henry Guilford and unimaginative officials such as Sir Richard Southwell, to the anonymous men and women who served these masters. Holbein himself complained that in England 'the arts freeze', and certainly he founded no native school of painters. It was instead through his designs for triumphal arches, gold and silver goblets, book-bindings, and similar applied decorations that he did most to plant the elements of a Renaissance style in England.

In the middle years of the century the court painters were still foreigners, William Scrots from Brussels, Antonio Mor, and the Flemish born Hans Eworth (1520–74), who provided a service, fulfilled a need, but left no followers. The Queen of Hungary lent Mary a portrait of Philip, painted by Titian, until she had 'the living model in her presence'. It was perhaps the only really great Renaissance painting in England at that time.

Whether it was due to the absence of example, or the lack of patronage, or the break with Rome, painting in the second half of the century did not share in the revival of the other arts.

Portraits of the aristocracy and gentry were still painted by foreigners such as Eworth[1] and Marc Gheeraedts of Bruges. The only significant English artists were minaturists, such as Nicholas Hilliard (*c.* 1547–1619) and Isaac Oliver (*c.* 1556–1617)—and the latter was the son of a Huguenot refugee. Their art derived from that of the medieval illuminators, but incorporated Renaissance naturalism and perspective. It owed something also to Holbein, who had himself produced a number of miniatures at the court of Henry VIII.

On the other hand the sixteenth century was one of the great ages of English music. Throughout the period important religious works were produced, ranging in time from the Masses of John Taverner (*fl.* 1530) and Richard Sampson (1470–1554), through the Responses and Litany of Thomas Tallis (*c.* 1505–1585), to the great works of Thomas Weelkes (*d.* 1623), Thomas Morley (1557–1602), John Bull (*d.* 1628) and, above all, William Byrd (1543–1623).

In secular music the madrigal, invented in Italy, became the most popular form. It was adopted by many of the composers already mentioned, and also by John Dowland (1563–1626). Between 1588 and 1630 almost two thousand original songs were printed in about eighty books, and of course there was a great deal of work which remained in manuscript.

Of all the composers Byrd was the greatest, a man able to stand comparison, particularly in his religious works, with international figures like Palestrina. He was a Catholic and himself gave a description of one of the sources of his inspiration:

> There is a certain hidden power in the thoughts underlying the words themselves, so that as one meditates upon the sacred words and constantly and seriously considers them, the right notes, in some inexplicable fashion, suggest themselves quite spontaneously.

Literature

As in the other arts so too in literature the hundred years from the mid-fifteenth to the mid-sixteenth century are best labelled 'Late Medieval'. The prose is simple and natural, the poetry is often metrically irregular. The most important imaginative

---

[1] Eworth worked in England *c.* 1545–72.

prose work is Sir Thomas Malory's *Morte d'Arthur*, the most original poet John Skelton (*c.* 1460–1529). Skelton was educated at Cambridge, was employed as tutor to Henry VIII, and was supported by the Countess of Surrey. The short, casual line of his verse is cumulative in its effect and curiously modern. His satires on Wolsey, *Speke Parrot* and *Why come ye not to Courte*, forced him at last to take sanctuary at Westminster where he remained until his death.

From the historian's point of view the most important writings are a group of chronicle-histories; Thomas Fabyan's *Chronicle* (1516), Sir Thomas More's *History of King Richard the Third* (*c.* 1513), Edward Hall's *Chronicle* (1548), and the *Anglica Historia* of Polydore Vergil (1534). They each represent different approaches to the problems involved in writing history. Fabyan was an alderman and sheriff of London and his book is largely a repetition and conflation of existing works, but it does attempt to be something more than a superior kind of diary. More's *History* has been described as an attack on the amoral statecraft of the early sixteenth century, and contrasts Edward IV with a Machiavellian Richard III. Hall's *Chronicle* has been called the first attempt to write history in the grand manner. He saw history as a pageant and his vision had significant consequences; Holinshed used Hall almost *verbatim*, and Shakespeare used Holinshed.

Polydore Vergil (*c.* 1470–1555) was an Italian from Urbino who came to England as a collector of papal taxes in 1502, was naturalized in 1510, and remained in England until 1551. Henry VII invited Vergil to write a history of England. The resulting *Anglica Historia*, begun in 1506, finally appeared in 1534. Critical of the legends established by earlier writers such as Geoffrey of Monmouth the new history was 'modern' in its analytical approach, its weighing of evidence, its careful organization and its original observation, though Vergil did not forget that one of his objects must be to present the Tudor monarchy as the restorer of order.

Poetry which looks forward to the age of the Elizabethans first appears in the works of Sir Thomas Wyatt (1503–42) and of Henry Howard, Earl of Surrey (*c.* 1517–47), but a mid-century period, which C. S. Lewis has labelled 'the Drab Age', stretches from the later years of Henry VIII's reign to the end of the seventies, a period in which, as he says, all the authors write like elderly men: 'The good work is neat and temperate, the bad flat and dry. There is more bad than good'.[1]

The significant years are the golden period which followed, the limits of which are approximately the half-century from 1580 to 1630. Important works follow so thick and fast that any attempt in a general history to deal with them all results in nothing but a breathless list of titles. It must be the object of the historian to try to explain the great efflorescence of Elizabethan writing rather than to describe it. Unfortunately there is no acceptable way of accounting for the remarkable change in quality between the writings of 1550 and those of 1580. Some influences may be hinted at, but their force cannot be proved: the universal use of English for temporal and spiritual instructions of the highest importance; the development of cheap printing; the increased wealth, leisure, and above all security of those who might compose or buy literary works of art; the concentration in London of these factors to such an extent that the pile reached a critical heat— all these may have helped to make possible the explosion of late Elizabethan literature.

A general point can be made about the nature of Elizabethan literature. The beauty of its poetry, the splendour of its prose, should not hide the fact that it often expresses an essentially bustling, active, practical interest in the real world and in contemporary developments. Romanticism, in the sense of looking to an imaginary past, is rare—Spenser is the only great romantic writer. On the whole the legendary gives place to the actual, King Arthur to Henry V.

Many 'Elizabethans' were, for at least half their career, 'Jacobeans'. Only four of the best-known writers—Sidney, Marlowe, Spenser and Hooker—died before the Queen herself, and of these two died prematurely, through violence. Exact dates for the golden age are clearly valueless, but it is equally clear that the approximate limits are from 1580 to 1630. The onset is marked by such key works in their respective fields as Holinshed's *Chronicle* (1577), Lyly's *Euphues* (1578), Spenser's *Shepherd's Calendar* and North's *Plutarch* (1579), and Kyd's *Spanish Tragedy* (*c.* 1585). At the other limit there stands the *Authorized Version* (1610), the last plays of Shakespeare (*The Tempest* was performed in 1612), Ben Jonson

[1] C. S. Lewis, *English Literature in the Sixteenth Century*, O.U.P., 1954, p. 64.

(*Bartholomew Fair* 1614) and Webster (*The White Devil* 1614), and the appearance of Chapman's *Odyssey* (1615).

Of particular interest to the historian are the historical and geographical writings of the period, especially William Camden's antiquarian survey, *Britannia*, of 1586—the Society of Antiquaries had been founded in 1572; the county surveys of William Lambarde (Kent) and Richard Carew (Cornwall), and Stow's *Survey of London*; the maps and text of Saxton's *Atlas of England* and Speed's *Theatre of the Empire of Great Britain*. More specifically historical are Holinshed's *Chronicle* including Harrison's *Description of Britain* (1577), Speed's *History of Great Britain*, Bacon's *History of Henry VII*, and the great Hakluyt's *Principal Navigations, Voyages, Traffics, and Discoveries of the English Nation* (1589). Interest and pride in the country helps to account for these works. For instance, in the preface to the second edition of his *Voyages*, Hakluyt wrote: 'What restless nights, what painful days, what heat, what cold I have endured; how many long and changeful journeys I have travelled; how many famous libraries I have searched into; what variety of ancient, and modern writers I have pursued . . .' continuing that 'the honour and benefit of the Commonweal wherein I live and breathe, hath made all difficulties seem easy. . . .' It was patriotism that 'as it were with a sharp goad provoked and thrust me forward. . . .'

Renaissance interest in the European world combined with the new muscular style of English to produce great translations, among them Florio's *Montaigne* and North's *Plutarch*. That prose also powered the first English novels. John Lyly's *Euphues* marked one line of development, the use of alliteration, conceits of metaphor and simile, and a Mannerist distortion of language, but the future lay with the precise, simple, real world described by Thomas Deloney in *Jack of Newbury* and, in a more ornate style, by Thomas Nashe in *The Unfortunate Traveller* (1594), works which anticipate respectively the writings of Defoe a century later and the picaresque novels of the eighteenth century.

The most unexpected achievements were those made in the field of drama. The ancestors of the Elizabethan plays were three. There were the Mystery cycles of episodes, based on the Bible, such as the forty-eight scenes performed at York and dating from the second half of the fourteenth century. The

Moralities developed slightly later: allegories such as *Pride of Life* (*c.* 1405) and *Everyman* (*c.* 1495) designed to remind their audiences that

> When thou art graven in green
>   There meeteth flesh and mould;
> Then helpeth little, I ween,
>   The gay crown of gold.

The early sixteenth century witnessed briefly the replacement of religious by political propaganda. About the year 1516 Skelton used the Morality form for an attack on Wolsey in his *Magnificence*, and reference has already been made to Bale's *King John* (1538) directed against the Pope. The third group of pre-Elizabethan plays were native productions of the Drab Age: Udall's academic imitation of Plautus, *Ralph Roister Doister* (1553); Sackville and Norton's *Gorboduc* (*c.* 1561), modelled on Seneca; and the native farce of *Gammer Gurton's Needle* (*c.* 1560). English plays written before 1580 and worth preserving could be comfortably contained in one volume.

Conditions were changing, however, and the old religious cycles of plays were frowned upon. In 1577 John Northbrooke attacked those who claimed 'that plays are as good as sermons, and that they learn as much or more at a play, than they do at God's word preached'. The Chester cycle came to an end in 1575, those of York and Wakefield in 1577. In the first years of her reign the Queen had restricted the topics with which plays might deal; 'permit none to be played wherein matters of religion or of Governance of the estate of the common weal shall be handled. . . '. A generation later, in 1589, Star Chamber was recording that '. . . the players take upon themselves to handle in their plays certain matters of Divinity and State unfit to be suffered, for redress whereof their Lordships have thought good to appoint some persons of judgement and understanding to view and examine their plays before they be permitted to present them publicly.' Censorship, however regrettable from a libertarian point of view, must have helped to free the drama from the aridities of political and theological argument. Meanwhile other opportunities presented themselves. In 1574 the first actors' company came into existence under the protection of the Earl of Leicester. Two years later the first public playhouses were opened, at Shoreditch (the

Theatre) and Blackfriars. Other patrons followed, other theatres were built. The first playwright to make his name was Thomas Kyd (1558–*c*. 95), whose *Spanish Tragedy* (*c*. 1585) marks the coming-of-age of Elizabethan drama. The flood-gates were now open. It is, of course, not feasible to deal adequately with Elizabethan literature within the limits of a few pages. As Professor Denys Hay has written: 'The literary specialist and the historian each gives a guilty acknowledgement that his world is only part of the world, and then proceeds as if it were the world in its entirety.'[1] The greatest playwrights are Marlowe, Shakespeare and Jonson. Christopher Marlowe (1564–92) made in *Doctor Faustus* (1588), the *Jew of Malta* (1589), *Tamburlaine* (1586) and *Edward II* (1592) studies in 'bragging blank verse' of men enslaved by the lust for power. Ben Jonson (1573–1637) was the most learned of the three. His characters are types rather than individuals and such plays as *Every Man In His Humour* (1598), *Volpone* (1605), *The Alchemist* (1610), and *Bartholomew Fair* (1598) are in effect generalized maps of social behaviour. From the point of view of the historian this is a positive advantage.

To confine Shakespeare (1564–1616) is proverbially impossible. All that can be attempted here is to peg out the ground-plan of the first playwright who was not a university man—one who was attacked as 'an upstart crow beautified with our feathers' who thought himself 'the only Shake-scene in the country'—a professional, not a well-born amateur. His first plays date from about the year 1590. By 1594 Shakespeare's rivals—Marlowe, Kyd, Greene, Lodge, Lyly and Peele—were dead or in retirement and he had the stage to himself. During the decade he wrote the majority of the histories, *King John*, *Richard II*, *Richard III*, the two parts of *Henry IV*, and *Henry V*; the comedies *A Midsummer Night's Dream*, *The Merchant of Venice*, *Much Ado About Nothing*, *As You Like It*, *Twelfth Night*, and *The Merry Wives of Windsor*, and the lyrical tragedy *Romeo and Juliet*. The years 1601–8 were the period when the great tragedies and the gloomy comedies were written; *Hamlet*, *Othello*, *Lear*, *Macbeth*, and *Timon of Athens*; *Measure for Measure*, *All's Well that Ends Well*, and *Troilus and Cressida*. To this decade belong also the Roman

---

[1] D. Hay, '*The Early Renaissance in England*', in *From the Renaissance to the Counter-Reformation*, ed. C. H. Carter, Cape, 1966, p. 96.

plays *Julius Caesar*, *Antony and Cleopatra*, and *Coriolanus*.   Finally (1608–16) there is a group of experimental romances; *Pericles*, *Cymbeline*, *The Winter's Tale*, and *The Tempest*.   His greatness lay in his characterization, his range of dramatic forms, his ability to remove from his works almost every trace of his own opinions.

The historian must naturally be particularly concerned with the nature of the historical plays.   Shakespeare wrote for an audience which had been brought up on the Tudor myth, originating in the time of Henry VII, that the union of York and Lancaster was the happy ending to a century of turmoil consequent on the deposition of Richard II.   The myth had been established by the historical writings of Polydore Vergil, More and Hall, securely based in the generally-held assumptions of the disastrous nature of disorder, the sanctity of monarchy, the enormity of rebellion.   The titles that Hall gave to the chapters of his *Chronicle* illustrate this view of history:

    i. The unquiet times of King Henry the Fourth.
    ii. The victorious acts of King Henry the Fifth.
    iii. The troublous season of King Henry the Sixth.
    iv. The prosperous reign of King Edward the Fourth.
    v. The pitiful life of King Edward the Fifth.
    vi. The tragical doings of King Richard the Third.
    vii. The politic governance of King Henry the Seventh.
    viii. The triumphant reign of King Henry the Eighth.

Accepting these assumptions, Shakespeare imposed a dramatic pattern on Holinshed's *History* and took advantage of the popularity after 1580 of Chronicle Plays based, as Nash said, on events 'that have long lain buried in rusty brass and worm eaten books', which saw history in the simple black and white of the earlier Miracle Plays, and in which even the bad English kings, for instance, exhibit nobility in the presence of foreigners.

These were the sources from which Shakespeare created the eight plays which cover the years from Richard II to Richard III (though the plays were not written in historical sequence).   They present a picture of disorder, arising out of a disruption of natural order, the deposition of Richard II, and culminating in the defeat of Richard III, who is seen as a great abscess on the body politic, a 'poisonous hunch-back'd toad', destined to be destroyed by the future Henry VII—inevitably, since 'God and good angels fight on Richmond's side'.

Education

In the middle ages education had been in the hands of the professionals—the clergy and the canon lawyers. In England its secularization began in the fifteenth century in the towns, with the growth of a demand for some instruction in writing and accountancy, technical-commercial skills of more practical value than a knowledge of Latin, canon law and philosophy. The Renaissance provided the intellectual stimulus, while the Reformation made it easy to break down the ecclesiastical monopoly, with the result that eventually education was taken out of the hands of the Church. In the sixteenth century the town merchant and the country gentleman were both, though for slightly different reasons, concerned to preserve, or to create, efficient lay schools.

There is only space to indicate one or two significant landmarks. St. Paul's School was established by the Dean, John Colet, but it was controlled by the Mercer's Company. In 1530 Sir Thomas Elyot (c. 1490–1546) produced his most important work, *The Governor*, in which he outlined a scheme of humanists education for the ruling class. Elyot laid emphasis on instruction in Latin and Greek, but added to these education in the arts and in sport—though not in the 'beastly fury' of football. An orator is of no value unless his words are accurate and his knowledge complete, exact information carries conviction:

> Undoubtedly, very eloquence is in every tongue where any matter or act done, or to be done, is expressed in words clean, propitious, ornate, and comely: . . . . Wherefore inasmuch as in an orator is required to be a heap of all manner of learning which of some is called 'the world of science', of others 'the circle of doctrine', which is in one word of Greek, *encyclopedia*, therefore at this day may be found but very few orators . . .   (Book I, Chapter XIII)

At court the humanists Sir John Cheke (1514–57) and Roger Ascham (1515–68) were tutors respectively to Edward VI and the Princess Elizabeth. Ascham was one of the first to condemn the Italianate Englishman, 'Some Circes shall make

him, of a plain Englishman, a right Italian. And at length
to hell, or to some hellish place, he is likely to go', and he
exhibits in his *Toxophilus* a sturdy nationalism which, one feels,
may have helped to inspire the future Queen's contemptuous
pride in being 'mere English':

> Rejoice England, be glad and merry,
> Truth overcometh thine enemies all.
> The Scot, the Frenchman, the Pope, and heresy,
> Overcome by Truth, have had a fall:
> Stick to the Truth, and evermore thou shall
> Through Christ, King Henry, the Book and the Bow
> All manner of enemies, quite overthrow.

Under the pressure of ambitious men of the middle sort,
education acquired a new function. Its object was no longer
to produce priests and canon lawyers, but to enable laymen to
find the road to promotion and wealth. In 1516 the humanist
Richard Pace attacked the traditional view that gentlemen
should confine themselves to sport and leave the study of
literature to 'the sons of peasants', while in 1529 another
humanist, Thomas Lupset, wrote of scholars 'our first study is
to get promotion, to get these goods, to live wealthily'. On the
other hand, Latimer declared, 'If ye will not maintain schools
and universities, ye shall have a brutality'. Gentleman and
scholar alike converged on the same goal.

Demand produced supply and many new lay schools were
founded, including Shrewsbury (1552), Westminster (re-
founded 1560), Merchant Taylors (1561), Felsted (1564), Rugby
(1567), Harrow (1571), Repton (1557), St. Bees (1583) and
Uppingham (1584). Education of a sort was not confined to
the upper and middle classes; it seems probable that in towns up
to 40 per cent of the adult male population had some degree of
literacy by the end of the century,[1] though the percentage in the
countryside was naturally far smaller.

During the century local schools administered by lay
governors under the silent supervision of the state were founded
in surprisingly large numbers. A contemporary, Richard
Mulcaster, believed that more schools had been set up between
1558 and 1580 than in the whole of England's previous history,
and it has been estimated that by 1600 England possessed 360
grammar schools, one for every 13,000 of the population,

[1] D. Hay, p. 100.

Y

though there were of course wide variations from one county to another.[1]

Above the schools, new and old, there survived the ancient Universities of Oxford and Cambridge and the Inns of Court which, apart from the establishment of the Regius Professorships at the time of the Dissolution, were unchanged in their methods. They offered to the gentlemen who attended them in increasing numbers a traditional curriculum and a useful social centre, combining some of the functions of a finishing school and a club.

'The science of Elizabeth's reign was the work of merchants and craftsmen, not of dons; carried on in London, not in Oxford and Cambridge; in the vernacular, not in Latin.'[2]   The new vehicle for this new learning was Gresham College, founded, posthumously, in London by Sir Thomas Gresham in 1596, and surviving until the middle of the eighteenth century.   The College was to deal with practical, applied knowledge: the professor of divinity was to refute the teaching of Rome; the professor of physic was to expound the modern theories of medicine 'for that every man for his health's sake will desire to have some knowledge in the art of physic'; the professor of astronomy was to lecture on geography, navigation and mariners' instruments; the law lectures were to have reference to subjects of special importance to merchants.   All were to teach in English.   The College gave impetus to the development of applied science in England.

Science

The link between pure and applied science, and the need to rest both on impartially observed experiments, two indications that the prehistoric period of science was at an end, were emphasized on the continent by Galileo and in England by Francis Bacon (1561–1626).

Bacon first outlined his views in 1605 in his work *Of the Proficiency and Advancement of Learning*.   Knowledge, he argued, should be sought for its own sake, but it brought with it power and the material improvement of man's life.   'Natural philosophy' (science) must learn from 'the mechanical arts' (technology), the latter must apply the new discoveries of the former, and

---

[1] See A. L. Rowse, *The England of Elizabeth*, Macmillan, 1950, pp. 496–501.

[2] C. Hill, *Intellectual Origins of the English Revolution*, O.U.P., 1965, p. 15.

both must divorce themselves from the 'barren virgins' of theology and metaphysics:

> The sciences stand where they did and remain almost in the same condition, receiving no noticeable increase, but on the contrary, thriving most under their first founder [Aristotle], and then declining.   Whereas in the mechanicals arts, which are founded on nature and the light of experience, we see the contrary happen, for these (as long as they are popular) are continually thriving and growing, as having in them a breath of life; at first rude, then convenient, afterwards adorned, and at all times advancing. . . (aphorism lxxiv).
>
> Let no man look for much progress in the sciences— especially in the practical part of them—unless natural philosophy be carried on and applied to particular sciences, and particular sciences be carried back again to natural philosophy . . . (aph. lxxx).
>
> Experiment will give a more true and real illumination concerning causes and axioms than is hitherto attained. For like as a man's disposition is never well known till he be crossed, nor Proteus ever changed shapes till he was straitened and held fast; so the passages and variation of nature cannot appear so fully in the liberty of nature, as in the trials and vexations of art [technology].[1]

Bacon developed the argument in his later works, especially in his *Novum Organum* (1620) and *New Atlantis* (1621), but the lines along which he argued had been worked out by 1605.

The history of scientific achievement in sixteenth-century England is the story of individual successes notched up by enquiring minds, but with little in the way of continuity between one discovery and the next.   Specialized works in what may be loosely termed natural history included Dr. Caius' work *On English Dogs* (1576), Gerard's *Herbal* (1597) and Moffet's *Theatre of Insects*, based on the work of Edward Wotton (1492–1555) and Thomas Penney (1530–88) though not published till the seventeenth century.

The greatest figure in what would later be known as physics was undoubtedly that of William Gilbert (1540–1603).   He was an odd mixture of the experimental scientist and the

---

[1] The first two extracts are from Book I of the *Novum Organum* and the third from *The Advancement of Learning*: the whole argument is contained in the earlier work, but less succinctly.

mystical philosopher, standing as it were with one foot in the old world and one in the new. His book *De Magnete*, published in 1600, is one of the first scientific accounts based on experimental work. In it Gilbert defined the earth as a great magnet, explained many of the problems of terrestrial magnetism, and distinguished between magnetism and the power of *electrics* (a word he invented) such as amber to attract objects after they have been rubbed. To help him in this investigation he constructed the first electroscope. Gilbert's work remained firmly rooted in the technical needs of the day—in this case the use of the magnet as an aid to navigation:

> We may see how far from unproductive magnetick philosophy is, how agreeable, how helpful, how divine! Sailors when tossed about on the waves with continuous cloudy weather, and unable by means of the celestial luminaries to learn anything about the place or region in which they are, with a very slight effort and with a small instrument are comforted, and learn the latitude of the place (Book V, Chapter 8).[1]

In 1543 the *Revolution of the Heavenly Spheres*, written by the Polish monk, Copernicus (1473–1543), was published. Copernicus argued that if it were assumed that the sun, and not the earth, was at the centre of the universe, the Aristotelian description of the movement of the heavens could be greatly simplified. It was not until the seventeenth century that Galileo was able with the aid of the telescope to provide experimental proof of the correctness of the Copernican model. Meanwhile all natural philosophers engaged in the great debate as to the truth or falsity of that model. In England the first scientist to come down firmly on the side of the Copernican theory was Thomas Digges (*c.* 1543–95). In *A Perfect Description of the Celestial Orbs* (1576) Digges described how 'in this our age one rare wit (seeing the continual errors that from time to time more and more have been discovered, besides the infinite absurdities in their Theoricks, which they have been forced to admit that would not confess any mobility in the ball of the Earth) hath by long study, painful practice, and rare invention delivered a new Theorick or model of the world'. For Digges 'the orb of the fixed stars

---

[1] *De Magnete*, S. P. Thompson, ed., London, 1900.

extendeth itself infinitely up in altitude' until it merges imperceptibly in Heaven 'the very court of celestial angels. . . . the glorious court of the great God'.[1]

Digges was also a practical scientist, one of the group, concerned particularly with geography and navigation, at whose centre lay John Dee (1527–1608). Dee, like many sixteenth-century thinkers, was a mixture of mystic and mathematician, astronomer and astrologer. He cast horoscopes, yet at the same time he was the organizing spirit behind most of the navigational theorizing of the second half of the century. In 1547 he went to the Netherlands to learn from continental mathematicians, and brought home examples of Mercator's new projection. Next year he journeyed to Louvain and to Paris, where he met others engaged in solving the problems, essential to map-making, of projecting a sphere on to a flat surface. Back in England mathematicians and practical sailors alike were in touch with Dee. Members of this circle include John Davis, who described the improved quadrant known as the backstaff in *Seaman's Secrets* (1594); Edward Wright, who described the making of projections in *Certain Errors in Navigation* (1598); and William Bourne who, in *A Regiment for the Sea* (1573), explained the ship's log, and 'how that you shall behave yourself with your Astrolabe'. As for determining longitude, Bourne advised sailors to leave that matter alone, for it was 'very tedious'.

John Napier (1550–1614) was responsible for the most significant mathematical development, the invention of logarithms. His work was not published until 1614, but the tables themselves had been worked out earlier.

The emphasis on efficient farming and the great land sales of the century created a demand for accurate large-scale maps. The first book in English on surveying was John Fitzherbert's *Book of Surveying* (1523). By 1562 the surveyor had at his disposal tables to work out areas and land values, and instruments, the plane-table and the theodolite, with which to carry out the work. The method of triangulation was understood, and it was possible to survey over 300 acres a day. The surveyor encountered both contempt—'Marry, he was a plumber, and had learned from a painter'—and mistrust—'The

---

[1] For Digges, see F. R. Johnson, *Astronomical Thought in Renaissance England*, Baltimore, 1937.

common people are in great fear when survey is made of their land' (1583).

Estate maps exist which date from the end of the sixteenth century, and at the other end of the scale there is the great series of county maps and atlases.   The first important engraved map of Great Britain and Ireland was produced by George Lily in 1546 when he was a Catholic exile in Rome.   He returned to England in Mary's reign and copies were produced in London in 1555.   Humphrey Lloyd, who died in 1568, was in touch with the Flemish map-makers Mercator and Ortelius, and himself produced one of the earliest maps of Wales.   The Yorkshireman, Christopher Saxton, produced his first county maps in 1574, and in 1579 completed his *Atlas* originally intended to accompany Holinshed's *Chronicles*.   Most of the maps were engraved by Flemish refugees.   The work of John Norden (1540–1625) of Somerset, the *Speculum Britanniae* (1593–8), was intended to be a new atlas with maps and archaeological and historical descriptions.   The scheme foundered from lack of money and maps of only five counties were published—but they were the first English maps to show roads or to have a grid for reference and a scale.   John Speed (1552–1629) of Cheshire summed up the earlier work when he published his *Theatre of the Empire of Great Britain* in 1611, an atlas which drew mainly on the work of Saxton and Norden.

Closely connected with the map-makers were the antiquarians, of whom the greatest was William Camden, who described his aims in his preface to *Brittania*:

> In my description of each country, I will show with as much plainness and brevity as I can, who were the ancient inhabitants, what was the reason for the name, what are the bounds of the country, the nature of the soil, the places of greatest antiquity, and of greatest eminence at present, and lastly, who have been dukes or earls of each, since the Norman Conquest.

Medicine in England lagged behind the other sciences.   On the continent Vesalius (1504–64), a Netherlander who lectured at Padua, had published the first book of modern anatomy, *On the Fabric of the Human Body*, in 1543 in Basle.   Yet as late as 1577 the surgeon of St. Bartholomew's Hospital was still content to rewrite a fourteenth-century treatise on the subject.

However some work based on personal observation was appearing in England. John Gale (1507–87) and William Clowes (1540–1604), who had both seen active service, wrote on the treatment of gunshot wounds, and Dr. Caius lectured and dissected at Gonville and Caius College, Cambridge. Earlier (1555) he had published a careful account of the sweating sickness. (This mysterious disease had appeared suddenly in 1485 and had reached epidemic proportions in 1508, 1517, 1528, and 1551. The people sardonically nick-named the sickness *Stoop-Knave-And-Know-Thy-Master*.) Prescription remained in the hands of the local apothecary, who sold 'druggy baggage' to his customers. Medicine and surgery as yet had no effect on the population structure. Infant mortality was very high, the first year of life immensely dangerous. If one survived that hurdle, there is some evidence to show that the average expectation of life rose from about thirty to perhaps forty years over the period—a consequence of better conditions rather than of greater knowledge.

Although there was an overall increase in population during the century, there were great fluctuations as killing epidemics, known indiscriminately as 'plague', swept through the country. Indeed in London plague of one sort or another was endemic rather than epidemic—it has been estimated that the city was only completely free during about a dozen years between 1500 and 1665. In 1554 the Venetian ambassador reported that 'they have some little plague in England well nigh every year, for which they are not accustomed to make sanitary provisions, as it does not usually make great progress. The cases for the most part occur amongst the lower classes, as if their dissolute mode of life impaired their constitutions.' It was dirt and starvation which made the poor susceptible. Plague followed bad harvests. Information is patchy, but there were certainly bad harvests in 1527, 1545, 1550–1, 1555–6 and 1594–6, and on each occasion these were followed by epidemics. Their effect should not be underestimated. Sir Thomas Smith, a man not usually given to exaggeration, wrote: 'God did so punish the realm with quartan agues, and with such other long and new sicknesses, that in the last two years of the reign of Queen Mary, so many of her subjects was made away, what with the execution of sword and fire, what by sicknesses, that the third part of the men of England were consumed.'

EXTRACTS

I.   *William Harrison, writing in 1577, describes changes in country architecture and comfort:*

The ancient manors and houses of our gentlemen are yet, and for the most part, of strong timber, in framing whereof our carpenters have been and are worthily preferred before those of like science among all other nations.   Howbeit such as be lately built are commonly either of brick or hard stone, or both; their rooms large and comely, and houses of office further distant from their lodgings.   Those of the nobility are likewise wrought with brick and hard stone, as provision may best be made; but so magnificent and stately, as the basest hound of a baron does often match in our days with some honours of princes in old time.   So that if ever curious building did flourish in England, it is in these our years, wherein our workmen excel and are in manner comparable in skill with old Vitruvius. . . .

There are old men yet dwelling in the village where I remain, which have noted three things to be marvellously altered in England within their sound remembrance;   One is the multitude of chimneys lately erected, whereas in their young days there were not above two or three, if so many, in most uplandish towns of the realm. . . .   The second is the great (although not general) amendment of lodging, . . .   The third thing they tell of, is the exchange of vessel, as of wooden platters into pewter, and wooden spoons into silver or tin. . . .

II.   *Robert Reyce, writing in 1618, contrasts old and new styles of building in Suffolk:*

. . . our ancientest houses. . . .   were always built low not with many rooms or above one or two stories, but these more in length than in largeness.   Thick were their walls, of squared or rough stone, brick, or strong timber, their windows small, their chimneys large, or instead of them to have round hearths in the midst of their great halls or rooms, with round holes or louvres aloft in the roof, which carried away the smoke never offending; whereas our building at this day is chiefly to place houses, where they may be furtherest seen, have best prospect, sweetest air and greatest pleasure, their walls thin, whether with brick, stone or timber, their lights large, all for outward show, their rooms square, raised high commonly with three and often four stories, their chimneys as many but small, their roofs square, . . . (*Breviary of Suffolk,* ed. Lord Hervey, 1902.)

III. *Cromwell's directions to Philip Hoby, sent to request the Duchess of Milan, in Brussels, to permit Holbein to paint her portrait, February, 1538:*

. . . to visit and salute her on my Lord's behalf and to require her that for the ministering to my Lord of a further occasion and to satisfy the ambassadors, It may please her grace to take so much pain at his poor desire to sit so long at some such time as herself shall appoint as a servant of the king's highness being come hither for that purpose may take her physiognomy.

Then shall he desire to know her pleasure when Mr. Hans shall come to her for the doing of his feat in the taking of his picture.   And having the time appointed he shall go with him or tarry behind as she shall appoint.   (R. B. Merriman, *Letters and Speeches of Thomas Cromwell*, Vol. II, p. 121.)

IV. *Hakluyt praises the Spanish practice of insisting that pilots take an examination in the art of navigation:*

. . . Charles the emperor and the king of Spain that now is, wisely considering, have in their contractation-house in Sivill appointed a learned reader of the said art of navigation and joined with him certain examiners, and have distinguished the orders among the seamen . . . none is admitted to the order [of master or pilot] without he have heard the reader for a certain space (which is commonly an excellent mathematician . . .), and being found fit by him and his assistants, which are to examine matters touching experience, they are admitted with a great solemnity and giving of presents to the ancient masters and pilots and the reader and examiners as the great doctors in the universities, or our great sergeants at the law when they proceed, and so are admitted to take charge for the Indies.

V. *Two accounts of the sweating sickness—*

1. *John Johnson, a London merchant in Calais, gives advice to a friend (1551):*
There is to be observed three things, that is, the sweat being begun, no air to be suffered to come in to the bed, but yet not to be kept over hot; to drink as little as may be . . . and the third and principal thing is to be kept from sleep so long as sleep is desired in the twenty-four hours . . . for he that sleepeth, dieth.

2. *John Caius describes its first appearance in England:*
In the year of Our Lord God, 1485, shortly after the seventh day of August at which time King Henry the Seventh arrived at Milford in Wales, out of France, and in the first year of his

reign, there chanced a disease among the people, which for the sudden sharpness and unwont cruelness passed the pestilence . . . that immediately killed some in opening their windows; some in playing with children in their street doors; some in one hour, many in two it destroyed; and, at the longest, to them that merrily dined, it gave a sorrowful supper.   As it found them, so it took them: some in sleep, some in wake, some in mirth, some in care, some fasting and some full, some busy and some idle; and in one house, sometime three, sometime five, sometime seven, sometime eight, sometime more, sometime all; of the which if the half in every town escaped, it was thought great favour. (*A Book against the Sweating Sickness*, made by John Caius, Doctor in Physic, 1552.)

Further Reading

C. H. Carter ed., *From the Renaissance to the Counter-Reformation*, Cape, 1966;
      D. Hay, *The Early Renaissance in England*
B. Ford ed., *The Age of Shakespeare*, Penguin, 1955
A. R. Hall, *The Scientific Revolution, 1500–1800*, Longmans, Green, 2nd ed.,
      1962
C. Hill, *Intellectual Origins of the English Revolution*, O.U.P., 1965
E. Lynam, *British Maps and Map-Makers*, Collins, 1944
E. M. Nugent, *The Thought and Culture of the English Renaissance*, C.U.P., 1956
E. M. W. Tillyard, *Shakespeare's History Plays*, Chatto and Windus, 1944
J. D. Wilson, *Life in Shakespeare's England*, C.U.P., 1944

XVI · THE FINAL YEARS

HISTORIANS differ in their interpretation of the last years of Elizabeth's reign. Was it a golden sunset, or does one see on the horizon clouds, no bigger perhaps than a man's hand, but nevertheless clouds that are the first signs of the coming storms of the seventeenth century? As so often in history the answer given will depend to a large extent on the facts selected.

There is no doubt that in many ways the closing years were triumphant ones. Culturally, a great part of what is claimed most magnificent dates from this time, in these matters it *is* the Elizabethan age. Politically, the Queen's cautious, conservative technique had triumphed; at home (always excepting Ireland) there was little danger of civil disturbance, while abroad Spanish power in France and in the Netherlands had been forced on to the defensive, Cadiz had been sacked, and golden Spain had gone bankrupt. Throughout England men were making money and were investing it in land and houses, building or rebuilding a multitude of homes, ranging in size from the yeoman's farm to the statesman's palace.

The State church was apparently triumphing over its adversaries. These years, which opened with the Marprelate Tracts (1589), saw the destruction of the Brownists (1593), the weakening of the prebysterians with the deaths of Field and Leicester in 1588, the exile of Cartwright, and the defeat of the final parliamentary attack by Morice (1593), the splitting of the English catholics after the death of Cardinal Allen thanks to Whitgift's offer of 1602, and the philosophical defence of the new Church's traditional foundations by Hooker.

Overseas activity continued. Expeditions reached Malacca in the east and the Orinoco in the west. Will Adams reached Japan in 1600 and in that same year the great East India Company was chartered.

There was continuous activity, too, in the world of the imagination. Drill through the year 1598 for a typical section and the intellectual core includes: in literature, the enlarged edition of Bacon's *Essays*, Chapman and Marlowe's *Hero and Leander*, Dekker's *Shoemaker's Holiday*, the completion of

Hakluyt's enlarged *Voyages*, Sidney's *Arcadia*, Stow's *Survey of London*, the first production of Jonson's *Every Man in his Humour*, the probable appearance of *Henry IV*, the publication of Morley's *First Book of Airs*, while Hardwick Hall had just been completed, and the Globe was soon to open. It is, by any standards, a remarkable list, but it becomes even more remarkable if one looks back half a century to 1548 or a full century to 1498. In the former year there appeared the second edition of Hall's *Chronicle*, a translation by Nicholas Udall of Erasmus' *Paraphrase of the New Testament*, and the Book of Common Prayer was nearing completion. In 1498 Linacre was translating Greek classics into Latin, and Colet was lecturing at Oxford on St. Paul's Epistles. The most important cultural event was the visit of a foreigner, Erasmus.

The Europe that was soon to face Elizabeth's successor was very different in character from that with which Edward IV had negotiated. Germany and Italy remained geographical expressions, but elsewhere political unification and national differentiation had tended to triumph. The partial medieval unity, based on the Catholic church and the Latin language, was gone and Europe was divided. The great divide was between a Protestant north and a Catholic south. France had lost the first round of her struggle with the Habsburgs, in central and eastern Europe the Counter-Reformation was winning converts and subjects for the latter's Austrian branch, but Spanish Habsburg power was more apparent than real.

The personal union of England and Scotland would soon close the back door to invasion and would unite the British Isles politically, though they would still remain deeply divided into a Catholic Ireland, a Catholic and Calvinist Scotland, and an Anglican England. Norway–Denmark had become Lutheran in 1536, Sweden had broken away, had become Lutheran in 1526, and had acquired a toehold on the other shore of the Baltic by her acquisition of Courland in 1561 from Russia. There Ivan IV (1533–84) had begun the country's expansion east into Siberia and south towards the Black Sea. Trade contacts with England and the west hinted at future developments. Russia's neighbour Poland, large and weak, was being won back to Catholicism. The Ottoman Turks were still within striking distance of Vienna, and had gained control of the eastern Mediterranean, capturing Rhodes (1522), Cyprus (1573) and Tunis (1574, but they had failed to take Malta (1565) and had been defeated at Lepanto (1571). Their expansion was at an end by land and sea. In Italy the Habsburgs controlled, directly or indirectly, Milan, Tuscany and Naples, while Venice and the Papal States were rapidly becoming political nonentities. Spain had absorbed Portugal in 1580 and ruled the whole peninsula. France had united her lands and was beginning her expansion towards the Rhine, having finally expelled the English and acquired Provence (1481), French Burgundy and Picardy (1492), Metz, Toul and Verdun (1552). The abortive state of Burgundy had been dismembered. Franche Comté and the southern Netherlands were held by Spain, while the northern Netherlands would soon (1609) become an independent Calvinist state. With the exception of Bavaria and the Habsburg lands the greater part of the Empire was Lutheran or Calvinist. Overseas the outlines of European expansion and of conflict between Spain, Holland, France and England were being drawn.

During the century there had come about a radical change in England's European policy. Engagement had given place to withdrawal. Although Elizabeth had played a most important part in the United Provinces and in France, it had been as an outside agent that she had operated. For England the conquest of Ireland, the union with Scotland, the loss of Calais, the reduced dependence on the Netherlands cloth market, the repulse of the political Counter-Reformation, the isolation of protestantism, the introduction of ships capable of acting as a striking force in their own right, all combined to make it possible for England to isolate herself from the continent and to devote her energies to overseas trade and colonial expansion, while the same ships which made possible this expansion could defend her from the armies of the continental powers.

One is hardly likely to overlook the glories of the late Elizabethan age. Yet there is another side to the picture. Tudor government, Professor Black has written, was 'entering a period of disintegration' and, he continues, 'a *fin de siècle* attitude, compounded of irritation and lassitude, hovered over the political landscape'.[1] The constitutional crises that dogged

[1] J. B. Black, *The Reign of Elizabeth*, O.U.P., 1959, p. 207.

the Stuarts were not solely due to the political insensitivity of
James I and Charles I.   'The geological fault in society which
underlay the Revolution of the seventeenth century had its
beginnings in the Elizabethan Age', writes A. L. Rowse.[1]

It is valuable to analyse the changing climate of the last
years, to examine the extent to which that feeling of what one
historian has termed 'disenchantment' was setting in, to search
for signs of the origins of that change in atmosphere which
became so startlingly obvious as soon as the Stuarts reached the
English throne.

The decade was one of unemployment, poverty—in 1597 real
wages touched rock bottom, famine in the years 1594–7, and
plague.   The war, and the consequent need to seek large
parliamentary grants, weakened the Crown's position.   The
Elizabethan religious settlement, that brilliantly successful
exercise in empirical compromise, had endured for a generation.   Temperamentally inclined to temporize, the Queen
and her ministers had no desire to do more than to defend
a position already won, but however suitable to the situation
of 1558 that was not necessarily the correct attitude to adopt
towards the problems of Church and State forty years later.
A new inflexibility is apparent in the government's reaction
to opponents of the *status quo*, in the execution of Catholics and
and Brownists alike, and in the imprisonment until his death
of old Peter Wentworth for his insistence on raising yet again
the matter of the succession.

The last years of the Tudors dissolve imperceptibly into the
first years of the Stuarts.   The ease with which the political
transition was made is one more tribute to the solidity of the
Tudor achievement, but James I also inherited the late Tudor
riddles.   These would in any case have perplexed his reign,
but their solution had often been made more difficult by Elizabethan conservatism and procrastination.

Above all the question of the relationship between Crown
and Parliament remained unanswered.   The period from 1588
to 1603 had seen four parliaments in which, partly because
they were war parliaments and partly because there was a
new atmosphere in the air, the Commons had shown themselves determined to defend their economic interests against

[1] A. L. Rowse, *The England of Elizabeth*, Macmillan, 1950, p. 90.

authoritarian prerogative, no matter how securely the latter might be founded in long-established usage. During the monopolies debate of 1601 John Hele, the Recorder of Exeter, defended the traditional political theory that 'all we have is her Majesty's, and she may lawfully, at her pleasure, take it from us. Yea, she hath as much right to all our lands and goods as to any revenue of the Crown', but the practical Members interrupted, coughing until he was forced to sit down. Elizabeth could make all smooth again with a Golden Speech, but the time when the Commons would allow themselves to be hushed by this means was coming to an end. James was in any case not equipped, either physically or psychologically, to employ such methods. Of Parliament he remarked, 'I am surprised that my ancestors should ever have permitted such an institution to come into existence.'

The Tudor government had depended for its smooth running on the financial and administrative co-operation of the Crown on the one hand and the aristocracy and gentry on the other. The co-operation was voluntary and that fact gave these groups in the last analysis great power. The financial position of the Crown was being seriously, perhaps fatally, weakened by expenditure on foreign affairs. The naval struggle with Spain, the subsidies to Henri IV, the maintenance of a force in the Netherlands, and above all the huge cost of the seemingly endless operations in Ireland involved not only an increasing dependence on parliamentary grants but also the exhaustion of the Crown's capital assets by the sale of Crown lands. The Crown was in debt at Elizabeth's death to the tune of £400,000. The early Tudors had been content to tinker with the financial machine which they found already in existence. In the critical mid-century years it had almost broken down, but under Mary and Elizabeth a combination of efficiency and parsimony had temporarily obscured the fact that, with new commitments and higher prices, the days were gone when the Crown could be expected to live of its own, without regular reference to parliament.

The attempt to run England as a medieval manor had other, potentially more serious, consequences. The rulers, and in particular Elizabeth, found it necessary to rely on men who were virtually unpaid amateurs for the administration of the realm. The power of the Crown to distribute office, privilege and land enabled the rulers to provide a recognized if unofficial reward for services rendered to the state. Talent and loyalty were available at Court because it was at that same Court that wealth and opportunity were to be found. Grants and monopolies, the farming of customs, the negotiation of loans, and the large perquisites of office rewarded the capable administrator who was also an acceptable courtier.

Elizabeth had inherited this form of administration. During her reign the old personal links were replaced by ones of economic self-interest. The Court became the royal exchange where the fortunate or the adroit might defend themselves from the continuing pressure of inflation by the acquisition of exemptions, concessions, monopolies and government commissions. The more that is known about the lives of such men as Sir Horatio Palavicino (see p. 319), or Mr. 'Customer' Smythe, who married into the family of Sir Andrew Judde of the London Skinner's Company, inherited the latter's business interests, became collector of tunnage and poundage in London as early as 1557, obtained a consession to work the Cornish mines, and from his great 'farm' of the national customs between 1570 and 1588 made a net gain of £50,000—the more it is clear that the corruption of the early Stuart administration was latent in the administrative and fiscal systems of the late sixteenth century.

The corruption was potential, and it was during a great part of the reign inactive. Like all the Tudors, Elizabeth chose her servants with care and made sure the government benefited from their activities. The Queen saw to it that her administrators should know their mistress, she 'would have her dogs wear no collars but her own', and she took care to balance one group against another. As Sir Robert Naunton observed: 'The principal note of her reign will be that she ruled much by faction and parties which she herself both made, upheld and weakened, as her one great judgement advised.' In the late nineties she began to neglect these safeguards and under James I they were not observed at all. Then the disadvantages of the existing methods of reward became only too apparent.[1]

The Queen herself remained attached to the principle—

---

[1] For the above, see J. E. Neale, *The Elizabethan Political Scene*, Raleigh Lecture, O.U.P., 1948 and J. Hurstfield, *Political Corruption in Modern England: The Historian's Problem*, History, 174, 1967.

some would say lack of principle—that had served her so well in the difficult days. Conservative by inclination, regal by conviction, procrastinatory by temperament, Elizabeth had discovered that most problems could be solved by giving free play to these aspects of her character. By elevating the Queen so that she towered like the white alps above her subjects and by attaching to that awe-inspiring eminence all the great questions of national importance she had been able to secure these matters from mundane debate and criticism. They became part of her personal prerogative. Thus isolated they could safely be left alone until they—or their critics—were removed by the passage of time. Had she cared to expose her methods Elizabeth might have echoed the words of her rival Philip II: 'Time and I are a match for any other two.'

It was not so easy for the Queen's ministers. Burghley complained constantly of delay and uncertainty; Sir Walter Ralegh, when the Queen was safely dead, observed that 'Her Majesty did all by halves'; Sir Thomas Smith complained as Secretary of State: 'I can neither get the other letters signed, nor the letter already signed. . . sent away, but day by day and hour by hour deferred till "anon", "soon" and "tomorrow".' Her moods were unpredictable: 'When she smiled it was pure sunshine that everyone did choose to bask in if they could; but anon came a storm from a sudden gathering of clouds and the thunder fell in wondrous manner on all alike.' No minister, not even Cecil, could be sure of a free hand. Her godson, Sir John Harington, writing about 1606, has left an invaluable account of her methods:

> Her wisest men and best councillors were oft sore troubled to know her well in matters of State: so covertly did she pass her judgement, as seemed to leave all to their discreet management; and, when the business did turn to better advantage, she did most cunningly commit the good issue to her own honour and understanding; but, when aught fell out contrary to her will and intent, the Council were in great strait to defend their own acting and not blemish the Queen's good judgement. Herein her wise men did oft lack more wisdom; and the Lord Treasurer would oft shed a plenty of tears on any miscarriage, well knowing the difficult part was, not so much to mend the matter itself, as his mistress's humour; and yet he did most share her favour and goodwill; and to his opinion she would oft-time submit her own pleasure in great

z

matters. She did keep him late at night, in discoursing alone, and then call out another at his departure, and try the depth of all around her sometimes. Walsingham had his turn, and each displayed their wit in private. On the morrow, everyone did come forth in her presence and discourse at large; and, if any had dissembled with her, or stood not well to her advisings before, she did not let it go unheeded and sometimes not unpunished. Sir Christopher Hatton was wont to say, 'The Queen did fish for men's souls, and had so sweet a bait, that no one could escape her network.' In truth, I am sure her speech was such, as none could refuse to take delight in, when forwardness did not stand in the way. I have seen her smile, sooth with great semblance of good liking to all around, and cause everyone to open his most inward thought to her; when, on a sudden, she would ponder in private on what had passed, write down all their opinions, draw them out as occasion required, and some time disprove to their faces what had been delivered a month before. Hence she knew everyone's part, and by this fishing, as Hatton said, she caught many poor fish, who little knew what snare was laid for them.

Time may have been the Queen's most potent instrument, but she herself was subject to this universal solvent and by the close of the century she had become, in Ralegh's later words, 'a lady whom time hath surprised'. The old magic was almost exhausted, so that it was possible for a courtier, Essex, to rage that 'her conditions were as crooked as her carcase'. The new men had had enough of caution, conservatism and cheese-paring. There were, though, reserves that might be drawn on when required, as witness the Queen's Golden Speech of 1601. Witness, too, the fact that, in 1597, she was still capable of trouncing a belligerent Polish ambassador in a brilliant display of fluent extempore Latin, finishing with an aside in English to her admiring courtiers, 'God's death, . . . I have been enforced this day to scour up my old Latin that hath lain long in rusting'. Essex, hearing of the episode, wrote 'I was happy for her Majesty that she was stirred, and had so worthy an occasion to show herself. The Heroes would be but as other men, if they had not unusual and unlooked for encounters; and sure her Majesty is made of the same stuff of which the ancients believed the heroes to be formed; that is, her mind of gold, her body of brass'.

The councillors and courtiers who had surrounded Elizabeth at her accession were now dead, or soon to die, and younger, lesser men who had never known the mid-century crisis—men such as Ralegh and Essex, Bacon and Coke, and the younger Cecil—were jostling for place and power.

Lord Burghley sketched aspects of the situation to his son Robert, 'I advise thee not to affect, or neglect, popularity too much. Seek not to be Essex: shun to be Ralegh'; and 'Trust not any man with thy life, credit or estate'. And again, in words that echo those of the Pastons a century earlier while at the same time pointing the difference that time had brought: 'Be sure to keep some great man thy friend. . . . Otherwise, in this ambitious age, thou shalt remain like a hop without a pole, live in obscurity and be made a football for every insulting companion to spurn at.' In 1592 Burghley noted the new climate of behaviour, 'all causes governed by bribes. Conscience least accounted', and six years later, a month before his death, in a final postscript to his son he set down his own unmatched political philosophy: 'Serve God by serving the Queen, for all other service is indeed bondage to the devil.'

The career of Robert Devereux, Earl of Essex (1567–1601), illustrates some of the strengths and weaknesses of this last Elizabethan age. His springboard was the men who had made that age possible; his grandfather had been the Queen's cousin; his stepfather was Leicester; Walsingham and Mildmay, Sidney and the Pembrokes formed part of the same cluster of families. Brave and conceited, ambitious and superficial, Essex himself attracted admiration without inspiring confidence.

Essex first saw service in the Netherlands under Leicester, fighting at Zutphen in 1586. In 1589 he ran away to join Drake's Lisbon expedition. In 1591 he defended Dieppe. His stepfather died in 1588 and Elizabeth spent ten years unsuccessfully trying to turn Essex into a second Leicester, a courtier who would love her from a distance and a soldier who would prove absolutely reliable, a watchdog not over-involved in politics, but she was too old and Essex was too ambitious and too impulsive, carrying as Camden observed 'his love and his hatred always in his Brow'.

There followed six years during which Essex tried to wrest the machinery of patronage and promotion from the hands of the Cecil family, and to give political weight to his own

followers, Anthony and Francis Bacon.   In 1593 he was made
a Privy Councillor.   In the following year the post of attorney-
general fell vacant and he made a bid to obtain it for Francis
Bacon, staking his reputation as a patron on the effort, 'the
attorneyship for Francis is that I must have; and in that I will
spend all my power, might, authority, and amity, and with
tooth and nail defend and procure that same for him against
whomsoever; . . .'   It was Edward Coke, the candidate of the
Cecils, who received the appointment.

In 1596 Essex led the brilliantly successful Cadiz expedition,
but two years later he failed to get the Mastership of the Court
of Wards, the office which modern research has shown to be
one of the supreme founts of patronage and wealth.   It fell
instead to Robert Cecil.

The struggle for power irritated the Queen, and alarmed
lesser men such as Roland Whyte, who wrote to the English
governor of Flushing: 'It is a very dangerous time here, for the
heads of both factions being here a man cannot tell how to
govern himself towards them.'   In fact, Essex had already lost,
though he was not prepared to accept the situation.

In 1599 Essex obtained for himself the Lord-Lieutenancy of
Ireland.   Once there he achieved nothing and, while the
Queen's sarcastic letters struck a raw nerve, the Earl's parley
with Tyrone[1] awakened the Tudor trait of distrust.   In September Essex made a dramatic, mud-stained reappearance
at Court, without his army and without victory.   'By God's
son, I am no queen.   That man is above me.   Who gave him
commandment to come here so soon?   I did send him on other
business' the Queen stormed.   Essex was put under the close
supervision of Sir Thomas Egerton, the Lord Keeper, while
the Queen pondered the possibility of a Star Chamber trial.
In the end she was persuaded to have Essex brought instead
before a private committee, where he was charged with deserting his army, with the unlawful creation of knights, and with
his meeting with Tyrone.   He threw himself on Elizabeth's
mercy, and was suspended from the Privy Council and confined
to Essex House.

The final blow came in September.   The Earl's monopoly
of sweet wines expired, and it was not renewed.   He was
disgraced, out of favour, ruined.   Some of the common people

[1] See Chapter IX.

were sympathetic and he was surrounded by desperate unemployed officers from Ireland and courtiers hopeful for patronage, gambling on his return to favour. Rumours reached the Court. At the beginning of February 1601 he was informed that he must explain matters to the council. His hot-headed friends paid Shakespeare's company to perform *Richard II*— was Essex another Bolingbroke? The Queen thought so, 'I am Richard II: Know ye not that?' she told William Lambarde. Four privy councillors were sent to arrest Essex. He seized them and, at the head of two hundred followers, set out for the city, shouting 'For the Queen! The Crown of England is sold to the Spaniard! A plot is laid for my life!' There was no support and by nightfall Essex had given himself up. He was quickly tried and executed.

The pointless rebellion is an echo of the fifteenth-century risings of overmighty subjects, it is also perhaps a precursor of the motives that inspired some men to take up arms against the crown forty years later—financial bankruptcy and the thwarted desire to share in the fruits of power and patronage.

The last two years of the reign were uneventful:

> Little Cecil tripping up and down,
> He rules both the court and the crown,

For six years Robert Cecil had enjoyed power without office. Then in 1596 he succeeded his father as Secretary to the Council and Master of the Court of Wards. The Queen gave him her confidence and after James I's accession Robert Cecil remained chief minister of the Crown until his death in 1612. In 1601 he had got secretly in touch with James VI of Scotland in order that, when the time came, there should be no break in the administration—nor, perhaps, in Cecil's tenure of office.

In that year, too, the Queen gave an interview to the antiquary William Lambarde. Speaking of former times she said: 'In those days force and wit did prevail; but now the wit of the fox is everywhere on foot so as hardly a faithful and virtuous man may be found.' In 1602 the Queen was still active and apparently immortal, well able to hunt over ten miles of countryside on horseback, but in January 1603 about the time that the court moved to Richmond, it grew much colder and men noticed a change in Elizabeth, who became less active, spending more time on her devotions, and listening to 'old Canterbury tales'. In February she made her last important public appearance when she received a Venetian envoy. She took the opportunity to rebuke him for the fact that Venice had had no permanent ambassador in England throughout the whole of her reign. In March she grew feverish and by the nineteenth it was clear that she was dying. Horses were posted along the road to Scotland. On the twenty-third Archbishop Whitgift told her to prepare her soul, to which she replied a little crushingly 'That I have done long ago'. Later she was persuaded to make a sign that James should succeed her. She died between two and three the following morning, 'mildly like a lamb, easily like a ripe apple from the tree', and Cecil's man, Sir Robert Carey, left at once on the great north road to Scotland:

> I . . . took horse between nine and ten o'clock; and that night rode to Doncaster. The Friday night I came to my own house at Witherington, and presently took order with my deputies to see the Borders kept in quiet; which they had much to do: and gave order, the next morning, the King of Scotland should be proclaimed King of England, and at Morpeth and Alnwick. Very early, on Saturday, I took horse for Edinburgh, and came to Norham about twelve at noon, so that I might well have been with the King at supper time. But I got a great fall by the way; and my horse, with one of his heels, gave me a great blow on the head, that made me shed much blood. It made me so weak, that I was forced to ride a soft pace after: so that the King was newly gone to bed by the time I knocked at the gate. I was quickly let in; and carried up to the King's Chamber. I kneeled by him, and saluted him by his title of 'England, Scotland, France and Ireland'. He gave me his hand to kiss, and bade me welcome.[1]

FURTHER READING

J. Hurstfield, *Political Corruption in Modern England: The Historian's Problem*, History, 176, 1967

J. E. Neale, *The Elizabethan Political Scene*, Raleigh Lecture, O.U.P., 1948

L. Stone, *An Elizabethan: Sir Horatio Palavicino*, O.U.P., 1956

[1] Sir Robert Carey, *Memoirs*, written at some date before 1627

INDEX

The more important Acts of Parliament, Battles, and Treaties are listed in the Index under those headings

Date D